Studies in Evangelicalism

Edited by Donald W. Dayton, Northern Baptist Theological Seminary, and Kenneth E. Rowe, Drew University Library

1. *The Holiness Revival of the Nineteenth Century,* by Melvin Easterday Dieter. 1980, 1996.

2. *The Lane Rebels: Evangelicalism and Antislavery in Antebellum America,* by Lawrence Thomas Lesick. 1980.

3. *Freedom and Grace: The Life of Asa Mahan,* by Edward H. Madden and James E. Hamilton. 1982.

4. *Evangelicals United: Ecumenical Stirrings in Pre-Victorian Britain, 1795–1830,* by Roger H. Martin. 1983.

5. *Theological Roots of Pentecostalism,* by Donald W. Dayton. 1987.

6. *The Law as Gospel: Revival and Reform in the Theology of Charles G. Finney,* by David L. Weddle. 1985.

7. *Spirit and Intellect: Thomas Upham's Holiness Theology,* by Darius L. Salter. 1986.

8. *The Woman Evangelist: The Life and Times of Charismatic Evangelist Maria B. Woodworth-Etter,* by Wayne E. Warner. 1986.

9. *The Chicago Revival, 1876: Society and Revivalism in a Nineteenth-Century City,* by Darrel M. Robertson. 1989.

10. *Sacraments and the Salvation Army: Pneumatological Foundations,* by R. David Rightmire. 1990.

11. *Sectarian Against His Will: Gerrit Roelof Polman and the Birth of Pentecostalism in the Netherlands,* by Cornelius van der Laan. 1991.

The Holiness Revival
of the Nineteenth Century

Second Edition

by
Melvin Easterday Dieter

Studies in Evangelicalism, No. 1

The Scarecrow Press, Inc.
Lanham, Md., and London

SCARECROW PRESS, INC.

Published in the United States of America
by Scarecrow Press, Inc.
4720 Boston Way
Lanham, Maryland 20706

4 Pleydell Gardens, Folkestone
Kent CT20 2DN, England

British Cataloguing-in-Publication Information Available

Library of Congress Cataloging-in-Publication Data

Dieter, Melvin Easterday.
The holiness revival of the nineteenth century / by Melvin
Easterday Dieter. —Second ed.
p. cm. — (Studies in evangelicalism ; no. 1)
Includes bibliographical refereces and index.
1. Holiness churches—United States—History—19th century.
2. Holiness churches—Europe—History—19th century. 3. Revivals
—United States—History—19th century. 4. Revivals—Europe—
History—19th century. 5. United States—Church history—19th
century. 6. Europe—Church history—19th century. I. Title.
II. Series.
BX7990.H6D53 1996 277.3'081—dc20 95-25919

ISBN 0–8108–3045–0 (cloth : alk. paper)
ISBN 0–8108–3155–4 (pbk. : alk. paper)

To Hallie,
for love, wisdom,
and a lot of hard work

Contents

Editor's Note

The current resurgence of interest in Evagelical religion has high-lighted the importance of Evangelicalism in the formation of American culture. This series seeks to explore its roots in the Evangelical Revival and the religious Awakenings of the 18th century, its 19th century blossoming in revivalism and social reform, and its 20th century development in both sect and "mainline" churches. We will be particularly concerned to emphasize the diversity within Evangelicalism—the search for holiness, the Millennial traditions, Fundamentalism, Pentecostalism, and so forth. We are pleased to publish this revised and expanded edition of Melvin Dieter's acclaimed study of the holiness revival in the 19th-century America, which launched out series in 1980.

Following undergraduate studies with honors at Muhlenberg College, Professor Dieter studied theology first at Eastern Pilgrim College and then at Temple University in Philadelphia where he took the doctorate in 1973. He took leadership in developing and writing the three-volume Wesleyan Theological Perspectives series 1981-1986, and edited an important collection of devotional writings of Hannah Whitall Smith (1986). For twenty years he has been a regular contributor to theological journals.

The former General Secretary of Educational Institutions of the Wesleyan Church, he taught church history at Asbury Theological Seminary in Wilmore, Kentucky, where he also served as academic vice president. He recently retired to Lyndhurst, Virginia.

Donald W. Dayton
Northern Baptist Theological Seminary
Lombard, Illinois

Kenneth E. Rowe
Drew University
Madison, New Jersey

Preface to First Edition

This journey through the nineteenth century began almost thirty years ago at a small college near Boston, Massachusetts. There, at a chance meeting, two fledgling history professors shared their common interest in someday writing the history of the American perfectionist revival movement.

Both men eventually used their doctoral research projects to that end. In 1957, Dr. Timothy Smith's thesis on revivalism and social reform brought the movement to the attention of the academic and religious world. That volume quickly took its place as one of the crucially definitive interpretations of nineteenth century religious and social history.

The other young man, after long involement in academic administration, finally got back to his own commitment to contribute to the history of the holiness revival; his doctoral research is summed up largely in the volume which follows. One of the joys of that research was to share the journey again with Tim Smith, now director of studies in American religion at Johns Hopkins University. Dr. Smith served on the doctoral committee.

Many others have shared in the venture. Dr. Franklin H. Littell graciously adopted a doctoral candidate at a critical point in his study. Dr. Earnest B. Stoeffler, whose loving concerns for pietism shaped not only that candidate's teaching but his life, and Dr. Elwyn Smith, who encouraged the original research, were good guides.

The kindness of the many librarians who shared the dusty recesses of their nineteenth century collections was always an encouragement. Special thanks go to Lawrence McIntosh and Kenneth Rowe of Drew University and to the librarians at Pasadena Nazarene College (now Point Loma College) who were especially helpful.

And all along the extended journey, Hallie was there encouraging, prodding, *typing*—sharing good times and bad. Very near to the beginning Judy padded along—Judy, who is now following her own research and teaching paths.

All of us, who have experienced the pleasures of the unexpected discoveries as well as the humdrum plodding which a professionally honed venture demands, hope that all who join us through the account which follows will share the joy of discovery and find little "humdrum plodding." It has been a purposeful journey, and attempt at a balanced and reliable view of a small but significant segment of life; it has all been *con amore*.

Melvin E. Dieter
Wilmore, Kentucky
June 6, 1980

Chapter 1

Introduction

The Special Promotion of Holiness: A New Force in American Revivalism

It is a commonly accepted truism in American church history that from the time of the Great Awakening until the close of the nineteenth century revivalism was the dominant force in the shaping of American Protestantism.[1] The first issue of a new religious magazine in Boston in July 1839 announced the presence of a struggling, new force within the American revival tradition. Claiming a certain novelty for the venture, the Rev. Timothy Merritt, founder and editor, noted that his *Guide to Christian Perfection* was the "first publication of its kind ever commenced."[2] Merritt was a New England Methodist minister already well prepared for editorial work through his extensive service to the publishing interests of his church.[3]

The title of an introductory editorial, "What Shall Be Done to Revive the Work of Holiness in the Church?"[4] spoke directly to the special purpose of the venture. It rooted the then incipient American holiness revival, which the paper soon came to represent, in the revivals of the experience of entire sanctification in certain Methodist societies in England in 1760 and 1762. Merritt noted that John Wesley, convinced of the religious validity of the professions of those who had then testified to being made "perfect in love," had predicted that the time would come when "sanctifications would be as common as conversions."[5] In eager anticipation of that day, the editor concluded, "O, what a day that will be! What shall be done to hasten it?"[6]

The publication of the *Guide* indicated the editor's determination to hurry Wesley's hopes on to reality within nineteenth-century American Methodism. Merritt had prepared the paper particularly for the "encouragement" of the "many" who were becoming involved in a renewed interest in the experience of Christian perfection within the Methodist Episcopal Church about that time. "God was advancing the work in many circuits, stations, and classes," he noted.[7]

The *Zion's Herald* for February 22 1837, reported that at a recent Methodist preacher's meeting at Stafford, Connecticut, there was a thorough conviction on the minds of the preachers present of the importance and necessity of a revival of holiness both in the ministry and in the membership of our church; and it was a matter of rejoicing that the subject of entire sanctification not in theory only, but in experience and enjoyment had occupied the...attention of preachers and people more fully, for a few months past than for some time previous.[8]

The next month the same paper carried a report of the Maine Conference of the Methodist Episcopal Church to the editors of the *Christian Advocate and Journal* which indicated that there was "an interest in the distinguishing doctrine of evangelical holiness, greatly increased from former years..., " "and that an unusual number of witnesses of sanctifying grace have been raised up in different parts of the state...."[9]

By fall of that year, camp reports such as that from Derry, New Hampshire were common: "Many [were] sanctified and cleansed from all sin The work of holiness seems to be advancing in a powerful manner on many circuits and stations on this district." [10]

Aware of this immediate interest in the doctrine, the first edition of the *Guide* urged Methodist pastors to make the revival of the work of Christian holiness a particular concern of semimonthly "*special meetings* of the church." It insisted that, "the importance of the subject demands *special attention* and *extra effort* at this time" [emphasis mine]. The *Guide* was to become a special vehicle for publishing the personal testimonies to those new experiences of Christian perfection which were being made with increasing frequencies in such meetings.[11]

A NEW BLEND: HISTORIC PIETISM, AMERICAN REVIVALISM, AND WESLEYAN PERFECTIONISM

What Merritt could not know was that in his call for "specialty" he was most accurately defining a new emphasis, a factor which lent uniqueness to the American holiness revival. As the story of the succeeding history seems to demonstrate, it produced shades of distinction which set it apart from earlier holiness movements within the Christian church in general and from the promulgation of the experience of holiness by the Wesleys in particular. It also set the pattern for a movement which developed special organizations dedicated to the promotion of entire sanctification. This eventually, led to the creation of "holiness churches" and other religious organizations which made this "specialty" their priority concern.[12] Merritt's publishing venture represented a particular sense of purpose and logical procedure in the pursuit of Christian holiness unparalleled in the history of the tradition which preceded it. It marked the meeting of the American mind, prevailing revivalism, and Wesleyan perfectionism in as widespread a popular quest for the beatific vision as the world had known.

The Holiness Message

The adherents of the revival, which was gathering momentum and developing its character in the quarter century prior to the Civil War, were rooted deeply in the same Biblical orientation as that of the Pietists, Spener and Zinzendorf. They shared in John Bunyan's Bedford jail dreams of a Christian existence on the borders of heaven itself—a spiritual plateau beyond "the Valley of the Shadow...out of the reach of the Giant Despair...[and] out of sight of Doubting Castle."[13] They claimed to have found a spiritual highland where "they heard continually the singing of the birds, and saw every day the flowers appear on the earth and heard the voice of the turtle....[They were called] holy people."[14]

But they were also planted firmly in the midst of unique religious soil, part of the very pragmatic American experiment. Their vision of holiness was not a mystical one. They were guarded from such tendencies by their largely Methodist roots. Their pietism was a Wesleyan pietism oriented much more towards Christian activity than pietistic introspection. These American perfectionist revivalists appropriated Bunyan's pleasant "highlands" of his Christian's pilgrimage not for the "then" of death but for the "now" of life. They claimed that "pleasant" country as their earthly spiritual homeland; its Biblical language and rich imagery they adopted as their mother religious tongue. A present possibility of a life of practical holiness, a "Beulah land" within the reach of every Christian, became the rallying cry of the movement's evangelism.[15] To "spread Scriptural holiness over these lands" was the watchword of all who were involved,[16]

Claiming biblical authority and experiential authentication for what they believed was Wesley's own teaching on Christian perfection, they preached the necessity for a second crisis of evangelical faith in the life of every Christian. This "second blessing," subsequent to the crisis of evangelical conversion, as understood in the revivalistic tradition, involved the Christian's utter consecration of himself or herself to God through Jesus Christ in the faith that God would free him or her from the inner disposition to willful sin and fill the believer with divine love. The holiness adherents always denied that this produced a state of absolute perfection or of *non posse peccare*; they did maintain that, as long as the entirely sanctified individual did not consciously and willfully transgress this new relationship, they would continue in the Christian life with an undivided love for God. As they developed the graces of Christian maturity; there could be an enduring relationship, they said, of *posse non peccare*. Wesley gave this definition: "Entire sanctification or Christian perfection is neither more or less than pure love; love expelling sin, and governing both the heart and life of a child of God, The Refiner's fire purges out all that is contrary to love."[17]

The American Context

The American milieu in the nineteenth century comprehended certain cultural and religious moods which encouraged the revival's attempt to adapt Bunyan's dreams to everyday Christian experience. The expansive thrust of American revivalism accompanied by its emphasis on the universal call of the Christian Gospel made every person a prospective citizen of "Beulah Land"; burgeoning American Methodism with its basic commitments to Wesleyan Arminianism was at the forefront of the movement challenging men and women to enter in.[18]

A transcendental thrust was also shaping American thought patterns.[19] It "represented an intellectual effort to overcome the base material world," and "created a tendency in American Christianity...[to emphasize] the spiritual and ideal side of life...."[20] A perfectionist trend was inherent in transcendentalism itself. When the transcendentalist wrote that the "absolute or natural religion" is that which produces "the normal development, use, discipline, and enjoyment of every part of the body, and every faculty of the spirit; the direction of all natural powers to their natural purposes,"[21] he was setting out concepts, the connotations of which were very near to those expounded by the Wesleyan perfectionist who proclaimed that the experience of entire sanctification would free men and women to be all that a loving God originally had intended them to be.

Another factor in the total milieu was the idealism which inspired the American national destiny—a divine destiny whose goal was to create a new society, free from the ills which had plagued the societies left behind when emigrants set out for America. The conviction of the New England pioneers that their colony was "the place where the Lord...[would] create a new Heaven and a new Earth in new Churches and a new commonwealth together" had fixed itself generally within the American mind.[22] In their new land they were part of a new Israel; this vision infused both politics and, later, technology.[23] The inherent optimism in this American dream was readily assimilated with the optimism of perfectionism in the holiness movement; the two were to be regular traveling companions throughout the nineteenth century— each undoubtedly helping the other along the way. For the holiness advocate it was all a part of a grand, divine plan to usher in the "most glorious and last dispensation"—the dispensation of the Holy Spirit.[24]

In the midst of these, often mutually serving, religious, social and political currents, those who professed this "second blessing" witnessed everywhere to the new depths of spiritual reality they believed the experience of "perfect love" had opened for them. They zealously invited all Christendom to share in their discovery. With unbounded expectation they proclaimed the advent of a new dispensation of spiritual power.

In this experience, Christians who felt increasingly threatened by the rapidly altering culture in which they lived, might discover new resources for personal endurance and collective counterattack upon the evils which these changes represented to them.

The power and the victory promised in the optimism of the holiness message, therefore, may be seen, from this aspect, as a natural and significant consequence of developing revivalism among individuals in whom the principles of perfectionism, puritanism and pietism were at work.[25] It was a response to an urgent desire for some effective, counterrevolutionary, spiritual force which could enable the individual Christian, other Christians, and through them the Christian church to cope with the disturbing changes in society as a whole. They were certain that this formula for Christian action promised a "panacea" for "all" their evils. It could "solve all the religious, social, and political problems of mankind."[26] Regardless of whatever other bastions of traditional Christianity might fall before the increasing onslaughts of its critics, they believed that as long as "Pentecostal effusions" continued to manifest themselves, "primitive Christianity survives in one of its chief characteristics and will...vindicate its reality and potency...."[27]

THE SIGNIFICANCE OF THE MOVEMENT
IN CHURCH HISTORY

The story of the holiness movement is not, consequently, a story of unique twists of unorthodox patterns of theology or of Christian life; it is rather an account of a movement at the center of an accelerating current of some of the steadily flowing streams of Christian tradition. The quest eventually resulted in bringing thousands of new converts into the Christian faith and churches, but its main thrust was to reform the church itself.

In the Christian reform tradition which sought to assert the claims of apostolic Christianity as the pattern for determining the nature of the church and its life, the movement, like Wesley and the Anabaptists before him, generally considered the church far gone from original Christianity.

Its professed primary aim was to bring the fallen church back to primitive New Testament standards. The revival call to the church to experience again the outpouring of the Holy Spirit, as received by the Apostles themselves on the day of Pentecost, was the focal point of this effort to restore the church to its pristine power and purposes. It gave the movement a compelling sense of mission; the goal was to "*Christianize*" Christianity. When one relates that goal to the prevailing concepts of American idealism, mentioned above, which cast Christian America in her role as the destined leader in the Christianizing of all society, he/she can better understand why the holiness advocates saw their own role as very crucial. The pages which follow will demonstrate that this challenge to Christians to discover higher levels of personal holiness and new sources of spiritual power in a second personal religious experience as definite and critical as their initial Christian conversion left a telling and permanent impact upon Protestant evangelicalism in both America and Europe.[28]

The Methodist Context and Influence

The preaching of the doctrine often created sharp division in congregations and denominations just as general revivalism, itself, had done throughout history. The Methodist-oriented churches were most deeply influenced; they eventually suffered the greatest loss of members to the churches which were organized out of the revival activity at the century's close. At the same time, the revival's influence continued to make itself felt within that church through the large number of adherents of the movement who chose to remain with the church in the welter of conflict on the "church question" in the course of the institutionalizing of the holiness revival.

This intimate relationship with the Methodist movement in America, undoubtedly accounts, in some degree, for the fact that until recently the significance of the movement in American church history has largely gone unnoticed.[29]

Because the early leaders were Methodists, their efforts were comprehended within the Methodist denominational colossus or in the smaller churches which circled like orbiting satellites around its strong Wesleyan-Arminian theological center of gravity. Historical views of American revivalism and evangelism have often majored in revivalists and revival movements from the viewpoint of Calvinistic revivalism. The leaders of these were commonly more independent of intense denominational involvements, thereby developing a personal ministry more easily identifiable in historical analysis of revivalism.

This involvement in the revivalism of a large, highly organized, revival church may account, in part, for the fact that we have heard more about the Moodys, Chapmans, and Sundays than we have about the Asburys, Caugheys, Palmers, and Inskips. Yet the latter group, in the history of American revivalism, represent holiness evangelists who not only set the stage for, or strongly influenced the main emphases of the former group, but also contributed directly to the American revivalist and evangelical traditions in a degree not yet adequately represented in American church history. In their efforts to reform the churches and bring them back to primitive holiness with all of its ethical implications, they were typically puritanistic: in that they were working within the structure of the church and not as independent or charismatic prophets, they were typically pietistic. They were puritan-pietists, but not separatists.

The holiness movement, which was fostered by them and their successors, today constitutes the seventh largest family of churches in Protestantism, according to *The Encyclopedia of World Christianity*—about 3 million of them in the United States and Canada.[30]

The effective constituency, however, numbers at least double that figure. Restrictive standards for membership in its component churches make it difficult to account accurately for thousands of nonmembers, actively involved in the institutional life, who in more latitudinarian churches would have been received into full membership.[31] In addition to the regular members of the organized holiness churches, one must include in the movement's statistics the supporting constituencies of the nondenominational and interdenominational agencies which draw support, not only from members of the holiness churches, but also from a less readily identified, but equally committed, holiness constituency within the older churches, especially within Methodism.[32]

The largest of the organized holiness groups is the Salvation Army, with a worldwide constituency of about 3 million; the smallest is probably a splinter group of ten or twelve members started yesterday, unrecorded in any statistical tables, yet clearly claiming allegiance to the theological and historical tradition under consideration. The majority of the organized bodies and many of the individual supporters within the United Methodist Church maintain cooperative holiness promotion through the Christian Holiness Association, formerly the National Holiness Association.

A CASE STUDY IN THE DEVELOPMENT
OF THE AMERICAN CHURCHES

In the degree that these groups vary in size and influence, so they also bear the demonstrable imprint of a variety of religious traditions, Quaker, Mennonite, Baptist, and Presbyterian influences all blended emphases of spirituality, simplicity, freedom and piety into the mainstream of Methodism to shape modern holiness life. The richly variagated design which one sees when one views these diverse threads of American evangelical tradition that have been woven into the fabric of the religious life of the holiness churches, may scarcely be found in any other clearly identifiable segment of American Christianity. A study of this mix and its major ingredients constitutes another central purpose of this dissertation. This heterogeneity has always given the whole complex a strong interdenominational flavor. Variety is a hallmark of the movement; it has tended to keep the movement more open and flexible in its responses to other religious movements than it might have been without such a multiplicity of religious inputs. However, at the same time, these inputs from so many traditions have consistently created differences of viewpoint which have hindered efforts to extend the organizational unity of the movement.[33]

One may find, then, in the holiness movement, a unique and distinct composite of the development of American evangelicalism of the past one hundred years. It is replete with instructive comparisons which can contribute to a more objective understanding of the movement itself, its place in American religious history and, therefore, to that history itself. The loose organization of the movement allowed the cultural and social forces which were shaping American religious life during that time to impinge upon, influence, penetrate and shape its component groups to a degree scarcely possible in the other orthodox, but already more highly structured churches of the nation. The resultant microcosm of American religious life demonstrates all of the forces that Sidney Mead identifies as factors active in the development of American denominationalism: historylessness, voluntaryism, mission, enterprise, revivalism, flight from reason, and the concomitant triumph of pietism and competition among the denominations.[34]

SUMMARY

The history which follows is a study in the "dynamic" orientation which H. Richard Niebuhr saw in American Protestantism[35]—the dynamic of a "creative" religious force "in the process of passing over into custom and habit."[36] The pre-Civil War story demonstrates the creativity of the movement in its development of a new emphasis in American revivalism by applying the logic of revivalism to the special promotion of Wesleyan perfectionism; the history of the postwar revival in America and Europe outlines the significant success of holiness revivalism in permanently placing this emphasis in the thought and life of all of evangelical Protestantism around the world. The final section relates and analyzes the "process of passing over into custom and habit,"[37] or the institutionalization of a spiritual movement into holiness churches and other holiness organizations. This study, in conjunction with the preceding sections, contributes to the movement's self-understanding, to its understanding by others, and to an understanding of nineteenth-century religious history, particularly in the revivalistic tradition.

NOTES

1. See H. Shelton Smith, Robert T. Handy, and Lefferts Loetscher, *American Christianity: An Historical Interpretation with Representative Documents* (New York: Charles Scribner's Sons, 1963), I, 194; *The Shaping of American Christianity*, ed. James Ward Smith and Leland A, Jamison ("Princeton Studies in American Religion: Religion in Life," Vol. I, No. 5; Princeton, NJ: Princeton University Press 1961), II, 194.

2. "Editorial Remarks," *Guide to Christian Perfection*, I (July, 1839), 23, Merritt rightfully limits the uniqueness of the publication to those of American and British Methodism, the *Oberlin Evangelist*, representing the perfectionist views of Charles G. Finney and others had begun publication in 1837. Future references to the *Guide to Christian Perfection* which became the *Guide to Holiness* in 1864 are cited hereafter as *Guide*.

3. For résumés of Merritt's life and work see Abel Stevens, *History of the Methodist Episcopal Church in the United States of America* (New York: Carlton and Lanahan, 1867), III, 504ff.; "The Rev. Timothy Merritt," *Advocate of Christian Holiness*, XIV (July 1882), 193-95; George Hughes, *Fragrant Memories of the Tuesday Meeting and Guide to Holiness* (New York: Palmer and Hughes, 1886), pp. 167ff. For a brief time in 1838 Merritt's name was carried as associate editor of *Zion's Watchman*, the abolitionist periodical published by La Roy Sutherland, also a Methodist minister. Because of failing health, Merritt never served the paper. See Edward D. Jarvey, "La Roy Sutherland: Zion's Watchman," *Methodist History*, VI (April 1968), 21.

4. *Guide* I (July 1839), 13.

5. *Ibid.*

6. *Ibid.*

7. *Ibid.*, p. 23. Merritt had considered the publication of such a periodical as early as the spring of 1825; see "Revival of Holiness in New London in 1824," *Zion's Herald and Wesleyan Journal,* XX (February 28, 1849), 33; this paper is cited hereafter as *Zion's Herald.* Sarah Lankford Palmer, who began the "Tuesday Meeting for the Promotion of Holiness," finally induced him to start the *Guide;* see Delbert Rose, *A Theology of Christian Experience* (Minneapolis, MN: Bethany Fellowship, Inc., 1965), p. 38.

8. *Zion's Herald,* VIII (February 22, 1837), 30.

9. *Ibid.,* (April 12, 1837), p. 60.

10. *Ibid.,* (October 4, 1837), p. 158.

11. *Guide,* I (July 1839), 13. Merritt had first urged such efforts two and one-half years earlier; see *Zion's Herald,* VIII (January 25, 1837), 16. The interaction between this Methodist revival movement and the parallel movement in the Congregationalist churches chiefly centering in the work of Charles G. Finney and Asa Mahan at Oberlin College is already evident. Merritt's publishing partner, D. S. King, published Mahan's *Scripture Doctrine of Christian Perfection* (Boston: 1839). Merritt quoted it in the first issue of the *Guide, loc. cit.*

12. *Infra,* Chap. VI.

13. As quoted by the *Guide,* X (July 1846), 20. Also see *Advocate of Christian Holiness,* VI (September 1875), 63.

14. *Guide, loc. cit.*

15. *Ibid.* A footnote to the *Guide*'s article illustrates the movement's common interpretation of this imagery from Bunyan's *Pilgrim's Progress:* "The pleasant country of Beulah, where the pilgrims 'solaced themselves for a season before they passed the river of death, seems to shadow forth the highest state of spiritual enjoyment attainable in the present life...." The name, "Beulah," is taken from Isa. 62:4; it means "married." The theme was widely used by the holiness movement in its songs, literature, and testimonies; see, e.g., Hughes, *op. cit.,* pp. 49-50; Harriet Beecher Stowe's "Review of Thomas Upham's *Interior Life," Guide,* VII (July,1845), 14; and I. N. Kanaga, "Visions of Beulah," *Bible Standard,* XII (August 1880), 8.

16. *Minutes of Several Conversations between The Rev. Thomas Coke, L.L.D., The Rev. Francis Asbury and Others ... in the Year 1784. Composing a Form of Discipline for the Ministers ... of the Methodist Episcopal Church in America* (Philadelphia: Chas. Cist, 1785), p. 4. This slogan represented Methodism's understanding of its mission as a church.

17. Thomas Jackson (ed,), *The Works of John Wesley* (Grand Rapids, MI: Zondervan Publishing House, 1959), XII, 432. It is not possible here to outline the varying interpretations of Wesley at this point; however, the summary in the text represents the traditional understanding of Wesley that prevailed in the American holiness movement. Harald Linström, *Wesley and Sanctification: A Study in the Doctrine of Salvation,* tr. H. S. Harvey (London: Epworth Press, 1946) and George Allen Turner, *The More Excellent Way: Scriptural Basis of the Wesleyan Message* (Winona Lake, IN: Light and Life Press, 1951) are two scholarly works that come to conclusions defending this general stance. W. E. Sangster, *Methodism*

Can Be Born Again (New York: The Methodist Book Concern, 1938), p. 86, said that Wesley admitted that in all the points in this complex question he could not "split the hair." Sangster commented: "Nevertheless, the ... centrality of this teaching to Wesley's mind, it would be difficult to exaggerate. In the hour when he was least satisfied with his exposition, he was most positive about the experience."

18. Timothy L. Smith concludes in his *Revivalism and Social Reform in Mid-Nineteenth Century America* (New York: Abingdon Press, 1957), p. 92, that by mid-century all the Calvinistic churches in the country except for the Scotch Presbyterian, Antimission Baptist, and German Reformed denominations "had moved decidedly to free will." Many of the former were also susceptible to the invasion of perfectionism. Also see William Warron Sweet, *The American Churches, an Interpretation* (New York: Abingdon-Cokesbury Press, 1947), pp. 130ff.

19. James E. Johnson, "Charles G. Finney and a Theology of Revivalism," *Church History,* XXXVIII (September, 1969), 357, notes that "optimism was the order of the day with an emphasis on the ultimate perfection of society through progressive movement in mankind." Also see Winthrop Hudson, *Religion in America* (New York: Charles Scribner's Sons, 1965), p. 342, and John B. Bury, *The Idea of Progress: An Inquiry into Its Origin and Growth* (London: Macmillan, 1928).

20. Jerald C. Brauer, *Protestantism in America* (Philadelphia: The Westminster Press, 1953), p. 160.

21. Theodore Parker, *Autobiography, Poems, and Prayers,* edited with notes by Rufus Leighton; his *Works* (Centenary ed.; Boston: American Unitarian Association, 1910), XIII, 335, as quoted in Sidney F. Mead, *The Lively Experiment: The Shaping of Christianity in America* (New York: Harper and Row Publishers, 1963), p. 92, T. Smith, *op. cit.,* p. 113, says that the transcendental "revolt" and the "quest for Christian holiness" were different expressions of the same "strivings."

22. Edward Johnson, *A History of New England or Wonder-working Providence of Sions Saviour* (London, 1654) as quoted by Willard Sperry, *Religion in America* (Cambridge: At the University Press, 1948), p. 249.

23. *Ibid.,* p. 250.

24. Lewis R, Dunn, *The Mission of the Spirit: Or the Office and Work of the Comforter in Human Redemption* (New York: Nelson and Phillips, 1871), p. 299. Dunn, a Methodist minister in New Jersey, was deeply involved in the postwar holiness revival, For further discussion on the "Age of the Spirit," see *infra,* p. 110.

25. It is difficult to distinguish sharply between Puritanism and Pietism because, as Ralph Bronkema says in *The Essence of Puritanism* (Goes, Holland: Oosterbaan and Lecointre, n.d.), p. 76, they are "religious tendencies." Their historical origins can be readily identified. Both were reactionary movements—Puritanism against impurities in the Church of England and then against immorality, and Pietism against the "dead orthodoxy" of the German Reformation churches. Both were reformatory. Both had the ability to combine with other systems, even systems opposed to one another such as Calvinism and Anabaptism. Both were able "to combine with different confessions and take root in

different countries"; *ibid.*, p. 77. Bronkema maintains that "it is impossible to draw a sharp line of demarcation between them, for they assimilated influences from each other." He notes that W. A. Visser't Hooft says that in America "the age of revivalism or pietism followed on the age of original Puritanism and in that sense the two can be distinguished, but the two eventually were fused and confused so that 'through revivalism, Puritanism became Pietism....'"; *ibid.*, p. 78.

In this study, therefore, pietism is the predominant term and is used within the definition given to it by F. Ernest Stoeffler in his study, *The Rise of Evangelical Pietism* (Leiden: E. J. Brill, 1971), p. 13-23; in summary, the four characteristics which he uses to identify the tradition are: (1) the essence of Christianity, a Pietist believes, is to be found "in the personally meaningful relationship of the individual to God." It is "inward" and "experiential." (2) He is committed to religious idealism or perfectionism; sanctification and a Christian life of good works follow conversion; the goal is Christian maturity. (3) His central focus is on the Bible with a consequent Christian ethic based squarely on the New Testament. (4) An "oppositive" or "over-against" element is always essential for the Pietist. Prevailing religion must be ignoring the views to a measure which calls out sufficient expression of protest by those who hold the above emphases to be able to identify a movement. These characteristics, Stoeffler maintains, may be used to identify an on-going "experiential tradition" in Christianity which should be a valuable tool in interpreting church history along with other categories commonly used such as the Anglican, Roman, Lutheran, or Reformed traditions. It has been especially neglected, he says, in efforts to understand the American pietistic churches and movements; *ibid.*, pp. 6-7.

The present work recognizes the validity of such an "experiential tradition" as most critical to proper understanding of the holiness movement in America. It may be best identified, perhaps, as a "puritan-pietist" movement with the "puritan" element generally used to denote the revivalist's concerns for morality, conduct, and the reform of the church and society according to the laws of God; "pietist" is used to refer to their concern for individual Christian experience, centering in both conversion and sanctification—all under the direct and personal guidance and power of the Holy Spirit. If revivalism tended to fuse the two in America as Visser't Hooft claims, then perfectionism with its concern for personal sanctification and its larger optimism for reform of the church and the world through the church infused new meaning into both puritanism and pietism. Perfectionism kept the puritan dream alive in the former's preachments concerning the new age of the Spirit and the coming millennium; at the same time, it put new emphasis upon the pietistic doctrines of experience in its insistence that only as each Christian realized the fullness of the blessings of the baptism of the Spirit in his own life could the age of the Spirit become a reality.

26. As quoted from *The Methodist Times* in "Timely Words for all the Churches," *Divine Life and International Expositor of Scriptural Holiness*, IX (May 1886), 305. Hereafter cited as *Divine Life*.

27. "Revivals of Religion, How to Make Them Productive of Permanent Good," Philip Schaff and S. Iranaeus Prime (eds.), *History, Essays, Orations, and*

Other Documents of the Sixth General Conference of the Evangelical Alliance Held in New York, October 2-12, 1873 (New York: Harper and Brothers Publishers, 1874), p. 351. It is interesting to note the emphasis which was given to revivalism and perfectionism at this Alliance meeting; Philip Schaff was the organizer of, and dominant figure in, this general conference; see "Evangelical Alliance," *The New Schaff-Herzog Encyclopedia of Religious Knowledge,* ed. Samuel Jackson et al. (New York: Funk and Wagnalls Co., 1909), IV, 221-23. Yet he was no friend of revivalism. Apparently, at this point the subject demanded attention.

28. The inscription on John Wesley's tombstone states that he revived, enforced, and defended "the pure Apostolic doctrines and practices of the Primitive Church." Quoted in *Zion's Herald,* XX (February 14, 1849), 25. For the development of the importance of the concept of the fall of the church and restoration teaching among early Anabaptists, see Franklin H. Littell, *The Anabaptist View of the Church: A Study in the Origins of Sectarian Protestantism* (Boston: Star King Press, 1958), pp. 46-108.

29. Merrill E. Gaddis, "Christian Perfectionism in America" (unpublished Ph D. Dissertation, University of Chicago, 1929), constituted the earliest attempt to evaluate the movement and provided the best source of general information until the 1940s. General surveys now have begun to recognize the movement as a distinct part of the history of American religion; see, e.g., Hudson, *op. cit.,* pp. 341-50 and Martin Marty, *Righteous Empire: The Protestant Experience in America* (New York: Dial Press, 1970), pp. 216, 226, 247; Smith and Jamison, *op. cit.,* IV, 327ff.; Sperry, *op. cit.,* p. 98, was one of the earliest to do so.

30. Barrett lists the Salvation Army, largest of the holiness churches, separately from the holiness movement. As Barrett projects, the present total membership for the holiness churches approximates 8 million to 10 million worldwide.

31. The statistics which the General Secretary-Treasurer of The Wesleyan Church reported to the Second General Conference of that church held at Lake Junaluska, N. C., in 1972 would be typical for most of the holiness churches. They show that while that denomination had a full membership of only 74,049, those churches which reported average attendance for the Sunday morning service listed 111,794 worshipers. Average attendance in the same churches on Sunday evenings was given as 66,961—only slightly less than the regular membership—while the average Sunday school attendance was listed as 135,030 out of a total enrollment of 219,497; "Statistical Report of the General Secretary-Treasurer of The Wesleyan Church to the Members of the Second General Conference of The Wesleyan Church," Statistics section, pp. 8-9.

32. The largest of these in the field of missions are The Oriental Missionary Society and the World Gospel Missionary Society. In higher education the largest nondenominational holiness colleges are Taylor University, Upland, Indiana; and Asbury College, Wilmore, Kentucky; Asbury Theological Seminary at the same place is one of the largest independent accredited seminaries in the United States. All of these, together with the other independent holiness-oriented organizations, are active with the holiness denominations, associations, and individual members mainly from Methodistic larger bodies, in the Christian

Holiness Association. The latter serves more as a point of common communication and fellowship than as an instrument of joint action.

33. These tensions surfaced most dramatically as the movement began to move into firm organizational patterns in the closing decades of the nineteenth century. See *infra*, Chap. VI.

34. Mead, *op. cit.*, p. 21.

35. H. R. Niebuhr, "The Protestant Movement and Democracy," Smith and Jamison, *op. cit.*, I, 22, 24.

36. Anton Boisen, *Religion in Crisis and Custom: A Sociological and Psychological Study* (New York: Harper Brothers, 1955), p. 93.

37. *Ibid.*

Chapter 2

1835-1865

The Developing Synthesis: American Revivalism and Wesleyan Perfectionism

To understand the essential character of the American holiness movement as a phenomenon in American and world religious history, it is as necessary to look back to Jonathan Edwards as it is to look back to John Wesley. It may seem to be enigmatic to refer to Jonathan Edwards before one mentions the name of John Wesley in searching out the origins of a modern perfectionist movement, for most historians of Protestant "holiness movements" of recent times would agree with W. E. Sangster that all of them in some way "stem down" from the founder of Methodism.[1] American believers in the doctrines of Christian perfection have consistently recognized such a debt. The movement always has struggled hard to maintain the label of "true Wesleyanism" in defense of its theological position. But the American holiness movement was just that—both "American" and "holiness." The implications of the latter have been recognized almost universally by those who have written about it; but the implications of the former have had less attention until recent years.

Thus Jonathan Edwards! For to speak meaningfully of the history and significance of the rise and development of the holiness movement in the United States is to speak of revivalism; to speak of revivalism is to speak of Edwards' revival theology and methods. They have become the principles which in fuller development, under successive New England revivalists, have shaped American revivalism. Robert Baird had already pointed this out in 1844 to his European readers.[2]

The basic principle of Edwards' evangelistic practice was the stress on repentance as the "immediate duty" of every sinner, "Now" became the moment of salvation for every non-Christian within the range of the urgent Gospel appeal of the American evangelist. "Responsibility" in the "old Calvinism" was matched with "ability" in the "new Calvinism," "The days of halfway covenants were numbered when New England divines established their doctrine of natural ability."[3] Revival activity became the hallmark of the American Church. It was not only essential because of the responsibility of the church to disciple all men, but in America it became equally essential to the structure of the voluntary church system which became the pattern everywhere after regular church establishment was no longer the rule in the United States. The winning of men to the voluntary support of the churches centered in revivalism.[4] Under the broadening influences of Jacksonian politics and this voluntarism, revivalism consistently developed, strong Arminian tendencies. Its opponents often labeled them Pelagian.[5]

By 1839, when Merritt put out his call in *The Guide to Christian Perfection* for special efforts for the revival of holiness in the Methodist Church, Arminian revivalism was well on its way to becoming the accepted and essential mode of evangelism and populating the churches. It was heartily accepted by certain churches such as the Methodist and Baptist; it became the cause of schism in others, such as the Congregationalists and the Presbyterians. Very few American churches were able to completely reject these "new methods" and the Arminianization of theological thought which accompanied them. Holiness advocates' hearts were gladdened to read in the *Beauty of Holiness* that Albert Barnes, a leader of the "New School" Presbyterians, was saying that he held "no doctrine which will seem to be inconsistent with the free and full offer of salvation to every human being...."[6] The pattern was so widespread that Methodist Bishop Morris could challenge the 1864 General Conference of the Methodist Episcopal Church to name any church at that time "where the five points of Calvinism...[were] plainly and pointedly and fully taught."[7]

THE PIETISTIC IMPETUS

To the Wesleyan perfectionists who believed that the sinner's response to the revivalist's appeal for justification by faith still left him, as a Christian convert, short of a life of uninterrupted love for God and man, it was but a short step, given the prevailing mood and methods of American revivalism, to move in with the "second blessing" message. The appeal to the spiritual advantage of a second crisis in the Christian's life was an extension of the basic revival call in every respect.

The invitation was a universal one. Every convert was a candidate. The sense of immediacy was also there; the time to enter into the "higher life" was "now."

Just as Edwards and his successors pressed upon the sinner the decision to forsake sin, so those who shared the sense of urgency expressed in Merritt's call for "special efforts" in the promotion of holiness, pressed upon the unsanctified Christians a decision to consecrate themselves entirely to God and be entirely sanctified, Harriet Beecher Stowe took note of the parallelism in a tract favorable to this new development in revivalism, She wrote:

> It has been found, in the course of New England preaching, that pressing men to an immediate and definite point of conversion produced immediate and definite results and so it may be found among Christians that pressing them to an immediate and definite point of attainment [i.e. entire sanctification] will, in like manner, result in marked and decided progress.[8]

The dynamic in both crises was the grace of God.

The application of the revivalist's methods to the promotion of this particular doctrine and the adoption by revivalism of the experiential goals and possibilities of a "higher Christian life," marks a change both in revivalism and the advocacy of Christian perfection. Those who look for the differences between original Wesleyanism and the tone and teaching of the American holiness movement will probably discover that there were no radical differences in theology and belief, but rather, they will find subtle differences in emphases that derive from the application of all that was America in the nineteenth century to the promotion and practices of the Wesleyan emphasis. Perfection in love or a "Divine fullness" was the remedy for the church's fitful periodic piety...[its] disgraceful alienation of revival and declension...." It would make the Christian church "as steady as Niagara."[9]

The pietistic essence of American revivalism also helped to create a religious and social climate favorable to the rise of a holiness revival during this period. Whatever else pietism has represented in its history of consistent influences on the Protestant churches, it has symbolized religious emphases which favored experience over theology and the call to individual commitment to a Christian life of witness and charity. It was not enough to be a "formal" Christian. Individuals had to know for themselves that they were "born-again" Christian. The logical goal of such a life was individual Christian perfection.[10]

The dominance of this pietistic view of the nature of salvation and the Christian life in the early nineteenth-century revival tradition and revival churches is a "commonplace" among church historians.[11] That this bent was especially evident in the Methodist Church with its own emphasis on experiential religion and perfectionist ideals, is also "a commonplace."[12] If the Great Awakening indeed ushered in "the Pietist or Methodist age of American Church History,"[13] as Robert Thompson concluded, then the special efforts to revive the pietistic, peculiarly Methodist doctrine of Christian perfection marked the high point of both these pietistic and Methodist tendencies; it was the "radical and popular expression of the new evangelism."[14]

OBERLIN PERFECTIONISM: WITHIN
A HAIR'S BREADTH OF WESLEYANISM

The Methodization of the Calvinistic wing of the revival tradition which culminated in a "New Theology" and "New Methods" reached its fullest expression in the revival efforts of Charles Grandison Finney. He, more than any other leading revivalist out of the Calvinistic churches, repudiated classical Calvinism's ideas of the inability of man to exercise himself in any degree for his conversion. Finney chided those in the churches who waited for salvation to come to them. He saw it following as a natural result of obedience to certain spiritual laws, laws just as fixed as the physical law of seedtime and harvest. The only impediment that hindered the sinner in responding to the Gospel invitation lay in the failure of the sinner's own volition to declare "I will believe and be saved."[15]

Obvious success in the practical application of these convictions concerning revival possibilities and methods to his own ministry gradually overcame most of the opposition to Finney's approach; the response to his appeals proved as effective in metropolitan New York City as in the "burned over" territory surrounding his home area in rural, western New York.[16]

In 1835, with the promise of substantial support from the wealthy Arthur Tappan of New York, Finney went west to take up the position of professor of theology at the newly founded Congregational college at Oberlin, Ohio.[17] Prior to that move, he had already considered Christian perfection and its possibilities in several sermons in his New York City church.[18]

Finney's agitation over the possibilities for the attainment of a higher experience of Christian life than he then enjoyed intensified with his move to his new post in Ohio. In his treatise on sanctification that was published in 1840, he summarized the basic issue: "Whether the provisions of the Gospel are such, that did the Church fully understand and lay hold upon the proffered grace, she might attain this state [Entire Sanctification]?"[19]

During the first year at Oberlin, he, with President Asa Mahan, began to look eagerly for an answer to that question. In 1836, both Mahan and Finney professed to experience a second spiritual crisis as radical as the latter's dramatic initial conversion experience.[20] The importance of these "second conversions" of the Oberlin leaders was that they constituted an explicit admission by prominent revivalists of the non-Methodist tradition of the inherent impulses within revivalism towards more intense Christian experience.[21]

The Oberlin evangelists' promotion of a perfectionist experience as the epitome of evangelical Christian life, brought a parallel impulse toward perfectionism into play along side the special efforts of Merritt and his friends to revive the testimony to the experience within its more familiar Methodist environment. Concurrent efforts of the two forces gave rise to a new movement that introduced change into both sides of the house; American revivalism gave perfectionist promotion new and effective methods, and Methodist perfectionism provided American revivalism with enlarged vision of the possibilities of normal Christian life.[22] "Beulah Land" was coming into view! On that common ground a new "higher life" movement was born. This advocacy by both Calvinist and Methodist revivalists assured a larger hearing and more vigorous leadership for the doctrine than it had ever enjoyed before.

In 1840, Finney wrote a widely read book setting forth his new views.[23] His critics maintained that these attempts to systematize the theology of his new relationship were never entirely successful. He attempted to retain distinctions from the purely Wesleyan view which he felt were consistent with his theological roots in Calvinism, but in true revivalist and pietistic fashion his experiential confessions proved more persuasive than his formal apologetics. The result was that he was probably closer to his Wesleyan sympathizers than to the theological turns which Oberlin perfectionism later took under the aegis of William Cochrane and President Fairchild.[24]

Mahan tended, even more than Finney, toward Methodist interpretations of the "higher Christian life" doctrines. He quickly entered into the growing controversy that the Oberlin revival had generated in Congregational circles. In the course of one of these exchanges with those who were questioning the propriety of the new turn at Oberlin, Mahan laid down the gauntlet for this arm of the new movement by declaring that the Church is now rising to ask of her spiritual guides, what degree of holiness she may rationally hope to attain in view of the commands of God, her natural powers, and the acknowledged provisions and promises of the Gospel? Till this question receives a specific answer, she will not and ought not to rest.[25]

Wesleyan perfectionism would attempt to give the "specific" answer. A new rising class of holiness evangelists in the revival tradition was to attempt to give what it believed to be specific answers; both were to give the Church no rest until there was some kind of decision.

RADICAL REFORM AND RADICAL PERFECTIONISM

Whether revivalism in its constant and essential activity in the American churches was at ebb or flow during these years is difficult to determine. It is certain that from the middle of the third decade of the century until the Layman's Revival of 1858 there was no general surge of popular revival similar to the floodtide resulting from Finney's preaching immediately prior to that period.[26] There were major diversions; financial panic, war, and a multiplicity of reforming movements weighed heavy on many men's minds. The reform movements of the 1840s in particular made a strong appeal to the puritan revivalistic mind, attracting to themselves much of the dynamic that commonly went into traditional revival religious activity.[27]

These reforming efforts were laced through and through with revivalistic impetus and ideals, particularly with a dynamic, perfectionist idealism that contributed significantly by the end of the century, to the rise of the social gospel.[28] They represented a turning outward of the concept of individual freedom from sin to the creation of a society free from evil as well. Emerson reported to his friend, Carlyle, during the 1840's: "We are all a little wild here with numberless projects of social reform. Not a reading man but has a draft of a new community in his waistcoat pocket."[29]

Among these reform movements were some which centered in a mystical perfectionism. The most publicized of these experiments that commonly involved radical expression of new social organization and interpersonal relationships was that of John Noyes and his Oneida community. The community's modification of the monogamous marriage relationship was first among a number of innovations that agitated Noyes' neighbors and the religious community in general.[30] Soon after Noyes finally located in Oneida, New York, the *Guide* complained that one could no longer use the term, "perfectionist" in its regularly accepted sense, because of a new class who are "wild fanatics...who have nothing in common with us except it be a few scriptural expressions."[31] This reference may have comprehended a number of less celebrated perfectionist groups as well as Oneida. The existence of all of them testified to the perfectionist longings moving through society during these decades. These groups were unrelated to the mainstream movements in orthodox Christian channels, except for their use of the term perfectionism and claims to its concomitant idealism. The relationship, mutually disclaimed and minimal as it was, was nevertheless, a source of concern for the perfectionist of the holiness movement. Any guilt by association which the *Guide* feared the Wesleyan perfectionist cause may have suffered from these associations, however, was more than compensated for by the encouragement that had come from Oberlin.[32]

A reforming thrust more amenable to the Wesleyan concepts of perfectionism permeated the abolitionist's crusade against slavery. Abolitionism was absolutist or ultraist in its moral perceptions; it was most natural for perfectionism to head that way. In its religious expression perfectionism demanded complete consecration to the known will and purposes of God. This level of dedication provided a ready springboard for insistence upon ultimate answers to moral and ethical questions. The relationship between perfectionism and the anti-slavery crusade therefore, was not coincidental. "Converts of revivalism saw that *the law of love...* was being vitiated by slavery. They had to act against it" (emphasis his).[33] John Noyes, the Oneida perfectionist, warned William Lloyd Garrison that the abolitionists could succeed in their efforts only if such efforts were closely related to perfectionist ideals. Garrison ultimately espoused perfectionism, but according to Benjamin B. Warfield it paralleled that of the more Wesleyan Asa Mahan, than that of the mystical Noyes.[34] Garrison's steady inclination toward revolution rather than reform, ultimately created a rift between himself and evangelical abolitionists.[35]

The defection of the Wesleyan Methodists, from the mainstream of the Methodist Episcopal Church in 1843 is another example of the interworking of the principles of Wesleyan perfectionism doctrines and the campaign to extirpate slavery as a moral evil. Declaring their complete frustration in their efforts to move the official stand of the church to a more positive stance against slavery. Orange Scott and other outspoken anti-slavery advocates in the Methodist Episcopal Church ultimately called a convention on the issues at Utica, New York in 1843,[36] which resulted in the organization of the Wesleyan Methodist Connection of America, sometimes known as "True Wesleyans."[37] Their perfectionist leanings were formalized in the adoption of an article of

faith on Christian perfection in the 1848 Discipline; they were the first
Christian community ever to do so explicitly. [38]

THE PERFECTIONIST REVIVAL IN METHODISM:
THE TUESDAY MEETING

There is strong indication that at the very time that perfectionist
impulses were surfacing in these patterns that traditional Methodist
revivalism and its witness to the doctrines of sanctified Christian experience were at low tide, John Peters, in his definitive work on the
relationships between American Methodism and the doctrine of Christian perfection, marshals evidences of the fact.[39] According to the 1832
General Conference Episcopal Address, the experience was "rarely met
with" within the church at that time.[40] Bishop Peck looked back on the
1830s as a period in the life of the doctrine in Methodism in which it
"received less and less attention...[and was in] danger of being regarded as a novelty...."[41] This period, then, witnessed a strange paradox
in relation to Christian perfection in the American revival churches: at
the very moment that non-Methodist revivalists were joining themselves to the doctrine it was suffering neglect in its native home.

If that point, however, marks the nadir of the decline of the doctrine
in Methodism, it necessarily marked as well the starting point for
holiness revival. In fact, from 1835 to 1858 the revival of the promotion
of the doctrine and the number of those who professed personal enjoyment of the experience appears to have expanded at almost unbroken
pace. In 1851, George Peck wrote that "within the last twelve
years...[men had] appeared in increasing numbers as open and fearless
advocates of entire sanctification...." (emphasis his). [42]

The most effective promotion of the doctrine centered in the activities of Methodist laypersons in New York City. Sarah Worrall Lankford,
one of the principals involved there, in a manner reminiscent of the
testimony of the famed Blaise Pascal, dated her entry into the experience
of holiness as of *"half past two p.m., the twenty-first day of May, 1835..."*
(emphasis mine).[43] Both experiences were datable. Her continuing
account of the event, however, bears little resemblance to the emotion-
packed record which the brilliant French scientist left us of his own
spiritual encounter. Aware of the spiritual ecstasy which many of her
Methodist forbearers had testified to at the moment they believed they
had entered into the perfection in love, she had anticipated a similar
surge of intense feeling of her own; but none came. Mrs. Lankford, like
Pascal, however, witnessed to the continuing realities of that crisis
during the rest of her life:

All was calm and stillness; I had none of the expected emotions.
I arose from my knees fully determined to rest in God,...if I had
not a joyous emotion in forty years. Since that...May 21st., 1835,
I think there has not been an hour in which my soul has not
been...resting in the...atonement.[44]

In August of the same year, Mrs. Lankford transferred the meetings
of certain prayer groups that she was sponsoring at the Allen Street and
Mulberry Street Methodist Episcopal Churches to the parlor of her
home at 54 Rivington Street in New York City. There the combined
meetings soon became known as the "Tuesday Meetings for the Promotion of Holiness;" they came to be the movement's focal point.[45] Sarah
Lankford's vivid religious change which she had just experienced,
probably helped to establish the continuing emphasis of the meeting
upon the instruction, attainment, and testimony to the higher Christian
life of heart holiness. The subsequent revival of the influence of this
doctrine within its home soil of Methodism and out to all of evangelical
Christianity in America and around the world flowed chiefly from this
"house-church." It constitutes one of the most unusual phenomena of
American religious history.

A New Approach to Holiness Evangelism:
The "Altar Theology"

Soon after the move to 54 Rivington Street, the sister of Mrs.
Lankford, Phoebe Worrall Palmer, also testified to a similar "rest of
soul."[46] She wrote that it had come after severe and prolonged inner
struggle. Mrs. Palmer emphasized three aspects of that experience: (1)
entire consecration, (2) faith, (3) confession. Out of these elements of her
experience and her understanding of the Scriptures, she developed
what has become known as her "altar" terminology or theology. It
constituted a *scala sancta*, for the achievement of entire sanctification
and the personal assurance of the reality of that experience. An understanding of its formulation and application supports the thesis that the
holiness revival represented a new blend of religious forces.

Mrs. Palmer believed that the Scriptures taught that Christ was
both the sacrifice for her sin and the altar upon which she could offer
up her whole heart in consecration to God. She reasoned that the divine
promise of fullness of spiritual life, release from self-will and the habit
of sinning could be realized in every Christian through entire consecration of the self offered as a gift of faith upon the "Altar, Christ. " The
New Testament, she said, told her that, "the altar sanctifieth the gift."
The sanctifying efficacy of Christ as the Christian's altar would enable

the believer to love God with one's whole heart and to freely love and seek to obey His commandments. This relationship of love remained constant as long as the individual continued to exercise faith and obedience.[47] She wrote:

> On everyone who will specifically present himself upon the altar...for the sole object of being ceaselessly consumed, body and soul in the self-sacrificing service of God, He will cause the fire to descend. And...he will not delay to do this for every waiting soul, for He standeth waiting, and the moment the offerer presents the sacrifice, the hallowing, consuming touch will be given.[48]

Or again, if one should ask, "How soon may I expect to arrive at this state of perfection?" she replied,

> Just so soon as you come believingly, and make the required sacrifice....When the Saviour said, "It is finished!" then this full salvation was wrought out for you. All that remains is for you to come complying with the conditions and claim it...it is already yours. If you do not now receive it, the delay will not be on the part of God, but wholly with yourself.[49]

On this straightforward appeal to immediate personal commitment rode much of the widespread response which Phoebe Palmer and others enjoyed in the special promotion of a second crisis in personal Christian experience that lay at the heart of the holiness revival.

The Significance of the "Altar Theology"

It is difficult to define the subtle differences which were involved in this critical restatement of the Wesleyan theology of entire sanctification from Wesley's own understanding of the experience and its attainment. Phoebe Palmer was a woman who always denied any inclination to theological hairsplitting. In that she stood squarely in good American religious tradition.[50] What she had done was to use her proven ability for concise, convincing expression to definitively record her own experience. She verified it, in true Wesleyan fashion, by what she believed to be the settled message of Scripture upon the subject and then called upon other Christians to walk in the light of that truth.

Nathan Bangs, one of her closest friends and regular attendant at the Tuesday Meetings in his later years, directly challenged Mrs. Palmer on her "altar terminology." Bangs feared that emphasis on the reliance upon a simple statement of faith by an individual as the basis of his claiming the experience of entire sanctification endangered the concept of the "witness of the Spirit" that constituted the ground for assurance of spiritual life in historical Wesleyanism. Bangs, in essence, said that one cannot claim to have believed until God witnesses the same to him/her; Mrs. Palmer, on the other hand, said God cannot witness to seekers until they have believed and refuse to waiver until the witness is given.[51] Two articles in the January 1857 issue of the *Beauty of Holiness* illustrated the tension on the question which prevailed within the movement. In a letter to Mrs. French, the editor, Dr. Bangs insisted that

> until this [work of entire sanctification] is done for me and in me, I have no right to believe I have complied with the condition, for he has promised that the moment I do this, he will receive and give me the spirit of adoption and, therefore, if I have not the spirit of adoption, I may rest assured that I have not believed with the heart unto righteousness....[52]

In her "Editorial Sketches," Mrs. French took up the very phraseology which Bangs was criticizing by saying: "If you do by grace now claim that promise, confess that you claim it, that it is yours....Your faith cannot go beyond the promise, power, willingness of God...."[53]

Those who defended the steps which Mrs. Palmer outlined for personal attainment of Christian perfection were able to match each of them with definite parallels in the regular teaching of John Wesley. In her book, *Incidental Illustrations of the Economy of Salvation*, she drew on Wesley's works to support her own positions on the immediacy of the experience, the distinction between the experiences of conversions and entire sanctification, the place of faith in acquiring the experience, and the necessity for public testimony if one is to retain the experience. In his sermon on "The Scripture Way of Salvation" Wesley had said, "If you seek it [entire sanctification] by faith, expect it *as you are* and expect it *now* (emphasis his)."[54] As a result of this congruity, the terminology and the steps she outlined for attainment of the traditional Wesleyan experience of perfect love were finally commonly accepted in Methodism.

The acceptance was not total, however. The main point of concern for most of those who hesitated to fully endorse the implications of this "altar theology," was the fear that the demand for "naked faith in a naked promise," too readily, inferred a kind of auto-suggestion or self-deception concerning spiritual attainment, which somehow was in conflict with, or was an unacceptable substitute for, the Methodist doctrine of definite assurance and the witness of the Spirit. Her own life and writings give no hint that she herself, suffered any problems at this point.[55] In an earlier conflict over the question in 1848, however, Mrs. Palmer had written to Mrs. L. L. Hamline that "the entire Scriptures are the voice of the Holy Spirit....The promises of God are fulfilled the moment the waiting one relies fully upon the Promisor, after having complied with the stipulations laid down in His word."[56]

It was because of her insistence on the qualifying limitations of the compliance, called for in the final clause of the preceding statement, that she denied ever having taught "only believe you have it and you have got it." Such phraseology, she contended," is not scriptural...." Wesley, himself, after struggling with the issue, had decided that his own difficulty in trying to explicate the question arose out of the tension between his earnest conviction that every man could believe "if he will"; and his equally earnest denial that every man could believe "when he will"; he finally relegated the matter to a condition of permanent tension, and concluded that "there will always be something in the matter which we cannot well comprehend or explain."[57]

Abel Stevens, editor of the *Christian Advocate and Journal*, was very sympathetic to the Palmer movement. In his biography of his close friend, Nathan Bangs, he concluded that Bangs, in spite of the strong remonstrance on Mrs. Palmer's "altar terminology," referred to above, nevertheless, had "pronounced her teachings substantially orthodox, and Wesleyan, and in his opinion he had the concurrence of many of our [Methodism's] best minds."[58]

Eventually the "altar theology" set the common, but not exclusive, pattern for further formulation of the experience in the theology and preaching of what became the holiness movement.[59] Both Charles Jones and John Peters agree that the "altar theology" introduced new emphases in Wesleyan perfectionism that produced permanent changes in Methodist teaching and in that of the developing movement.[60] Ivan Howard maintains that Phoebe Palmer was really struggling with a contradiction in Wesley's own definition of the witness of the Spirit and his doctrine of assurance; he wavered, Howard contends, in defining the permanence and persistence of his subjective "inner persuasion" in the heart of the believer. Mrs. Palmer's approach, he concludes, appears to be more consistent in that she laid the greater emphasis on the individual's more objective reliance upon what she considered to be the clear Scriptural truths of the possibilities of personal holiness.[61] The newness then, essentially was a change in emphasis resulting from a simple, literal Biblical faith and the prevailing mood of revivalism combined with an impatient, American pragmatism that always seeks

to make a reality at the moment whatever is considered at all possible
in the future.

*Edwards' "immediateness" and Finney's "directness" joined with
Wesley's claim to full release from sin to create a powerful logic for the new
perfectionist movement's challenge to Methodism and the whole Christian
church.* If one accepts the conclusion of William Warren Sweet that the
new revivalism of Finney "made salvation the beginning of religious
experience in contrast to the older revivalism which made conversion
the end,"[62] then one could contrast Mrs Palmer's view of the attainment
and meaning of entire sanctification with the prevailing tone of Wesley's
teaching in similar terms, and that in spite of Wesley's use, at times, of
the "now" element in the experience. For the Palmer movement, perfection in love was the beginning of days for the Christian and, therefore, an urgent necessity of the moment; in the English Wesleyan
Revival it obviously had carried less urgency and might not become a
reality until the end of the Christian's days. The understanding of this
distinction is fundamental to the understanding of the American revival
in relation to its original Methodist roots.[63]

There is little question that some who sought to follow the Palmer
path too literally, failed to achieve her own balance at these points.
Those who accused her of setting up a theological syllogism were not
completely in error, for one of the patterns into which the theology and
preaching of the ensuing holiness movement often fell, was to press
upon seekers after holiness a too simplistic, stereotyped formula for the
promised attainment of so existential a spiritual experience.

Henry Clay Morrison, a leader in the southern holiness movement
at the turn of the century, took note of this tendency toward what he,
with Bangs before him, felt was spiritual presumption. He said:

> I sometimes meet people who say when asked if they are sancti-
> fied, "Yes I have taken it by faith." Well where is the witness?"
> Brother you have no right to stop crying to God until the baptism
> consciously falls." [64]

There is evidence, on the other hand, however, that other holiness
preachers, in an exactly opposite tack, used the failure to accept the
experience within the terminology and pattern of the Palmers' revivalistic formulation of it, as de facto evidence of willful unbelief on the part
of a halting hearer; they then concluded that such indecision threatened
to keep the conscientious, but confused, individual not only out of the
experience, but out of heaven itself. Granted the urgency which characterized the revivalistic message, it was not difficult for some to take

up such a statement by Mrs. Palmer as, "if you delay presenting the sacrifice from any cause whatsoever, you make food for repentance, God demands present holiness,"[65] and press it unduly into a pattern of "holiness or hell" preaching which appeared early in the movement; it maintained that those who die without a personal conscious crisis experience of entire sanctification would not be saved. Mr. Wesley's admonition to avoid "harshly preaching perfection" and to always place it in "the most amiable light"[66] was sometimes lost sight of.

The Specter of Separatism

Probably sensing an essential shift in emphasis, some of her contemporaries charged that her promotion of entire sanctification represented a position a step beyond that of Wesley, himself. They continued to maintain outspoken opposition in spite of strong protestation by Mrs. Palmer, herself and her prominent friends in the church who defended her as being strictly Wesleyan.[67] One who expressed fear was Professor Hiram Mattison of Falley Theological Seminary in Fulton, New York. He became a severe critic of Phoebe Palmer and her terminology and promotion of Christian perfection. He bitterly chided her for her "new theory" and her "shorter way," and he charged in the *Christian Advocate and Journal* that she was the cause of the controversy of "the last ten years" in the Methodist Church.

The developing holiness movement in the churches, he said, was an exact parallel to the disruption created by George Bell and Thomas Maxfield in Wesley's day. They too, he said, "began to preach sanctification as a specialty with great zeal and vehemence." His judgment of Mrs. Palmer and her followers as theological separatists who claimed to possess superior knowledge and refused criticism and instruction, raised all the ghosts of that old heresy in Mattison's Methodist mind. All this bode nothing but ill for the church, he contended, unless one of several things happened; either Mrs. Palmer had to change her position, withdraw from it altogether, or be properly disciplined.[68]

Mattison's concerns for the separatism potentially inherent in the extraparochial nature of Mrs. Palmer's meetings were shared by some more friendly to the movement than he. Jesse Peck, upon hearing of efforts to establish a special organization for the promotion of holiness in New Brunswick, Maine, quickly sought to lay any such ideas to rest. He saw nothing but schismatic possibilities in such a move. But the atmosphere was too charged with concern for the doctrine for such fears to slow down the momentum of the movement. The Tuesday Meeting soon became the pattern for holiness meetings both inside and outside of the churches.[69]

In the course of the ongoing holiness revival, the struggle to resist the divisive tensions feared by the movement's friend and foe was to prove long and valiant but only partially successful. Those Methodists who defended the growing popularity of these special meetings often held outside of the church and, therefore, generally free from direct ecclesiastical supervision, called upon the societies which the Wesleys themselves had established within the eighteenth-century Anglican Church as the prime witnesses to the integrity and regularity of their own efforts.[70] Others, however, remembered that, regardless of the integrity of Wesley's motives, his movement finally led to schism in the Anglican ranks and the formation of the Methodist Church.[71]

There is no proof that the early promoters of special means and meetings for Christian perfection in the Methodist Church had any schismatic intentions or even tendencies; they did everything to avoid any such accusations. At the same time, there is ample proof that those who harbored real fears about the ultimate divisive consequences of such efforts were accurate prophets of future possibilities. As early as 1845, Thomas Upham, a Tuesday Meeting convert, was warning the holiness people that in spite of the difficulties they might encounter in their efforts to live and promote their experience within their denominations and the consequent tendency to division and separation, they should remain within their local fellowships and bear patiently with the infirmities and even the sins of others in the churches.[72]

The beginning, then, of the long road at the end of which lay the loss of many holiness adherents to the church, was part of the microcosm which was the Tuesday Meeting. The close personal relationship between Dr. and Mrs. Palmer and their friends high in the Methodist bureaucracy, along with the restricted response to the more restrained promotion of holiness doctrine in these early stages of the movement, tended to restrict the tendencies to divisiveness which both the movement's friends and foes had already identified.

In the postwar movement and beyond, other persons with less influential relationships in a rapidly changing ecclesiastical climate would not allow similar viability to those who carried on the mission of these pioneer meetings. It was Mrs. Palmer's hope that "this church in the house" would be "one of the nurseries of the general church."[73] The unfolding history of the holiness revival and the holiness churches will reveal the fulfillment of that dream, but in a way quite different from what she, herself, may have anticipated. Her death, in 1874, precluded her involvement in the struggle between movement and church which began to demonstrate more definite patterns of conflict and even separation only a short time thereafter.

Most of these fears concerning the Palmer movement, however, eventually were apparently pushed aside by a massive outflow of spiritual activity. The age was increasingly pressed with problems which, many Christians seemed to feel, challenged the church and individual Christians to seek for more dynamic inner resources than they then commonly enjoyed. This, the movement's message promised. The quiet discourse and boundless activity of a woman who felt she had found the means of making these resources available to all Christians now, by a single act of consecration and faith, became the major impetus in setting off a worldwide movement. Whether the seeker for holiness was a Methodist bishop or the most ordinary camp meeting attendant, her directness seemed to work, and to the pragmatic American mind, that was what really mattered.[74]

By 1867, both the *Christian Advocate and Journal* and the *Northern Christian Advocate* were promoting Phoebe Palmer's major book on her concept on entire sanctification, *Faith and Its Effects;* the former commented that in that work, the author exposes and corrects the errors into which some have fallen, points out *the good old ways* of attaining this state of grace and supports all she advances by direct and incidental appeals to the Word of God. (Emphasis theirs.)[75]

The ensuing prominence of the "altar" theology or terminology in later Methodist, holiness and other higher life movements is the major, but not sole, indicator that the promotion of holiness by the Lankfords and Palmers in their Tuesday Meeting, represents a pivotal point for the understanding of these movements and revivalism as a whole. The patterns of the Tuesday Meetings portray a rather stark microcosm of the holiness revival and institutions which followed after the Civil War and beyond to the present. Much that continued to shape the character of the expanding revival forces found its roots here. It will be shown that it also left telling influences on the general concepts of evangelical Protestantism as well.

Although Mrs Palmer never replied directly to the assaults made by Mattison, her friends stoutly defended her position.[76] Nathan Bangs said, "The prejudices which have existed against her have arisen chiefly from misapprehension of her opinions."[77] Phoebe Palmer apparently evaluated the situation in a similar fashion, for she held to her positions and by extensive publication sought to explain them not only to doubting Methodists, but to the whole world.

The Testimony Controversy

Another feature of the Tuesday Meeting, prophetic of future traits of the American holiness movement, was the prominence given to public, personal testimony to the work of God in the individual's heart. Much of the journalistic reporting in the holiness periodicals which publicized the weekly proceedings of the "holiness meetings" consisted of verbatim accounts of individual experiences of the higher life. The *Guide* had been established mainly for that purpose.[78] Compilations of personal accounts of individual experiences of sanctification were widely circulated in promotion of the doctrine.[79] Here also, it would be difficult for one to define any major break with the traditional position of Wesley. Although Wesley, himself, nowhere leaves a specific testimony to his own perfection in love, he did overcome, in principle, his natural reticence to open up his inner experiences to others by encouraging guarded, humble testimony by those whose experiences he estimated to be genuine. In fact, his whole system of discipline in the band and class meetings was dependent, in a great part, upon the individual's subjective, public evaluation of his own state of grace and Christian experience. This critical reality of Methodist history was perhaps the strongest refutation of the position taken by those opponents, who in the heat of often futile argument, set up the absence of any recorded personal public confession by Wesley over against the often exuberant public witness of those of his spiritual descendants who felt that a whole new world of spiritual victory had been ushered in for them through this "second blessing."[80]

With mass evangelism and mass response there was additional opportunity, however, for modification or advance on the Wesleyan position, choose as one will. Even in Mrs. Palmer's time there were hints of a hardening of the line on this question which seemed to be such an essential part of the whole higher life experience and its effective promulgation. Her emphasis on public testimony usually took the form of varying degrees of insistence that testimony was not only essential to the promulgation of Christian holiness, but even more essential to the personal retention of that grace. One had to give public testimony in order to be "clear in his experience." Indeed if personal testimony lagged, it was one of the most certain signs of a lack of religious life which would finally culminate in complete apostasy.[81] The narrowing down of this position runs concurrently with the ongoing development of the holiness tradition within the total context of revivalism; that revivalism encouraged public profession of grace and religious attainment. Some degree of public confession was required to become a member of every revivalistic church. In reply to the critics, the movement also attempted to validate its basic claims concerning the essential nature of public confession in the lifestyle of evangelical Christians by appealing to non-Methodist authorities as well as to Wesley.[82]

Such testimonies of certainty and affirmation of personal experience, even in their moderate forms, frequently produced reaction against "enthusiastic" religion. Extravagance of expression afforded unsympathetic critics ample excuse to write off the genuineness of it all. Examples of public, personal testimony, which at times seemed to smack of hypocrisy, often made the most sympathetic, yet honest, observer cringe and draw away. Nevertheless, a movement such as this, which made a strong appeal to Biblical authorities and to primitive Christianity in justification of its practices, easily identified itself with the early Christians, who, when asked to relent in their propagandizing replied. "We can but speak of the things we have seen and known." In its strong emphasis on public testimony and spiritual assurance, the American holiness movement was a normal child of the pietistic, revivalistic, Wesleyan biblical tradition.[83]

Interdenominationalism

Another important facet of the Tuesday Meeting that demonstrates a dominant characteristic of American revivalism and also permeated the holiness movement was the strong interdenominational influence which it exhibited in spite of its predominantly Methodist origins. The centrality of the Methodist relationship was always evident in the support that the special efforts for the promotion of holiness enjoyed among the highest circles of that church's leadership. Less than a decade after the Tuesday Meetings commenced, Phoebe Palmer recorded in her diary that she had "…witnessed the ordination of Rev. L. Hamline and E. S. Janes to the office of Bishop of the M. E. Church." "They are," she said, "in no ordinary degree, lovers of holiness…."[84]

These new bishops joined two others of its supporters who, in that year, 1844, were already serving the church in its highest office—Thomas Morris and Elijah Hedding.

Bishop Leonidas L. Hamline and his wife became the Palmer's closest friends. Both the bishop and his wife were instrumental in spreading the doctrine and the literature of the holiness movement throughout the midwest prior to the Civil War.[85] Nathan Bangs, one of Methodism's most highly honored leaders, was a stout friend of the doctrine.[86] So too, was Stephen Olin, who was one of the most influential delegates in the founding of the Evangelical Alliance in London in 1846, and was a former president of Wesley University.[87]

The Methodist educators, Wilbur Fisk and John Dempster, were also strong proponents of Wesleyan holiness.[88] The former served as president of Wesleyan University, Middletown, Connecticut, the oldest Methodist college in the United States; the latter founded both Concord and Garrett Seminaries for the Church. Most of these men were among the growing number of the top Methodist leadership who frequently shared the Tuesday Meeting with the Lankfords and the Palmers; some came to be personally instructed more perfectly "in the way of holiness." All came because they were concerned for its revival throughout the Church which historically had practically claimed it as its unique glory.

But all of this Methodist influence apparently did not exclude from the movement the many non-Methodists, who in their own way, and sometimes using their own terminology, were seeking the same blessing in their own religious communions.[89] Thomas Upham, a Congregationalist professor from Bowdoin College, claimed to be sanctified as a result of attending a Tuesday Meeting in 1839.[90] Henry Belden, a Congregationalist, was a regular attendant; William Hill, also Congregationalist, who with Belden, was removed from the Presbyterian ministry because of his espousal of the holiness revival, came before his untimely death.[91] William E. Boardman, author of *The Higher Life*, was frequently there; Asa Mahan, colleague of Finney, and Oberlin College president, was a close friend, as was the Rev. Isaac M. See of the Dutch Reformed Church.[92] Boston evangelist, A. B. Earle, and the Rev. Dr. Levy of Philadelphia, both prominent Baptist leaders, were frequently involved in the services.[93] Dr. Charles C. Cullis, of the Episcopal Church, a Boston physician, participated in the New York Tuesday Meetings and promoted interdenominational holiness conventions over the northeast and England.[94]

Phoebe Palmer noted that "the time is past for the doctrine of holiness to be characterized as the doctrine of a sect. It is the crowning doctrine of the crowning dispensation."[95] Experiences such as that which she related to her friend, Mrs. Hamline, during the Palmer's prewar ministry in Toronto, seemed to her to substantiate such conclusions. She wrote that she had attended one of the "Conventions of Holiness" held at "an old established Episcopal Church." It had been "a season of Holy Ghost power...[in which] Congregational, Episcopal, Baptist, Presbyterian, and Methodist ministers as one [were] witnessing the great salvation." She added, "The Tuesday Meeting seems to be the general rallying point with these...."[96] The Palmer home and the weekly meetings for the promotion of holiness, thus became the nerve center of a general holiness movement outside of Methodism and a developing international holiness revival.

The contributions of Phoebe Palmer and other holiness promoters to the fostering of the growing unity movement among the denominations in the two decades prior to the Civil War, have gone largely unrecognized. But given her strong feelings on the direct relationships between the doctrine and experience of holiness and Christian unity and her widespread influence in evangelical Christianity through her personal evangelism publications, the views which she promoted through these channels and the Tuesday Meeting are worthy of note.

References are sprinkled all throughout her accounts of her evangelism in which she and other reporters relate her work and that of the movement as a whole to the ecumenical spirit which was then most prominently represented by the Evangelical Alliance founded in London in 1846. One of the most extensive descriptions of her hope for Christian unity and the role of holiness promotion in achieving it, is given in an 1857 report on the characteristics of the Tuesday Meetings written for the *Beauty of Holiness*. Their "unsectarian character" was one of the "crowning excellences" of these meetings, she said. The common experience of holiness united "Presbyterians, Baptist, Methodist, Episcopalians, Quakers, United Brethren in Christ, Jews and proselytes" in a single language of praise and a common desire for "free, full, perfect, immediate salvation"[97] To her mind, in such a fellowship lay the answer to the sectarian evils so strongly lamented by so many. She wrote

> We may long to see the happy, glorious era when God's people shall see eye to eye—...all united, heart, and hand, and soul, in the worship and service of God; all laboring...to do away the superabounding evils that curse the world...! But will this happy, glorious, joyful period ever be, till gospel holiness prevail.[98]

In describing the founding of the Christian Alliance [Evangelical Alliance] in London when more than thirty different sects were represented as a "marked success," she said:

> Every soul present, at one time, was cemented in love.... The room seemed filled with the Holy Spirit. It was a truly pentecostal season. Souls were on fire!—and they spoke as it were with other tongues as the Spirit give them utterance.[99]

The secret of the successful union of the churches, she continued, is the promotion of the experience of holiness which will leave no room for "selfishness or sectarianism." Granted this, she inquired, "Are not these meetings for holiness...the germs, the dawnings of millennial glory? Are they not strikingly imitative of the pentecostal?...Is not this the baptism now called for...ere the world blossoms as a rose."[100]

> If the union of the churches and consequently the salvation of the
> world and the ushering in of the millennium depended upon the
> promotion of the holiness of the churches, how vastly important
> then that meetings for this special object should be established in
> every city, village, country, place, throughout the land and world,
> by every church and people...?[101]

This natural relationship between a doctrine that heralded the
conquest of selfish interests through the promotion of perfect love and
the overcoming of the sectarian interests by the infilling of the Holy
Spirit as outlined here by Phoebe Palmer continued to remain prominent in the life of the movement. It especially haunted the leaders of the
nineteenth-century holiness forces as they sought to organize the divisive elements among the revival's converts into a common holiness
force. The implication for modern ecumenical efforts of this appeal to a
common spiritual language of perfect love which might overcome the
babel of sectarian interests are yet to be fully explored. The influence of
holiness revivalism that helped to give impetus to the beginnings of
efforts toward Christian unity along with other evangelical input into
the thrust for Christian unity was muted somewhere along the way.[102]

Along with this persistent impetus toward unity which was inherent in the doctrine of perfect love and the experience of entire sanctification, the common meeting of this heterogeneous group, with their
diverse theological and religious backgrounds, also displayed, in mini-
ature, the future pattern of the breadth of the coming post-war revival.
It also heralded a still more distant diversity of thought which would
be introduced into the later movement, often to plague its efforts to
unify under a single banner. Many of the "side issues," which the aging
Methodist leadership of the late nineteenth-century movement fought
hard to keep in the background at national holiness conventions, were
channeled into significant sections of the movement through men who
represented or at least were strongly influenced by non-Methodist
traditions that were rooted in the broader evangelical currents flowing
outside of institutional Methodism.[103]

Lay Involvement

An additional point at which the Tuesday Meetings participated in
a developing current of American religious life was the manner in
which they contributed to a growing consciousness of a new role for the
laity in the church. The Palmers and the Lankfords, at whose common
residence the meetings were held, were all laypersons. Both ministers
and laypersons were always in attendance after the meetings were

opened to men in 1839. Long before the great lay-evangelist, Dwight L. Moody, gave leadership to the revivalism of the last quarter of the century, these lay evangelists were demonstrating the potential for such leadership in the renewal of the church.

The promoters of holiness who gathered at Dr. and Mrs. Palmer's house every Tuesday met in a fellowship in which as an observer noted, "the ministry does not wait for the laity, neither does the laity wait for the ministry."[104] This blurring of the lines of the usual pattern of preacher-leader, layperson-follower was not an entirely new thing in American religious life.

As Howard Grimes points out in his essay on the place of the laity in the American churches, laypersons have assumed "considerable control" from earliest times.[105] It was fostered mainly by the voluntaryism which formed the basis of the American churches, especially the Disciples of Christ movement.

Alexander Campbell insisted that the "Protestant priesthood...stood between the people and the Bible." In addition to the Disciples of Christ, the other two large revivalistic churches also played a major part in the laicizing of the American religious life—the Baptists in their radical lay orientation and the Methodists with their lay preachers, class leaders, and exhorters. To these must be added the transplanted "Free Churches"—the Brethren, Dunkers, Mennonites, etc.[106]

The added significance of the Palmer's lay movement, however, did not relate to the question of the laity's place in church government, but rather to that of their personal responsibility for the mission of the church. To these individuals the position of the professional minister was, to borrow Spener's terms, one of "director and elder brother" along side the lay member.[107] Both were responsible for the evangelization of the world and the work of the church.

One can distinguish in this development another example of how Methodism and revivalism both permeated with Biblicism and Pietism, in combination with American democracy and activism tended to produce new emphases in revivalistic Protestantism. Singularly prominent in this theology of the lay Christian's place was the concept of the work of the Holy Spirit who cleansed and equipped each sanctified Christian, minister and laypersons, alike, for Christian vocation. This sense of responsibility and ministry of each spirit-filled individual believer was the dynamic which lay behind the ministry of the Palmers and other laypersons. Their lay activity constituted a dominant contribution to the outburst of revival activity in the Lay Revival of 1858 around the world and in the revivals of the last half of the century. Like its earlier counterparts in Europe had done, it released a massive flow of zeal for foreign missions and social reform as well.[108]

The Role of Women

The leadership role exhibited by Phoebe Palmer and Sarah Lankford in the Tuesday Meetings and subsequent holiness evangelism came at a time when the whole question of women's rights was being newly agitated. Lucy Stone made her first public address in 1847, and Antoinette Brown was refused the right to speak at the World Temperance Convention in New York City in 1853. This milieu may have contributed to their role.[109]

However, the greater freedom which commonly has been given to women to witness and exercise their spiritual gifts in lay and pietistic revival movements must be looked to to account for the fact that these women leaders of the early holiness movement could hold the effective places of leadership which they and others who followed them held. It was the theology of the movement and the essential nature of the place of public testimony in the holiness experience that gave many an otherwise timid woman the authority and the power to speak out "as the Holy Spirit led her."[110]

To those who allowed the theology, the logic was irrefutable. Although Mrs. Palmer never claimed to have preached, she wrote a widely read book in which she took to task anyone who would deny the rights of public testimony to any woman on purported scriptural grounds. She herself, probably "testified" more frequently to more people than many of the leading ministers of the day. One of the most outstanding consequences of her own ministry was the encouragement which she gave to Catherine Booth, wife of the founder of the Salvation Army, to begin her public preaching ministry.[111]

The camp meeting preachers of the post-war movement commonly advanced similar arguments. One of them chided a Presbyterian minister who refused to attend a camp meeting love feast because a woman was to preach by insisting that "She may—she will speak for the cross. We will listen to her testimony and profit from her experience. But not alone from potency of influence or dignity of her nature, but because of Pentecost."[112]

William G. Godbey, a fiery evangelist of the Methodist Episcopal Church South, the nineteenth-century holiness movement's most prolific author, prosaically summed up the persistent feeling of the movement; he took exception to the ancient Hector's address to his wife, Andromeche:

> My wife, go back to your home to quid the spindle and direct the
> loom
> Me, Glory summons to the martial plains; ...

Godbey commented: "That will do for a heathen warrior on whom the 'Sun of Righteousness' never shone. Not so in the army of the Lord...."[113]

Given this persistent tradition within the revival from Phoebe Palmer's time on, the new holiness churches, which were organized out of the movement in the closing decades of the century, were among the first to grant full ministerial rights to women. In the mid-1880s the Mennonite Brethren in Christ, a peace church group associated with the holiness movement, made full provision for women ministers.[114]

After a visit to Phineas Bresee's Church of the Nazarene in 1899, H. C. Morrison, editor of the *Pentecostal Herald,* wrote that "women are ordained to preach, and may sit in yearly conventions as delegates."[115]

Seth Cook Rees, a Quaker evangelist and co-founder with Martin Wells Knapp, of the Apostolic Holiness Union and Prayer League at Cincinnati, Ohio in 1897, wrote more directly about the question of women's place in a "Pentecostal Church":

> Nothing but jealousy, prejudice, bigotry, and a stingy love for
> bossing in men have prevented woman's public recognition by
> the church. No church that is acquainted with the Holy Ghost will
> object to the public ministry of women....[116]

At the same time, at least some of the holiness advocates who were active members in the Methodist Episcopal Church, lent their influence toward the attainment of similar status for the women of that church. Bishop Gilbert Haven, a friend of the holiness movement, defended the rights of Maggie Van Cott to her evangelistic ministry within the church; in her interests he questioned the judgment of Methodism's most able Bible commentator, Adam Clarke. But Methodism and others were not ready to ordain women.[117]

Phoebe Palmer's Biblicism

Phoebe Palmer claimed to have found her way out of spiritual confusion and weakness to an assurance of perfection in love because of the testimony of the Word of God to her soul. Her Biblio-centricity reveals another fundamental root of this early holiness revival which continued to feed the ongoing movement. In discussing what she considered the primary characteristics of her Tuesday Meetings, she said her theological and experiential foundation was not on "Wesley, not Fletcher, not Finney, not Mahan, not Upham, but the Bible...[which is] first, last and in the midst always."[118]

She rooted her own experience in that fact:

> I...covenanted with God that I would be a Bible Christian and most carefully seek to know the mind of the Spirit as recorded in the written Word, though it might lead to an experience unlike all the world beside....My highest and all consuming desire was to be a Bible Christian.[119]

This strong commitment to the written Word undoubtedly served to lend intransigence to some of her positions when more capable theologians sought to caution her on some of her expressions of her experience; but it also guarded her, just as it had her spiritual forbearer, John Wesley, from the many radicalisms so common to spiritual movements in the history of the church. Later on, the formalization of holiness theology often tended to restrict this immediate reliance on Biblical reference with the result that stereotypes, with their attendant proof texts, became the common authoritative staples that the faithful were fed. Nevertheless, following Mrs. Palmer's pattern, the movement became basically a fundamentally Biblical movement in that it sought its experiences and spiritual motives in the experiences of the Biblical New Testament Church and tested both its theology and experience by what it felt was the most accurate interpretation of the Scriptures.[120]

The interpretations on the essential nature of certain aspects of spiritual truth were not always uniform. Varying theological and historical predispositions brought into the movement from other than Methodist traditions were not always overcome by the appeal to Biblical authority. The differing views concerning the sacraments illustrate the fact. There is no indication that Phoebe Palmer, herself, held anything other than the prevailing view of the sacraments in the Methodist Church of her day. Other holiness adherents, however, held views which ranged from the traditional Quaker position that spiritualized the question to the views of some of the smaller groups who elevated foot washing to sacramental status.[121] Neither common insistence upon Biblical authority nor the spiritualizing impulses of the doctrine of the Baptism of the Holy Spirit to which the varying groups in the movement have been mutually committed have been able to submerge these differences sufficiently to provide an adequate basis for their complete organic union. Their continued close association in their common commitment to the authority of Scripture and the promotion of Christian holiness in spite of the tensions created by differences in other areas, produces a community in diversity which affords a unique opportunity to explore variations both in faith and practice among groups which, with such differences, ordinarily would be opposed to one another, not only in concept, but in context as well.

THE FIRE SPREADS

It was not long before many of those who had received personal benefits from the "social religious company" at the Palmer home were seeking to reproduce its usefulness in the promotion of Christian perfection in their own localities. Professor and Mrs. Upham of Bowdoin College established a weekly meeting for holiness at Brunswick, Maine very soon after Upham had testified to sanctification under Phoebe Palmer's influence.[122] By the 1850s, such meetings were common to a majority of the major cities of the east and midwest. All of them had one particular purpose:

> ..."Holiness unto the Lord." These meetings were not for debate, controversy, or speechifying, but for holiness. Everyone that enters these consecrated halls is expected to conform strictly to the objects and purport of the meeting....[123]

The format of the meetings was usually that of informal religious dialogue: "Many inquirers after the 'Way of Holiness' gather, and it is not unusual for the meeting to assume something like the form of an inquiry meeting."[124]

It is certain that the attractiveness of these Tuesday Meetings and similar holiness meetings was enhanced by all the religious and psychological benefits recognized in the "small group" and "neighborhood group" methods being used by churches as well as sociologists and political propagandists today.

When one analyzes the fellowship patterns of those holiness meetings by utilizing the categories suggested by Raymond J. Corsini and Bina Rosenberg in their studies of the psychotherapeutic values of small group dynamics, namely: acceptance, altruism, universalization, intellectualization, reality testing, transference, interaction, spectator therapy, and ventilation, one can identify the forces at work.[125]

In such interplay, communication was possible that was not possible under the more formal atmosphere of the larger meetings held for either religious or political purposes; prejudices were more easily overcome; the subjective feelings of those who were involved were more readily opened up to the common concern of the group; and unity of purpose and action were more easily achieved. Theological concerns were subsumed within a common experience; moreover, considerable imprecision of theological expression could be tolerated in the small, intimate situation such meetings tended to create. These were "family gatherings"; one could patiently overcome tensions in the family, where communication might result as readily from nonverbal understanding, which otherwise might be sources of conflict. In this kind of context there was also an interaction at work which made ordinary people often quite extraordinary.[126]

These small group meetings for the promotion of holiness teaching and the encouragement of the spiritual life of Christians parallelled in many significant ways both the purpose and practice of the "house churches" of the "spiritualists" or "sectaries" in the Lutheran and Reformed Churches of Germany of the Reformation period, and the religious "cells" of the Pietists which followed them. The service to the Christian community was similar. They generally represented a concern for the quality of Christian life rather than purity of doctrine and often served as centers of Christian lay activity.

Bishop Willard Mallilieu's description of the character of the meetings at the Palmer-Lankford home illustrates the parallelism: "It has not been a school where great skill and wisdom have been displayed in analytical definition of terms....It has not been a place of controversy, but a place where...a really new...life commenced."[127]

The Tuesday Meeting and the Class Meeting

But the pattern and meaning of these meetings must be related even more directly to the Methodist class meetings. The successful use of the small holiness meeting represented one positive effort, all unconscious as it may have been, to find a substitute to fill the spiritual and social void which was being created in the changing Methodist religious community by the declining significance of the class meeting. The latter served Methodism as an organizational unit which provided the opportunity for the small group dynamics discussed previously. The consistent appearance of similar evangelical "cells" within the larger structures of formal church organizations throughout church history indicates their proven utility and possibly their basic importance to religious life.

The Tuesday Meetings and similar holiness meetings, therefore, fulfilled many of the functions of Wesley's "special societies." Bishop John P. Newman called the class meeting "the nursery of Scriptural Holiness" (emphasis his). In his mind Phoebe Palmer was "following the example of...Wesley."[128] However, in the later movement, gathered together in a home as frequently as in a church, and a step removed from official pastoral care, instead of contributing to the unity of the denomination while they were filling the small group role, they tended to become centers of separate interests rather than instruments for strengthening the church itself. All that was needed was to take the holiness meeting to the masses, and that is essentially what the revived camp meeting movement, which became the leading edge of the tide of post-war holiness revival, was to do.[129]

The Importance of the *Guide*

The Tuesday Meetings and their patterns of holiness promotion could not have become the revival force they did become in Methodism and certainly not beyond it, without the instrumentality of a "special voice." As has already been noted. Timothy Merritt's *Guide to Christian Perfection* became that voice.[130] Its inception was a part of the special nature of the new methods to promote Christian holiness. Its pages provided the means to broadcast accounts of revival activities and, more particularly, "Accounts of such as have attained the enjoyment of this blessed state, especially such as have died in the possession of it....And let not modesty of any stand in the way of their complying with our request."[131]

In 1853, the *Beauty of Holiness*, printed at Delaware, Ohio, joined the Guide in the field of holiness journalism. In 1864, both the *Guide* and the *Beauty* were acquired by the Palmers, eventually becoming known as the *Guide to Holiness.*

By 1870, circulation had jumped to thirty-seven thousand. It tied the movement together until the official house organs of rapidly developing holiness associations began to enter the field. That competition from more strongly based organizational strength and interest might have forced it out of competition were it not for an endowment fund for its continued publication created by Mrs. Joseph Knapp, wife of the president of the Metropolitan Life Insurance Company, and daughter of Dr. and Mrs. Palmer. It survived until early in the next century.[132]

CONFLICT IN METHODISM

The years following the beginnings of the Tuesday Meeting and the *Guide* were "a period of unusual trial" according to the report of the statistical committee to the New England Centenary Convention meeting in Boston in 1866. It indicated that the decade from 1840 to 1850 had produced an increase of only one-half percent in that conference's membership. The committee attributed this inertia to "the reaction and deadness which followed the Millerite excitement, the losses of the Wesleyan secession, and the violent controversies connected with the Church South...."[133] From Massachusetts to Kentucky the same conditions prevailed. The historian of Methodism in Kentucky has indicated that although from 1835 to 1844, the churches had experienced revival growth in that state, by the latter date, "the agitation over the subject of slavery sapped the spiritual vigor and brought about an actual decrease of 1500 members."[134] The prevalence of these conditions across the church caused William Warren Sweet to call this period leading up to the Civil War "the tragic era" of American Methodist History.[135]

In the midst of this milieu the effects of the activities of the Palmers, the Lankfords, and the Merritts began to make themselves felt. The pattern of the growing revival is a checkered one. However, the general conclusion of men like Sweet and Gaddis that the doctrine was in decline during the two decades before 1860 is open to question."[136] The reasons for their conclusions undoubtedly lie in such testimony as that of E. A. Hazen, a Methodist minister, who recounted that when he was a student at Indiana Asbury University in 1846 he "seldom" heard the experience of entire sanctification "referred to in a sermon," heard anyone give "clear testimony to its possession," or saw anyone "invite Christians...to seek the great blessing...."[137]

Even as late as 1856, S. H. Platt noted that, "with a single exception the fundamental doctrines of the Bible are still retained by our [Methodist] people. The exception is Christian perfection!"

He said that the doctrine is still retained in standard authors, and preachers are required to emphasize it. "But unless appearances greatly deceive, there are thousands upon thousands...who utterly ignore it or regard it of little consequence as to be unworthy of their attention."[138]

On the other hand, there are many indications that although the fortunes of the doctrine were low they were definitely responding to the new revivalists' thrusts. In 1841, George Peck wrote that "the subject of entire sanctification is exciting great, great interest...."[139] In 1850, Nathan Bangs, a consistent proponent of Wesleyan perfectionism, reported that within the space of six or seven years there were more people than before professing "the blessing of perfect love."[140]

Moreover, a review of the many Methodist publications of antebellum years indicates the increasing frequency with which articles emphasizing the centrality of the experience to the Methodist's mission and the necessity for its revival began to appear. The *Christian Advocate and Journal*, Methodism's official voice; the *Zion's Herald*, one of the church's oldest publications; the *Methodist Quarterly Review*, and many other area publications took notice of the growing emphasis. Not all of the new attention was favorable, but it was publicity in any case.[141]

In addition to the periodicals within the church, which publicized the developing revival of Methodist perfectionism, books defending the doctrine, published during this period, indicated that some of the most forceful voices in American Methodism were showing a new concern for the subject. George Peck, editor of the *Methodist Quarterly Review* (1840-1852) lectured and wrote in its cause. [142] His younger brother, who later was elected bishop in 1872, published *The Central Idea of Christianity* in 1856.[143] Another influential spokesman was Randolph Foster, whose views were heard widely throughout the church through his book, *Christian Purity,* and through his work at Garrett Biblical Institute (Evanston, Illinois) and Drew Theological Seminary at Madison, New Jersey; he served as president of both of these institutions. He, too, became a bishop in the church in 1872.[144]

At the close of the forties, Bishop Hamline, also an active proponent of the new holiness cause, foresaw the potential for conflict which the revived interest in that doctrine would create. He wrote to a friend: "I am more than ever convinced that a conflict impends over the M. E. Church on the doctrine of holiness, but the results will be glorious. Where no war rages, no victories await her. If her foes are still, it is because her friends are idle...."[145]

He was writing about the time of the controversy in the church over Phoebe Palmer's "altar theology" and "the shorter way" to holiness; it was obvious that the "friends" had not been idle and the "foes" had not been still. The conflict was to prove an enduring one.

The opposition to the attempt to restore holiness in its traditional Wesleyanism to the church developed a twofold thrust by midcentury. The one already referred to of the Mattison variety attacked the new-revival efforts as un-Wesleyan; the second front against the holiness revival was opened up by a succession of men[146] who openly or by inference turned to a Zinzendorfian concept of sanctification which undercut the restoration efforts on theological grounds. In the developing conflict within the church, the holiness proponents generally suffered as much from the shift of the church away from Wesley as they did from those who tried to deny that they were his rightful followers. The dual lines of opposition created strange bedfellows in the anti-holiness camp in the Methodist Church. Men who considered themselves Wesleyan perfectionists, but not of the new "variety" found themselves joined in their opposition by a school which denied Wesley at the very point of the holiness conflict.

The controversies developing around the renewed interest in the subject were sufficient to command a warning from the Methodist bishops at the 1852 General Conference of the church. They urged all the protagonists to avoid both new theories, new expressions and new measures on this subject, and adhere closely to the ancient land-marks.[147]

Hamline's prediction of impending conflict was a reality. The tensions were real and would not go away even at the bishop's command. Both the "new theories" and the "new measures" persisted throughout the developing history of the movement in Methodism.

Whether the results of such controversy were as "glorious" as Bishop Hamline had anticipated in his remarks noted above, must be judged in the light of the bitterness of the polemics which tended to produce weariness with the question in the church; this noise of persistent rejoinder undoubtedly produced waning concern for the whole matter among many, who under other circumstances, may have given a more sympathetic ear to the appeal which to thousands of others appeared so winsome. It is certain that the debate, which continued with greater or lesser intensity for the balance of the century, indicated the strength of the movement and the centrality of the issues it was raising in Methodism.

The Free Methodist Separation

As the year 1859 began, the *Guide* took notice of a developing crisis in the Genesee Conference of the church. It reported that it was apparent that "a struggle [was] going on, not in the Genesee Conference merely, but in the churches of the land, between a modern phase of piety and the spiritual element for which our fathers contended..."[148] The Rev. Benjamin T. Roberts, a pastor of the Genesee Conference, stood at the center of the controversy because of his leadership among a group of pastors and laymen who protested a "New School Methodism" which had become dominant in the conference. Among other charges against this "New School," Roberts noted the new theological trends mentioned above, and claimed that they held that "justification and entire sancti-fication or holiness are the same...."[149] This concern for what Roberts and his sympathizers believed to be the Wesleyan doctrine of perfec-tionism, together with the closely related concerns for the abolition of slavery, and the enforcement of a more stringent discipline in the churches became the dominant theme of the protest of the new move-ment. When Roberts and others associated with him were eventually disciplined and forced out of the Methodist Episcopal Church, they took the name of Free Methodists because of another issue in their expressed discontent with the church—the growing tendency to build more elaborate church edifices financed in part by rented pews; this practice, they claimed, kept the common man out of the congregation and out of reach of the church's message. The *Discipline* of the new sect which was formed in 1860 out of a union of dissenters in the Genesee Conference and others who had expressed similar opinions in other sections of the Methodist Episcopal church, uniquely tied them to the Wesleyan perfectionism promoted by the growing Palmer movement. It played a significant continuing role in the advancement of the post-war revival and the organization of its converts.[150]

WESLEYANS OUTSIDE THE METHODIST CAMP

New literature in the perfectionist camp outside of Methodism, which fanned the fires of the revival interest in the experience, added other converts to the "second blessing" forces. Both Finney and Mahan contributed treatises in defense and explication of the Oberlin revival.[151] It was more natural that their writings should produce negative reactions among their fellow ministers than those of the Methodist proponents produced in their circles. But, as the impetus to general revival once more was generating strength in the nation prior to the Panic of 1857, the opposition to their perfectionism in Presbyterian and Congregational churches diminished. As Smith has shown even where the "second conversion" concept was rejected, many ministers in these circles espoused a strong emphasis on the place of Christian holiness in Christian conversion.[152]

The Influence of Thomas Upham

During this same period several books by Professor Thomas Upham of Bowdoin College substantially enlarged the perimeters of the new movement's influence in the churches.

His wife's urgent insistence that he seek the help of Phoebe Palmer in his spiritual quest led him to the Tuesday Meeting at the Palmer's residence in New York in 1838. That visit marked the opening of those meetings to men as well as to women. Following the pattern of consecration, and immediate faith, and public testimony, which Mrs. Palmer taught, Upham finally became an ardent member of the movement.[153]

His Congregational background, his scholarship, and his irenic spirit gained an entrance for his essentially Wesleyan perfectionist teaching where normal prejudice would otherwise have excluded it. This was particularly due to the historical relationships in which he saw the American movement. Upham believed that what was being experienced in the holiness meetings in America in the 1840s was part and parcel of a long tradition in Christianity. It reached back, not only to Wesley and the Pietists before him, but beyond the Reformation to Catholic traditions of piety as well. His book on the life and experiences of Madame Guyon, the French Catholic mystic and friend of Fénelon, received wide-spread publicity and review.[154] All his writings on the Christian life delved heavily into the relationship of the life of Christian perfection and classical mystical concepts, particularly those of the Catholic Quietists. He permanently infused into the holiness tradition in America a deep sense of experiential kinship with such Catholic perfectionists.

Upham's sympathetic emphasis on the importance of the inner, contemplative, devotional life of holiness possibly reminded some Methodist friends of John Wesley's warnings concerning the quietistic character of Catholic perfectionists.[155]

Even Phoebe Palmer warned her close friend that he was moving beyond the clear teachings of the Scriptures in some of his teaching concerning the possibilities of "divine union."[156]

A careful reading of Upham's writings does not seem to bear out the intensity of these fears or the continuing charge of "heresies." The reaction may have been intensified by the fact that his emphasis on the inner life of holiness was in quite direct contrast with the radical perfectionism which was then expressing itself in the reform movements of the same period.

Harriet Beecher Stowe defended Upham's strong appeals to inner holiness and a life of devotion. She felt they afforded an essential balance to the activistic mood of the times. She noted in a review of the book in the *New York Evangelist* that in spite of some difficult metaphysical and philosophical principles in the book, "The Christian may ...rejoice that such a work has been given to the church. The whole state of the times seems to call forth an effort to bring back the Christian mind to a deeper internal scrutiny...."[157]

The church, she said, was finding out that the mere organization of a voluntary movement to correct evils in society or the church did not automatically mean that "Satan was...outvoted." The book was a reaction to an age whose spirit was conveyed In the following:

> Only keep on *acting* for Christ and your *heart* will keep right....But while the church has been...enabled to do great and glorious work in...developing a system of efficient energetic action, are there not signs which show that she must turn her attention again *within*?...The experience described in Professor Upham's work

may be looked upon as utterly hopeless as a mark of personal attainment. Yet the history of the church in all ages shows instances how it has been attained [emphasis hers].[158]

Through the pages of the *Guide*, Upham also called attention to other Christian traditions which he considered to be in the vanguard of the revival of holiness during his time.

John Arndt's pietistic classic, *True Christianity*, appeared to him "to be everywhere favorable to the doctrine of evangelical holiness." Noting its influence upon the origins of Pietism, he concluded that, "the great power and charm of the work...consists in the prominence which it gives to the doctrine of entire sanctification. Not in a formal way, it is true, but in such a way that there can be no mistake as to the views; the desires and aims of the author."[159]

This type of interpretation led Benjamin Warfield to severely criticize Upham. Of the rapport which the latter established with the Catholic Quietists, Warfield said: "He undertook...nothing less than the amazing task of evangelizing...[them]."

He had really assimilated Quietism to Wesleyanism. He further said that Upham used "Miguel de Molinos to Antoinette Bourignon" adapting them to his own purposes "with utmost freedom, not to say violence."[160] Upham's writings were published widely in England as well as America. They prepared the way for the English holiness evangelism of the Palmers during the war; their influence moved on into the seventies opening doors for the holiness revival of the Smiths, Mahan, and Boardman. They continue on the active reading lists today. Through them Madame Guyon, Molinos, St. Catherine, Fénelon, Catherine Adorna and others in the Christian mystical tradition remain on the active list of holiness "saints" as well.

Harriet Beecher Stowe's sympathetic review of Upham's work indicates the growing desire among a significant number of people at that time for a different quality of Christian experience than that which the churches were then experiencing. Her brother, *Henry* Ward Beecher, too, expressed similar perfectionist sentiments: "Now this steadfastness of God's presence is both to be prayed for and possessed. There is provision in the Gospel for that very blessing. It is the promise of the Father.... It is made to be the Christian's duty to pray for it and expect it].[161]

Favorable, if not entirely approving, reviews of Upham's works also appeared in the *Biblical Repository*. Henry T. Cheever said of Upham's two-volume work on *The Life and Writings of Madame Guyon:*

These volumes make their appearance as the legitimate demand
and offspring of the times, because there is arising in the religious
mind of the evangelical Christendom generally a strong desire to
know more of that form of holiness, or phase of religious experience....The important truths wrapped up in mysticism, Quietism,
Pure love, or Perfectionism so-called should be carefully un-
folded....[162]

Cheever rejoiced in what he felt was divine purpose in allowing
"the ideas that have revolutionized the world...[to originate] in the cells
of obscure enthusiasts...." In the new interest in these subjects he saw
a potential for greater religious discoveries than the church had realized
to that time. The Harvards, the Oxfords, and the Sorbonnes would have
to systematize it all, he admitted, but it will originate "in the conscious
wants...and fulfilled aspirations of everyday Christians."[163]

In the same journal in January 1848, the Rev. Erskine Moore struck
a note which was not unrelated to Cheever's encouragement to the
churches to give the perfectionists a hearing. Erskine anticipated that
"as we draw near to the consummation of all things...we may expect
more wonderful spiritual achievements and more magnificent results,
than the world has ever seen."[164]

This expectation of expanding Christian experience and spiritual
achievements fitted hand-in-glove with the prospects promised by the
holiness evangelists.

William E. Boardman's Influence

These rising religious aspirations of the 1840s did not wane with
the approaching shadows of the Civil War conflict which was to test the
very existence of the nation. They found a measure of fulfillment in the
Revival of 1858. Their continued persistence in the life of the churches
right up to the outbreak of the war in 1860 is best indicated by the
enthusiastic response to the publication of a new book on Christian
holiness in 1858, William E. Boardman's *The Higher Christian Life*.[165] This
book opened the doors of non-Methodist churches to the revival's
teachings more widely than any volume which had preceded it. It had
none of the sophistication of the books of the scholarly Upham. Denying
any pretensions to systematic statements of theology and drawing upon
his own experience and spiritual longings, Boardman apparently
caught up in significant measure all the religious longings which were
coursing through the popular temper of much of Christendom in
America, Canada, and Europe at the time.[166]

Boardman, a Presbyterian, had had intimate contact with the mainstream of Wesleyan and Oberlin perfectionism. The writings of Finney and Mahan had been given to him by an itinerant Methodist minister. His first glimpses of the experience of the higher Christian life had come to him while he was reading the life of James Brainerd Taylor. He finally professed to enter his own "second conversion" through Methodist influences. This combination of both Methodist and Oberlin teaching and expression flowed through his work to produce a statement of the nature and reality of the life of holiness which was more widely received than the expositions in the more classic traditions.

The book enjoyed unusual popularity. It went through repeated editions in England where it was one of the chief influences in stirring up the religious awakening of 1859 and following. Within the movement and beyond, only Hannah Whitall Smith's later classic, *The Christian's Secret of a Happy Life*[167] sold so quickly.

In spite of his efforts to stay away from the traditional Wesleyan terminology, Boardman was essentially a part of the Wesleyan holiness movement. He was a frequent attendant at the Tuesday Meetings and for a time was the leader of Union Holiness Conventions in conjunction with other holiness advocates. He participated, although only in a lesser public role, with Robert Pearsall Smith in the famous English holiness conferences at Brighton and Oxford in 1874 and 1875. After a brief return to America, he returned to England in December of 1885 to make his permanent home there. The later years of his long life were spent in a healing ministry.[168]

A. B. Earle's profession of the experience of holiness in 1859 also secured a hearing for the doctrine in non-Methodist circles, especially among members of his own Baptist faith. His books on the subject emphasized the central idea of the doctrine as a "rest of faith."[169]

THE PALMERS' WIDENING REVIVALISM

The widespread preparation for holiness revival was not due only to these effective instruments of publicity, or the small group fellowships such as the Palmers promoted. The rooms where the groups met for mutual encouragement in the experience were too small, and the circulation lists of the periodicals devoted to its publications were too limited to accomplish all of that. The use of larger public mass meetings to emphasize the doctrine added their influence in this preparatory period. Methodist camp meetings and holiness conventions everywhere gave new attention to the teaching. Accounts by the camp meeting reporters of sanctifications reported along with the more usual conversions became increasingly common at the midpoint of the nineteenth century.[170] Prewar holiness associations and their public meetings in the churches already predicted the later pattern of more extensive organization within the postwar movement.[171]

As it is shown in a later section, the Methodist camp meeting, though much larger than the Tuesday Meetings, was able to keep alive many of the latter's small-group communicative and therapeutic values within its own structure; however, its more public nature necessarily brought charges which tended to a more rigid formulation of theology, practice, and standards by which the orthodoxy of true holiness faith and life were measured.[172]

During the 1850s, the Palmers moved the experience and the teaching of the Tuesday Meeting out into this arena through their evangelistic activities. Aided by the growing acceptance of interdenominational evangelism by the churches and the generally prevailing longing for some new transcendental word, they were invited to many non-Methodist as well as Methodist churches and conventions to speak to eager audiences about the way of faith into the higher Christian life. Together with the books already listed, Phoebe Palmer's own popular works had gone through edition after edition creating a ready audience for these two laymen throughout Canada and the United States and beyond. Edwin Orr who chronicles the worldwide revival which ensued in 1858 as the Second Evangelical Awakening roots the beginnings of the revival movement in the work of Dr. and Mrs. Palmer in Canada in 1857.[173]

Toward the end of the latter year, letters from Phoebe Palmer to Mrs. French, co-editor of the *Beauty of Holiness,* were filled with glowing reports of the revival upsurge which they were seeing in their work among Canadian Methodists. From a camp meeting at London, in then Canada West, she wrote:

> The meeting we have just attended has been one of the most remarkable for the displays of saving mercy, of any we have ever attended....Perhaps we have never before been quite so abundant in labors. Meetings have been kept up with scarcely any intermission....[174]

The usual response to the Palmers' ministry continued from the September of the incident above on into the winter. The very last page of the *Beauty* for 1857 carries a hurried insert of a two-line note: "Glorious News From Hamilton, C. W. too late for insertion; 700 converted and sanctified." [175]

This was the eve of what Timothy Smith calls "Annus Mirabilis,"[176] the year of the well publicized revival of 1858. The revival had strong perfectionist tendencies; it marked the beginning of a decade of renewed revivalism which was interrupted briefly in America by the spiritual barrenness born of war.

However, the eruption of the civil strife in America did not bring revivalism to a complete standstill. There were significant revivals in both the Northern and Southern armies during the war period. Some holiness adherents, mostly Methodist ministers, served as military chaplains. William E. Boardman served as Executive Secretary of the United States Christian Commission early in the war.[177]

Revival in England

The Palmers were in England during much of the war; their attitude, and that of other holiness movement leaders, toward the issues of the day may rightfully be criticized for its inclination to follow rather than to lead the public mind as the Wesleyan Methodist perfectionists had. The former were too closely linked with the leadership of the Methodist Episcopal Church to follow an activist line. The Methodist bureaucracy, on the whole, saw the slavery issue as a threat to the institutional organization; they wanted mainly to keep antislavery controversy from rending the fabric of the church. The Wesleyan Methodist schism in 1843 and the separation of the Southern church a little while thereafter showed how unrealistic this approach was under the temper of the times.[178]

If the revival progress in America was at least temporarily delayed by the war, the same was not true of holiness evangelism in England and Scotland during that period. After their successful public ministry in the United States and Canada, the Palmers went to England and Scotland to participate in the 1859 awakening of the religious interest there which was encouraged by the revival upsurge in America the previous year. They remained there for most of the Civil War period ministering in those Wesleyan Churches which chose to ignore the general ban put on the Palmers' work by the main English Methodist body. The constant flow of reports on their successful campaigns and the length of their stay indicated that the official Methodist apprehensions were not widely shared by local church congregations. The ecumenical character of the slowly rising English revival movement undoubtedly assured them their wide hearing.[179]

Influences upon the Salvation Army's Founders

Both the Palmers and Caughey had considerable influence on the beginnings and temper of the Salvation Army movement during their visits. William Booth was converted as a young man under Caughey's revival ministry in an earlier English campaign. In the Civil War period revivals, the Booths, Palmers, and Caughey worked closely in cooperative or alternating campaigns in England and Northern Ireland. It was at one such series of meetings that Booth's "Hallelujah Band" was first formed out of his converts; these lay organizations were one of the first concretizations of Booth's conviction that Christianity could be communicated to the common man most effectively by his own kind and through cultural media he naturally understood.[180]

But perhaps the most important influence of the Palmer-Caughey holiness evangelism in connection with the founders of the Salvation Army was that in these associations Phoebe Palmer's widely accepted and effective revival preaching overcame whatever reluctance Catherine Booth may have retained in following her husband into the public Christian ministry. She began her preaching career in the wake of the Palmer meetings.[181] The current work of the Salvation Army testifies to the significance of these contacts of early responsible representatives of the American holiness movement with the founders of the Salvation Army during its formative years.

The influences of the Americans for the strengthening of the Army's Wesleyan holiness position fed back into the American movement with strength and vigor when the Army began its American work in 1880; the Army's active influence within the movement continues to this day.[182]

Finney, another representative of the American perfectionist movement, also took part in the British revival. He was old and his stay was brief, but the accounts of evangelistic successes he leaves in his *Memoirs* are generally supported by local contemporary reports.[183]

According to James Orr this "second evangelistic awakening" effected every county in Ulster, Scotland, Wales and England, adding a million members to the evangelical churches, accomplishing a tremendous social uplift, and giving an effective impulse to home and foreign missionary enterprise. [184] The presence of the American holiness evangelists as part of the English revival activity proved to be part of the preparation for the influence of the movement in the later surge of revival in which holiness evangelists such as the Robert Pearsall Smiths, Asa Mahan and William E. Boardman joined Moody and Sankey in the 1870s. In 1864, the Palmers came home to a war-weary America, longing "for the dawn of peace." The initial ground swells of the post-war revival which moved to high tide within ten years of the close of the conflict were already being felt in the nation's churches.

SUMMARY

This chapter has attempted to outline the developments by which American revivalism, in the tradition from Jonathan Edwards to Charles Finney, and Wesleyan perfectionism, in the tradition of the American Methodists, each took up the emphasis of the other to form a new blend of American revivalism and Wesleyan perfectionism. One can maintain that to properly understand either revivalism or the holiness movement, he must take into account the results of the wedding of these two forces.

Given the American voluntaristic church system, which encouraged revivalism, and given pietistic revivalism's inherent tendencies towards perfectionism, the continuum was a very natural one. The call of the revivalist to the sinner, for an immediate faith decision for his evangelical conversion, was paralleled by the holiness evangelist's call to the Christian for an immediate faith decision for his entire sanctification. Out of this new urgency in perfectionist revivalism, reinforced as it was by the transcendentalism, the progressivism, and the optimism which were seething in the national mind at the time, a new holiness movement arose in the American churches. At its heart, it was a puritan-pietist movement which lived very comfortably, by the nature of those tendencies, in its predominantly American-Methodist, perfectionist environment.

The main focal point for these dynamic elements, in their initial interaction was the holiness promotion of Phoebe Palmer, her family, and friends. The practice, promotion, and teaching of holiness, as developed in the Tuesday Meetings at her home and in her ministry, became normative for the movement. It is difficult to overestimate the importance of a proper understanding of the nature of that incipient history to all further efforts to interpret the ensuing movement, or its proper place in the history of revivalism. Within its activities, the Palmers' Tuesday Meeting best comprehends the religious, cultural, and social forces which fed their input into the structure, teaching, and methodology of the holiness revival.

Phoebe Palmer's Biblical orientation carried strong Methodist and, therefore, pietist overtones, as also did her insistence upon the centrality of personal experience, and the individual's witness to it, as the essence of the Christian life. The movement's contention that the ministry must be "fully sanctified" to be effective and fruitful, the emphasis upon the priesthood of every believer, as demonstrated in the common ministry of laypersons and ordained ministers, the place given to the ministry of "Spirit-led" women, the ease with which men and women of differing creeds promoted a common concern within the nontheological context of the small group meetings—all categorize the whole as highly pietistic. It is not surprising that all of these should come out so boldly in a revival which had as its goal, the goal of all pietism—the sanctification of the Christian, and that, "entirely." Nor is it surprising that the movement should arise in Methodism, under the leadership of a woman whose father was a personal convert of John Wesley. The perfectionist, the pietist, the puritan elements—all were part of him also. These were ingredients that went into the dynamics of the special promotion of holiness, as fostered by its pre-Civil War proponents.

The terminology, the methodology, and the *praxis pietatis* which were fixed on the movement during the first thirty years, were both used and abused by those who followed. Whichever way it may have been, they strongly determined the future course and nature of the postwar revival and the holiness sects and other institutionalized forms of the movement which followed. Out of the same ingredients, the ongoing movement demonstrated, at various times and in various sectors, most of the well-known weaknesses, characteristic of pietistic traditions. Inherent in the Palmer emphases were the tendencies to deemphasize any theological definition, to overemphasize the validity of subjective experience as the norm of the Christian life, and to become introspective and quietistic. Phoebe Palmer, herself, maintained a better balance in these areas than did some of her followers in the later movement.

With all of the above, Phoebe Palmer and her friends, in the special promotion of holiness prior to the Civil War, set the patterns of a new evangelical pietism, commonly known as "the higher Christian life." Its essential dynamic was the one word heard most at the Tuesday Meetings—"definite." That was the keynote; from that platform a new revivalism had been launched.

NOTES

1. W. E. Sangster, *The Path to Perfection* (London: Epworth Press, 1943), p. 7.

2. Robert Baird, *Religion in the United States of America* (New York: Arno Press and the New York Times, 1969), p. 459. Baird's work, originally published in 1844, noted that Edward's principles had prevailed from 1735 to that time. Martin Marty, *op. cit.*, pp. 84-85, outlines the development of these principles in such men as Nathaniel Taylor, probably the most effective advocate of the "New School"; Timothy Dwight, President of Yale University; Samuel Hopkins, and men who followed a similar pattern in Presbyterianism such as Albert Barnes

and Lyman Beecher. On Edwards' principles also see C. C. Goen, "The Methodist Age of American Church History," *Religion in Life,* XXXIV (1965), pp. 564-65 and C. C. Goen, *Revivalism and Separatism in New England 1740-1800* (New Haven: Yale University Press, 1962), pp. 13-14.

3. Daniel T. Fiske, "New England Theology," *Bibliotheca Sacra,* XXII (July 1865), 512.

4. Franklin H. Littell, *From State Church to Pluralism: A Protestant Interpretation of Religion in American History* (New York: Macmillan, 1971), p. 55, notes that the American churches often violated this pattern of voluntaryism by seeking aid from the state. Voluntaryism also required a revivalism that would win individuals to the churches. In this sense Littell also maintains that the American churches essentially paralleled the mission churches more closely than their European counterparts; *ibid.,* pp. 57-8; the call to Christian perfection was closely related to the success of the revivalists in flooding the churches with new, but at best, immature Christians.

5. T. Smith, *op. cit.,* pp. 25-83, 88-92; also see Jackson, *Church History* (September 1969), p. 357.

6. *Beauty of Holiness,* VIII (February 1857), 36. Goen, *Religion in Life* (1965), p. 565, discusses the developments from Edwards down to the Methodization of revivalism.

7. *Journal of the General Conference* (New York: Carlton and Porter, 1864), p. 283.

8. Harriet Beecher Stowe, *Primitive Christian Experience* as quoted by Jacob Hoke, *Holiness: or the Higher Christian Life* (Dayton, OH: United Brethren Printing Establishment, 1870), p. 38. Henry Ridgeway, the biographer of Rev. Alfred Cookman, attributes this sense of definiteness which pervaded holiness promotion not to "New England preaching, but to Methodism; in the course of its history, he said that that tradition held "that when an object ought to be effected, there is a way to effect it, and that this way is usually the one that goes straight to the object and deals specifically with it." See Ridgaway, *The Life of Rev. Alfred Cookman* (New York: Harper and Brothers, 1873), p. 321. That same definiteness was carried into the English movement later by American holiness evangelists. Hannah Whitall Smith advised Lady Cowper-Temple that to have a successful holiness conference, "the call to it must be very *definite.*" (emphasis hers.) She continued, "It has been proved a thousand times that meetings held expressly for the definite purpose of the promotion of holiness or the Higher Christian Life are infinitely more blessed than the same people meeting indefinitely." As quoted in J. C. Pollock, *The Keswick Story* (London: Hodder and Stoughton, 1964), p. 20.

9. *Divine Life* (July 1879), p. 3. Thirty years earlier Henry T. Cheever had looked to the renewed interest that Thomas Upham had excited in the experience of Christian Holiness by his book, *The Life, Religious Opinions, and Experience of Madame Guyon* (London: H. R. Allenson and Co., Ltd., 1961 [originally published in 1846]), in almost exactly the same light. "This good book," he said, "[would accelerate] the pulse of the church, without the intermittent fever...of revival and declension; enlarging its faith...and adding to its...momentum in the on-

ward movement for the world's evangelization, until the Kingdom is given to the People of the Saints of the Most High, and the conquest of the world is accomplished for Christ." "Life and Writings of Madame Guyon," *The Biblical Repository and Review,* IV (October 1848), 642.

10. See Smith, Handy, Loetscher, *op. cit.,* II, 312-14, 421-22; Jamison, *op, cit.,* II, 202, says that revivalism "dynamically stimulated...the desire for absolute perfection....William Warren Sweet sees this combination of individualism, German pietism, and interior moralism as the factors which produced the American spiritual awakenings, and eventually, the social gospel. See William K. Anderson (ed.), *Protestantism: a Symposium* (Nashville, TN: Commission on Courses of Study, the Methodist Church, 1944), pp. 99-109. Sloeffler, *op. cit.,* pp. 3-6, R. Newton Flew, *The Idea of Perfection in Christian Theology: an Historical Study of the Christian Ideal for the Present Life* (London: Oxford University Press, 1934), p. 275.

11. Mead, *op. cit.,* p. 115.

12. See A. W. Nagler's *Pietism and Methodism* (Nashville, TN: Publishing House of the Methodist Episcopal Church South, 1918). *Ibid.,* pp. 35-36, has a summary of the perfectionism of Jacob Spener, one of the fathers of Pietism; he acknowledged that a wholehearted service to God in this life did allow for a relative Christian perfection. Nagler also demonstrates, *ibid.,* p. 128, that the connection between perfectionism and pietism is indicated by the fact that the latter's opponents in Germany always considered that perfectionism was the one common ground on which the otherwise quite diverse pietistic groups stood together. See Stoeffler, *op. cit.,* p. 17.

13. Robert Ellis Thompson, *A History of the Presbyterian Churches in the United States* (New York: Charles Scribner's Sons, 1895), p. 34.

14. Smith and Jamison, *op. cit,* IV (Parts 3, 4, 5), 679. Glenn C. Atkins, who was no sympathetic critic of revivalism in his *Religion in Our Times* (New York: Round Table Press, 1932), p. 19, claims that "if one adds the influence of Wesleyanism in England to the force and outcome of evangelism in America, one has the religious dynamic of almost two hundred years among the English-speaking peoples." The holiness movement was most representative of that combination of forces and the resultant dynamic.

15. Charles G. Finney, *Views on Sanctification* (Oberlin, OH: James Steele, 1840), p. 59: "It is self-evident that entire obedience to God's law is possible on the grounds of natural ability." James E. Johnson, *op. cit.,* p. 342, observes that neither A. T. Swing's claim that Finney's theology was developed independently of "New Haven Theology" made in *Bibliotheca Sacra,* LVII (1900), 465, nor R. H. Foster's indictment of it as "pure Taylorism" in *A Genetic History of New England Theology* (Chicago: University of Chicago Press, 1907), p. 457, is entirely accurate. Johnson, *loc. cit.,* claims it was probably both. Finney did have contact with Nathaniel Taylor. See Sidney E. Mead, *Nathaniel Taylor, 1798-1858: A Connecticut Liberal* (Chicago: The University of Chicago Press, 1942), p. 167. Cf. also James E. Johnson, "Charles G. Finney and Oberlin Perfection," *Journal of Presbyterian History* (March 1968), 42-57 and *ibid.* (June 1968), pp. 128-38, *Finney's Revivals of*

Religion (New York: Fleming H. Revell, n.d.), his most extensive treatment of his revivalistic methods, is still widely read in holiness circles.

16. This in spite of the fact that his followers had feared he would be shorn of his strength in the city. Whitney R. Cross, *The Burned-over District; the Social and Intellectual History of Enthusiastic Religion in Western New York, 1800-1850* (Ithaca, NY: Cornell University Press, 1950), p. 147. For Finney's early work see ibid., pp. 151-69.

17. Tappan offered to give all of his annual income of "about a hundred thousand dollars a year" (except what was needed to provide for his own family) if Finney would go to John Sheperd's new college at Oberlin, Ohio. Tappan was unable to fulfill his promise because of the financial panic which set in soon after Finney had made the move. Charles G. Finney, *Memoirs of...* (New York: Fleming H. Revell, 1908 [originally published in 1876]), pp. 334, 336-37. Finney was president of Oberlin from 1851-1866.

18. *Ibid.*, pp. 340-41.

19. Finney, *Views on Sanctification*, p. 193.

20. For accounts of the Oberlin revival, see Finney, *Memoirs*, pp. 336-41; 349-51. Asa Mahan, *Out of Darkness into Light or the Hidden Life Made Manifest* (Louisville, KY: Pickett Publishing Co., n.d. [originally published Boston: Willard Tract Repository, 1876]), pp. 180ff. *Zion's Herald*, VIII (March 15, 1837), p. 42, rejoiced that Finney had "recently come out in favor of *Christian perfection* as taught by Mr. Wesley." (emphasis theirs.)

21. *Ibid.* (September 13, 1837), p. 146, noted that "many Calvinists [were] thinking favorably of the doctrine as held by the Methodists and some...[were] publically teaching it." In 1837 the *Oberlin Evangelist* was begun to promote the doctrine from that center. In 1839 Mahan published his *Scripture Doctrine of Christian Perfection* (Boston: D. S. King, 1839), and in 1840 Finney published *Views on Sanctification* cited above.

22. See *supra*, p. 20. James H. Fairchild, "The Doctrine of Sanctification at Oberlin," *The Congregational Quarterly*, LXX (April 1876), 238-39, notes that the desire was to find an establishment in Christian experience beyond the ups and downs of the revivalistic pattern. George Hughes, *The Beloved Physician, Walter C. Palmer M. D....* (New York: Palmer and Hughes [ca. 1884]), pp. 239ff., speaks of Oberlin and the beginning of the holiness revival; also see T. Smith, *op. cit.*, pp. 103-113.

23. Finney, *Views on Sanctification* cited above.

24. George Peck, editor of the *Methodist Quarterly Review*, commented that Finney did not express himself "Methodistically" in his work on sanctification, but Peck was satisfied that, "the *thing* which we mean by *Christian Perfection* is truly set forth in that work." (emphasis his); *Methodist Quarterly Review*, XXIII (April 1841), 308. Paul Rader, "A Study of the Doctrine of Sanctification in the Life and Thought of Charles G. Finney" (unpublished B.D. thesis, Asbury Theological Seminary, 1959), p. 103, concludes that the Wesleyans and Finney are in "substantial agreement" on the doctrine and experience. T. Smith, *op.cit.*, pp. 108-111, gives a concise summary of the fluctuations in Finney's emphases

on faith and natural ability. James H. Fairchild, *op. cit.*, pp. 252-59, outlines the shades of difference within the views of the Oberlin men themselves.

25. *Guide*, III (January 1842), 15. *Ibid.*, pp. 153-86, gives the whole of Asa Mahan's reply to the criticism leveled against the Oberlin School by Professor Woods of Andover Seminary. See Mahan, *Out of Darkness*, pp. 245-48, for Mahan's observations on some of the distinctions between Finney's and his views on perfectionism. Smith, Handy, Loetscher, *op. cit.*, II, 42-48, is a ready source on Mahan's perfectionist persuasions. The *Zion's Herald*, XX (July 25, 1849), 118, commends Mahan to Methodist pulpits as a preacher of entire sanctification, for "he differs but slightly from the Wesleyan view of the subject...." Smith's comment on Mahan's standing as an example of Christian perfection in *Revivalism and Social Reform*, p. 11 could be expanded by the feelings of the Wesleyan Methodists toward Mahan after he was influential in moving the Michigan Union College in 1859 from Leoni, Michigan, to a new campus in Adrian, Michigan. The library of the Leoni school was moved to Adrian by ox-cart at night to escape the wrath of the local populace who had supported Michigan Union College. Mahan, who served the new Adrian College as a Wesleyan Methodist, left the college after five years, although his title of president continued into the spring of 1864. The trustees at last decided that his absence during the 1864-65 term, together with his attachment to the Methodist Protestant Church and one of their colleges, warranted a call for his resignation. He was replaced in 1865. Adrian College became a Methodist Protestant College in 1868. For the fullest account of these events, see Willard Garfield Smith, "The History of Church Controlled Colleges in the Wesleyan Methodist Church" (unpublished Ph.D. thesis, School of Education, New York University, 1951), pp. 47-53. Also Ira Ford McLeister, *History of the Wesleyan Methodist Church*, ed. R. S. Nicholson (Rev, [i.e., 3rd ed.]; Marion, IN: Wesley Press, 1959), pp. 334-36; and Fanny A. Hay, Rugh E. Cargo, and Harlan Freeman, *A History of Adrian College, The Story of a Noble Devotion* (Adrian, MI: Adrian College Press, 1945), p. 21.

Mahan probably became acquainted with Wesleyan Methodist leaders even before their separation from the Methodist Episcopal Church in 1843; the *Guide*, III (September 1841), pp. 70-71, reports on a "convention of those interested in the doctrine of entire sanctification." Mahan and other Oberlin leaders joined with Upham and Methodist perfectionists in these, the very first conventions for the promotion of holiness.

See also Cross, *op. cit.*, pp. 261, 278-81; and T. Smith, *op, cit.*, pp. 116-17.

26. Clifton E. Olmstead, *History of Religion in the United States* (Englewood Cliffs, NJ: Prentice-Hall, 1960), p. 90; James Edwin Orr, *The Second Evangelical Awakening* (London: Marshall, Morgan and Scott, 1955), pp. 11-40; William Warren Sweet, *Methodism in American History* (New York: Abingdon Press, 1953), p. 254. All of these general conclusions comparing this period with previous revival surges must be modified by the fact that during the whole time revivalism was far from dead as evidenced by the continuing work of Finney and Mahan together with the activities of Caughey and the Palmers.

27. Reviews of these reform movements can be found in Alice F. Tyler, *Freedom's Ferment. Phases of American Social History from the Colonial Period to the*

Outbreak of the Civil War (Minneapolis: University of Minneapolis Press, 1944) and Cross, *op. cit.*, T. Smith, *op. cit.*, pp. 148-237, treats extensively with revivalistic or evangelical reform efforts.

28. Sidney F. Mead, *The Lively Experiment*, pp. 92-98, describes the mind of the National Period: "Central was the figure of the free individual..." *Ibid.*, p. 92. Therefore, a perfect society was created by free individuals voluntarily developing organizations which in turn could exert reform pressure to produce a "paternalistic response" from those who would have to make reform possible; *ibid.*, p. 97.

William Warren Sweet, *Protestantism in American History*, p. 108, observes that "it was out of this background of emphasis upon the practical and experiential [in revivalism] that the social gospel arose." Cf. Winthrop Hudson, *op. cit.*, p. 343, for the relationship of perfectionism and reform. Also see Johnson, *Religion in Life*, p. 357. Sweet, *American Churches*, pp. 121ff., traces much of this social action back to Jonathan Edwards' concept of "disinterested benevolence."

29. As quoted by Ray Strachey (ed.), *Religious Fanaticism: Extracts from the Religious Papers of Hannah Whitall Smith* (London: Faber and Gwyer. 1928), p. 74. Strachey reviews some of the more bizarre reform efforts of the period.

30. See Tyler, *op. cit.*, pp. 184-95.

31. *Guide*, VI (December 1844), 131. Noyes was just as careful to dissociate himself from the more orthodox perfectionists whom he called "semi-perfectionists." See Benjamin Warfield, *Perfectionism* (New York: Oxford University Press, 1931-1933), II, 252-53; Cross, *op. cit.*, pp. 238-51; and Asa Mahan, *Scripture Doctrine of Christian Perfection*, pp. 7-13. Noyes' career is portrayed in Robert A. Parker, *A Yankee Saint: John Humphrey Noyes and the Oneida Community* (New York: Macmillan, 1935).

32. The views of Antinomian Perfectionists at New Haven, Conn. in *The Perfectionist* originally raised the perfectionist questions at Oberlin; they were rejected, but applied differently in the context of "natural ability." See James Fairchild, *The Congregational Quarterly*, p. 238.

33. Brauer, *op, cit.*, p. 179.

34. Garrison was a friend of Noyes. Warfield, *op. cit.*, II, 331, refers to the *Liberator* (December 1839).

35. For general treatments of the antislavery crusade and the churches, see T. Smith, *op. cit.*, chap. xii; Brauer, *op. cit.*, chap. xi; G. H. Barnes, *The Anti-Slavery Impulse: 1830-1840* (New York: Appleton-Century-Crofts, 1933), *passim*.

36. That the perfectionist mind did not necessarily lead on to abolitionism is demonstrated by the lively debate between holiness advocates such as Wilbur Fisk and Bishop Hedding vs. Orange Scott and Timothy Merritt in the pages of the *Zion's Herald*. See *ibid.*, VIII (1837), *passim*. Scott was charged with leaving the main "business" of the church which was "to save souls"; *ibid.* (February 22, 1837), p. 30; and with a "manifest exchange of the gospel for politics...."; *ibid.*, p. 32. Fisk in replying to Merritt, *ibid.* (March 1, 1837), p. 33, prophesied that the issue would "rend the church." Scott replied to Fisk, *ibid.* (March 8, 1837), p. 38: "I despise that time-serving, cringing policy which can sacrifice millions of

human beings on the altar of *peace;* and which is less affected by the groanings of the prisoner than with a little excitement and agitation...."

37. See Orange Scott, *The Grounds of Secession from the M. E. Church* (New York: Arno Press, 1970 [originally published in 1848]).

38. Arthur T. Jennings, *American Wesleyan Methodism* (Syracuse, NY: Wesleyan Methodist Publishing Association, 1902), pp. 189-90, closely relates the struggle against slavery with the perfectionist leanings of the Wesleyans. "The essence of liberty," he says, "is found only in perfect conformity to the will of God, hence we find the Connection, early in its history, adopting an article of faith on the subject of entire sanctification.... The doctrine...was as much a logical necessity for a church which would be free from bondage to their fellow man as any logic ever noted among men."

Also see Peters, *op. cit.,* pp. 124-27; Cross, *op, cit.,* pp. 263-267. The holiness emphasis was prominent in the early conventions and conferences, The "Pastoral Address" to the Utica Convention in 1843 concluded with it: "But above all, brethren, we exhort you to make holiness your motto; it is holiness of heart and life that will arm you against every assault....It is holiness that will assure success in our enterprise....'And may the very God of peace sanctify you wholly....'"; "Record of the Wesleyan Convention," original copy in The Wesleyan Church archives, Marion, IN. An article on entire sanctification was also presented to the same convention but not acted upon; *ibid.* The General Conference adopted a statement on the doctrine and sent it to the conferences for approval; it was subsequently placed in the *Discipline* cast in language strongly favoring a per-fectionist stance; "Record of the Minutes of the Proceedings of the First General Conference of the Wesleyan Methodist Connection in the United States of America Held in Cleveland, Ohio...October 2, a.m., 1844," pp. 7, 10, original copy in the same archives. Mead, *The Lively Experiment,* confirms the relationship; "Central," he said, "was the figure of the free individual....The perfect individual was the fully free individual...."

39. See Peters, *op, cit.,* pp. 99-101 and T. Smith, *op, cit.,* pp. 114ff.

40. *Journal of the General Conference of the Methodist Episcopal Church, 1832* (New York: 1832).

41. *Guide,* XX (August 1851), 2.

42. Peck, *ibid.,* pp. 1-7, outlines this progress; *ibid.,* p. 3; "The doctrine is preached more than for at any period for probably the last thirty years, *ibid.,* p. 4, Nathan Bangs, *Prospects and Responsibilities of the Methodist Episcopal Church* (New York: Lane and Scott, 1850), p. 288, confirms this conclusion: "[The] work of holiness...[has] revived in the six or seven years past, more people than before seeking and finding 'the blessing of perfect love.'" Allan Coppedoe offers another view of the revival in his "Entire Sanctification in Early American Methodism: 1812-1835," *Wesleyan Theological Journal* 13 (Spring 1978); 34-50. He does not see any major decline of the doctrine in the first decades of the century.

43. *Guide,* LXXVI (July 1880), p. 11 of "Supplement." Pascal recorded his experience in these words: "In the year of Grace, 1654, on Monday 23d of November...from about half past twelve, FIRE, God of Abraham, God of Isaac,

God of Jacob, not of philosophers and scholars." Emile Calliet, *Pascal: The Emergence of Genius* (New York: Harper and Brothers, 1961), p. 131.

44. *Guide,* III (July 1841), 13; John A Roche, *The Life of Mrs. Sarah A. Lankford Palmer, Who for Sixty Years Was the 'Able Teacher of Entire Holiness'* (New York: George Hughes [1898]), pp. 32-33. For further details of her life see George Hughes, *Fragrant Memories of the Tuesday Meetings and Guide to Holiness* (New York: Palmer and Hughes [1886]); Thomas C. Oden, ed., *Phoebe Palmer: Selected Writings* (New York: Paulist Press, 1988); Harold E. Roser, *Phoebe Palmer: Her Life and Work* (Lewiston, NY: Mellen Press, 1987); and Charles Edward White, *The Beauty of Holiness: Phoebe Palmer as Theologian, Revivalist, Feminist, and Humanitarian* (Grand Rapids, MI: Francis Asbury Press, 1986).

45. See *ibid.,* pp. 10-13; Roche, *op. cit.,* pp. 105-129, R. Wheatley, *The Life and Letters of Mrs. Phoebe Palmer* (New York: W. C. Palmer, Jr., 1876), pp. 238-57.

The meeting was a ladies' meeting until 1839, In that year Professor Thomas Upham, professor at Bowdoin College, was allowed to attend; thereafter, the meetings were open to everyone. *Ibid.,* p. 238; Roche, *op. cit.,* p. 111.

46. Wheatley, *op. cit.,* pp. 36ff. Wheatley's work is as much an apology for Mrs. Palmer's teachings as a biography. Her description of her experience reminds one of the moment of enlightenment of the mystics: "O! into what a region of light, glory, and purity was my soul at this moment ushered. I felt I was lost as a drop in the ocean of infinite love, and Christ was all in all." *Ibid.,* pp. 43-44.

47. *Ibid,* pp. 15-26. For typical summaries of the "altar theology" see Phoebe Palmer, *The Way of Holiness* (New York: Palmer and Hughes, 1867), pp. 52ff.; the same, "The Act of Faith by which the Blessing Is Obtained and Retained," in J. Boynton, *Sanctification Practical: a Book for the Times* (New York: Foster and Palmer, Jr., 1867), pp. 115-130; "We Have an Altar," *Guide,* XXIII (May 1853), 158-59.

48. *Ibid* (June,1853), p. 176.

49. Phoebe Palmer, *Faith and Its Effects: or Fragments from My Portfolio* (New York: Published for the Author at 200 Mulberry St., 1854), pp. 52f.

50. See Sweet, *The American Churches,* pp. 110ff.

51. See *Beauty of Holiness,* VII (January 1857), pp. 1-3. Also see John L. Peters, *Christian Perfection and American Methodism* (New York: Abingdon Press, 1956), p. 113, and T. Smith, *op cit.,* pp. 126-127. Abel Stevens, *Life and Times of Nathan Bangs, D. D.* (New York: Carlton and Porter, 1863), pp. 396-402.

52. *Beauty of Holiness,* VIII (January 1857), 3.

53. *Ibid.,* pp. 14ff.

54. See Phoebe Palmer, *Incidental Illustrations of the Economy of Salvation, Its Doctrines and Duties* (Boston: Henry V. Degen and Son, 1860); she draws directly on Wesley to support her positions on the immediacy of the experience, the distinction between the experiences of conversion and sanctification, when it may be received, its reception by faith, and the necessity for testimony for the retention of the experience. *Ibid.,* pp. 37-41. *The Works of John Wesley* (Grand Rapids, MI: Zondervan Publishing House, n.d.), VI, 53.

55. See Wheatley, *op. cit.*, p. 583: "Neither would she tolerate for a moment the phrase, 'Believe that ye have it, and ye have it.'"

56. *Ibid.*, p. 516; also see Palmer, *Faith and Its Effects*, p. 190.

57. As quoted by Peters, *op. cit.*, p. 113.

58. Stevens, *Life of Nathan Bangs*, p. 351.

59. J. Wesley Corbin, "Christian Perfection and the Evangelical Association through 1875," *Methodist History*, VII (January 1969), 41, says that her phraseology and methodology were "almost taken as normative...." After 1869, Phoebe Palmer's "altar theology" became the means by which the holiness teaching of the denomination was expressed, *ibid.*, 39. Abel Stevens recommended it sympathetically in the *Christian Advocate and Journal* which he edited; see *ibid.* XXXIII (December 30, 1858). By this time the Wesleyan Methodists were also recommending Mrs. Palmer's books and using her terminology; see *The Wesleyan*, XVII (March 21, 1885), 7; "hundreds all over the land are testifying that the altar, Jesus, sanctifies their gift, and the blood of Jesus Christ cleanseth from all sin." On this terminology the holiness message was introduced into the mainstream of European evangelicalism; *Record of the Convention for the Promotion of Scriptural Holiness Held at Brighton, May 29 to June 7, 1875* (Brighton: W. J. Smith, n.d.), p. 370.

60. Charles E. Jones. *Perfectionist Persuasion: The Holiness Movement and American Methodism, 1867-1936* (Metuchen, NJ: Scarecrow Press, 1974), p. 5; Peters, *op cit.*, pp. 112-13.

61. Ivan Howard, "Wesley Versus Phoebe Palmer: Extended Controversy," *Wesleyan Theological Journal*, VI (Spring 1971), 31-40.

62. Sweet, *The American Church*, pp. 126-27.

63. Jones, *op. cit.*, aptly makes this point by contrasting Charles Wesley's hymn, "Jesus Thine All-Victorious Love," with Phoebe Palmer's "Cleansing Wave." The former speaks of the relationship in terms of "Till...all renewed I am," the latter in terms of "now" with all verb tenses in the present. See Robert G. McCutchan, *Our Hymnody: A Manual of the Methodist Hymnal* 2nd ed. (New York: Abingdon Press, 1937), pp. 279-80.

64. Byron Ress, *Halleluyahs from Portsmouth Camp-meeting, Number Three: A Report of the Camp-meeting Held at Portsmouth, Rhode Island, July 29 to August 8th, 1898* (Springfield, MA.: Christian Unity Publishing Co., 1898), p. 53. Morrison was only repeating what R. S. Foster had said in 1851 when he wrote in his *Nature and Blessedness of Christian Purity* (New York: Lane and Scott, 1851), pp. 130-31: "Persons seeking the blessing have been told that they must believe they are sanctified, and they will be sanctified. What a misfortune that so great, so dangerous an error should be taught in connexion with so important a subject...I trust it will no more find place in the language of the friends of this glorious doctrine."

65. Palmer, *Faith and Its Effects*, p. 104. Corbin, *Methodist History*, p. 31, notes that already in 1856 the *Botshafter*, a German holiness periodical of the Evangelical Association, carried an article by "An Old Evangelical," which held that the view of the Association was that those who die without entire sanctification will be lost. William Nast, the leader of German-American Methodism in an article

of the *Catechism* of the Methodist Episcopal Church and its teachings on sanctification, commented: "Then to refuse to be cleansed from all filthiness of the flesh
and spirit, is to imperil one's justification"; see the *Christian Advocate and Home
Journal,* VIII, No. 41, 321.

66. Richard Watson, *The Life of the Rev. John Wesley, A. M., Sometime Fellow
of Lincoln College, Oxford and Founder of the Methodist Societies* (New York: G. Lane
and C. B. Tippett, 1847), p. 159. Jack Ford, *In the Steps of John Wesley: The Church
of the Nazarene in Britain* (Kansas City, MO.: Nazarene Publishing House, 1968),
p. 228, in speaking of the groups which formed the Church of the Nazarene in
Britain said that "in all three movements the alternative of 'Holiness or hell' was
sometimes vigorously put....In so far as these movements made fear a motive
for seeking entire sanctification they departed from the counsel of Wesley."

67. See *supra*, p. 30; other than such men as Abel Stevens and Nathan Bangs,
Bishops Matthew B. Simpson, Willard F. Mallilieu, and John P. Newman, all
testified to the essential soundness of her Methodism; see Wheatley, *op, cit.,* p. v;
Hughes, *op, cit.,* p. iv; and Roche, *op. cit.,* p. 11. Bishop E. S. Janes tied it to "the
Pauline doctrine of sanctification, as defined by Wesley...." See the same, Ser-
mons on the Death of Nathan Bangs (New York: Carlton and Porter, 1862), p. 27.

68. Hiram Mattison, "Deceived Professors of Sanctification," *Christian Advocate and Journal,* XXX (August 2, 1855), 121. Mattison's heaviest attack fell three
months later; see *ibid.* (November 29, 1855), 189. Wheatley, *op. cit,* pp. 93ff.,
discusses the controversies and Mrs. Palmer's reactions to them. She tells of
having a terrifying nightmare-dream in which he was viciously attacked by a
lion immediately before the first attack was published. Also see *ibid.,* 115ff.

69.*Guide,* XXI (April 1852), 113; *ibid.* XXII (July 1852), 5; *ibid.,* XXIII
(May,1853), 153, encourages the expansion of such meetings in spite of the
criticism of some; *ibid.,* p. 157, gives an account of one in Vestry, N.Y., attended
by representatives from thirty churches. *Ibid.* (June 1853), p. 175, calls for one in
Cincinnati; also see *ibid.,* XXIV (October 1853), 126-27; and *ibid.,* XXV (April 1854),
125-28.

70. Bishop Newman saw them in this relationship. Speaking of Sarah
Lankford Palmer, he said, "following the example of the illustrious Wesley, this
Christian lady maintained for years the Tuesday meeting...." Roche, *op. cit.,* p.
11.

71. *Guide,* XXI (April 1852), 112-14, announced that a Brunswick, Maine,
"Christian Union" had been formed for "those desiring a more thorough knowledge of the theory and experience of Scriptural Holiness...." Jesse Peck, then
president of Dickinson College, Carlisle, Pa., came out with a strong warning
against "*any organization of the friends of holiness as a distinct work....*" He labeled
it "undesirable and highly dangerous." He said that he was not against special
meetings but as far as holiness organizations were concerned the Methodist
Church was an adequate institution dedicated to those interests. See the same,
"To Professors of Perfect Love," *Guide,* XXII (July 1852), 5-6.

72. *Guide,* VII (November 1845), pp. 97-101. Also see Thomas Upham,
"Peculiar Dangers Attending A State of Holiness," *Advocate of Christian Holiness,*
III (July 1872), 13.

73. Wheatley, *op. cit.*, p. 243.

74. By 1867, both *Northern Christian Advocate* and *New York Christian Advocate and Journal* were commending her *Faith and Its Effects:* "The author clearly shows that it is the will of God that believers should be wholly sanctified." See Phoebe Palmer (ed.), *Pioneer Experiences* (New York: [Walter C. Palmer,] 1867), advertisements at end of volume. The pragmatism and practicality of the "New methods" continued to prove themselves in the later movement. See a very clear defense of the terminology and its practical effects in E. F. Walker, "The Altar Sanctifieth the Gift," *Nazarene Messenger,* XIV (March 3, 1910), 2. Walker notes that when the altar terminology was presented to a group of people who were seeking holiness "the effect was electrical. At once victory came to a number of seekers. Thus did God approve, as he constantly has done, the application of the text to personal sanctification and most clearly and emphatically condemn opposition to it." Walker, *loc. cit.*, claims support of such non-Wesleyan scholars as Alexander Cruden, William Milligan, and Matthew Henry to the defense of the terminology. In *Ibid.*, (February 24, 1910), p. 3, he also quotes Dr. Lightfoot in its defense.

75 Palmer, *loc. cit.*

76. See *infra*, p. 133. Stevens, *Life of Bangs*, p. 352, commented: "It may indeed be doubted whether any one occasion of social devotion...has in the last twenty years had more profound and wider influence in favor of the special doctrines of Christian experience as taught by Methodism....At no place have those doctrines been more thoroughly and devoutly discussed...."

77. *Ibid.*

78. *Supra*, p. 2.

79. Phoebe Palmer's *Pioneer Experiences* became the best known of these. As well known in the later movement was S. Olin Garrison (ed.), *Forty Witnesses Covering the Whole Range of Christian Experience* (Freeport, PA: The Fountain Press, 1955 [Reprint of 1888 ed.]).

80. Wesley's "Plain Account of Christian Perfection," *The Works of John Wesley,* XI, 399, cautions all who testify to their religious experience to "avoid all appearance of boasting." The most complete essay on the question of Wesley's own direct testimony to a personal experience of entire sanctification is in Peters, *op. cit.*, pp. 201-215. George Croft Cell, *The Rediscovery of John Wesley* (New York: Abingdon-Cokesbury Press, 1946), p. 181, believes that Wesley "must have set an example of that *sharing of Christian experience* which he inculcated in season and out of season upon all his followers and was the dynamic of early Methodism. To suppose that he stood outside and aloof from the *experience-sharing* [emphasis his] into which he labored indefatigably to draw every member...would render the Wesleyan Reformation historically unintelligible." Cell refers particularly to Wesley's *Rules of the Band Societies* drawn up in December 1738. Also see J. Peck, *The Central Idea of Christianity* (Boston: H. V. Degen, 1856), pp. 289ff., for a basic Methodist defense of the place of public personal testimony. See Jack Ford, *op. cit.*, pp. 230-31, for a general summary of the same in the modern movement.

81. The experience of Bishop L. L. Hamline illustrates this emphasis. In early life he had failed to testify to the experience of entire sanctification; he says, "For some eighteen months I was like Sampson [*sic*] shorn, because I didn't fully confess God's goodness towards me." As quoted in Walter C. Palmer, *Life and Letters of L. L. Hamline, D.D.* (New York: Carlton and Porter, 1866), p. 101. Hamline advised his ministers to not neglect public testimony. *Ibid.*, pp. 206-212. The 1901 General Holiness Assembly at Chicago encouraged testifying "moderately and unassumingly" but also warned that the withholding of testimony can lead to "darkness and relapse." S. B. Shaw (ed.), *Echoes of the General Holiness Assembly Held in Chicago May 3-13, 1901* (Chicago: S. B. Shaw Publisher [1901]), p. 32.

82. See Phoebe Palmer (ed.), *Pioneer Experiences*, pp. vii-viii; she defends the strong emphasis on testimony by calling on men from the non-Methodist camp such as Matthew Henry and Dr. Thomas Scott. The latter is quoted: "I likewise learned the use of experience in preaching, and was convinced that the readiest way to reach the hearts and the consciences of others was to speak from my own!" *Ibid.*, p. vii. Bishop Latimer is also called as a witness.

83. Mead, *The Lively Experiment*, p. 136, says that the nation was given over to pietistic emphases on experience with a strong holiness appeal. He quotes Bushnell, who spoke of a heart secure from "speculations of the philosophers and the literati"; *loc. cit.* The more the movement became inbred, the less caution was given to "bold" testimony; e.g., one can note a difference in tone and semantics between the testimonies as published in the *Guide, passim*, and those in the *Revivalist*, published by Martin Wells Knapp, one of the founders of the Apostolic Holiness Union and Prayer League. See *God's Revivalist and Bible Advocate*, XIII (September 9, 1901), 4-5. This is an ever-present danger in pietistic groups. See Emil Brunner's caution on the Oxford Movement in Sangster, *Methodism Can Be Born Again*, p. 54. This pietistic emphasis exerted a strong influence on the psychology of William James, according to Sperry, *op. cit.*, p. 152. Sperry says: "The importance which he attaches to experience…matches an emphasis which is wholly familiar to us. Admission to membership in most of the congregationally ordered denominations has always traditionally seated upon the candidates ability to give satisfactory proof of his own spiritual state."

84. Wheatley, *op. cit.*, p. 61.

85. Melinda Hamline wrote to Phoebe Palmer from Mt. Pleasant, Iowa, December 30, 1864: "Both our preachers here receive subscriptions for *Guide* and *Beauty*. I have written to many friends abroad to enlist them in this good cause." "Hamline-Palmer Letters," Drew University Manuscript Collection, Madison, N.J. Also see Walter C. Palmer (ed.), *The Life and Letters of Leonidas L. Hamline, D.D.* (New York: Carlton and Porter, 1866).

86. Wheatley, *op cit.*, p. 252. Janes, *op. cit.*, p. 27, says that Bangs, during his "late years," presided over the Tuesday Meetings. Also see Matthew Simpson (ed.), *Cyclopedia of Methodism* (Philadelphia: Everts and Stewart, 1878), p. 86.

87. Phoebe Palmer recorded in her "Diary," October 27, 1844: "Dr. Olin now enjoys the blessing." Quoted by Wheatley, *op. cit.*, p. 244. Also see the *Methodist Quarterly Review*, XXXIII (1851), 654. *Ibid.*, XXXVI (1854), 17-18.

88. William McDonald said that Wilbur Fisk was sanctified and lay five hours under the power of the Holy Ghost under a sermon preached by Timothy Merritt. E. Davies, *Illustrated History of Douglas Camp Meeting* (Boston: McDonald Gill and Co., 1890); also see Simpson, *op cit.*, p. 363; *ibid.*, p. 285.

89. Cf. Palmer, *Pioneer Experiences*, p. vi; Wheatley *op. cit.*, pp. 196-98, 247, 248, 250; and *Beauty of Holiness*, VIII (December 1857), 364, for the interdenominational influences of the Tuesday Meeting.

90. Wheatley, *op. cit.*, pp. 238-39. Phoebe Palmer had made a vow that if the Lord would sanctify Upham, she would make it a special subject of praise. Upham testified that in response to that vow he considered himself "consecrated and pledged forever!" *Ibid.*, p. 241. See complete statement on his experience in Garrison, *op cit.*, pp. 226-36.

91. Wheatley, *op. cit.*, pp. 66-67, indicates Mrs. Palmer first met Belden and Hill at a camp meeting. She described the two ministers, then still Presbyterians, as "flaming torches filled with the Spirit." In 1844 both men were deposed from the Poughkeepsie, N.Y. presbytery. They then became Congregational pastors, although Hill died soon thereafter. Cf. also *ibid.*, pp. 578-79; *Guide*, XX (January 1847), pp. 5-6; *Divine Life* (July 1879), pp. 12-13. The Rev. J. A. Wood, later one of the most prominent men of the National Camp Meeting Association, took his ministerial apprenticeship under William Hill.

92. See's volume on Christian Holiness, *The Rest of Faith* (New York: W. C. Palmer, 1871), was reviewed in the *Guide*, LX (July 1871), 35.

93. Levy joined "the sanctificationists," as he once called them, while he was preparing a sermon to oppose them. When he informed a deacon in his church of his intention, the layman replied, "I think any minister has mistaken his calling when he preaches against anything that has for its only object the making of people better." Adam Wallace (ed.), *A Modern Pentecost: A Record of the Sixteenth National Campmeeting for the Promotion of Holiness Held at Landisville, Pa., July 23 to August 1st, 1873,* (Philadelphia: Methodist Home Journal Publishing House, 1873), p. 201. Levy also claimed to have been instrumental in having Charles Wesley's holiness hymn, "Love Divine," with its phrase, "take away the bent to sinning," placed in the Baptist *Hymnal, ibid.*, p. 72. Levy was pastor of the Berean Baptist Church.

94. *Guide*, LXXV (March 1880), 94; *The Christian Standard and Home Journal*, VIII (September 6, 1874), 311.

95. Palmer, *Pioneer Experiences*, p. vi.

96. Wheatley, *op. cit.*, p. 57.

97. Phoebe Palmer, "Meetings for Holiness—Sectarianism," *Beauty of Holiness*, VIII (December 1857), pp. 364- 65. Mrs. Palmer sometimes used a verse to express her hopes for Christian unity:

"Names and sects and parties fall,
And Christ alone is all in all."

See Wheatley, *op. cit.*, pp. 197-98.
98. *Beauty of Holiness, loc. cit.*

99. *Ibid.*, p. 365.

100. *Ibid.*

101. *Ibid.*

102. The institutionalization of the revival, particularly in the second generation, tended to create a "turning inward" and isolationism. Timothy Smith, *Called Unto Holiness: The Story of the Nazarenes, the Formative Years* (Kansas City, MO: Nazarene Publishing House, 1962), p. 297, notes that "the denominationalism which the founders [of the Church of the Nazarene] thought inappropriate for men seeking a reformation of American Christianity became for their successors the hallmark of orthodoxy."

103. For example, faith healing, prudentials of Christian life and conduct, millennialism.

104. Wheatley, *op. cit.*, p. 254. See Phoebe Palmer, "A Laity for the Times," *ibid.*, pp. 554-57, for a full treatment of her views. See T. Smith, *Revivalism and Social Reform*, pp. 66, 80ff. Orr, *op cit.*, pp. 95ff.

105. Howard Grimes, "The United States: 1800-1962," in Stephen Charles Neill and Hans-Ruedi Weber (eds.), *The Layman in Christian History: a Project of the Department of the Laity of the World Council of Churches* (Philadelphia: The Westminster Press, 1963), p. 240; Grimes notes that exceptions must be made for "Lutheran bodies,...Roman Catholicism [and]...Eastern Orthodoxy; *ibid.*

106. *Ibid.*, pp. 245-46.

107. *Ibid.*, p. 166. William Arthur's *Tongue of Fire or the True Power of Christianity* (New York: Harper and Brothers, 1880 [first published in 1856]) is one of the most reasoned treatises in the movement on the characteristics of the Spirit-filled church. He says on this point, "A church wherein, from the pulpit down, every man in his order...is called to exercise his gift...can alone answer to the New Testament ideal of a Church." *Ibid.*, pp. 128-49. Also see *ibid.*, p. 87: "The greater should never attempt to extinguish the less, and to reduce the exercise of spiritual gifts within the limits of the public and ordained ministry. To do so is to depart from primitive Christianity."

108. For example, see *Ladies Repository*, XXVI, No. 5, 66, *et passim*, for Mrs. Palmer's involvement in social work, particularly in New York City. T. Smith, *Revivalism and Social Reform*, pp. 169-73, gives an excellent summary of these; Mrs. Palmer, through her own projects and participation in those of others, took a place of leadership in such agencies as The New York Female Assistance Society for the Relief and Religious Instruction of the Poor, and more particularly in the founding of the Five Points Mission. Smith indicates that the latter represents the beginnings of Protestant institutional work in the slums.

109. Tyler, *op. cit.*, pp. 424-62.

110. See Phoebe Palmer, *The Promise of the Father, or a Neglected Specialty of the Last Days* (New York: Foster and Palmer, 1866); Lewis R Dunn, *The Gospel in the Book of Numbers* (New York: Hunt and Eaton, 1889), pp. 264ff.; Dougan Clark and Joseph H. Smith, *David B. Updegraff and His Work* (Cincinnati, OH: Published for Joseph H. Smith by M. W. Knapp, Revivalist Office, 1895), pp. 219-26; all these deal with the question on this premise. The subtitle of Palmer's book speaks directly to it; the "last days" were upon them; the Holy Spirit was inspiring both

the "sons and the daughters." See also the *Beauty of Holiness*, XI (July 1860), p. 379, "Women Prophesying," a column of news items on women who were speaking out in the churches of Europe and America. William A. Clebsch, *From Sacred to Profane America: The Role of Religion in American History* (New York: Harper and Row, 1968), p. 192.

111. Bernard Watson, *A Hundred Years' War: The Salvation Army, 1865-1965* (London: Hodder and Stoughton, 1964), p. 30, says that Mrs. Booth was so stung by a Methodist paper's attack on Phoebe Palmer that she wrote the first of her numerous pamphlets on the subject of women's ministry and their rights to preach the gospel. See Orr, *op. cit.*, p. 121; however, in her own account of how she began to preach she said that her husband had been urging her to do it for ten years and that she had had strong impressions to do so since she had been fifteen or sixteen years of age; Catherine Booth, *Aggressive Christianity* (Boston: McDonald and Gill, 1883), pp. 126-32.

112. Amos P. Mead, *Manna in the Wilderness: or the Grove and Its Altar* (Philadelphia: Perkinpine and Higgins, 1860), p. 242. *Advocate of Bible Holiness*, I (August 1882), on the inside of the back cover carried the notice of "A Holiness Campmeeting, LED PRIMARILY BY WOMEN of the Various Christian Denominations, who believe in ENTIRE SANCTIFICATION as a distinct work...."

113. William B. Godbey, *The Woman Preacher* (Atlanta, GA: Office of the Way of Life, n.d.), p. 12.

114. Jasper Abraham Huffman, *History of the Mennonite Brethren in Christ Church* (New Carlisle, OH: Bethel Publishing Co., 1920), pp. 150ff.; Everck Richard Storms, *History of the United Missionary Church* (Elkhart, IN: Bethel Publishing Co., 1958), p. 251. Storms says that one out of every eight churches in the denomination was started by women preachers. *Ibid.*, p. 253.

115. H. C. Morrison, "Editorial, The Church of the Nazarene," *Pentecostal Herald*, XI (January 25, 1899), 8.

116. Seth Cook Rees, *The Ideal Pentecostal Church* (Cincinnati, OH: Revivalist Office, 1897), p. 41.

117. The American Lutheran Church was among the latest to grant full ministerial rights to women. See "Lutherans Ask New Standards," *Chronicle-Tribune* [Marion, IN] (October 6, 1972), p. 11. The Methodists gave full rights to women ministers in 1956. Exactly seventy years before that, Bishop Gilbert Haven, a "holiness" bishop, had written in the "Introduction" to Maggie Van Cott's *The Harvest and the Reaper: Reminiscences of Revival Work* (New York: N. Tibballs and Sons Publishers, 1876), p. xix, that women should have such full rights although he did not expect many of them to exercise them. He held up Susannah Wesley as an example, within Methodism, who had exercised practically every ministerial right except that of the pulpit in assistance to her son, John; "her silver treble" chimed in with "his manly bass." He chided Adam Clarke, the Methodist Biblical commentator, for allowing such rights to women in his exegesis and then qualifying it in its application in order to throw "a sop" to the men whom he may have offended. "Offset the demon Woodhull with the saintly Palmer and Van Cott," he cried; *ibid.*, p. xxvi. It was "time," he said, "to

fight fire with fire." Mrs. Van Cott was licensed by a local church; she evangelized extensively.

118. Wheatley, *op. cit.*, p. 257; see an almost identical statement in the *Beauty of Holiness*, VIII (December 1857), 365.

119. Hughes, *op. cit.*, p. 16. Mrs. Palmer exercised this principle in her sharp judgment of Professor Upham, who, she felt, was becoming too mystical in his writings on holiness. Warning him about the implications of his thoughts on "Divine Union," she said: "Surely the excellency of a religious experience is only to be treated by conformity to the Word of God." Wheatley, *op. cit.*, p. 522. Bishop Matthew Simpson had had some fears that Mrs. Palmer may have "imbibed something of that mysticism which affects Madame Guyon." Wheatley, *op. cit.*, p. v. But he found that "her constant effort was to persuade friends to trust…the simple Word of God. This preserved her, on the one hand, from wild fanaticism, and on the other from the depths of mysticism." *Ibid.*, p. vi.

120. This was true to the Methodist tradition. See Humphrey Lee, *The Historic Backgrounds of Early Methodist Enthusiasm* (New York: Columbia University Press, 1931), chap. vi, "Methodist Enthusiasm."

121. One of the largest groups in the movement, The Salvation Army takes a position very similar to the traditional Quaker position. Milton S. Agnew, *Manual of Salvationism* (n.p.: The Salvation Army, 1968), p. 61, says, "It is the Salvation Army's firm conviction that the ceremonies commonly known as 'the sacraments' are not necessary to salvation nor essential to spiritual progress…." Religion is spiritual and inner and "in spirit and in truth." Also see Robert David Rightmire, *Sacraments and the Salvation Army: Pneumatalogical Foundations.* Studies in Evangelism; No. 10 (Metuchen, NJ: Scarecrow Press, 1990).The revival elements of the movement were strongly affected by this. Even George Hughes, the Methodist editor of the *Guide*, could ask, "Is it right to deprive a congregation for twelve Sabbath mornings in a year to hold sacramental services?"; *ibid.*, CIII (November 1898), p. 158. The Mennonite elements in the movement favored foot washing; see Walter L. Fleming, "The Religious and Hospitable Rite of Feet Washing," *Sewanee Review*, XVI, No. 1, pp. 1-13; especially see p. 11 on the River Brethren and the Brethren in Christ who were part of the holiness movement.

122. *Advocate of Christian Holiness*, XI (April 1880), 77-78.

123. Hughes, *Fragrant Memories*, p. 39. See *Guide*, XXIII (May 1853), 156-57; *ibid.* (June 1853), 175; *ibid.*, XXIV (October 1853), 126-27; *ibid.*, XXV (April 1854) 125-28, for the spread of the Tuesday Meeting's influence.

124. Hughes, *Fragrant Memories*, p. 40.

125. Raymond J. Corsini and Bina Rosenberg, "Mechanisms of Group Psychotherapy: Process and Dynamics," in *Group Psychotherapy and Group Function*, ed. Max Rosenbaum and Milton Berger (New York: Basic Books, 1963), pp. 340-48. Jerry Sproul used the above to study the Methodist class meeting. The same, "The Methodist Class Meeting: a Study in Its Development, Dynamics, Distinctions, Demise, and Denouement," (Unpublished Master's thesis, Asbury Theological Seminary, 1967). Also see J. L. Morento (ed.), *Sociometry Reader* (Glencoe, IL: Free Press, 1960), pp. 15-16, *et passim*.

126. *Guide*, XXIII (May 1853), 156-57; the same, VII (December 1857), 364-65. Wheatley, *op. cit.*, pp. 238-57. This has been a common result of such small spiritual groups. W. E. Mann, *Sect, Cult, and Church in Alberta* (Toronto: University of Toronto Press, 1955), pp. 3-4, observes that two premiers of Alberta had been active members of the small Prophetic Bible Institute. Neill and Weber, *op. cit.*, p. 165, also take note of this phenomenon in the "spiritualist" tradition of the sixteenth and seventeenth centuries in European Protestantism.

127. Hughes, *Fragrant Memories*, p. iv.

128. Bishop John P. Newman, "Introduction," Roche, *op. cit.*, p. 10. Also see Janes, *op. cit.*, p. 27.

129. See chap. iii. The problems were not uniquely American or limited to the Palmer Movement in Methodism. See the dispute at this point between Karl Barth and Emil Brunner over Buchman's Oxford Movement in Sangster, *Methodism Can Be Born Again*, pp. 52-53. Barth felt they could not be integrated. Brunner felt they could be.

130. *Supra*, pp. 1-3.

131. *Guide*, I (July 1839), 23.

132. Jones, *op. cit.*, p. 19. Hughes, *The Beloved Physician*, p. 259; the same, *Fragrant Memories*, pp. 167ff. Publication was finally discontinued in the fall of 1901.

133. *A Phonographic Report of the Debates and Addresses together with the Essays and Resolutions of the New England Methodist Centenary Convention Held in Boston, June 5-7, 1866* (Boston: B. B. Russell Co., 1866), pp. 159ff., "Report on Committee of Statistics," Rev. D. Dorchester, Chairman.

134. W. E. Arnold, *A History of Methodism in Kentucky* (Louisville: KY: Herald Press, 1936), I, 310.

135. Sweet, *Methodism in American History*, p. 254. Also see Orr, *op. cit.*, p. 11; Olmstead, *op. cit.*, p. 90.

136. Sweet, *op. cit.*, p. 340; Gaddis, *op. cit.*, pp. 375-76. Gaddis probably reads too much of the trends of postwar Methodism into the pre-Civil War Period. See *ibid.*, pp. 384-97.

137. E. A. Hagen, *Salvation to the Uttermost* (Lansing, MI: Darius D. Thorp, Printer and Binder, 1892), p. 40.

138. Smith H. Platt, *The Gift of Power: or the Special Influences of the Holy Spirit, the Need of the Church* (New York: Carlton and Porter, 1856), p. 95. Platt felt that the tendency toward stationed rather than itinerant ministers was isolating local congregations in the face of increasing social evil, leaving each one to fight alone; the danger was great enough "to prevent us from preserving our ancient purity."

139. George Peck, "Christian Perfection," *Methodist Quarterly Review*, XXIII (January 1841), p. 123. *Ibid.* (April 1841), 307: "The discussion of the subject of *Christian Perfection*...is a matter of no small interest to the church of Christ in general."

140. See *supra*, n. 42. Also Palmer, *Life and Letters of Hamline*, pp. 184, 207. The question of the evaluation of spiritual activity in the churches is such a relative one that one consistently meets very contradictory conclusions concerning the revival activity at any given period. See Paul A. Carter, *The Spiritual Crisis*

of the Gilded Age (DeKalb, IL: Northern Illinois University Press, 1971), pp. vii-ix; especially note the statement of William R. Hutchison to the author concerning the religious faith of the end of the century: "Faith was both growing and declining; the point is to figure out the special form (if any) in this age, of perennial paradox." *Ibid.*, viii. The same may probably be said of the 1840s and the revival of holiness.

141. A review of the *Zion's Herald* during this period reveals the tensions mentioned above, n. 140. A letter to the editor in *ibid.*, VIII (January 25, 1837), 13, asks "why so few of our vast church have experienced this work [entire sanctification]...?" But in *ibid.* (February 8, 1837), p. 21, L. Pierce writes that "the time is not far distant when the cry will become general in the ministry and the membership, '0 Lord' cleanse me from all sin.'" A similar review of *Zion's Herald* for 1849-1850 reveals the same contrast. The editor, Abel Stevens, consistently carries reports of revival of interest in holiness; yet these first-page reports are followed by an editorial decrying the fact that "revivals are occasionally reported, but they are seldom, and seem not to be extensive and profound." *Ibid.*, XX (September 1849), 134. Articles on entire sanctification in the *Christian Advocate and Journal* appeared in increasing numbers, especially during the Revival of 1858, e.g., *ibid.*, XXXII (February 18, 1858), 25; *ibid.* (March 18, 1858), p. 41; *ibid.* (April 8, 1858), p. 53, *ibid.* (May 13, 1858), p. 72, *et passim.*

142. George Peck, The Scripture Doctrine of Christian Perfection (New York: G. Lane and P. P. Sanford, 1842). Simpson, *op. cit.*, p. 698.

143. Jesse Peck, *The Central Idea of Christianity* (Boston: H. V. Degan, 1856), Simpson, *op. cit.*, pp. 698-99.

144. Randolph Foster, *Nature and Blessedness of Christian Purity* (New York: Lane and Scott, 1851), Simpson, *op. cit.*, pp. 371-72.

145. *Beauty of Holiness*, VIII (May 1867), p. 154.

146. For a concise summary of these controversies, see Peters, *op. cit.*, p. 122, and T. Smith, *Revivalism and Social Reform*, pp. 127-29.

147. *Journals of the General Conference of the M. E. Church, 1848-1856* (New York: Lane and Scott et al., 1848- 1856), p. 160.

148. *Guide*, XXX (January 1859), 31.

149. B. T. Roberts, *Why Another Sect: Containing a Review of Articles by Bishop Simpson and Others on the Free Methodist Church* (Rochester, NY: "The Earnest Christian" Publishing House, 1879), p. 91.

150. In addition to Roberts, *op. cit.*, see F. W. Conable, *History of the Genesee Annual Conference of the Methodist Episcopal Church, 1810-1872* (New York: Nelson and Phillips, 1876), pp. 618, 620-21, 635-36; Ray Leslie Marston, *From Age to Age a Living Witness: a Historical Interpretation of Free Methodism's First Century* (Winona Lake, IN: Light and Life Press, 1960), Simpson, *op. cit.*, pp. 379-80; it was Robert's reaction to Simpson's *Cyclopedia* article on the Free Methodists which prompted him to write *Why Another Sect. Ibid.*, pp. 15-21.

151. *Supra*, p. 22.

152. See T. Smith, *Revivalism and Social Reform*, p. 113.

153. Thomas C. Upham, *The Christian Experience of Thomas C. Upham, D. D. (of the Congregational College, Brunswick, Maine, America) in Reference to Entire*

Sanctification and the Full Assurance of Faith (Liverpool: W. Sanderson, 1858), is a pamphlet relating his experience; the copy at Drew University is personally autographed to Dr. and Mrs. Walter Palmer. Also see *Advocate of Christian Holiness*, XI (April 1880), pp. 76-78. See Darius L. Salter, *Spirit and Intellect: Thomas Upham's Holiness Theology* (Metuchen, NJ: Scarecrow Press, 1986) for the fullest integration of Upham's views.

154. Thomas C. Upham, *The Life...of Madame Guyon*. See reviews: Henry T. Cheever, "Life and Writings of Madame Guyon," *The Biblical Repository and Review*, IV (October 1848), 608-44; and George Peck, "Upham's Works," *Methodist Quarterly Review*, XXVIII (1846), 248-65. Peck's article, *loc. cit.*, also reviews other books by Upham: *Principles of the Interior or Hidden Life...* (New York: Harper and Brothers, 1854 [originally published in 1843]); *The Life of Faith...* (Boston: n.n., 1847 [originally published in 1845]); *Life of Madame Catherine Adorna...*(New York: Waite, Pierce, 1845); later came his *Treatise on Divine Union...* (Boston: Charles H. Pierce & Co., 1852). He also published a book of poems, *Christ in the Soul* (New York: Charles H. Pierce, 1872).

155. See Cell, *op. cit.*, chaps. iv and v, for a summary of Wesley's stance in regard to the Catholic mystics and mysticism. Wesley "acquired his interest in Christian perfection from [them]...," *ibid.*, p. 113, but accepted the state and goal only, not the means. "Among all of Wesley's antagonisms in religion [antinomianism, predestination, etc.] the opposition to mysticism is easily the strongest...." *Ibid.*, p. 117; this in spite of some modifications in later life. Regardless of this strong Methodist tradition, the *New York Christian Advocate and Journal* defended Upham's perfectionism and recommended his works to Methodists; see "To Ministers and Others. Upham—Faith—Perfect Love," *ibid.*, XXXIII (September 23, 1858), p. 149. J. Agar Beet, *Holiness, Symbolical and Real* (London: Robert Culley, 1910), pp. 167-68, agreed that there was a "profound agreement" and "a similarity of phrase" between Madame Guyon, Molinos, Fénelon, and Wesley, which "suggests that he learned this great truth of holiness, in part, from them." Dean Inge's conclusion in W. R. Inge, *Mysticism in Religion* (Chicago: University of Chicago Press, 1948), final chapter, that "Blessed are the pure in heart" is the essence of religion is also instructive here. The goal was Christian perfection and thereby the relationship between the Mystics and American perfectionism was established. See also Anne Freemantle (ed.), *The Protestant Mystics* (London: Weidenfeld and Nicolson, 1964); she includes Wesley and Hannah Whitall Smith in the book. Stephen Hobbhouse, *Wm. Law and 18th Century Quakerism* (London: George Allen and Unwin, 1927), also has a good section on Wesley and Law's mysticism—chap. xi.

156. Wheatley, *op. cit.*, pp. 518-523. Nevertheless, she herself had had a mystical experience described in *ibid.*, pp. 96ff. Of it she said, "I never felt before in such blessed unity, the unity of Godhead....No voice issued but love—infinite love." Thus the *unio mystica* of the Catholic mystical tradition in its evangelical expression through a faith experience rather than a *scala sancta* filtered into American experience just as it had into the Pietists' beforehand.

157. Harriet Beecher Stowe, "A Review of The Interior Hidden Life," *Guide*, VII (May 1845), p. 114.

158. *Ibid.*, pp. 114-15.

159. *Guide*, VIII (September 1845), p. 49-51; *ibid.* (October 1845) , 73-76; *ibid.*, IX (January 1846), 6-7. Upham undoubtedly was reading Arndt differently from what Warfield did below. The former was reading him existentially as a man who had come through an experience of sanctification similar to his own. Arndt was "testifying" to him from his heart "as the 'father of Pietism' who transformed the doctrine of the Word, as Luther understood it, into an ethical doctrine, and thereby changed the experience of justification into one of sanctification." As quoted by Stoeffler, *op. cit.*, p. 203, from R. Friedman, *Mennonite Piety Through the Centuries* (1949), p. 24. This is a good example of the necessity for using Stoeffler's concept of an experiential tradition in any analysis of the development of American pietistic churches.

160. Benjamin B. Warfield, *Perfectionism* (New York: Oxford University Press, 1931-1932), II, 373; *ibid.*, 342; Warfield concludes that it was all "just Wesleyan doctrine...." *Ibid.*, p. 360. Ronald Knox, *Enthusiasm: a Chapter in the History of Religion with Special Reference to the XVII and XVIII Centuries* (New York: Oxford University Press, 1961), pp. 235-38, also claims that Upham misread Madame Guyon completely. Both missed the experiential tie which existed between them in the "emphasis on inner identification with God." Stoeffler, *op. cit.*, p. 15, says this is why mysticism infiltrated Pietist ranks. See Flew, *op. cit.*, p. 277.

161. *Beauty of Holiness*, VIII (February 1857), 48.

162. Henry T. Cheever, "Life and Writings of Madame Guyon," *The Biblical Repository and Review*, IV (October 1848), 608-609.

163. *Ibid.*, pp. 610-11.

164. *Ibid.* (January 1848), pp. 84-85.

165. William E. Boardman, *The Higher Christian Life* (Boston: Henry Hoyt, 1858).

166. Jacob J. Abbott, in a negative review of *The Higher Christian Life* in *Bibliotheca Sacra and Biblical Repository*, XVII (July 1860), pp. 508-35, ridicules the optimism and the sense of expectation which the book exudes. "The air and tone told us all along...that the author was almost beside himself under the inspiration of a new and extraordinary discovery which he was trying to make known." *Ibid.*, p. 511. "His theory claims to be a new and grand discovery, the time having come now for this morning star of the millennium to rise." *Ibid.*, p. 529. Regardless of Abbott's feelings, the mood of the book was much closer to the mood of the day than his own.

167. Warfield, *op. cit.*, II, 465, attributes the rise of the whole "Higher Life" revival to its influences. That statement is too broad in that Warfield was not well informed on the work of the Palmers, but it does reveal the impact of the work. Warfield, *loc. cit.*, quotes Mark Guy Pearse on the importance of Boardman's book: "[It was] perhaps the first popular treatise on the subject that has won its way among all denominations; and its vast circulation, both in America and England, not only melted the prejudice of hosts against the subject, but made it possible for other writers to follow in the paths which he opened...." Mrs. William E. Boardman, *Life and Labors of the Rev. W. E. Boardman ...* (New York: D.

Appleton and Co., 1887), p. 105, gives her own rather enthusiastic account of the demand for the book.

168. *Ibid.*, 136-37, 156-60.

169. See A. B. Earle, *Bringing in the Sheaves* (Boston: James H. Earle, 1870), for an account of his revivalism. Chap. xviii defends his union meetings; chap. xxviii, "The Rest of Faith," outlines his own religious experience.

170. See continuous flow of reports in *Beauty of Holiness*, VIII (1857), *passim*; the *New York Christian Advocate and Journal*, XXXIII (October 1858), 161.

171. See, *e.g.*, *Zion's Herald*, XXI (February 6, 1850), p. 18.

172. *Infra*, p. 112ff.

173. Orr, *op. cit.*, p. 62. A report from Canada says, "The whole of 'Faith and Its Effects' was published in successive numbers of the *Christian Guardian*, the official organ of the Church. Her other works were scattered broadcast through every part of our country....The popularity of these works...created...an earnest desire to become personally acquainted with their author." *Beauty of Holiness*, VIII (November 1857), 321. *Ibid.* (September 1857).

174. *Beauty of Holiness*, VIII (December 1857), 366.

175. *Ibid.*, p. 368.

176. See T. Smith, *Revivalism and Social Reform*, chap. iv, for an account of the 1858 Revival, often called the Layman's Revival because of the dominance of a rising lay leadership. For the relationship of the financial panic of 1857 and the course of the revival, see Timothy Smith, "Historic Waves of Religious Interest in America," *Annals of the American Academy of Political and Social Science* (1960), No. 332, pp. 9-19. Olmstead, *op. cit.*, p. 90, says that "the revival of 1858 bore powerful indications of the influence of perfectionist doctrines...." T. Smith, *Revivalism and Social Reform*, p. 69, notes that the revival "evoked support from Old School Presbyterians, Episcopalians and even Universalists and Unitarians." For example, *The Church Journal*, the Episcopalian High Church paper, urged revival methods upon its pastors because people were not attending services which were not "manifestly...of a *character* more or less extraordinary....Crowds will everywhere attend a definite *series of special services* when no persuasion will get them to come to Daily Prayer." [emphasis theirs]. As quoted by the *New York Christian Advocate and Journal*, XXXIII (March 25, 1858), 46. Also see William C. Conant, *Narratives of Remarkable Conversions and Revival Incidents...* (New York: Derby and Jackson, 1858); John Hall (ed.), *Forty Years' Familiar Letters of James W Alexander! Constituting with notes a Memoir of His Life...*, 2 vols. (New York: Scribner, 1860); James Waddell Alexander, *The New York Pulpit in the Revival of 1858: a Memorial Volume of Sermons* (New York: Sheldon, Blakeman and Co., 1858), James Waddell Alexander, *The Revival and Its Lessons* (New York: Anson D. F. Randolf, 1859). The *Christian Advocate and Journal* for 1858 carries especially interesting accounts of the revival and commentaries by Nathan Bangs and others on its implications for the Wesleyan doctrine of Christian perfection. See *ibid.,passim.*

177. See William W. Bennett, *A Narrative of the Great Revival which Prevailed in the Southern Armies...* (Philadelphia: Claxton, Remsen, and Haffelfinger, 1877); J. William Jones, *Christ in the Camp, or Religion in Lee's Army* (Richmond, VA,

1887); Harrison W. Daniels, "A Brief Account of the Methodist Episcopal Church South in the Confederacy," *Methodist History,* VI (January 1868), 34. A. B. Earle, the Baptist evangelist, continued his meetings throughout the war; see Earle, *op. cit.,* pp. 100-106, 187-97.

178. The divided house which existed among Methodist holiness adherents in the New England Conferences (see pp. 20-21) also existed elsewhere. Alfred Cookman and John Inskip, both founding members of the postwar National Camp Meeting Association for the Promotion of Holiness, stood for a time on opposite sides of the antislavery debate in the church. Cookman favored anti-slavery legislation in the church. Ridgaway *op. cit.,* pp. 218-21. Inskip "felt averse to the discussion of slavery by ecclesiastical bodies...." That was 1844; by 1858, he was calling himself "a thorough abolitionist...." William McDonald and John E. Searles, *The Life of Rev. John S. Inskip, President of the National Association for the Promotion of Holiness* (Chicago: The Christian Witness Co., 1885), p. 49; *ibid.,* p. 130.

179. Walter and Phoebe Palmer, *Four Years in the Old World Comprising the Travels, Incidents and Evangelistic Labors of Dr. and Mrs. Palmer in England, Ireland, Scotland and Wales* (New York: Foster and Palmer, Jr., 1867), is the most complete account of the Palmers' efforts. Orr, *op. cit.,* pp. 62-77 *et passim,* is a more modern English account of the revival. Strangely enough, Orr admits to having little information available to him on the Palmers themselves. *Ibid.,* p. 12. See Orr, *op. cit.,* p. 121. B. T. Roberts, still smarting from his own battles with the Methodist Episcopal establishment, noted that the English Wesleyan Methodist Conference of 1861 called on its superintendents to keep the Palmers out of their chapels, and that the Conference of 1862 prohibited "all continuous revival services by visitors from America or elsewhere; President Prest ...reprobated the spirit, teaching, and services of Dr. and Mrs. Palmer as being fraught with immense mischief to the interests of Methodism." *The Earnest Christian,* IV (December 1862), 185. The Palmer Meetings were often called "Evangelical Alliance Reviv-als." See Palmer, *Four Years in the Old World,* p. 105; Orr, *op. cit.,* p. 63. Caughey also took part in this revival during the American war years. Orr, *op. cit.,* p. 73. The opposition was not so strong as it had been earlier when the English Methodists had complained to the American Methodist Episcopal Church in an official letter "against the unofficial visits of American ministers to the European Connection." "Methodism in Earnest," *Zion's Herald,* XXI (March 1850), 37. For a brief summary of Caughey's earlier English revivals (1841-1847) see Daniel Wise, "Sketch of the Life of Rev. James Caughey." James Caughey, *Earnest Christianity Illustrated; or, Selections from the Journal of the Rev. James Caughey...* (Boston: J. P. Magee, 1855), pp. 9-19. Also see James Caughey, *Methodism in Earnest: Being the History of a GreatRevival in Great Britain...,* ed. R. W. Allen and Daniel Wise (Boston: C. H. Pierce, 1850).

180. Orr, *op. cit.,* pp. 58, 71, 103, *passim;* Ford, *op. cit.,* p. 29.

181. F. de L. Booth-Tucker, *The Life of Catherine Booth, the Mother of the Salvation Army* (New York: Fleming H. Revell Co., 1892), pp. 117-23, 343ff. "Prejudice and lordly usurpation" may be limiting the "sphere of women's

religious labors," and imposing "restrictions upon the operations of the Holy Ghost." *Ibid.*, p. 22. Also see *supra*, p. 42.

182. The Salvation Army in one of the largest and most active bodies in the Christian Holiness Association whose annual meetings bring together representatives of the holiness denominations and other holiness institutions.

183. Finney, *Memoirs*, chap. xxxv, *Beauty of Holiness*, XI (December 1860), 379; Orr, *op. cit.*, pp. 47-66.

184. Orr, *op. cit.*, p. 81, says 200,000 members were added to the English Methodist Churches alone; but the Baptists and Congregationalists gained even more. Orr attributes this to the fact that neither of them "troubled to pass resolutions of exclusion against free lance revivalists." *Loc. cit.* This may explain, in part, why the Keswick or non-Methodist holiness movement became the more dominant force in England and Europe. Orr concludes that the Roman Catholic Church was the only English religious body unaffected by the revivals; *ibid.*, p. 125. However, see Palmer, *Four Years in the Old World*, p. 663; the Roman Catholic Church at Walsall, along with the revival churches and the Church of England, announced special services continuing daily for four weeks with five services every Sunday. A Catholic revival bill declared: "A mission is a message from…God to His people to put them in mind that 'one thing' is necessary,…the salvation of their souls….What must I do?…I must prepare to make a good confession. 'Behold now is the accepted time; now is the day of salvation.' "

Chapter 3

1867-1877

The Post-War Holiness Revival

REVIVAL AND THE AMERICAN DREAM

Abraham Lincoln's prayer at Gettysburg for a new birth of freedom for the American nation helped to establish the postwar mood. William Clebsch concludes that "a cleansed nation now greeted this worldly, millennial dawn for which all history had been preparing."[1] For some, this "millennial dawn" became the occasion for unscrupulous ventures into materialism—a quest for individual wealth and the power which polarized around it.[2] To many others, however, the deep religious overtones of Lincoln's own concerns were a new challenge to begin again on the American utopian dream. It was a perfectionist dream which involved an optimistic anticipation of individual, national, and world redemption which would usher in a Christian millennial order. The bustling activity in every area of national life provided a ready rationalization for the bitterness of the recent conflict; it was a catharsis for four years of fevered illness. These post-war aspirations were "palpably religious, for in most cases they appealed to a divine vocation laid upon Americans through their peculiar experiment in human freedom."[3]

This religiously oriented dream of national destiny was already firmly fixed in the American mind in the perfectionist revivalism of pre-war years. In 1856, Nathan Bangs regarded America's "future greatness and consequent responsibility" as, "a pleasing anticipation to the believing Christian and the zealous patriot, of the rising glory of our country, and the important part she is to take in the emancipation of mankind from the thralldom of sin."[4]

If the Christians of his day would persist, he said, "in striving after pure and perfect love...they may look forward...and joyfully anticipate the day when the knowledge of the Lord shall cover the earth..." [emphasis his] .[5]

This dream of the divine restoration of man and his world has lived in most movements which have emphasized the work of the Holy Spirit. Bangs' sentiments could be duplicated again and again from the literature of the revival movement from 1840 to the end of the century. In his *Sermons, Speeches and Letters on Slavery and Its War*, Bishop Gilbert Haven, also a strong proponent of the need for holiness revival in Methodism, foresaw the same remedy for the pressing problems of the nation and "the nations";

> Let Christ abolish sin from your souls...Labor to make all other hearts equally perfect. Strive to bring the laws of society into subjection to His control....Root up the gnarled tusks of prejudice...toil cheerfully...to bring in the Grand Sabbatic Year....[6]

This prevailing mood, as it was projected by such perfectionist advocates, was bound up with a secular cast provided by the growing materialism and humanism. This, by the end of the century, was to produce a tragic gap in society between barons of wealth and the masses of the poor, as well as an earthward turn of mind which looked less to transcendental roads to the "Grand Sabbatic Year" and more to innate power of man to gradually perfect his own state. Darwinism, developmentalism, and a mystique of progressivism were all seething in mid-century America in what Martin Marty calls the "metaphysics of Progress."[7]

The tenor of it all strongly permeating postwar American society provided fertile soil for holiness revivalism. Holiness advocates were aware of this although they often expressed the issues in more negative tones. In response to a charge that the sense of urgency which characterized the movement was only an annoying "hobby," the editors of the *Beauty of Holiness* replied that "it is high time that all concerned should wake up to the idea that the spread of Scriptural holiness is the only thing that can save the church from utter apostasy. Indeed it is the only instrumentality that can save the world from ruin."[8]

The triumph of holiness constituted the instrument of the world's salvation in each of the references noted above; the last one, however, carries the seeds of the apocalypticism which tended to become increasingly prominent in the movement as the century wore on, especially as premillennialism became generally dominant in American evangelicalism.[9] This element kept dwelling on the first step of the perfectionist formula as expressed by both Bangs and Haven—the sanctification of the individual to save the church from apostasy. A second group, out of the same perfectionist visions, fastened on to the hope for societal redemption which interlaced these mid-century dreams. The eventual result was the development of the social gospel.[10] Each element carried off with it a part of the dream of perfectionist revivalism into the twentieth century. The adoption of premillennialism allowed the holiness movement to live with its postponed dream. Prevailing optimism, centered in progressive and evolutionary activism, buttressed by technological progress, fed the hopes of the social gospel. Two major world wars and modern technology "made perfect" in atomic destruction were to bring both up short.

THE RISE OF THE NATIONAL CAMP MEETING ASSOCIATION

As noted above, the four years of the war dampened the revival interest which had been fanned into a blaze so shortly before the start of the conflict.[11] The "Pastoral Address" of the Methodist bishops to the 1864 General Conference decried a loss of spirituality in the church and called for revival. Even before its formal ending, however, signs of the renewal that was coming were breaking out across the North. In April of 1865, while Lee and Grant were holding their fateful rendezvous at Appomattox Court House, Methodist Episcopal papers were reporting spiritual awakenings all through the church. The editor of the *Western Christian Advocate*, Dr. J. M. Reid, wrote that within the circulation area of his paper, mainly Indiana, there had been eleven thousand, four hundred and ninety four converts in a six-week period.[12]

The enthusiasm which the Palmers and Caughey, fresh from unprecedented revival activities in England, brought back to the war-weary nation the year before the "stillness at Appomattox" added impetus to renewal.[13] The expanding circulation of the *Guide to Holiness* and the *Beauty of Holiness*, now combined under the Palmers' editorship, broadcast the success of their English missions.

The rapid expansion of organized meetings for the promotion of holiness also helped to generate growing interest in the doctrine. The 1865 issues of the Guide and Beauty contained long lists of these; most of them were held in the larger urban centers, and in many of those, at several locations.[14] New York, Philadelphia, and Boston were the homes of the Palmers, the Inskips, the Levys, and the McDonalds. The fact that the holiness movement began and for two generations was fostered mainly in the larger urban centers of the northeast raises serious doubts about the common generalization that this movement attracted chiefly the poorer and uneducated classes.

NEW LEADERSHIP: JOHN S. INSKIP

The Rev. John S. Inskip was one of the leading young pastors of the Methodist churches in New York City at the end of the war. His sometimes critical attitudes toward the special efforts to revive the experience of entire sanctification in his denomination up until 1864 scarcely predicted any possibility of the central leadership role he was to play in the post-war revival. They were not atypical of the feelings of many another Methodist pastor at that time: "his denominational pride led him to tenaciously contend for the doctrine, while he virtually discarded the experience."[15]

In 1832, while a student at Dickinson College in Carlisle, Pennsylvania, he appears to have accepted the doctrine and briefly professed the experience. He attributed his loss of that new life to his "failure to confess frankly what God had done for him...." Again in 1853, now a Methodist pastor, he testified to an experience similar to that of his student days; but for the second time, he felt that a lack of public confession of it dissipated its effects on his life.[16]

For the next twelve years his interest in the higher life movement centered mainly in complaints against those who presumed to actively promote it within the church. In *Methodism Explained and Defended*, published in 1851, Inskip acknowledged the Methodist doctrine of "the more excellent way."[17] However, he charged many of the higher life advocates in the church with being "wild and deluded enthusiasts," full of "practical inconsistencies." This type of holiness adherent, he maintained, could not "endure the least contradiction, [but] in the most uncharitable manner possible pass judgement upon all who do not happen to be as he is."[18] His own subsequent demands, once he had moved inside the movement, for discipline and moderation, together with the policy of avoiding public controversy over any personal criticism directed against the members of the National Committee may have been influenced by these early concerns.

Martha Inskip was the critical agent in her husband's religious turnabout in 1864. Dissatisfied with the level of her Christian experience, she went to the Methodist camp meeting at Sing Sing, New York, in August of 1864, with the definite intention of finding a more stable and satisfying inner life. On Friday, August 19, 1854, she claimed "the blessing" by consecration and faith in the manner taught by the Palmers. The spiritual erraticisms of his wife greatly "afflicted and mortified" the rising young minister.[19]

From that time, however, his antiperfectionist stance began to weaken. The desire for "more religion," "a deeper work of grace," and a "baptism of the Spirit" began to appear in his diary. The convincing manner in which Mrs. Inskip related the effects of her camp meeting experience to a prayer meeting congregation in his church, pressed him further; the occasion, he wrote, was a "glorious" one.[20]

Only nine days after his wife's spiritual crisis, John Inskip confessed his own complete commitment to the religious experience urged upon the church by the holiness advocates. On Sunday morning of August 28, 1864, the "South Third Street pastor" was strongly exhorting his congregation with a vigor even beyond that for which he was commonly noted; his text was Hebrews 12:1. He urged his hearers to consecrate their lives totally to God With Methodistic enthusiasm, he exhorted:

> Brethren, lay aside every weight! Do it now. You can do it now, and therefore should do it. It is your privilege and therefore your duty at this moment to make a consecration of your all to God, and declare you will henceforth be wholly and forever the Lord's.[21]

In these terse phrases, Inskip captured the essence of the synthesis of American revivalism, Wesleyan perfectionism, and even evangelical pietism which formed the heart of the movement.

He later asserted that while he was emphasizing the *now* and the need for immediate, personal commitment, that a voice within him seemed to say, "Do it yourself!" He hesitated; the voice said again, "Do it yourself, and do it now." Calling upon his members to follow him, he made his way to the altar rail at the front of the chancel of the Methodist church; surrounded by his parishioners, he cried out, *"I am, O Lord! wholly and forever thine!"* [emphasis his.][22]

Too much must not be read into or out of this account of John Inskip's personal espousal of the holiness cause. But, in the attempt to trace out the development of the movement, the record left by him at the time does merit comment. One may note here many of the emphases which put Inskip in the Palmers' succession; he in turn, during the next twenty years, deepened the impression of these on the movement as a whole. The urgency of the "now," the call for "entire" commitment, the provision become a "duty," all were already part of revivalistic holiness preaching. They called for the Christian to fix his attention on Christian perfection and seize it by faith at any cost.

Very soon thereafter, Inskip attended the Tuesday Meeting at the Palmer's home; he told the group of recent experience. The next day, he visited the Palmers to invite them to hold special meetings for the promotion of holiness in his church. Later, in reviewing that visit, he admitted that his "mind had been prejudiced against the efforts made by a few...to keep this flame alive in [the] church." He knew the doctrine was "of God. But their manner of promoting it," he confessed, was "a rock of offence." "It pleased God, however, to reveal his grace to me...." he concluded.[23]

Inskip was destined to general the main forces of the postwar movement in its challenge to the churches to recognize not only the validity of the Palmers' call to holiness, but also the necessity for a broader response to that call; this alone could guarantee the reform of the church, the nation, and the world. The changes that the new phase was to bring would be, in the main, advances or enlargements upon the new promotional methods of the earlier phase. The intimate Tuesday Meetings in the parlor, became "National Camp Meetings" with their clouds of dust or seas of mud stirred by the feet of the thousands in attendance; the informal lay emphasis fostered by the Palmers as lay leaders was to be overshadowed by the more formally organized efforts of the ardent ministerial advocates who maintained a loosely structured, but tight control over the movement for more than thirty years.

The winsome, yet urgent appeal of personal testimony in the earlier parlor meetings which invited men of widely differing creedal stances to personal dialogue on the deeper Christian life was often to be replaced in the approaching camp meeting promotion by a more polemical, definitively dogmatic proclamation of the doctrine in terms that tended to become stereotypes. At its extremes this zeal lent itself to the appearance of driving men into an experience of perfect love with the naked alternatives of *holiness or hell*. Beulah Land was often lost sight of.

The theological tolerance which the more intimate atmosphere of the smaller group meetings could practice without diversion from the main issue also suffered in the midst of larger meetings and the later institutionalization of the revival; differences of terminology were to become points of issue as Calvinist and Methodist wings of the movement each began to define the higher life more definitively within the context and terms of their own theological biases.

The terms, the theology, the process would not change significantly from that of the Palmer period, but the tone and the tempo would vary. Furthermore, in spite of the best efforts of sincere leaders, the irregular meetings which spurred on the revival tempo as that leadership began to lose its grip on the movement were to encourage the irregularity of schism. Here were the beginnings of the conflicts that eventually led to the reorientation of loyalties for thousands of Methodists and members of other established churches.

These proponents of Christian perfectionism developed a sense of homelessness as the popularization of church membership, through the very success of revivalism itself, brought masses into the American churches for the first time in the nation's history. As Franklin Littell points out, "converts" were often received into the Christian fellowship without a sense of Christian commitment and without concern for the basics of Christian life, much less a higher Christian life; these masses had little time for spiritual zealots who in their puritanism and pietism insisted that the church was a fellowship of believers and Christian experience comprehended every aspect of a man's existence.[24]

All of these trends and potentialities were there in embryo in John Inskip's expression of his own mind and experiences as he turned himself without reserve to the holiness cause. It was a holiness crusade which participated in all the strengths that other moral crusades in America have generated by the unswerving dedication of their members to the achievement of an all consuming goal; it also shared in many of the weaknesses which result from the tendency to create imbalance of view and misunderstanding and intolerance of those who do not see the issues in so narrow a framework.

The strengths and the weaknesses tended to show their full potential in this movement which was not alone a crusade against the evils of alcohol or other social ills which have often caught the attention of a particular group; this was a crusade against the last vestiges of evil itself in the hearts of men. Holiness revivalists sought to redeem them from that inner evil and bring them to the possibilities of the grace of Christian perfection. This would restore the power of primitive Christianity to the churches and through them the Holy Spirit would redeem the whole of mankind. It was, at heart, a reexpression of enduring Christian faith in the adequacy of divine grace for the complete moral redemption of men now; but that expression was often clothed with the accoutrements of its nineteenth-century milieu.

Inskip joined the "revival" in the closing months of the war. He had served as a chaplain in the Northern Army, but he now confessed that he was excited "very little" by the dying struggle. After his August 28 experience, he wrote: "I am interested in the government of my country...nevertheless, I do not feel myself particularly called to that work: my business is of a different character entirely....This business will occupy all of my time and call out all my energies."[25]

Vineland: the First National Camp Meeting

A brief notice in the *Philadelphia Public Ledger*, "Local Affairs" section for Thursday, June 27, 1867, carried news that: "a meeting of Methodist ministers from New Jersey, New York, Baltimore and of this city, was held a few days since at 1018 Arch Street, and it was agreed to hold a camp meeting at Vineland, New Jersey, commencing July 17th."[26]

The Methodist ministers who met at Philadelphia on June 13th, were there in response to a call to help to plan a camp meeting, "the special object of which should be the promotion of the work of entire sanctification."[27] This concept of devoting an entire ten-day camp to the preaching of that doctrine was undoubtedly as unique to the camp-meeting tradition as the men who met seemed to consider it to be.[28] Special services in camp meetings had sometimes been set aside for particular instruction on the experience, but never had it been made the central goal of the entire meeting.

A conversation between the Rev. J. A. Wood and Mrs. Harriet Drake of Wilkes Barre, Pennsylvania, in August 1866, had sparked the June 13, 1867 meeting which planned the Vineland National Camp Meeting. While the two were traveling to a small camp near Red Bank, New Jersey, Rev. J. A. Wood had observed that the holiness cause often was ignored or ridiculed in the camp meetings of the day. In response, his parishioner, a member of one of the leading families in her home community, offered to pay for half of the expenses for a camp meeting devoted especially to that cause if one could be arranged. During the Red Bank camp, John Wood relayed the concern to Rev. William B. Osborn, an ardent supporter of holiness doctrine within Methodism in southern New Jersey; the latter carried the idea to John Inskip at his New York church. Inskip received the suggestion enthusiastically and prepared for the June meeting in Philadelphia.[29]

The men who conceived this "new method"[30] for holiness promotion were well-known pastors in their home conferences in the New York and Philadelphia areas of the Methodist Episcopal church. Rev. A. E. Ballard, a presiding elder, was active in the planning. Dr. George C. M. Roberts, Baltimore, Maryland, served as president of the *ad hoc* committee. Rev. J. A. Wood, Wilkes Barre, Pennsylvania, pastor, suggested that the special camp be held at Vineland, New Jersey from July 17 to July 26. Rev. Alfred Cookman, revered by the church for his piety and irenic spirit,[31] wrote out the call for the camp, addressed to the "friends of holiness,"[32] which appeared in the church and secular press. It invited "all, irrespective of denominational ties, interested in the subject of the higher Christian life, to come together and spend a week in God's great temple of nature."[33]

The call to this "National Camp Meeting for the Promotion of Holiness" was careful to point out that although the meetings would seek for the conviction and conversion of sinners, its special object would be

> to offer united and continual prayer for the revival of the work of holiness in the churches...to strengthen the hand of those who feel themselves comparatively isolated in their profession of holiness...to realize together a Pentecostal baptism of the Holy Ghost—and all with a view to increased usefulness in the churches of which we are members.[34]

The call for the Vineland camp produced a reaction indicative of the mixed fortunes of the movement in the Methodist Episcopal churches in the summer of 1867. The old fears for the unity of the church first raised two decades before by a friend of the movement, Jesse Peck, and later by many others less sympathetic to it, were resurrected in the face of this most dramatic suggestion for special holiness promotion. Appeals were made to Presiding Elder Ballard to withdraw his sanction of the special camp meeting. Like Peck before them, these concerned Methodists still looked upon their church itself, as a great holiness church. Its declared purpose was the proclamation of Christian perfection and they saw little need for these urgent special measures within the church structure. Many of them took affront at any such intimations of the declension of the purpose or the effectiveness of the denomination.[35]

These critics failed to turn the mind of the Vineland committee, however; the latter seemed to be confident that they were advancing a theme whose time had come. They appear to have been convinced that there was a special desire in the land for a deeper spiritual answer to the problems the postwar nation was facing; and that Methodism, in particular, because of its high pretensions, was the first to require renewal. Statements from the upper echelons of the church's leadership reinforced their concerns. In 1866, during Methodism's centenary year, Rev. John McClintock, one of the church's most respected scholars, had warned American Methodism that the measure of its success was its dedication to the preaching of holiness. "And that," he urged, "in the face of any who would choose to call it 'fanaticism'." He concluded that this was Methodism's "glory...[and] power...and there shall be the ground of our triumph."[36]

The critics of the special efforts were correct in looking on the Methodist Church as a holiness church; that was its commitment and message. But the "friends of holiness" proved to be equally correct in maintaining that there was something lacking in the response of that church and others to the rising tide of demand for a quality of Christian experience beyond that which the revivalism of the past hundred years had produced in the church. They shared deeply in the national sense of expectancy released by the change from war to peace. For them the proposed meeting at Vineland promised to serve as an effective new measure for advancing Christian experience and preparing the people of the nation for whatever personal and collective challenges the realization of that expectation might produce.[37]

Thousands of people poured into Charles Landis's model town in the pine flats of southern New Jersey, for the beginning of the Vineland camp on July 17, 1867.[38] Crowded trains stopped at the Cape May Railroad station; long lines of buggies thronged the roads which led to the forty-acre public park on the edge of town which served as the camp site. Overnight the town's population swelled to almost double its 10,000 regular inhabitants as hundreds of tents sprang up around the speaker's stand on the camp ground. For ten days the campers listened to sermons and exhortations on the theme of Christian holiness by members of the organizing committee and Bishop Matthew Simpson. The camp closed with the observance of the Lord's Supper. The meeting had more than met the expectations of the organizers. The *Philadelphia Public Ledger*'s earlier prediction that the camp meeting would be the largest ever held in the area proved to be accurate.[39] The enthusiastic pastor of the Spring Garden Methodist Episcopal Church of Philadelphia wrote to his sister that it "had only one disadvantage—it made every other service seem tame by comparison."[40]

The Organization of the National Association

The enthusiastic response to Vineland led to the demand that another special holiness camp meeting be held the following year. During the meeting of a committee called for that purpose at the close of the Vineland camp, the decision was made to create the National Camp Meeting Association for the Promotion of Holiness.[41] Its object was "to glorify God in building up the church in holiness and saving sinners."[42] The nature of the almost impromptu inception of the organization and the fact that it operated without a constitution or by-aws for the three decades during which it was most influential in the holiness movement, both left their own impact on the movement. It was publicized widely that the organization had been born while the committee was on its knees in prayer and the idea had come not through any human planning but by the inspiration of the Spirit.[43] This example of nonstructure and Spirit guidance combined with the consequent success of the association, often set a pattern for the approach of holiness groups to the organization of meetings, rituals of service, and institutional planning as well. There was a consistent tendency to keep definition of organization and duties loose and fluid. Tensions frequently arose between the strong commitment to openness, to spiritual leadership, and the necessity for some kind of human initiative in programming and, above all, internal discipline.[44]

This formation of the National Camp Meeting Association for the Promotion of Holiness in Vineland, after the close of the camp there, marks the formal opening of a new phase of activity and influence for the movement within the American churches and evangelical Christianity around the world. John S. Inskip was chosen as president of the new, loosely structured, but extremely durable, organization of Methodist ministers dedicated entirely to holiness revivalism. Its leadership in the movement was practically unquestioned for the next fifteen years. Its structure was a significant prototype in the organization of American evangelism. *It was possibly the first team of revivalists working jointly in extended revivalistic efforts in the history of modern evangelism.*

Manheim and Round Lake: the Success of the "New Methods"for Holiness Promotion

Six hundred tents dotted the campground near Manheim, Pennsylvania, at the start of the second National Camp Meeting in the summer of 1868. Alfred Cookman, to whom the Association had given the responsibility of selecting the site for the camp, had decided to engage these grounds in Lancaster County, Pennsylvania, for the camp because of his own familiarity with that area. Representatives had come to this "Pennsylvania Dutch" country from most of the states of the union. More than 300 ministers and 25,000 other attendants crowded into the camp area for the Sunday services. Twelve thousand pressed around the preaching stand to hear the morning sermon by Bishop Simpson. A reporter noted that, "the weather was oppressively hot; dust was abundant, water scarce, and board most miserable."[45]

The Manheim meeting was significant to the American holiness revival, not only because of the large crowds who gathered there, but also because of the interdenominational influences. In one of the meeting tents Presbyterians, Methodists, Baptists, Dutch Reformed, Congregationalists, and Quakers all gave testimony to a common experience of a work of God in their hearts which knew no denominational distinctions. The site of the camp was central to the churches of the Evangelical Association, already strongly conditioned by Methodist influences in their early history. A renewed emphasis on Wesleyan perfectionism in the denomination followed Manheim through the influence of the large numbers of Evangelical Association ministers and laity who attended the meetings. Reuben Yeakel, prominent editor and leader of the holiness movement in the Evangelical Association, says that the National Camp Meeting Association rescued camp meetings in America and "the result [of Manheim and successive meetings] was a great improvement in holding and conducting camp meetings through the Evangelical Association beyond her borders."[46] The Wesleyan perfectionist views which were beginning to develop in small segments of the Mennonite people of the area of eastern Pennsylvania also received new impetus from the camp.[47]

The National Camp at Manheim ranks as one of the largest convocations in American nineteenth-century religious history, perhaps the greatest in number of attendants at a single meeting until the Moody-Sankey revivals which followed it by a decade. In these holiness meetings the extreme physical manifestations which had marked the first Great Awakening and the early camp meeting movement, were almost nonexistent; nevertheless, the atmosphere was packed with emotion, typically Methodist enthusiasm, and spiritual expectancy. As two thousand people bowed in prayer after a sermon by the Rev. John Thompson on Monday afternoon, Dr. G. W. Woodruff began to pray aloud,

> when, all at once, as sudden as if a flash of lightening from the heavens had fallen upon the people, one simultaneous burst of agony and then of glory was heard in all parts of the congregation; and for nearly an hour, the scene beggared all description....Those seated far back in the audience declared that the sensation was as if a strong wind had moved from the stand over the congregation. Several intelligent people, in different parts of the congregation spoke of the same phenomenon....Sinners stood awestricken and others fled affrighted from the congregation.[48]

The people were convinced they were "face to face with God."[49]

Although the leaders of the National Committee always took special note of the presence of members, particularly ministers of other denominations at the meetings, the difficulties of ordering so diverse a crowd of non-Methodists as appeared at the Manheim encampment may have given them second thoughts about the possible complexities of setting up and administering their own camp meetings; there was also the additional concern that too much broadening of the movement might carry them too far into an irregularity of program which could excite further reaction from their already vocal critics in the Methodist Church. Subsequent to the 1868 camp, the members of the National Association, therefore, decided to take their holiness ministry only to regular Methodist camp meeting grounds upon invitation from the local camp meeting administrators.[50] Furthermore, since the members of the association were full-time pastors, the summer vacation times which they devoted to those efforts did not allow time for both evangelism and the organizational details involved in administering camps teeming with thousands of campers and visitors.

The 1869 camp was held at Round Lake, New York. Spiritual response still ran at full flood. Although the Committee had stipulated that no trains should be run to the campsite on Sunday, no less than twenty thousand people were reported to be on the grounds. Bishop Peck was there and preached "a most powerful sermon."[51] Following the Bishop's sermon, one of the ministers present declared:

> I am glad that I was not born before I was...I have a big programme before me for I begin to see how God is going to spread His work by the instrumentality of a holy church....This is a wonderful meeting. It seems I could afford to stay out of heaven for this. This meeting has rolled the world a hundred years towards the millennium....This is the outflow of heavenly influence—God's great Amazon—which is to flow around the globe. Let the nations make way for the coming of God.[52]

The remark was typical of the optimistic enthusiasm which often swept the crowded campgrounds. These happy participants gave further proof of the persistent belief within the movement that the rising holiness revival was sweeping the world toward the dawn of the millennium with quickened pace. Even close-communion Baptists were carried along by the tide and shared in the closing communion service conducted by Bishop Simpson.[53]

THE AMERICAN CAMP MEETING AND THE SPECIAL PROMOTION OF HOLINESS

American church historians who contend that revivals and camp meetings were fading in influence in the religious life of America after the Civil War have been challenged to reconsider their thesis as the full extent of the national and worldwide enlargement of Christianity in the latter half of the nineteenth century comes into clearer historical focus. Actually, both revivalism and camp meetings were both very much alive and growing. As Timothy Smith points out, they had moved from rural to urban American.[54] In spite of a continual undercurrent of doubt on the part of some as to their further usefulness[55] and questions as those which Horace Bushnell raised concerning the quality of the Christian life which their methods produced[56] there was no slackening of the revival pace.[57]

If camp meetings were not fading out as a religious institution, many of them were changing, nevertheless. The changes were disconcerting to those who looked upon these gatherings as the main evangelistic arm of the church, particularly the Methodist Church. To these individuals such innovations as the Chautauqua program of popular education, patterned after the camp meeting idea, but varying from its spiritual purposes, represented a radical departure.[58] This deviation was not so alarming, however, as was the inclination to make camp meetings as much recreational as evangelistic centers. To those who were already fearful for the quality of Christian piety within the church this represented another step backward—a concession to an increasingly noncommitted church membership. *Harper's Weekly* took note of the changing conditions as 1873 summer camp season approached:

> The fervent Methodists are all through the month of August holding their camp meetings. Near the great cities their once primitive assemblies have changed their form. The camp is sought for its sanitary as well as religious advantages....Boating, bathing, fishing, have a place with religious worship in the round of occupations.[59]

The Use of Camp Meetings for Holiness Promotion

Such changes in some camps, together with the outright opposition to, or neglect of, specific promotion of the doctrine of entire sanctification in others, concerned the leaders of the postwar Methodist revival. Their decision to use the institution as a special instrument for the promotion of holiness was a significant factor in the continued growth of the American camp meeting as an evangelical instrument. Indeed, the American camp meeting movement became dominantly a higher life movement thereafter. Many existing camps and the hundreds of new, specifically holiness, camps which the movement spawned all across the country became centers of holiness evangelism.[60]

When one reads the history of the movement it becomes evident that a more suitable instrument for such evangelism than the open air meetings of the camp meeting groves could scarcely be conceived. The wedding of the two was another step in the specialization of the promotion of the holiness which makes up so large a part of the development of Christian perfection in America. Through the institution of the camp meeting, then mainly Methodist dominated and well established, though never recognized in the *Discipline* of the church, the holiness revivalists were able to get their message out to larger numbers of church and nonchurch people than otherwise ever would have been possible in the face of the opposition which developed within the structure of the churches themselves.

The prewar evangelism of the Palmers in the camps of Canada and the United States had already proven the potential for holiness work in such summer gatherings. As has already been noted, the glowing success of their ministry in Canadian camps in the summer and fall of 1857 had marked the first signs of the 1858 Layman's Revival in the United States and its counterparts in other parts of the world, especially England.

Shortly before her death in 1874, Phoebe Palmer had had to remind George Hughes, one of the leaders of the National Camp Meeting Association, of this history. His review of the first five years of the promotion of holiness cause through camp meetings held especially for the purpose, Mrs. Palmer indicated, drew too dark a picture of the fortunes of the cause and the prewar relationship of the doctrine to the work of Methodism's camps. She charged that the contrasts were drawn much too sharply to suit the facts. Her editorial went on to note that prewar editions of the *Guide* had carried frequent reports of camp meetings which had served as centers of holiness promotion, not by special design, but because of the place of the doctrine within Methodist tradition and preaching. She further pointed out, that as early as 1853, she had observed that "the Spirit had never before been so largely poured out upon the churches." It was this history, she added, which had prepared the way for the obvious success of the National Camps in which she too rejoiced.[61]

Postwar Life and the Postwar Camp Meeting

The continued effectiveness of the camp meeting after the Civil War as an instrument for holiness revivalism was probably abetted by the milieu of postwar American life. Little has been said about the relationship of these outdoor tented grounds and the potential nostalgia related to other encampments, under other circumstances, which undoubtedly attracted many war veterans and their families to the country groves. The families who "roughed it" through a ten-day camp meeting may have heard many a tale of camps at Vicksburg, Harper's Ferry, Richmond, or even Andersonville.

The American view of nature, one of the dominant ideological patterns in the development of American history, also clearly played its part in the camp meeting mystique. Nature was "a splendid system of signs,"[62] American society was also still a rural one—tied to the open sky, the trees, the earth.[63] The growth of large camps, close to urban centers, attended mainly by residents of rapidly expanding cities supports this. When the editors of the holiness journals called these people to come, "away to the tented grove! Away from the busy scenes, from the din and conflict of earthly strife! Away to the place of holy convocation...."[64] most of the people to whom they were appealing were city residents who had either recently left their rural homesteads or older residents who still maintained strong ties with rural residents and friends. The camp meeting was the time to annually renew these relationships. A camp meeting advocate wrote long before the postwar rush to the cities that "without some such meeting, the members of a large city church will, to a great extent, remain strangers to each other and though they might be seated side by side in heaven, would need the angel Gabriel to give them an introduction." He noted further that given such surroundings it was easy to see the campers became "one happy family,"[65] Charles Jones concludes that "to the nostalgically satisfied believer, fellowship in the suburban camp meeting communities seemed like reaching Beulah Land."[66]

The strong and enduring relationship between the camp meeting and the holiness groups was not only due to their historical use in Methodism and the rural posture of American life, however; just as important to the union was the easy meshing of the setting of the meetings and the transcendental and spiritual elements of the theology and experience of perfectionism. They were convinced that the same God who created and controlled the natural settings in that they met was also able to order their inner lives in a way which would create a world of peace and harmony. The introduction to a book of camp meetings sermons observed that,

> there is a peculiar charm about camp meetings. We worship in God's great Cathedral, in nature's magnificent temple, arched over with brilliant heavens, and floored with beautiful green earth—under the foliage of the trees planted by God's own hand.

There is a kind of grandeur about such a temple that accords with man's own noble origin and lofty destiny [emphasis mine].67

Andrew Manship, frequently engaged in Methodist camp meetings of the Civil War period, reported to the *Christian Advocate and Journal,* in 1858 from a camp meeting he was attending that

the stately trees afford a delightful shade; the beautiful vallies [*sic*] that environ the "holy mount" afford places suitable for the members of the Church in the wilderness to "steal away awhile" for secret prayer. The numerous springs and running brooks were well calculated to remind us of the well of salvation and the "springs that never run dry."68

The "noble origin and lofty destiny" of man and the "springs that never run dry" were dominant themes in holiness message; they blended easily and effectively with the natural setting of this semiurban revival of the frontier camp.

The "Church in the wilderness" concept also carried special meaning with it. Many of the campers did not feel fully at home in their home churches, particularly those in the cities; their enthusiastic holiness promotion often struck a discordant and lonely note in the fellowship of urban congregations moving toward more liturgical patterns of worship. As Jones has pointed out, the holiness revival was strongly based among the people who were migrating from rural to urban centers in the latter half of the nineteenth century. The camp meeting was more like the church "back home." "The camp meetings encouraged the nonliturgical, subjective bent of American Methodist worship...."69

The campers met in God's free fields; there was room to breathe and room to move. As has been noted above, the extreme physical demonstration of the early frontier camps and revivals was generally absent; however, traditional Methodist enthusiasm was commonly expressed. In defense of such spiritual zeal, the Methodists reminded their detractors that "you could not endure to see men laboring to save immortal souls from unending death with the cool gravity of a Turk sipping coffee."70

Camp meeting experience could range all the way from the high emotionalism of a whole congregation, one moment on its feet waving handkerchiefs in ecstatic praise, and the next lustily singing as it marched around the tabernacle, to the awesome solemnity of a midnight communion service with a thousand communicants.71 Musical selections ranged from the staid hymn to the latest revival song; the musical accompaniment may have been by "professor Mitchell, educated in music in Germany and now filled with the Holy Ghost in Rhode Island," or by an "old colored brother" who "rattled a tambourine in a most marvelous way."[72] The campers also tolerated such typical camp meeting eccentrics as a "Crazy Elisha," a "Shouting Harris,"[73] or the little Jewish convert who showed up year after year in his black mohair suit, poking every piece of litter on the camp ground with his long, everpresent umbrella and challenging every minister he could corner with his superior knowledge of the Bible—usually successfully.[74] The whole, at times, constituted a "glorious confusion,"[75] At camp, the evangelist and the people were in a community of life and worship which was ordered to their own religious and cultural commitments. It provided identity, meaning, and purpose. This milieu was the most favorable one in which the holiness evangelists could find a platform with relative freedom to proclaim their message to the membership of the churches as opposition to the movement increased among many pastors and local congregations.

One reporter declared:

> We thank God in these days of ecclesiastical bondage and pastoral despotism there are camp meetings...where the children of God can seek, find, and bear witness, to the Scriptural experience of entire sanctification without having their shoulders lashed by self-constituted bosses.[76]

If one allows that the camp meeting freed the worshipper from the lashes of "self-constituted bosses," he cannot allow that there were not any "bosses" at all. A recognized authority figure, be he evangelist or platform manager carrying either charismatic or administrative credentials or both, generally kept a firm, if not dictatorial hand on all activities.

The observations of Wallace concerning Inskip at the National Camp at Landisville, Pennsylvania, in 1873 are not atypical of the prevailing camp meeting patterns. Obviously giving personal acknowledgment to the charisma of the leader of the National Committee, he said:

> *The management is a depositum.* Everybody and everything must bow to the control of one master mind. That mind infused by a fervor extraordinary and guided by a supernatural wisdom and power, holds the congregation in a steady unrelaxing grasp. To

rebel in any case, is to mar the grand end in view, so far as it relates to the individual and the universal good to be attained [emphasis his].[77]

The same author notes that the day-to-day camp life outside of the actual meetings were more obviously regulated by "arbitrary" rules, which made the encampments, "models of management, good order, and the highest social privilege....Obstinate, or narrow-minded men [who]...found them too exacting...[should] either stay away or yield at once and move with the mighty current as it flows onward...."[78]

An account of the daily schedule at the 1875 National Camp Meeting on the Newburgh District of the New York Conferences of the Methodist Episcopal Church lists the typical camp routine.

The bell rang at five in the morning for the benefit of the sleepy. Half-past five a prayer meeting was held in the pavilion; after breakfast, at eight o'clock, prayer and experience meeting; half-past two, preaching from the stand; after tea, a six o'clock prayer meeting; and then the closing public service at seven o'clock. At ten the bell rang for all to retire.[79]

Only the Holy Spirit could interrupt the regimen. Rowdyism, less a threat than in the frontier camps, was not tolerated.[80]

The religious mystique created out of these elements combined with the psychological and spiritual intensity generated by ten days of direct spiritual exercise was readily felt by the friends of holiness who annually responded to the summer call to local and national camp meetings. The air of the camps sometimes was recognized even by disinterested observers. A newspaper reporter gave the following account of his visit to a Texas holiness camp meeting:

The increasing years see no diminution of the numbers of so-called holiness people as they answer to the roll call of the great annual assembly on the thither side of the Brazos...."

Whatever may be said of the beliefs of the Holiness people or of their relations to other worship, the simplicity of their nature, their profound belief in the actual presence of the Spirit of God in their midst, the intensity of their piety, and it may be safely said the integrity of their lives, make them a pleasing study and the hours spent with them are profitable ones. To escape from the arid doubts and sneers and materialism of daily life and sit among a people who whether in reality or imagination walk and talk with

God, is, as if one, lost in an arid desert, should suddenly find himself on the banks of a great river, amid the umbrageous shade of laughing trees and the aroma of singing flowers.

The exercises of the first day or two...are devoted to prayers for the appearance of the Holy Ghost....There is hardly a moment when from the quivering voice of holy women, grizzly good men and even children, the throne of God is not dynamited with burning and fiery supplications, all of one tenor and one purpose, that of the coming of the Holy Ghost. It seems as if heaven could not stand the bombardment. "The kingdom of heaven suffereth violence and the violent take it by force."

The Holy Ghost does come or seems to come. There is no doubt of the presence of an afflatus, weird, powerful and overwhelming. It comes as the sound of a mighty rushing wind....The presence lasts for days in a mad, spiritual, but always beautiful revel and one so full of bliss and rapture and inexpressible glory that, if it be God, one day with God is worth a thousand years of mundane life.

The reporter concludes: "To the curious in recondite and abstruse studies the phenomena of the Holiness camp meeting is worth going a thousand miles to observe."[81]

Few people came a thousand miles to observe the phenomena of the holiness camp, but many a holiness camper went a thousand miles, even in the postwar era to attend and take part in the religious activities. Dr. William Godbey, one of the most prominent holiness evangelists of the last quarter of the century, tells of his visit to the Texas campgrounds referred to above, when four thousand tenters were on the grounds and sixteen thousand people were in attendance at the meetings.[82]

The adoption of the camp meeting by the National Committee as centers of higher life evangelism broadened the utility and influences of the camps. They became focal points for personal communication between areas of the movement which were otherwise out of contact with one another;[83] such communication became very critical to the progress of their common cause. The broad spectrum of representation from practically every state in the country in the first National Camp Meetings, established a means by which the movement stabilized around certain pivotal patterns of faith and order in spite of geographical discontinuity. Traveling evangelists moved from camp to camp spreading the propaganda of the cause from point to point; the camp meeting circuit became more than a round of meetings, it became a communication and fellowship circuit by which the fluid movement found coherence and a measure of informal but very effective inter-group discipline. Timothy Smith, in reviewing a portion of the later history of the movement in the Church of the Nazarene, the largest of the "camp meeting churches," says: "Here in the tented grove they [the Nazarene fathers] forged the unity, the interdependence, and the common front against 'worldliness' out of which a new denomination was born."[84]

THE HIGH TIDE OF THE REVIVAL

The Methodist pastors who formed the National Camp Meeting Association for the Promotion of Holiness were as ardent Methodists as they were holiness advocates. They were completely honest in their consistent denial that there was anything schismatic in their adoption of the Methodist camp meeting for their own special purpose. They were sure that here was the most suitable platform for the sounding of the call to bring that church back to its central message and the only insurance of its continued blessing and usefulness. What they were really accomplishing, was to transplant a revivalistic doctrine and way of life with strong roots and vigorous new shoots into the structure of the only established institution congenial enough to the doctrine to nurture and preserve it through the tumultuous late nineteenth century. Meetings in the camp meeting pattern also produced vigorous trans-plants of the movement which found root and flourished among non-Methodist churches of America, England, and Europe.

By 1870, the tempo of holiness evangelism through the camp meeting medium was rapidly increasing. Three National Camps were held that year. The reports of the first one at Hamilton, Massachusetts indicate that the revival activity at Hamilton excited "Unitarians and others" to hold special meetings, but probably the most significant work done for the promotion of the cause of holiness was the large number of ministers who professed to enter into the experience of perfect love.[85]

The reports of success at the second 1870 camp meeting at Oak-ington, Maryland, indicate that the relation between the pleasant sur-roundings of the open grove and the Beulah Land experience of the campers was not an absolute one. The weather there was unbearably hot; the preachers preached with the temperatures above one hundred degrees, but with "mental clearness, propriety of utterance, and far-reaching power. The people were in high spirits; no wearying, no sign of exhaustion..."[86] By 1871, the summer editions of the *Guide to Holiness* were filled with reports of holiness camp meetings within Methodism and beyond.[87]

A NEW EVANGELISM

In the spring of that year, Inskip, leaving the pastorate, toured the Methodist conferences of the southwestern states at the invitation of, and in company with, Bishop Ames. At Council Bluffs, Iowa, Inskip was joined by other members of the National Committee who, together with other friends, traveled to California where the pattern of successful evangelism, which had marked the summer camps, was now repeated in smaller, but equally successful, meetings in Methodist churches and conferences.[88]

John Inskip and Brigham Young

The high point of the return trip was the meeting held at Salt Lake City at the invitation of Rev. C. M. Pierce, Methodist missionary on station there. Brigham Young and most of the other Mormon leaders, as well as the territorial officials, crowded into the large tent for the closing service. According to the National Association's reporter, the converts in this center of Mormonism were few, but significant. The wives of Bishop Hunter, president of the board of Mormon bishops, and of the leader of the Mormon Godbieite sect, together with the wife and daughter of Orson Pratt, one of the able prophets of Mormonism, responded to the call.[89]

The account of the stay of the National Committee in the capital of Mormonism, indicates that the holiness evangelists did not stay as close as usual to their commitment to the particular promotion of holiness as their central theme. The evangelists seem to have been too much aware of where they were and who was present. The preaching was almost exclusively directed to Brigham Young and the evils of Mormonism; the record clearly indicates that the cause of Christian holiness was scarcely advanced. The participants and some other contemporary observers saw it differently, however. Inskip's biographers who also took part in the meetings conclude that, "Mormonism has never recovered from the terrible bombardment it received from the batteries of the National Camp Meeting Association. The authority and influence then lost by the Mormon rulers, have never been regained, and never will be."[90]

The Rev. Dewitt Talmage agreed with them; to *The Christian at Work* he wrote, "We have never seen the brethern of that religious storming party but we hail them...for the glorious work that they have accomplished in Salt Lake City."[91]

In spite of the overtones of the Salt Lake City meeting which was the last of the 150 public meetings of the seven thousand mile tour, the revival results had been good; but more significantly the pattern had been set for the peripatetic holiness evangelists who, in their own way, would become the new circuit riders of Methodism, spreading the holiness message and literature across the spiritual wilderness of the church just as the Methodist circuit rider had done across the unchurched wilderness of the American frontier.[92]

Continued Interdenominational Influence

Although the work of the National Committee was distinctively Methodist in its background and its organization, the interdenominational element which has always been a distinct feature of the revival movement continued to involve other communions in the developing holiness revival. Reports of holiness revivals among Quakers, United Brethren, Moravians, Mennonites, Lutherans, and from evangelical missionaries in China and India appeared in the *Guide*.[93] Henry Belden and William E. Boardman and others who were regular attendants at the Palmer's Tuesday Meeting continued their ministry of the Wesleyan holiness emphasis in the postwar period into numerous Baptist, Congregational, Presbyterian, Episcopal, and Lutheran churches and especially through Union Holiness Conventions. The May 1842 issue of the *Guide* announced that the two of them were going to enter evangelistic work on a full-time basis.[94] In Philadelphia, the Baptist, Dr. Edgar Levy, maintained his active position in the Friday meetings held at the headquarters of the National Association on Arch Street.[95] In the fall of 1871, Finney, now an elder statesman of perfectionist revivalism, preached on the "baptism of the Holy Ghost" before the National Congregational Council, representing three thousand churches.[96]

The growing use of the camp meeting service, as special means for promoting holiness doctrine, allowed ministers and laymen from non-Methodist churches much greater freedom to participate in perfectionist gatherings, than would have been possible to them in meetings held for a similar purpose in the denominational churches themselves; there was less of the sectarian emphasis in the former.

Influences upon the Evangelical Alliance

The presentation of two papers to the international meeting of the Evangelical Alliance in New York City in 1873, further demonstrates the fact as well as the extent of the penetration of the general evangelical community by the revival's doctrines of higher Christian experience. In one of them, the speaker, Richard Fuller, directing his remarks to the quality of Christian life required by dangers threatening the Church of that day, called for a total response throughout Christendom to a new piety. The nature of that piety, the means for its achievement, and the terminology used to describe it were completely within the patterns of Wesleyan perfectionism then being utilized by the holiness movement.[97]

The address was important because it spoke particularly to the relationship between Christian activism and the quality of the life of the Christian who engaged in that activism. He observed that one of the most "remarkable features" of the age was the energy with which men in that day were combining "their efforts in every sort of enterprise" in both the religious and secular worlds everywhere forming special societies to do whatever "they wish to do...." As a result of this constant doing, he concluded, the peril in religion is "the mistaking what we *do* for what we *are* and consequently the neglect of our spiritual health...while we engage in the diversified systems of concerted movements which incessantly claim our attention" (emphasis his). Fuller then launched into a lengthy appeal to the Christian church to disallow its traditional excuses for a lack of consistent Christian life and to promote a piety whose "fruit" was "holiness." The church "can scarcely adopt a system which...mocks the highest, holiest aspirations of the 'new creature,'" he continued. One genuine "act of faith," he said, "[was]...worth a whole lifetime of attempted *faithfulness*, in subduing the depravities which diluted the quality of usual Christian life" (emphasis his). The question he was raising, he observed, was a most critical one at the moment because the "state of the world" indicated to him such a rapid expansion of Christianity that nothing less than the quality of Christian piety he had described would be demanded of Christians themselves.[98]

Thus the pietistic thrust of the movement again raised the question of the quality of devotion required for effective Christian action. It had been raised before by Harriet Beecher Stowe as a consequence of the strong emphasis upon the "interior life" raised by Thomas Upham's works. Both Beecher and Fuller concluded that the revival's call to the inner life of the Christian in a perfection and purity of love was a necessary antidote to the tendency of the social activism of the churches to divorce both its content and methods from its "Christianess." The tragedy for the Christianity of the latter part of the century was that the viable tension between Christian devotion and Christian activity frequently broke down under the pressures that the churches faced as part of a revolutionary social order.

The tragedy for the holiness revival in America was that it let its pietism, some elements of which tended toward pious passivity, overcome its Wesleyan perfectionism, which inclined toward activity rooted in the inherent optimism of its broad universal concepts of the designs of divine redemption for man and society. Neither was ever completely submerged, but the scales commonly tipped toward *being* rather than *doing*. Its activism centered in evangelism and such efforts at social reform as contributed to that end, the goal, as has been already noted, was to "Christianize" Christianity, to prepare the church for whatever activity it put itself to.[99]

The second holiness address to the Evangelical Alliance was by William Nast, father of the German Methodist work in America, and an active participant in the development of the Methodist Church in Germany as well. Nast, at this time was a member of the National Association for the Promotion of Holiness. His sermon, typical of that of the National Association for the Promotion of Holiness evangelists, reinforced the conclusions drawn by Fuller concerning the desire and demand for higher, more potent, Christian experience which was abroad in the churches.[100]

It is impossible to ascertain what elements of these appeals may have been carried home by the European delegates present at the meeting. In both England and on the continent the Palmer's work had left its influence. The Methodist churches of England and the newly developing Methodist movements in Germany contained active holiness elements. These together with the influences of the movement's literature and periodicals helped to pave the way for the strong response to the holiness ministry of Robert Pearsall Smith which began that same year in England.

The National Committee in the South

The year 1872 marked the first venture of the members of the National Committee into the South. The cause of Wesleyan perfection had suffered more in the South than in the North during the immediate prewar period. The Methodist Episcopal Church South, after the division of the Methodist Church in 1844, looked upon the holiness papers and other means of promotion for the doctrine, such as the Tuesday Meetings, as tools of the northern church; furthermore, the close relationship between perfectionist teaching and the moral issues concerning slave-holding scarcely lent popularity to any advance of the doctrine in the southern church. The anti-slavery cause had been a religious crusade. The Wesleyan Methodists and the Free Methodists, now clearly allied with the holiness cause, had stood firmly in the middle of that agitation. The whole movement was suspect.[101]

The South too had been only slightly affected by the Revival of 1858, in part, because that revival had been most effective among the working men of the industrialized areas of the country and the South shared few of those; in part, it was also due to a general apathy against revivalism, itself, which always was strongly moralistic, and by then, commonly activistic.[102] Nor could the Methodist Episcopal Church South quickly forget what they considered to be undue efforts by the Methodist Episcopal Church to take advantage of the reconstruction period and the poverty of the southern church to reestablish itself in the south at the cost of the latter.[103] The National's evangelists preaching in the South reported that the Methodist Episcopal Church South, "Understood that we were there to make a raid upon the church for the purpose of enlarging our own territory...and that the Methodist Episcopal Church had loaned to the committee, not only its official sanction but also its money."[104]

It was not surprising then that when the National Committee decided that some of its members would hold the last of the five National Camps for 1872 in Knoxville, Tennessee, there was a raising of eyebrows in the North and rumblings of discontent in the South. In the latter area some claimed that the principal aim of the camp meeting was to "make proselytes" for the northern church. Others felt that it was "a grand electioneering trip...." The use of the term "National" in the name of the organization also misled some.[105]

In spite of all these concerns the National Camp Meeting Association's efforts produced numerous confessions to conversions and sanctifications especially among the ministry of the area. The *Methodist Advocate,* published at Atlanta, Georgia, gave a favorable report on the meeting, noting that doctrine was Wesleyan and everything was in "good order." The following year the last National camp of the season was again held at Knoxville. This time the committee was sure enough of its grounds to invite Bishop Gilbert Haven of the northern church to participate in the meetings.[106]

The revival of the preaching of entire sanctification in the South was abetted in this same period by the establishment of new publications "to advance the cause of holiness." The pace of the holiness revival would prove to be slower than that in the North and the officials of the southern church were less open to the holiness movement within the church. Nevertheless, the aged Dr. Lovick Pierce, whose seventy years in the Methodist ministry allowed him to reach back to the very beginning of Methodism, linked hands with the new movement. He reported to Inskip in 1875, that a new periodical on the same plan as the *Christian Standard* was out with its first issue and already the "spring buds of holiness are putting out, at the lowest points of sapped life."[107]

The National Committee and the Perfectionist Churches

The two smaller Methodist bodies, the Wesleyan Methodists and the Free Methodists, who openly espoused Wesleyan holiness doctrine by incorporating articles concerning it in their *Discipline* were not in a strong position to take leadership in the expanding revival. The increase in articles on the subject in their religious papers indicate that both were influenced by the activities of the National Committee; but during the postwar decades, the Wesleyans were depleted by a severe loss in leadership and membership, due to the return to the parent body of those who felt that the purposes for the church's existence had been obviated by the successful conclusion of the "war against slavery."[108] Those who chose to continue the movement were concerned chiefly with anti-secret society reform.[109] The Free Methodists, organized in 1860, were busy developing and establishing their work which was still in the formative stages. As already noted, the Free Methodist Church was the first organized church in history to specifically identify itself with the doctrine of Christian perfection as its founding. But the controversy which had surrounded its founding, and its popular identification of the doctrine with the intense puritan ethic of Finney and the western New York "burnt over" district, limited its influence in the general movement. In fact,[110] in some circles the critics of the holiness movement used the "Nazarite" affair in the Methodist Episcopal Church's Genesee Conference in 1860 as a certain illustration of the divisive nature of the holiness specialists within the church. Too intimate an identification of the mainstream Methodist holiness movement with such a group would hardly have been expedient for the National Committee.[111]

The Holiness Revival in Methodism: Flow Tide

The participation of bishops, presiding elders, and large numbers of Methodist laymen in the National Camp meetings testified to a growing acceptance of the methods by the organized church.[112] This acceptance was undoubtedly widened by the ability of the National Association leaders to avoid many of the extreme physical and emotional demonstrations which had always been played up by critics of the camp meeting movement. Commentaries on the services in the Methodist *Advocates* were cast in increasingly favorable tones. Typical of these is the guarded but positive language of the report of Dr. Reid, editor of the *Northwestern Christian Advocate;* of his observations on the closing service of the first Midwestern National Camp Meeting held at Des Plaines, Illinois, he wrote,

Silence was a wonderful power with them; the vast assembly
awaiting on God, just waiting....Not a word said, but every heart
opened heavenward, and God pouring his blessing in. The results in bringing souls to Christ estimating no other good that was
done, marks the meeting a signal success. It has evidently marked
an era in the religious experience of Northwestern Methodism;
and thus far there is in it great promise of good, and little promise
of evil.[113]

An enthusiastic report to the *Philadelphia Home Journal* said: "The
whole Northwest is in a blaze of salvation. Holiness is the theme in
every direction....I have heard that ministers have gone home covered
with sanctified power, and whole churches are at the altar seeking
holiness."[114]

In 1872, five years after the Vineland meeting, the president of the
National Committee could report to the annual meeting of the Association in New York City that:

Never before in the history of Christianity has there been so great
and widespread an interest in this important subject as within the
last four or five years. All denominations have been so aroused
as to assure the most skeptical that this is truly the "work of
God."[115]

He rejoiced that not only the church in general, but the Methodist
Church in particular had been largely won to the movement: "The
church in a degree, perhaps beyond what, all things considered, we
would have expected, has given us countenance and appreciated our
endeavor."[116]

Less than ten years after the end of the Civil War the following facts
about the holiness movement in America were evident: that the tide of
revival was rising in America, that it was commonly, but not exclusively
oriented toward Methodist Wesleyan perfectionism, that the National
Camp Meeting Association Committee was playing the leadership role,
and that those who had predicted schism for the church because of
increased organization of the holiness party within it were obviously
wrong. There was a genuine basis for Inskip's optimism for the cause.

The influence of the movement was also making itself felt at the
administrative center of the church's life. Bishop Morris testified at a
love-feast at the Urbana, Ohio National Camp Meeting in 1871: "There
are a number of things I praise God for. The first is, that I have lived to
see a National Campmeeting in Ohio."[117]

He later wrote about the Urbana Camp: "The final results of this campmeeting will never be known fully till the great day of reckoning."[118]

The Methodist Episcopal General Conference of 1872 elected eight new bishops, six of them were friendly with the holiness cause. Randolph S. Foster had been selected by John McClintock, the first president of Drew University, to head the theological studies of the new school; his theology was pronouncedly Wesleyan; at the time of his election he was serving as president of Drew.[119] Stephen Merrill maintained an open and close relationship with the friends of holiness.[120] Jesse T. Peck, the younger brother of George Peck, the Methodist editor, had written one of the major defenses of the doctrine of Christian perfection contributed regularly to the *Guide*, and had participated in the National camps as noted above. He openly proposed that the church should incorporate the "second blessing" view of the revival into its doctrinal statement.[121] Gilbert Haven, the fourth of the holiness bishops elected that year, had defended the activities of the National Committee during his editorship of the *Zion's Herald*, the voice of New England Methodism.[122] Thomas Bowman[123] was the fifth and William L. Harris, the sixth; the latter joined Asa Mahan and Asbury Lowrey in a special call to entire sanctification addressed to the ministers and laymen of all denominations.[124]

The Holiness Revival in Methodism: Ebb Tide

But even the groundswell of approbation for the movement which helped to carry these men into ecclesiastical power, did not silence the voice of the opposition. John Inskip's report to the National Association in 1872 recognized the continuing conflict concerning the special promotion of holiness within the church. The doctrine of entire sanctification, he noted, had "in large measure" been put aside by Methodism. This fact accounted for the criticism and censure which the work of the National Committee had met. In the face of this misunderstanding and misrepresentation he reminded the committee members that "the vow taken at Vineland not to answer anything that might be alleged against us has been the occasion of much unfair dealing towards us; but it has saved the Church from the shame and dishonor of an acrimonious controversy."[125]

The Vineland vow, of course did not prevent "acrimonious controversy" in the church, for it applied only to nonretaliation against attacks made upon members of the Association as persons. The thrusts against the movement sometimes became *ad hominum* by nature, but, on the whole, they were otherwise—first, doctrinal, and second, methodological. Charges related to these two categories heightened the tensions for the movement within its Methodist home. In controversies over doctrine, the movement ultimately established its broad contention that the doctrinal positions it held were essentially those which primitive Methodism had affirmed and which the Methodism of their day continued to hold to in its official utterances and exhortations.[126] Bishops north and south declared the mission of the church to be the spreading of Scriptural holiness. Even modern Methodism has not completely ignored the traditional holiness emphasis of the church.[127]

But when the movement tried to establish the appropriateness of its special methods for the promotion of holiness within the increasingly bureaucratic structure of burgeoning Methodism, they lost the day. The intensity of the opposition, which had refused to yield the field completely, even under the more informal "irregularities" of the layman's movement under the Palmers continued to increase in direct proportion to the transfer of leadership to pastors who were more deeply involved in the power structure of the church. The critics became especially vocal as the summer-camp evangelism moved back into the churches after the close of the camp meeting season.

The intense debates covering the propriety of holding special meetings for the promotion of holiness again agitated Methodist ministers' meetings, especially in New York City. Unhappy critics maintained that every Methodist service was a holiness meeting; proponents of the new measures, however, contended that in reality this was no longer so; they insisted that the backsliding of the church on this theme and the critical problems which she currently faced, mandated and justified even extraordinary agencies for the restoration of the doctrine and the experience throughout the denomination.[128]

In 1873, Dr. Asbury Lowrey, pastor of Wesley Chapel in Cincinnati, Ohio, invited John Inskip and William McDonald to his church to hold a meeting "expressly for the promotion of personal holiness." Night after night capacity audiences crowded the large church in a remote area of the town. Even concurrent nightly lectures in the city by Henry Ward Beecher failed to diminish attendance at the holiness meetings. In spite of the popular success of the meeting, Lowrey came under heavy criticism for his encouragement of those "special agencies." His reply to these objections in the *Advocate of Christian Holiness* for June 1873 is a classic example of the many apologies which were made by the movement's defenders from the time of the Palmers on. The propriety of the methods of specialization used by the holiness reformers was the issue.

Lowrey's arguments centered in three basic points. The first question at issue was, "Are specific and extraordinary efforts needed at the present to revive personal holiness?" Lowrey said: "I unhesitatingly answer, yes, Nay more, I affirm that the conservation of our distinctive features, and the efficient perpetuity of our church, can only be secured by a diffusion of experimental holiness...."[129]

This was the basic rationale for the movement; in that day it was applied generally by Methodist to the Methodist Church, but the continuing story will reveal that the interdenominational nature of the revival, combined with the general hunger in the churches for new spiritual power, gradually broadened that theme to promote the revival of personal holiness in all of Christendom as the only hope for a redeemed world.

Lowrey then turned to his second question: What is the posture of affairs in the church? He listed six developments which he believed were militating against the future usefulness of the church, a church that in more normal times would have encouraged people into a life of Christian holiness. These six in summary are (1) *The expansion of "ecclesiastical machinery."* He warned that it threatened to "break down with its own weight." The threat here was toward externality without spiritual depth. (2) *The increased wealth and popularity of the church.* "We are numerous, wealthy, educated, and damagingly respectable. From these sources, influences are constantly springing adverse to holiness." He saw the tendency to "commute benevolent deeds for heart purity—to sink substance in the symbol, and exchange life for a name." (3) *The neglect of holiness literature.* "Very few of our own people now read Wesley, Fletcher, Clarke...." They were regarded as obsolete. (4) *The abandonment of the spiritual means of grace.* In some localities "the class meetings, prayer meetings, bands, fasting, family and secret prayer," were generally or totally given up. (5) *The tolerance by the church of "respectable vices."* Papers were received on Sunday, the children of the church went to dancing schools; dancing, games of chance, and even drinking were tolerated in the homes of many in the church. Visiting theaters, circuses, and horse races was common as also was the participation in fairs, excursions and public festivities. (6) *The admission of large numbers of unconverted members.*

His concluding question was: "If such is the true posture of affairs in our church is it probable that a general revival of personal holiness will ever take place without the use of special and extraordinary agencies?"

Lowrey appealed to the church not to rule out this holiness "irregularity." If the church should do so, he warned, "the brightest star of hope that has shown upon the church for a half a century will be struck from the heavens of Methodism."[130]

In a contrary vein, an article in the *Western Christian Advocate* in the fall of 1875, entitled "Holiness Then and Now," argued that special meetings for the promotion of holiness were "un-Wesleyan and should be suppressed." The author contended that such meetings were "not exactly in harmony with the old time-honored and well-tried Methodism." Such effects, he said, were "incompatible with the spirit and genius of Methodism, and altogether schismatical and revolutionary in its tendency."[131]

Inskip, editor of the *Advocate of Christian Holiness*, replied that not only were such efforts fully in accord with the practice and theology of Methodism, but that John Wesley, himself, used similar measures when the testimony to the experience of Christian perfection began to wane in his societies. He made reference to Wesley's *Journal* entry for January 29, 1767, in which the latter noted: "At five in the morning I began a course of sermons on Christian Perfection; if haply that thirst after it might return which was so general a few years ago. Since that time how deeply have we grieved the Holy Spirit of God."[132]

Inskip also argued that according to Tyerman's *Life of Wesley*, Methodism's founder, had organized special meetings for the promotion of holiness and then had given them into the charge of laymen in his absence. The "band" meetings and the "very select societies" were all meetings for the special encouragement of Christian holiness; the rules for such meetings, he pointed out, were carried in the *Discipline* of the Methodist Episcopal Church until 1852.[133]

PHOEBE PALMER'S DEATH

In December 1874, at the height of the revival and in the midst of the increasingly sharp conflict it was causing in the Methodist Episcopal Church, Phoebe Palmer died. After she and her husband had returned to America from their evangelistic work in England ten years earlier, they continued their holiness evangelism through the Tuesday Meetings, in conventions, camps, and in the churches assisted by the Lankfords. Mrs. Palmer had accepted gracefully the organization of the National Camp Meeting Association in 1867; recognizing a new era in the movement, she blended her own ministry with that of the new leadership. She and her husband were regular workers in the National camp meetings and consistently promoted the work of the Association in the pages of the *Guide* which she continued to edit until her death in December of 1874. Occasionally she had mildly rebuked the enthusiasm of the reporters of the National Committee for their overzealous claims,[134] which, as indicated above, tended to be too unconscious of the flow of history and too enthusiastic for "now" and the "tomorrow" which their efforts would insure. When the National had begun publication of its own periodical, the *Advocate of Christian Holiness,* she had expressed regret that the resources and constituent readership so vital to the holiness periodicals' survival had to be divided by even friendly competition, but she had wished the new venture every success.[135]

The penname "Shepherdess," which she used in her first writings, might aptly describe her religious activities and informal, but influential, position in American Methodism and the holiness movement. Bishops and ministers were part of the flock. Twenty to thirty of them were regularly in the congregations at the Tuesday Meetings. She became a spiritual guide to thousands more in the American churches through her public ministry and her numerous books. In the Palmer's ministry in England and Scotland during the war years, twenty thousand conversions and ten thousand sanctifications were recorded among people of all classes. Milton Lorenzo Haney, a later leader in the movement, said that to Phoebe Palmer, more than to any other single individual, must be given the right to the title of founder of the modern holiness movement. In granting such recognition to Mrs. Palmer, he went on to say that it was nevertheless probable that she would not have acknowledged all that was bound up in the movement in his time.[136] Like all great leaders, she has been read variously by both friends and followers, onlookers and opponents. Her largeness of spirit and ecumenical viewpoint often did not suit the character or the times of many who took up her concerns for the work of holiness in the ongoing movement.

There is possibly some relationship between movements which are centered in the perfection in Christian love and the dominant positions they have often granted to the leadership of women.[137] Undoubtedly, it was partly due to her feminine persuasiveness that she was able to convince so many listeners of the possibilities and values of the higher Christian life after so many others failed to do so. But the religious sentiments of Phoebe Palmer went considerably deeper than the romanticism of the language of the mid-nineteenth century in which she expressed herself and by which others described her life and work would indicate. A double-page spread of pictures in the *Ladies Repository* for February 1866 which shows a full page portrait of Phoebe Palmer seated opposite a composite arrangement of the pictures of outstanding representatives of Methodist Church's first one hundred years in America, symbolizes her influence in her day.[138] Her sturdy chin and set features seem to express the cool determination of a woman who for almost thirty years made a simple gathering in a private home at a dull hour on a weekday, a center of spiritual renewal in the face of incessant criticism, neglect, gibes, and ridicule. It was for Wesley to first bring the Protestant church at large to ask the questions concerning the possibilities of practical holiness in the Christian life; he said, "If there is grace for entire sanctification at the moment of death, why is not the same grace available in life." He began to preach it and testified to finding some genuine recipients of such grace in his lifetime; it remained, however, for an American woman to introduce into that Wesleyan theology the urgency of the revivalist call for immediate decision and promise of perfection in love to the masses. For her the "now" in the "if at death, why not now" of Wesley, stood out in capital letters; she insisted that present faith and entire consecration made Christian holiness a possibility in grace for every Christian. In writing of her and her sister, Sarah, Bishop John P. Newman said that "no two women of...[the Methodist Episcopal Church] have left a deeper...impress upon their day and generation."[139]

The direct relationship between her application of American revival methods to the promotion of Christian holiness and the questions which arose among friends and opponents who evaluated her efforts is illustrated in a summary of her work by her friend, Dr. Asbury Lowrey upon her death:

> Mrs. Palmer, we think, was strictly Wesleyan in her views and inculcations. In order to lift individuals over the bar of constitutional, habitual, or creed-bound unbelief, she would seem to lead them out, sometimes, to the very crest of presumption; but in such cases she always left the bridge of orthodoxy in good repair behind her....They were seen by her keen insight to be necessary to success....Indeed, every great revivalist has found it necessary to provoke action by cutting dull informalities, fossilized faith and perfunctory services at right angles. Such exploits, considered hyper-critically, may easily be magnified into heresy and delusion; and yet, according to the verdict of history, they are indispensable to success.[140]

When one attempts to explain the varying individual stances taken towards the movement, in Methodism at least, then one must take into account the fact that the pros and cons may have been determined by sympathy or antagonism toward revivalistic methods as much as toward the theology involved.

It is for this emphasis that the higher life movement in all of Protestantism looks back to her life and work. DeWitt Talmage recognized her interdenominational influences. She had been a Methodist, he said, but denominational walls could not contain her; some "caricatured" her higher life evangelism, he observed, but, "she lived long enough to see the whole Christian church waking up to this doctrine...."[141] Asbury Lowrey's memorial in the *Christian Advocate* upon her death, in the literary pattern of the day, is couched in prose too flowery for the modern ear, but the closing sentence is solid and long since proven by subsequent history: "Whoever promotes holiness in all this country, must build upon the foundations of this holy woman."[142]

CONTINUING CONTROVERSY IN METHODISM

Not every one in Methodism was as enthusiastic as Lowrey over Mrs. Palmer's work. By the time of her death Dr. Daniel D. Whedon,[143] editor of the *Methodist Quarterly Review,* had become the chief antagonist of the movement which continued the special methods for holiness promotion which she had fostered. He charged it with a theology of "hyper-Wesleyanism."[144] In response to an objection by George D. Watson, one of the movement's main advocates, to a *Quarterly Review* article on holiness by Dr. J. O. A. Clark, Whedon defended Clark's article as, "Less perniciously divergent from Wesley than Inskip, McDonald, or this Dr. Watson."[145]

In regard to the special methods used by the advocates of holiness in the church, the holiness association, the holiness periodical, the holiness prayer meeting, the holiness preacher, Whedon charged that they "are all modern novelties. They are not Wesleyan. We believe that a living Wesley would never admit them into the system."[146] In an earlier controversy with Asbury Lowrey over Jonathan T. Crane's book, *Holiness: the Birthright of All God's Children,* Whedon repeated the original charges which Mattison had made against the movement and the work of Phoebe Palmer in the debates of 1857. The whole movement, he claimed, smacked of the flavor of the enthusiastic George Bell. The "Nazarites" of central New York were still fresh in his mind as an example of the potential evil which could result from such holiness propaganda as the *Guide* and the *Standard of Holiness* poured out; he forecast that this movement like Bell's could lead to nothing but disloyalty and division.[147]

The controversy continued on into 1878. In March of that same year William McDonald's editorial rejoinder to Whedon's attack is one of the sharpest to be found anywhere in the polemical writings of the proponents of holiness; the personal inference and the biting irony of the reply to Dr. Whedon pushed the nonretaliatory vow of the Vineland organizational meeting to the limits and probably beyond. McDonald wrote,

> If Dr. Whedon is not the chief umpire in Methodism, he is a greatly mistaken man. Never did the occupant of the fancied chair of St. Peter speak with greater constituted authority. Whenever he utters his dictum, every Methodist preacher...must gracefully bow and silently submit.[148]

In his reply to Dr. Watson's tract against the position taken by Dr. Clark, in the *Quarterly Review,* Whedon was charged with letting his "Shillalah" fall "without special care as to whose head is broken." Whedon's views, McDonald continued, had been rejected by "hundreds of our ablest and best ministers" as well as by a then recent action of the Wisconsin Conference.[149]

The sharpest retort of all was his reference to the efforts of certain ministers to excuse Whedon's alleged "unchristian spirit" by attempting to "Explain it on the ground that he is old and broken down and is not to be held to a strict account for what he has to say under such circumstances."[150]

The strong reaction of McDonald for the National Committee was probably prompted not only by Whedon's objections to the work of the National Association, but because, although the editor of one of the powerful papers in Methodism, McDonald claimed Whedon's theology of Methodist perfectionism was pure "un-Wesleyan heresy" and "clear as mud."[151]

These exchanges not only demonstrate the depth of the continuing controversy over the movement in the church, but also its acrimonious spirit was prophetic of the extreme polarization which was taking place both in the National Association and the institutional churches. There was a developing breakdown of communication between the growing movement and the church structures. Within the next few years the strictures would be drawn sufficiently tight to give the more radical fringes of the movement a rationale for forsaking the church structures to pioneer the narrow paths of schism which finally became broad roads of separation. There would be Methodists whose ties to the officialdom of the church were not so warm and direct as those of the Palmers and the Inskips or even the McDonalds, and whose optimism for restoring the church to her holiness testimony would be considerably less evident. Jones concludes,

Well recommended in the church, early leaders became patri-
archs in the holiness cause...but failed to father spiritual sons to
lead a movement in the church. Despite their intentions, they
were unable to save Methodism from change, and unwittingly
became agents of faction rather than fraternity within its ranks.[152]

SUMMARY

The formation of the National Camp Meeting Association for the
Promotion of Holiness in 1867, in many aspects, was a very typical
American action. The organization took its place as one among many
special groups within the nation which were created by volunteer
activists to propagandize some particular concern, or to seek a desired
reform. In this context, the National Association was in the company of
such other evangelical reform organizations as the American Bible
Society, the Women's Christian Temperance Union, or any other of the
hundreds of reform movements which dot and even clutter the social
history of nineteenth-century America. In its revivalistic activism, it
undoubtedly shared in the attitudes of suspicion with which reforming
movements of any kind were commonly met by those who are not as
urgent about the issues as the reformers themselves may be. Some of
the persistent opposition in Methodism, to the work of the National
Committee, can probably be read in that light. However, it was hard for
the advocates of the holiness experience to refrain from regarding such
hesitation to accept their methods as anything but negativism toward
perfectionist teaching itself.

Another sense in which the Association was also strongly in step
with a current mood was in its strong sense of mission. Most of the
reform efforts of such groups as the National Camp Meeting Association were deeply rooted in the New England, American tradition which
sought to bring a new order to all society by means of the application
of Christian principles and law. As we have seen, this idea was deeply
ingrained in the national purpose. Although the National Association
had as its immediate reformatory goal, the restoration of the experience
of Christian holiness to the general life of the Methodist churches, its
ultimate sense of purpose fully participated in that Puritan purpose,
strengthened, as it was, by the movement's inherent perfectionism. Its
goal, too, was the reformation of all society. The holiness evangelists
hoped to accomplish this through a purified Methodist Episcopal
Church; that church, in turn, could give leadership to a revival of
holiness which would Christianize America; the nation and the
churches could then fulfill America's redemptive mission to the whole

world. The age of the Holy Spirit and a new millennium would be ushered in. They were true Puritans.

But, as we have also indicated, more than that, they were a new breed of pietists. It was already evident to the National Committee, in the second National Camp Meeting at Manheim, that their message had a much broader appeal than to Methodism alone. They had caught hold of a new evangelistic method in the Palmer pattern. In combination with the innately American institution of the camp meeting, it created a new urgency in the promotion of Christian perfection. The call for immediate consecration, immediate faith, and personal witness had a common appeal to an essential Pietism, which had infused the Calvinistic as well as the Arminian camps in America. The strength of that concern was demonstrated in the Evangelical Alliance meeting of 1873.

The appeal, therefore, of Asbury Lowrey, a member of the National Committee, to the Methodist Episcopal Church to not reject the Committee's special revival methods, was not merely a response of a nineteenth-century American pastor to his church and society; there was a much older and broader tradition pressing through. He was speaking to problems, which others with concepts of the Christian faith very similar to his own, had faced before him. He was reflecting a Christian tradition of concern for a particular Christian approach to the world, the Christian's relationship to it, and the most effective means for its redemption.

Finally, both its revivalistic formulation and its essential pietistic nature made the whole movement extremely experience centered. Its commitment to holiness primarily as an experience facilitated the extension of the revival beyond Methodism. It produced an interdenominationalism, mainly grass-roots in character, which survived extreme variances in creed and denominational polity. At the same time, it laid the foundation for future conflict, not only within the movement itself, but also between the movement and the churches represented by its adherents. The success of the revival, by the mid-seventies, created increasingly sharp tensions between the members of the National Committee and the Methodist Episcopal Church. More and more, the Association with its subsidiary organizations and periodicals was being regarded as an irregular agency. The strident words between Daniel Whedon and William McDonald, at the very zenith of the movement's success, plainly announced that reality.

NOTES

1. William A. Clebsch, *From Sacred to Profane America: the Role of Religion in American History* (New York: Harper and Row, 1968), p. 192.

2. William Warren Sweet, *Methodism in American History*, p. 298, observes that "the four bloody years of the War left their brutalizing effect upon society...and exercised a blighting effect upon the life of the nation for the years that were to follow." Also see Boisen, *op, cit.*, p. 128.

3. Clebsch, *op. cit.*, p. 199.

4. Platt, *op. cit.*, pp. vi, vii. Also see *ibid.*, p. 231.

5. *Ibid.*

6. Gilbert Haven, *Sermons, Speeches and Letters on Slavery and Its War* (Boston: Lee and Shephard, 1869), pp. 629-30. Out of such statements T. Smith, *Revivalism and Social Reform*, p. 7, concluded that "revivalistic religion and Christian Perfection lay at the fountainhead of our nation's heritage of hope...." Clebsch, *op. cit.*, p. 199, notes that Father Isaac Hecker, famed as the center of the Americanism Controversy in the Catholic Church, near the end of his life in 1888 had written that Calvinism with its pessimism and determinism was inadequate to support the American ideal. On religious optimism also see Sperry, *op. cit.*, p. 14.

7. Marty, *op. cit.*, p. 189. Also see Russell B. Nye, *The Almost Chosen People, Essays in the History of American Ideas* (n.p.: Michigan State University Press, 1966), chap. i, "The American Idea of Progress."

8. *Beauty of Holiness*, VIII (April 1857), 104.

9. See Louis Gasper, *The Fundamentalist Movement* (The Hague: Mouton and Co., 1963), pp. 7-8, 53-54.

10. This development is the theme of T. Smith's *Revivalism and Social Reform*. Also see Smith, Handy, and Loetscher, *op. cit.*, II, chap. xii, and the literature there cited; S. Mead, *The Lively Experiment*, chap. vi.

11. Anton Boisen in his classic study, *Religion in Crisis and Custom*, indicates that religious concern is often associated with social as well as personal crises with constructive results. War, however, he says, "seems to be an exception to this principle." Prevailing reactions in war time are "malignant"; Boisen, *op. cit.*, p. 5. See also the whole of "War as Social Crisis," *ibid.*, pp. 95-107. On the Civil War and the holiness revival see W. C. Muncy, Jr., *Evangelism in the United States* (Kansas City: Central Seminary Press, 1945), p. 128.

12. *Guide*, XLVII (April 1865), 91-93.

13. *Ibid.*, XLVI (October 1864), 93-94, reports on the completion of Caughey's latest English campaign in which 3,300 converts were reported in nine months.

14. *Guide*, XLVII (May 1865), 15, and *ibid.*, XLVIII (July 1865), 28-29, show typical lists.

15. McDonald and Searles, *op. cit.*, p. 147.

16. *Ibid.*, p. 148.

17. John S. Inskip, *Methodism Explained and Defended* (Cincinnati, OH: H. S. and J. Applegate, 1851), p. 61.

18. *Ibid.*, p. 60, Also see McDonald and Searles, pp. 147-48. It is interesting to note that the very questions which later became distinctive parts of his teaching on the doctrine, at this period of his life he considered "questions of but little consequence." See Inskip, *op. cit.*, p. 61.

19. McDonald and Searles, *op. cit.*, p. 150, as quoted from Inskip's "Diary."

20. *Ibid.*, p. 151.

21. *Ibid.*, p. 152.

22. *Ibid.* For eight years after this religious experience, Inskip kept a full journal record of his activities; at the top of each page printed in beautiful letters was the motto, "I am, O Lord, wholly and forever thine!"; *ibid.*, p. 160.

23. *Ibid.*, pp. 154-55, as quoted from Inskip's "Diary."

24. Littell, *op. cit.*, pp. 93ff., develops the thesis that the rapid growth of the churches "was accompanied, indeed in part accomplished, by the abandonment of the traditional standards of discipline."

25. McDonald and Searles, *op. cit.*, p. 157, as quoted from Inskip's "Diary."

26. The *Philadelphia Public Ledger* (June 27, 1867).

27. McDonald and Searles, *op. cit.*, p. 118.

28. The Rev. Alfred Cookman, a member of the *ad hoc* committee, called it "a bold move for the friends of holiness." Ridgaway, *op. cit.*, p. 315.

29. McDonald, *The Double Cure*, pp. 5-6; McDonald and Searles, *op. cit.*, pp. 185-88; Rose, *op. cit.*, pp. 50-53; *Autobiography of J. A Wood* (Chicago: Christian Witness Co., 1904), pp. 73-74; Adam Wallace, *op. cit.*, p. 202, wrongly makes William B. Osborne the main instigator of the movement; see Rose, *op. cit.*, p. 50.

30. Inskip noted in his "Diary" that "it is a new idea, yet it forcibly impresses me." Quoted in McDonald and Searles, *op. cit.*, p. 187.

31. George Roberts was a local preacher, physician, and founder of the Historical Society of Baltimore; Simpson, *op. cit.*, p. 759. Cookman was pastor to Bishop Matthew Simpson and his family in pastorates in both Pittsburgh and Philadelphia; Ridgaway, *op. cit.*, p. 47.

32. A term used frequently by Cookman and the movement; it indicates the polarization in the churches on the question.

33. McDonald and Searles, *op. cit.*, p. 190. The terms "higher Christian life" and "life of holiness" or "victorious Christian life" were used interchangeably at these early stages. Later with the birth of the Calvinistic holiness movement attempts to distinguish between the Wesleyan movement and the former tended to use "higher Christian life" in relation to the Calvinistic holiness movement and "holiness" in relation to the Wesleyan camp.

34. *Ibid.*

35. *Ibid.*, p. 188; McDonald, *Double Cure*, p. 6. Cookman, however, found less reaction than he had anticipated; see Ridgaway, *op. cit.*, p. 316.

36. Quoted by Daniel Steele, *A Defense of Christian Perfection or a Criticism of Dr. Mudge's Growth in Holiness toward Perfection* (New York: Hunt and Eaton, 1896), p. 14. The holiness advocates also were encouraged by the Episcopal Address to the General Conference of the Methodist Episcopal Church in 1864 in which the Bishops prayed for "the outpouring of the Holy Ghost upon the Church, the nation, and the world" as their only hope. They had exhorted: "Let faith command it and it shall be." *Journal of the General Conference of the M. E. Ch., 1864* (New York: Carlton and Porter, 1864), p. 436.

37. One cannot help but be impressed with the expectant optimism of the holiness proponents. Cookman wrote to Inskip of his anticipation that Vineland Camp would begin a revival of religion that "spreading North, South, East and

West, may wrap the nation, the continent, and the world in a flame of devotion to Jesus"; Ridgaway, *op. cit.*, p. 316. Wallace, in preparing for the printing of an account of the National Camp at Landisville, Pennsylvania, in 1873, even prior to the meeting, was "so confident that God would baptise the assembled people with the Holy Ghost and fire sent down from heaven that the plan of [his]...prospective book embraced the title, 'Pentecost Repeated.'..." The final notice of the Vineland Camp in the *Philadelphia Public Ledger* (July 15, 1867), was cast in the same optimistic tones in phrases such as "Grand Camp Meeting" and "the largest [camp meeting] ever [to be] held in South Jersey."

38. The first stake had been driven for the development of the town only six years previously. The sale of alcoholic beverages was prohibited; this undoubtedly contributed to the choice of the town as the camp site. As a land promoter, Landis was happy to welcome national organizations and their conventions to his development. "The Friends of Progress Society," made up mainly of Spiritualists and a few Quakers, an anti-Masonic group under Rev. Charles Blanchard, and "women's rights" associations followed in the train of the National Camp Meeting Association. The frequent appearance of feminist leaders such as Mrs. M. E. Tilloston, Spiritualist, Free Love advocate, and dress reformer, who often walked the streets of Vineland in her trousers and frock coat, stamped it as a "Free Love Town" only a few years after the camp meeting there. See *Vineland, N. J. Centennial* (Vineland Centennial Inc., c.d. [*ca.* 1961]), pp. 16-24; Charles K. Landis, "The Settlement of Vineland in N.J.," *Fraser's Magazine*, XI (January 1875), 126ff.; and D. O. Kellog, *Illustrated Vineland* (n.p.: L. L. Buckminster Printer, 1897). The last named provides descriptive materials on the life and layout of the town at the time of the 1867 camp.

39. McDonald and Searles, *op. cit.*, pp. 191-94; Ridgaway, *op. cit.*, pp. 317-18.

40. See his letter as quoted by Ridgaway, *op. cit.*, p. 327. One should note the implications of this enthusiastic reaction to the holiness camp meeting experience by the pastor of the Spring Garden Methodist Episcopal Church in Philadelphia for any attempts to properly evaluate the tensions which developed between many holiness Methodists and the regular Methodist congregations pursuing their usual routine of religious service in the local church. The intensity of the religious experience in the camp, oftentimes unjustly, made the church services appear dead and lifeless.

41. McDonald and Searles, *op. cit.*, pp. 194-95; *Advocate of Christian Holiness,* III (July 1872), 3-4; Ridgaway, *op. cit.*, pp. 317-18; J. E. Searles, *A Sermon Preached by the Request of the National Camp Meeting at Pitman Grove, N. J., August 5, 1887 on the History of the Present Holiness Revival* (Boston: McDonald and Gill, 1887), pp. 4-5.

42. As stated by George Hughes in the *Methodist Home Journal* (October 12, 1872) and quoted both in Ridgaway, *op. cit.*, p. 323, and Searles, *op. cit.*, p. 12.

43. *Ibid*, p. 10; McDonald and Searles, *op. cit.*, p. 194.

44. "Waiting for the Spirit to move" had traits of Quakerism in it. Val B. Clear in "The Urbanization of a Holiness Body," *The City Church*, IX (July-August, 1958), 8, illustrates the end to which it sometimes came; Church of God (Anderson, Iniana.) preachers sat on the front row of camp benches, each with hand in

Bible at his favorite text, waiting for a chance to preach. This same Spirit-led order of unstructured services was also adhered to in the Holiness Church of California. Searles, *op. cit.*, p 10, says this arose out of the movement's emphasis on Spirit direction as they believed it operated in the primitive, post-pentecostal church.

45. McDonald and Searles, *op. cit.*, p. 199. For a general description of the Mannheim meeting see the article from the Columbia, Pennsylvania, *Daily Spy* (July 20, 1868), quoted in *ibid*, pp. 201-202, and Ridgaway, *op. cit.*, pp. 349-50. Lizzie R. Smith, a camp meeting minister long active in the National Holiness Camps, described her experiences at Manheim in Leander L. Pickett, *Faith Tonic I and II Combined* (Louisville, KY: Pentecostal Publishing Company, n.d.), pp. 34-42.

46. H. J. Bowman, compiler, *Voices on Holiness from the Evangelical Association* (Cleveland, OH: Publishing House of the Ev. Assoc., 1882), p. 205. *The Living Epistle*, the holiness periodical of the Evangelical Association, edited by Reuben Yeakel and Elisha A. Hoffman (September 1871), p. 95, carried a report on the Easton, Pennsylvania, district camp meeting which noted that "A new camp-meeting spirit has been infused into the members...." The change was attributed to *"Holiness"* (emphasis theirs). Thirteen out of the seventeen ministers on the district had made a public confession "of having experienced this great salvation." *Ibid.* (1871), *passim*, reveals the growing influence of the movement on evangelicalism. Toward the end of the century, official promotion of the doctrine flagged following a pattern parallel to that of the holiness emphasis in Methodism. An excellent summary of the movement in the Evangelical Association up to that turning point may be found in J. Wesley Corbin, "Christian Perfection and the Evangelical Association through 1875," *Methodist History*, VII (January 1969), 28-44. Also see Raymond W. Albright, *A History of the Evangelical Church* (Harrisburg, PA: The Evangelical Press, 1942), pp. 268-78, W. Horn (comp.), *Yearbook of the Evangelical Association* (Cleveland, OH: Publishing House of the Evangelical Association, 1907), p. 48.

47. The holiness emphases in the Mennonite Brethren in Christ Church and other smaller Mennonite holiness bodies who affiliated with the movement developed out of these influences: Storms, *op. cit.*, p. 201.

48. McDonald and Searles, *op. cit.*, p. 201.

49. *Ibid.*, p. 202.

50. *Ibid.*, p. 197.

51. A correspondent for *The Methodist* (July 17, 1869), as quoted by Ridgaway, *op. cit.*, p. 360, reported that the meeting had attracted natives of every state except Louisiana, Florida, and Texas, as well as some Europeans; among the latter was the English publisher D. Morgan, Esq. One hundred fifty ministers attended.

52. McDonald and Searles, *op. cit.*, pp. 203-204. Nye, *op. cit.*, pp. 164-207, speaks of "The American Sense of Mission." That "the United States [was to] serve as an example to the rest of the world of God's plan" was part of the nation's definition of its purpose.

53. *Ibid.*

54. Smith notes in his *Revival and Social Reform* that Charles Johnson, *The Frontier Camp Meeting, Religious Harvest Time* (Dallas, TX: Southern Methodist University Press, 1955), discussed the decline of the frontier camp, while camps in eastern urban centers were growing in number and importance. In the post-Civil War period a good railroad became a prime consideration in the location of a camp. Special rates were frequently provided by the rail lines for the campers. See Wallace, *op. cit.*, pp. 12-13.

55. For typical discussions of the subject see *Christian Advocate and Journal*, XXXIII (August 26, 1858), 133; *Beauty*, VIII (June 1857), 161-63; *ibid.*, VIII (August 1857), 228-29.

56. In his *Christian Nurture* (Hartford, CT: n.n., 1846), Bushnell proposed that the Christian education of children in the home and the church would be more effective in producing Christians than the crisis conversion experiences of the revivalists.

57. In 1868, in Philadelphia alone, the Methodists announced fifteen area camp meetings for the summer. See *Philadelphia Public Ledger* (July 9, 1868), "Local Religious News."

58. Sweet, *Revivalism*, p. 166; the same, *The American Churches*, p. 56. After 1874, Chatauqua, one of the oldest Methodist camps, became largely an educational institution.

59. *Harper's Weekly*, XVII (August 23, 1873), 742. Also see "Amusement, Religion and Recreation Combined at Chester Heights," Chester (PA) *Times* (July 26, 1883); James F. Reisling, "Some Ocean Grove Observations," *Christian Advocate and Journal*, LXXIII (September 22, 1898), 1542; the latter reported that there were no "sinners or unsaved" at Ocean Grove, N.J. camp, and that the holiness camp founded by National Association leaders in 1869 was becoming "more and more …a Christian seaside resort and less a camp meeting…" in spite of the fact that seventy-eight holiness meetings had been held during that season. For the history of Ocean Grove, see Morris S. Daniels, *The Story of Ocean Grove* (New York: Methodist Book Concern, 1919).

60. R. Yeakel attributed "a great improvement in holding and conducting camp meetings throughout the Evangelical Association and beyond her borders" to the influence of the National camps; H. J. Bowman, *op. cit.*, p. 205. Gaddis, *op. cit.*, p. 445, claims that "the camp meeting from the close of the Civil War on passed almost entirely under perfectionist auspices.…" It was through a camp meeting that the Mennonite Brethren in Christ became a holiness denomination; see Huffman, *op. cit.*, pp. 148-49.

61. *Guide*, LXIV (October 1873), 117-18; *ibid.*, LX (August 1871), 62; *ibid.*, II (September 1840), 70; *ibid.*, XLVIII (September 1865), 87.

62. Nye, *op. cit.*, pp. 256-304, "The American View of Nature." Also see a more extended development of the concept in American history in Hans Huth, *Nature and the American* (Berkeley, CA: n.n., 1957). Perry Miller, *The New England Mind* (New York: n.n., 1939), chap. viii, gives a brief analysis of the Puritan and nature.

63. In 1860, four out of five people lived in rural areas; in 1870, three out of four. *Historical Statistics of the United States: Colonial Times to 1957* (Washington, DC: Government Printing Office, 1961), p. 9.

64. *Advocate of Christian Holiness*, III (July 1872), 19.

65. *Zion's Herald*, XXI (July 31, 1850), p. 1.

66. Jones, *op. cit.*, p. 110.

67. S. Mead, *op. cit.*, p. ix.

68. *Christian Advocate and Journal*, XXXIII (September 9, 1858), 141.

69. Jones, *op. cit.*, p. 63. For an excellent interpretation of the significance of the place of the camp meeting within the holiness movement, see *ibid.*, pp. 93-110. It is limited only by the restrictions of Jones' main thesis that the holiness institutions were shaped mainly to suit the nostalgia of rural immigrants to the city for situations similar to those they once knew "back home."

70. *Beauty of Holiness*, VIII (August 1857), 253.

71. B. Rees, *op. cit.*, p. 110. "The effect was tremendous. It was as if a great white lily had burst into full bloom in an instant"; *ibid.* Ridgaway, *op. cit.*, p. 366.

72. B. Rees, *op. cit.*, p. viii. Camp meeting commentators usually referred to the place of music in the camps. In 1850, H. C. Atwater noted that one could learn there "the mighty power of congregational singing over the human heart, and what it would do...if adopted in all...churches." *Zion's Herald*, XXI (July 31, 1850), p. 1. In 1857, Rev. T. M. Eddy urged that "No man should be allowed to sing his fugue tunes, his opera music, or to flourish through his demi-semiquavers—No! We want good, old stirring tunes full of melody, full of soul—tunes in which the congregation can join," he concluded; *Beauty*, VIII (August 1857), p. 228.

73. S. Mead, *op. cit.*, pp. 52-58. One of the most famous camp meeting characters was "Camp Meetin' John Allen," the Rev. John Allen of Farmington, Maine. He attended 374 camps during his lifetime; he died in 1887 at the age of ninety-three at the Methodist Episcopal Church camp at East Livermore, Maine.

74. From the writer's personal experience at Beulah Park Camp Meeting, Allentown, Pa.

75. Wallace, *op. cit.*, p. 215.

76. B. Rees, *op. cit.*, p 24.

77. Wallace, *op. cit.*, p. 29. Clark and Smith, *op. cit.*, pp. 173-80. Wallace, *op. cit.*, p. 12, notes that at Manheim "rowdyism was met and on its own chosen field completely conquered."

78. *Ibid.*, p. 31.

79. C. S. Eby, "Wesley Grove National Camp Meeting," *Earnest Christianity*, I (October 1875), 583. For typical variations in this schedule, see *ibid.*, II (February 1874), 48; also, Wallace, *op. cit.*, p. 28.

80. Wallace, *op. cit.*, p. 12. Also see Jones, *op. cit.*, p. 103.

81. *Methodist*, IX (August 4, 1897), 8-9, as quoted from the Waco (Texas) *Telegram*. For another account of the same meeting, see Jones, *op. cit.*, p. 398, taken from the *Pentecostal Herald*, IX (August 11, 1897), 4. Wallace, *op. cit.*, is the best description of all the aspects of a National Camp Meeting as seen by one in the movement.

82. William B. Godbey, *Bible Theology* (Cincinnati, OH: Revivalist Office, 1911), p. 100.

83. T. Smith, *Called Unto Holiness*, pp. 63, 76, 130. Editor G. Hughes looked to the 1872 National Camps "to give the keynote that shall send its powerful vibrations through all our ranks." *Advocate of Christian Holiness*, III (July 1872), p. 19.

84. T. Smith, *Called Unto Holiness*, p. 66. Daniel D. Williams in his article, "Tradition and Experience in American Theology," *The Shaping of American Religion*, Smith and Jamison, *op. cit.*, I, 454, says that "It was inevitable that pietists would discover in the camp meetings...that the emotional patterns of the conversion experience could become the liturgy and sacrament of the religious fellowship."

85. McDonald and Searles, *op. cit.*, p. 207.

86. *Ibid.*, pp. 207-208.

87. *Guide* for 1871, *passim*. In 1872, the *Guide* began a systematic listing of the camp meetings.

88. McDonald and Searles, *op. cit.*, pp. 220ff.

89. For the full account of the Salt Lake meeting, see *ibid.*, pp. 263ff.; the Godbieites were one of three Mormon factions in Salt Lake at that time according to McDonald and Searles, *op. cit.*, p. 265. They, with the members of the Reorganized Church of Jesus Christ of the Latter Day Saints under Joseph Young, welcomed the evangelists to the city. Godbie was a "wealthy merchant," whose aims seemed to be "political"; *ibid.* Brigham Young, himself, appeared friendly toward the party; *ibid.*, p. 264.

90. *Ibid.*, p. 271.

91. *Ibid.*, pp. 270-71, as quoted from the *Christian at Work*. It was pioneering work; Pierce had arrived only a year before and the first Presbyterian church in the city was not started until the month following the National Committee's meetings in the middle of June 1871.

92. In 1871-1872, Inskip and his band traveled 20,000 miles, held 600 services, and claimed 1,200 converts and 3,000 Christians who sought entire sanctification. Among the latter was the industrialist W. C. DePauw, an Indiana glass manufacturer who claimed the experience of sanctification in one of Inskip's tabernacle meetings in Indianapolis, Indiana, September 21, 1871. DePauw became treasurer of the National Association. He is best remembered through DePauw University, a Methodist college in Greencastle, Indiana, named in his honor. McDonald and Searles, *op. cit.*, pp. 278-81. Also see Michael F. O'Brien, "A Nineteenth Century Hoosier Business Man; Washington Charles DePauw" (unpublished B. A. thesis, DePauw University, 1966).

93. See *Guide* and *Advocate of Christian Holiness* for 1871 and 1872, *passim*. Also see David Bundy, "Bishop William Taylor and Methodist Mission: A Study in Nineteenth Century Social History." *Methodist History*, 27, 28 (July, October 1989): 197-210; 3-21. Edward Davis, *Illustrated History of Douglas Camp Meeting* (Boston: McDonald, Gill and Co., 1890), pp. 1-2. Wallace, *op. cit.*, p. 63. Holiness work in India centered in the work of Methodist missions under James Mills Thoburn, missionary to India from 1859-1908. Later missionary bishop of India,

Thoburn was directly involved in the postwar holiness revival through the faith missions work of William Taylor, a Methodist irregular in missions, who was widely known for his independent work in starting Methodist missions in India, Africa, and South America. Taylor, later a Methodist missionary bishop, became an active member of the National Camp Meeting Committee; the holiness movement inside and outside of the Methodist Episcopal Church was the main source of funds for his work through what was known as "The Transit Fund." T. B. Welch, M. D., Vineland, N. J., who gave his name to the famous nonfermented grape juice, was treasurer of the fund and associate editor of Taylor's *African News*. See *ibid.*, I (January 1889), 1; William Taylor, *The Story of My Life: an Account of What I Have Thought and Said and Done in My Ministry of More than Fifty-three Years in Christian Lands and Among the Heathen* (New York: Eaton and Mains, 1898); the same, *Four Years' Campaign in India* (New York: Phillips and Hunt, 1880 [originally published 1876]). Jones, *op. cit.*, pp. 151-59, has a good summary of Taylor's work and influence in the movement and Methodism. On Thoburn, see Simpson, *op. cit.*, 858-59; *Webster's Biographical Dictionary* (Springfield, MA: G. and C. Merriam Co. Publishers, 1943), p. 1460.

94. *Guide*, LIX (May, 1871), 157. Among others listed were layman Robert Pearsall Smith, Presbyterian from Philadelphia; layman Charles Cullis, M.D., Boston; Rev. Dr. Daniel Steele, Methodist, professor at Boston University; and New England Baptist Evangelist A. B. Earle. *Ibid.; Advocate of Christian Holiness*, III (February 1873), 185-86; a letter from Boardman in *ibid.* (January 1873), p. 159, also refers to "one of the pillars of the Central Baptist Church of Providence, and one of the trustees of Brown University," who was a believer in the holiness experience, together with the holiness convention work in the Providence area in the Congregational, Baptist, and Methodist churches.

95. *Guide*, XVI [New Series] (February 1872), 58.

96. *Advocate of Christian Holiness*, III (February 1873), 185.

97. Richard Fuller, "Personal Religion, Its Aids and Hindrances," Schaff and Prime, *op. cit.*, p. 335.

98. *Ibid.*, pp. 335-36.

99. *Supra*, p. 6. Not all Pietism was quietistic, however; the beginnings of the social outreach of Protestantism lay "in no small part" in Pietism. Stoeffler, *op. cit.*, p. 4.

100. Schaff and Prime, *op. cit.*, pp. 338-40. Jones, *op. cit.*, appendix C3, pp. 451-52, lists the membership of the National Camp Meeting Committee for the years 1869, 1873, and 1894.

101. See Gaddis, *op. cit.*, p. 426. Roy S. Nicholson, *Wesleyan Methodism in the South: Being the Story of Eighty-Six Years of Reform and Religious Activities in the South as Conducted by the American Wesleyans* (Syracuse, NY: Wesleyan Methodist Publishing Association, 1933), pp. 1-113, gives a full account of the opposition experienced by Wesleyans in the South prior to the Civil War. Wesleyans had also been active in the Underground Railroad system, particularly in Indiana and Michigan. McLeister, *op. cit.*, pp. 424-25.

102. Gaddis, *loc. cit.*

103. See Jones' summary in, the same, *op. cit.*, p. 53; Bishops Simpson, Janes, and Haven, all sympathetic to the holiness cause, envisioned southern expansion after the war. Alfred Cookman and Gilbert Haven, after whom Cookman Institute in Jacksonville, Fla., and Haven Normal School in Waynesborough, Ga., were named respectively, identified the movement with the Negro cause and northern "carpetbaggers." See Simpson, *op. cit.*, pp. 256, 380-81. Also see Jervey, "Motives and Methods of the Methodist Episcopal Church in the Period of Reconstruction," *Methodist History*, IV, 17-25.

104. *Advocate of Christian Holiness*, III (November 1872), 108. "The Churches and Reconstruction," Olmstead, *op. cit.*, pp. 400-404.

105. *Ibid.* (September 1872), p. 69.

106. *Ibid.* (November 1872), 108-10. Also see McDonald and Searles, *op. cit.*, p. 292. Haven was especially rejected because of his close association with radical New England movements; Jervey, *loc. cit.*

107. *Ibid.* (September, 1872), 69; *Christian Standard and Home Journal*, IX (November 27, 1875), 382. See also Henry Clay Morrison, *Life Sketches and Sermons* (Louisville, KY: Pentecostal Publishing Co., 1903), p. 33. Morrison lists some of the early holiness leaders in the south as: Dr. Lovick Pierce, William B. Godbey, B. A. Cundiff, W. A. Dodge, W. S. Grinstead, and J. S. Keen. For biographical notes on Pierce, see Simpson, *op. cit.*, p. 717.

108. McLeister, *op. cit.*, pp. 86-9.

109. *Ibid.*, p. 85.

110. The Free Methodists, who were noted especially for their stringent standards of dress, were expressing the direct instructions of both Wesley and B. T. Roberts, their founder. The latter pointed out in *The Free Methodist* that Wesley had laid down the rule that no ticket for admission to a class meeting should be given " 'to any, until they have left off superfluous ornaments. Allow no exempt case, not even of a married woman....Give no tickets to any that wear high heads, enormous bonnets, ruffles, or rings.'" "If this rule were carried out today, how many would they [the Methodists] have in their love-feasts? Were they fanatical then on the subject of dress, or are they backslidden now? Times may change but God does not change" (emphasis his). As quoted from *ibid.*, in *Pungent Truths, Being Extracts from the Writings of the Rev. Benjamin Titus Roberts, A. M., while Editor of the* Free Methodist *from 1886-1890*, ed. William R. Rose (Chicago: The Free Methodist Publishing House, 1915), pp. 78-79; also see comment in *ibid.*, p. 80, on not wearing a necktie. This became a prominent characteristic of male Free Methodist dress, especially among the clergy. The degree to which times do change and "God" with them is shown by the fact that a piled-up hair style undoubtedly quite similar to Wesley's "high heads" which kept women out of the class meeting is currently the only one commonly accepted by some of the very conservative holiness and pentecostal sects today, and in the Free Methodist and other larger holiness bodies, the average member's contemporary styles would also ban him.

111. Robert Pearsall Smith, the Philadelphia holiness layman who led the holiness revival in Europe in the mid-1870s, judged that the extremes which had been exercised on both sides in the controversy had resulted in "one side, taking

the doctrine of full salvation…to be swept past the tender, gentle, forbearing spirit of love into contentiousness and separation; while the other side reacted into prejudice against the experience of 'holiness.' " See the same, "The Great Revival of 'Christian Perfection' as a Life in America," *Earnest Christianity*, II (1876), 46. See T. Smith's conclusions, pp. 132-33. The Methodist Episcopal Church's Genesee Conference sought to make amends for its part in the controversy when it restored Roberts' ministerial parchments to his son, Benson Howard Roberts, in 1910 at the conference's centenary celebration. Roberts had died seventeen years previously. Marston, *op. cit.*, pp. 582-88.

112. Among these was Bishop Matthew Simpson. Robert D. Clark, Simpson's biographer, discusses the bishop's personal struggles over the experience; *The Life of Matthew Simpson* (New York: Macmillan, 1956), pp. 175-77. Simpson counseled with Phoebe Palmer in 1852; she urged him to no "longer let the tempter to hinder you from laying hold upon the promise…." Clark observes, "Perhaps it was of significance to Methodism that the most eloquent of the Bishops never discovered the satisfying spiritual condition of which she wrote." *Ibid.*, p. 176.

113. McDonald and Searles, *op. cit.*, pp. 210-11.

114. *Ibid.*

115. *Advocate of Christian Holiness*, III (November 1872), 111.

116. *Ibid.*

117. McDonald and Searles, *op. cit.*, p. 277.

118. *Ibid.*

119. Simpson, *op. cit.*, pp. 371-72. Also see *supra*, p. 50.

120. Simpson, *op. cit.*, pp. 585-86.

121. *The Advocate of Christian Holiness* was certain that the bishop sympathized "most deeply with the work of the National Committee." In reporting on a visit by Peck to the Thirty-first National Camp held at Clear Lake, Iowa, the paper said, "If all our bishops would do as Bishop Peck has done…they would then be able to see for themselves whether there was any peril to the church in this movement." *Ibid.*, IX (August 1878), 188.

122. Simpson, *op. cit.*, pp. 434-35.

123. Simpson, *op. cit.*, p. 128. Bishop Bowman was still involved with the movement in 1901 when he signed the call to the General Holiness Assembly at Chicago in 1901; see S. B. Shaw, *op. cit.*, p. 13.

124. See *infra*, p. 211; Simpson, *op. cit.*, pp. 430-31. Jones, *op. cit.*, pp. 56-57, comments, "Having denounced fanaticism and avoided schism, holiness believers had strong representation in the church's progressive vanguard. Their year of majority had arrived." Note that Jones does not list Harris among the sympathizers with the movement who were elected in 1872. In light of this joint action with Lowrey and Mahan, it seems he should be added to the list. *Divine Life* (October 1879), 61-67; *ibid.* (March 1880), pp. 161-66.

125. *Advocate of Christian Holiness*, III (November 1872), 111. Mrs. Hamline wrote to Phoebe Palmer in 1867 of the conflict over the holiness revival of the postwar period. She observed that "Dr. Bannister…is marked as an advocate of 'Christian Perfection'…[and] Dr. Kidder…is sinking deeper in the ocean of

Salvation [*sic*]. But there are those who stand exactly in the way, of the work of Holiness—'Stumbling blocks, indeed.' " Letter of Mrs. L. Hamline to Phoebe Palmer from Evanston, Ill., November 17, 1867, in manuscript collection of Drew University.

126. T. Smith, *Called Unto Holiness*, p. 42. Smith contends here that "this, in part, explains the unanimity with which Methodist officialdom professed loyalty to the doctrine whole opposing measures to promote it." See L. L. Pickett, *Entire Sanctification from 1799 to 1901* (Louisville, KY: Pickett Publishing Co., 1901), for a summary of the doctrinal continuity of the movement with Wesley. See Jones, *op. cit.*, "Appendix C4: Official Methodist Pronouncements on Holiness," pp. 454-56, for excerpts from numerous episcopal addresses to the general conferences of both the Methodist Episcopal Church and the Methodist Episcopal Church South on the question. Sweet, *The Story of Religion in America*, pp. 405-406.

127. Bishop John P. Newman's statement in the "Introduction" to Roche's biography of Sarah Lankford Palmer is typical of many others: "For this purpose they were called to be a Church. To give preeminence to this central, subjective doctrine, was Wesley chosen by Providence…and the universal spread of these sentiments is now esteemed the high mission of the Church which has survived him over a hundred years." Roche, *Sarah Lankford Palmer*, pp. 8-9. Kenneth W. Copeland, "The Magnificent Purpose," *Asbury Seminarian*, XXVI (January 1972), 31-33.

128. *Advocate of Christian Holiness*, III (November 1872), 150. *Ibid.* (December 1872), 142. *Ibid.* (January 1873), 160. *Perfect Love, or the Speeches of Rev. E. L. Jane; Rev. H. Mattison, D.D.; Rev. D. Curry, D.D.; Rev. J. M Buckley and Rev. S. D. Brown in the New York Preacher's Meeting in March and April 1867, upon the Subject of Sanctification…* (New York: N. Tibbals and Co.), 868.

129. *Advocate of Christian Holiness*, III (June 1873), 265.

130. *Ibid.*, pp. 265-67.

131. *Advocate of Christian Holiness*, VI (October 1875), 86.

132. *Ibid.*

133. *Ibid.* Also see William McDonald, *John Wesley and His Doctrine* (Boston: McDonald, Gill and Co., 1893), pp. 136ff. Simpson, *op. cit.*, pp. 84-85. All of these were essentially pietistic.

134. *Supra*, p. 111.

135. *Guide*, LX (August 1871), 62.

136. M. L. Haney, *The Inheritance Restored: or Plain Truths on Bible Holiness* (Chicago: Christian Witness Co., 1904), p. 215.

137. Ernest Wall compares and contrasts her life with that of Catherine of Siena. Ernest Wall, "I Commend unto You Phoebe," *Religion in Life*, XXVI (Summer 1957), 396-408.

138. *The Ladies Repository*, XXVI (February 1866).

139. Roche, *op. cit.*, p. 8.

140. *Advocate of Christian Holiness*, V (December 1874), 136.

141. *Guide*, LXVII (January 1875), 9.

142. *Advocate of Christian Holiness*, V (December 1874), 137.

143. Simpson, *op. cit.*, p. 936.

144. *Methodist Quarterly Review,* LX (January 1878), 176.

145. *Ibid.*

146. *Ibid.* (October 1878), 688ff. In this same article, Whedon says: "Many of us do not believe that Christian Perfection is a second special blessing 'gained instantaneously by an act of faith....' " *Ibid.,* 696. He also attacked the "altar terminology" of Phoebe Palmer; *ibid.,* 697.

147. *Ibid.,* LVI (October 1874), pp. 662-81. Crane's book, *Holiness the Birthright of All God's Children* (New York: Nelson and Phillips, 1875), had been reviewed in the *Methodist Quarterly Review,* LVI (July 1874), 490-92. The reviewer noted that the book seemed to support sanctification of the believer at the time of his conversion. This was more Zinzendorfian than Wesleyan.

148 "Methodist Quarterly Review," *Advocate of Christian Holiness,* IX (March 1878), 64.

149. *Ibid.,* p. 65.

150. *Ibid.,* p. 85. In the *Methodist Quarterly Review,* LVI (October 1874), 662-63, Whedon defended his definition of Wesleyan and Methodist doctrines which he had first outlined in *Bibliotheca Sacra,* XIX (April 1862), 241-74. He says the article still stood and had been republished in the *Advocate* and *Zion's Herald* and was commended by McClintock in *Cyclopedia of Methodism* as a standard statement of "our Arminianism." He noted that part of the statement on Christian Perfection was included in the above. Whedon's statements on the topic were far too general to satisfy the holiness party in the church.

151. *Ibid.,* p. 64.

152. Jones, *op. cit.,* p. 89.

Chapter 4

From Vineland and Manheim to Berlin and Brighton: The European Holiness Revival

THE BACKGROUND OF THE ENGLISH REVIVAL

The intercourse in religious revival movements between England and America presents an interesting study in itself. From the revivalism of George Whitefield to that of Billy Graham, there has not been a significant revival of religion which has not crossed and sometimes recrossed the Atlantic. The postwar revival of holiness evangelism by the Palmers in England and Scotland after the American Revival of 1858 had done as much as anything else to prepare the way for the great higher life conventions which were to cause an explosion of that doctrine across England and the Continent in the 1870s. The revival meetings of James Caughey, the Methodist holiness evangelist, and the visits of American evangelists, Charles Finney, Asa Mahan, and William Boardman during the Second Evangelical Awakening,[1] also helped to spread the dominantly Wesleyan perfectionist revivalism from the American movement across the British Isles. As noted above, the Palmers alone saw thousands of sanctifications recorded in their campaigns;[2] however, there was a lack of any organized effort at that time to conserve the results of those meetings or to promote the doctrine in the special manner popularized by the work of the National Camp Association in America.

Some called the revival which ensued with the Palmer's wartime ministry in the British Isles an Evangelical Alliance Revival because of its ecumenical character;[3] although there was considerable opposition to the American evangelist within the official circles of the Wesleyan Methodist Churches of the country, as well as by the Camp Meeting or

Primitive Methodists.[4] From 1860 to 1870, however, the mood in these churches was changing providing another opportunity for the holiness revival to penetrate British Methodism with its message.

New holiness literature and periodicals complemented the standard Wesleyan writings on the doctrine and experience; they contributed to the growing religious expectancy which finally issued in the dramatic responses to the appeals of Dwight L. Moody and Ira D. Sankey and the American holiness evangelists, R. Pearsall Smith, William E. Boardman, and Asa Mahan. The call for a new outpouring of the Holy Spirit upon the churches came from as diverse sources as Edward Golburn, the Dean of Norwich, and William Arthur, an influential leader in the Wesleyan Methodist Conferences.[5]

INITIAL MOVEMENTS

Regular reports of the English religious scene began to appear in the *Guide to Holiness* and the *Advocate of Christian Holiness* in the late 1872 editions. The *Advocate's* British correspondent in the December 1872 issue, noted the remarks of the retiring conference president to the members of the conference:

> By what has recently come under my own notice...in proclaiming the truth on this point [entire sanctification], you will preach to appreciative and sympathizing audiences. I believe there is a revival and wide-spread yearning among our people for full salvation....Therefore, let this subject receive your special attention. *You can hardly do the church any service equal to that of urging upon our people that they seek to be cleansed from all sin, to love God with all their heart*...[emphasis his].[6]

The King's Highway reported at the close of 1872 that there was appearing a "movement of the evangelical churches for united and earnest prayer arising chiefly from the influence of the Evangelical Alliance."[7] As a result, the last conference of the Wesleyan Methodist Church had formed a prayer union among its membership. The union appealed to all who had "the purity of the church...and the welfare of soul at heart."[8] It was, in essence, a holiness association on the pattern of the numerous similar groups which were already rising all over the United States and Canada in the wake of the well-publicized work of the National Camp Meeting Association. The members of the union received a card reminding them to pray for certain specific results:

For myself that I may be sanctified wholly and preserved blameless. For ministers that bearing the vessels of the Lord they may be clean. For Methodism, that it may rightly SPREAD SCRIPTURAL HOLINESS through the land. For all churches that the doctrine and experience of holiness may prevail among them. And for our TIMES that they may be marked by a CONTINUING REVIVAL OF RELIGION ensuing in the salvation of multitudes both at home, and abroad....[9]

The patterns of the holiness revival dominated by Methodist teaching and National Camp Meeting influences were appearing in Wesley's homeland. To many it appeared to be "carrying coals to Newcastle," but it was a fact, commonly acknowledged, that the religious fires of Wesley's land and his church had not been burning very brightly.[10] The almost spontaneous gathering up of the spiritual hunger of evangelicals in all churches of the land into the desire for a deeper Christian experience during these few years in the mid-1870s, is the strongest evidence of that.

The introduction of the idea of special meetings for the promotion of holiness into the English religious scene produced opposition equal to any that had been experienced in America. W. G. Pascoe, the English correspondent who most regularly reported to the American holiness journals on the progress of the revival in the British Isles, wrote to the *Advocate of Christian Holiness* in March 1873, that "there is yet a large amount of prejudice against them." Even the friends of the doctrine, he said, were reluctant to encourage such special measures, "lest the charge of 'cliqueism' should be brought against them...."[11]

In May of the same year, the *Advocate* carried a private letter from the north of England which reported that, "the two works of conversion and entire sanctification were going on together...."[12] In June 1873, Pascoe again noted that there was more mention of "entire sanctification in the past six months than some ministers have heard in their whole previous ministry"; nevertheless, he admitted that "the few meetings held distinctly in the interest of holiness are small...." The advocates, he said, had to move ahead "against the stream of prejudice which flows rapidly along."[13] The prejudice was diminishing, however, for even some established church parishes were using religious missions. Pascoe regarded these protracted meetings as "a remarkable proof of the mighty religious stir which is now affecting all religious circles..." in spite of their promotion, at times, "of the confessional and other pernicious Romish teaching."[14]

ROBERT PEARSALL AND HANNAH WHITALL SMITH

If the lay evangelists, Walter and Phoebe Palmer had represented the heart of the spiritual dynamic at work in popularizing the revival of Christian holiness in the Methodist and other churches in the United States another husband and wife team, Robert Pearsall and Hannah Whitall Smith, also laypersons, represented the spark which finally ignited the holiness revival movement in England and throughout the continent of Europe.[15]

The Smiths were Quakers—her family from rural, and his from urban Philadelphia. They were the first among several evangelists of the Quaker faith who were to take a prominent part in the spreading holiness revival. In spite of their non-Methodist religious affiliations, they were, nevertheless, exponents of Wesleyan perfectionism; both had learned of the experience of entire sanctification in Methodist holiness meetings in Philadelphia and southern New Jersey where they lived.

Mrs. Smith had gone through a period of religious skepticism early in her married life in which she had seriously doubted the orthodox teachings of Christianity, particularly the doctrine of the atonement. Her rejection of this religious skepticism and her search for the "God [who was] making Himself manifest [to her] as an actual existence" are part of the story of the Revival of 1858. It was at one of the popular noonday prayer meetings of that revival that she discovered God. Her description of her experience has a mystical ring which is illustrative of a theme that sounds its muted, but identifiable, note throughout the story of the movement. It readily suited an experience of inner devotion, centered, as it was, so strongly in pursuit of the fullness of the Holy Spirit in the individual life. She said of that day in 1858:

It was not that I felt myself to be a sinner needing salvation, or that I was troubled about my future destiny. It was not a personal question at all. It was simply and only that I had become aware of God, and that I felt I could not rest until I should know him....*All I wanted was to become acquainted with the God of whom I had suddenly become aware* [emphasis mine].[16]

She did not claim to have become a Christian until after a member of the Plymouth Brethren sect helped her to believe that her new grasp of God and the joy which had ensued in her life were the result of her being "born of God." She later described the certain conviction which followed that moment of personal commitment: "There it was—the grand central fact of God's love and forgiveness, and my soul was at rest about this forever."[17]

Both because of this experience and the failure of her reserved Quaker friends to understand the newfound enthusiasm she demonstrated in telling others of her spiritual discovery, she turned to members of the Plymouth Brethren sect for continuing spiritual advice. Their simplistic approach to belief and the Bible were, she confessed, a settling factor in her life, but gradually their emphasis on the Calvinistic doctrine of "election" began to raise questions in her mind concerning their overall system of Christian doctrine. Perhaps her inbred Quaker latitudinarian instincts reacted against a doctrine that was much too restrictive for them. The warm relationships with the Plymouth Brethren began to cool.[18]

It was not until she and her husband moved to Millville, New Jersey, where he was to assist in the management of her father's glass factory, that Hannah Whitall Smith claimed to discover what she commonly called the "secret" of a happy Christian life. One Saturday evening, as Mrs. Smith slipped into a Methodist ladies prayer meeting, she heard a "factory woman" testifying to her friends that previous to her sanctification the "whole horizon used to be filled with great big *Me*." But that when she "got sight of Christ…great big Me wilted down to nothing."

Mrs. Smith acknowledged that these words brought a "profound conviction" to her, and "that this must be real Christianity…that it was, perhaps, the very thing I was longing for." She said that the truth came to her as a discovery and without any definite crisis of spiritual experience.[19]

She began to testify to having found the secret of a happier state of Christian experience which she later elaborated in the book that very soon became and still remains one of the great religious classics, *The Christian's Secret of a Happy Life*.[20] In those early years of discovery, she declared that she had

> found that the gist of it was exactly what Paul meant when he said, "Not I but Christ,"…the victory I sought [she said] was to come by ceasing to live my own life and by letting the power of God "work in me to will and to do of his good pleasure…."
>
> It is a Methodist doctrine, and I have been used to hearing Methodists much objected to on account of it, but it seems to be the only thing that can supply my needs, and I feel impelled to try it.[21]

In spite of considerable initial concern that his wife had fallen into some dangerous heresy, Robert Pearsall Smith gradually yielded to the convincing personal testimony and the scriptural proof texts she provided for him in reply to his questions concerning the experience. He claimed the "blessing" in "true Methodist fashion" very soon thereafter at the National Association's first camp at Vineland in July of 1867. His wife describes his experience:

> Suddenly from head to foot he had been shaken by what seemed like a magnetic thrill of heavenly delight, and floods of glory seemed to pour through him, soul and body, with the inward assurance that this was the longed-for Baptism of the Holy Spirit. The whole world seemed transformed to him, every leaf and blade of grass quivered with exquisite color, and heaven seemed to open out before him as a present blissful possession. Everybody looked beautiful to him, for he seemed to see the Divine Spirit within each one without regard to their outward seemings. This ecstasy lasted for several weeks...[22]

Hannah confessed that for some time after observing her husband's emotional experience she was

> rather jealous that she did not receive a like blessing, for I felt that I needed it quite as much as he did, and I renewed my efforts to obtain it. But it was all in vain...I became convinced at last that the reason of this difference between my experience and that of some others was not that they were peculiarly favoured by God above me, but that their emotional nature received with these floods of emotional delight, the same truths that I received calmly, and with intellectual delight; the difference being, not in the experiences but in the different natures of the recipients of that experience.[23]

Regardless of intellectual or emotional variations, Mr. and Mrs. Robert Pearsall Smith of Millville, New Jersey, had joined the holiness revival. They had discovered what Hannah, thereafter, commonly called "the unselfishness of God." The news of their enthusiastic witness to this new experience rapidly spread across the movement in the United States and Canada, but most significantly to England and Europe.[24]

The Smiths' Early English Ministry

In 1873, Robert Pearsall Smith was informally introduced into the English evangelical circles, which were increasingly agitated on the question of the higher Christian life. He was not there in response to any call for his religious services, but rather was traveling after a period of severe sickness resulting from an accident which he had suffered in 1871.[25] But the news of his espousal of the "blessing" and his inability to resist testifying to it soon deeply involved him in the already incipient tide of English revival. The movement there was gradually overcoming its opposition and building up strength for the unusual spiritual response which Moody and Sankey experienced in their ministry on their first evangelistic tour of England in 1873. Informal meetings with Smith's English friends soon led to more formal breakfast meetings, especially with the ministry of the non-Methodist churches of England and the Established Church. As a result, invitations multiplied for him to address groups seeking deeper life instruction.[26]

Initially, some English evangelicals were hesitant to allow Mrs. Smith as free a range on the religious conference speaking circuit as her husband; hints of her espousal of a universalist view of eternal destiny had already begun to steal across the Atlantic along with her much more widely known reputation for evangelistic effectiveness.[27] It is most remarkable that in spite of a long-standing commitment to a universalist view of the restitution of all things, not only was she widely used in the meetings, but soon she became known to English friends as "the angel of the churches."[28]

Hannah Whitall Smith's universalist tendencies not only did not restrict her English ministry, but even appeared to enlarge it. Her honest response to a chance remark at the home of Mrs. Cowper Temple, later Lady Mount Temple, opened up the door to the Smith's holiness evangelism among the English upper classes.

The incident occurred at an informal meeting of a group of evangelicals who were considering the endorsement of the Smiths for meetings among them. A passing funeral procession turned the group's conversation to the question of eternal destiny. The subject evoked an expression by Mrs. Smith of her basic belief in the final salvation of all men and women. Attracted by her candor in the face of the possible opposition it might arouse, Mrs. Temple invited the American woman evangelist to Broadlands, the family estate in Hampshire, formerly the estate of Lord Palmerston, Temple's father. This relationship evinced strong support among the upper class of England for future holiness conferences and the subsequent work of the Smiths in England and Europe.[29]

The fact that her ministry and books continued to be influential in the holiness and higher life movement, in spite of her divergent views, is probably due to several factors: to her own attitude in the matter, to her personal effectiveness and winsomeness, and to the general disposition of a spiritual movement such as she was involved in to lay considerably more stress on experience and lifestyle than on doctrinal rectitude. Or again, it may have been that her rock-ribbed Quaker character simply squelched much of the potential controversy. This clearly shows in a letter to her husband after he had successfully overcome pressure by a committee preparing for the Brighton Convention in 1874 to compromise the issue of her universalist views. The committee had agreed to invite her to attend, but wanted to restrict her public participation at the meeting. In reply to the invitation which finally came without the desired restrictions, she said:

> I am glad thee has got out of thy difficulty about thy heretical preaching wife with so little trouble. But the idea of B[_____] with shaky views of his own, undertaking to excommunicate me. I really do not think it was honest. I do not choose to sail under false colours, and I am a thousand times stronger in my views of restitution, every day I live. If they let me alone in England I shall probably not say much about it, but if there is the least hint of any compromise or underhanded secrecy on my part, I shall blaze on in perfect conflagration....So you must please bear this in mind, ye Lords of Creation. Soberly, however, I do not feel at all drawn to preach or to teach restitution over there, and if the dear frightened Orthodox friends do not make any fuss about it I shall not be likely to. Their difficulties do not annoy me in the least. I believe I actually enjoy being the victim of "odicum theologicum." I guess there is something of the war horse in my composition.[30]

With the active help of the Smiths, the holiness forces in England were coalescing and new allies were joining the cause. Pascoe's own holiness journal, the *King's Highway*, first published in 1873, was beginning to serve the English movement in the same manner that Timothy Merritt's *Guide* had done in the beginnings of the American revival. Robert Pearsall Smith and William E. Boardman, who was now also working on the English scene, seconded that initial effort in 1874 with their paper, *The Christian's Pathway of Power*. This paper, under the editorship of Evan H. Hopkins, later became the *Life of Faith*, voice of the Keswick movement.[31]

By the fall of 1873, a now-regular column on the "Work of Holiness in England" in the *Advocate of Christian Holiness* told the readers that Robert P. Smith is "doing a good work in London in connection with the holiness movement, especially among the Calvinistic churches."[32] Dr. Charles Cullis of Boston, and the aged Asa Mahan, also, were assisting Smith and Boardman by this time. A prominent London Baptist minister, Henry Varley,[33] who had made a public profession of his own entrance into the "rest of faith" only a short time before, also became active in the movement. These non-Methodist men formed an effective force for introducing the movement's message into circles which may otherwise have arbitrarily denied it a sympathetic hearing.[34]

The traditional official reserve which the British Methodist bodies had shown to American holiness evangelists such as Caughey and the Palmers now began to break down under the expanding interest in spiritual revival. Holiness meetings began to become a part of some official Methodist conference gatherings; holiness associations were formed. Smith was invited to bring his essentially Wesleyan message, conditioned, as we have seen, by American revivalism, back to its original home in special meetings with Methodist ministers of London and other urban centers. He was not unaware of whom he was addressing. At one such meeting with Methodist clergymen, Smith reminded them that

There were deep inward yearnings for an outpouring of the Spirit upon the universal Church. In the Establishment here and in the other denominations in England and Scotland this was the prominent subject. There was not a church in this great city which has not the subject of consecration to God as the leading subject before its members and a very prominent subject in its ministry.

He then inquired,

Should they as Methodists be behind them in this entire consecration? He expected to see the church of which John Wesley was the father in Christ rouse itself, and be more than it had been before....The great Establishment of England was getting into Methodist ways—holding after-meetings, singing in the power of the Spirit...upon their knees; going round and talking to inquirers—they were close upon their heels; would they [the Methodists] continue in the van in their great mission?[35]

Besides the reserved opposition of conservative forces in the English churches which hesitated to commit themselves too readily to these "new doctrines" flowing into England from the camp meeting movement in the United States, there was also outspoken questioning of Smith and Smith's message by other critics. In the columns of the English *Christian Standard*, Mr. Grant, a newspaper man, wrote a series of sixteen articles attacking Robert Pearsall Smith. He quoted John Wesley's teachings in contradiction to Smith's and charged that the evangelist was a teacher of new doctrine, the possessor of an experience greater than the Apostle Paul, and that he must have reached absolute perfection. Reluctantly, Grant admitted, however, that caught up by the growing momentum of the English revival, "some of the holiest men of the land have adopted these views which are yet 'altogether unscriptural and dangerous....'"[36]

THE BROADLANDS AND OXFORD CONVENTIONS FOR THE PROMOTION OF HOLINESS

The support of Lord and Lady Mount Temple and other evangelicals prominent in English society provided a strong base of operations for the evangelism of the Smiths. The Temple's Broadlands estate was the scene of crucial meetings in the promotion in England from July 17-23, 1874. "Union Meetings for Consecration" held in Mildmay, Dublin, Manchester, and finally in Cambridge, had preceded these Broadlands meetings. The Broadlands meetings were held at the request of some Cambridge students, who, influenced by the Union Meeting at the University, wanted to spend time in prayer and meditation in some secluded spot. Cowper Temple opened up his 6,000-acre estate to them, entertaining one hundred guests for the six days of a convention designed to suit the students' purposes. At the conclusion of the conference, Sir Arthur Blackwood, Earl of Chichester and president of the Church Missionary Society, suggested that another, but more extensive meeting for the promotion of holiness should be held at Oxford during the summer vacation time.[37]

The call for the Oxford Union Meeting for the Promotion of Scriptural Holiness went out on August 8, 1874. The list of conveners for this special conference was much more extensive and represented a much broader scope of social, religious, and political life than the list of the names of the thirteen American Methodist ministers who sent out the call to the first special holiness camp meeting at Vineland, New Jersey, only seven years earlier. The Oxford list delineates the broadening patterns of the higher life movement. In addition to the names of

ministers prominent in the promotion of holiness at that time in England, such as William Arthur, William E. Boardman, and Henry Varley,
the rising British Baptist evangelist, a fair representation of English
society headed the list. Among them were Sir Arthur Blackwood, Lord
Farnham, Sir Thomas Bart, Arthur Kinnard, M.P., Stephenson A. Blackwood, Esq., Henry Kingscote, Esq.; and Charles Lloyd Braithwaite, Esq.
Among leading churchmen from England, France, and Germany, were
the Very Rev. Dean of Canterbury, Theodore Monod, son of the prominent French Free Church pastor, Fred Monod; Paul Kover and Otto
Stockmayer of Switzerland, and from Germany, Theodor Jellinghaus
and V. von Niebuhr of Halle, whose father was one of the most influential diplomats of the nineteenth century.[38]

The complexion of the company that gathered from the first day's
meetings at Oxford on August 29, paralleled that of sponsors mentioned
above. Many were from the English upper classes. The revival of this
period affected these groups more than the former movements of 1864
had. A foretaste of the international flavor of Brighton a year later was
provided by the twenty or thirty Continental pastors who participated
along with the ministers of both the established and nonconformist
churches of England.[39]

It is very probable that a careful comparison of the obvious appeal
of the holiness message to the complex social and cultural pattern,
portrayed by the groups that participated in the English holiness revival, with the conclusions of sociologists of religion who have interpreted the American holiness sect development in strongly sociological
terms would cast a note of caution into some of their conclusions. It
would appear that, granted the appeal of the movement to the most
basic religious desires, a poor man in America may have responded to
the holiness evangelist's call out of the same existential impulses as did
Lord Mount Temple, who obviously was not among "the disinherited."
At least, more tolerance must be allowed for such a possibility. The
appeal and the response, in both cases, probably arose out of a common
pietistic and Biblical orientation which strongly permeated both English and American evangelical Protestantism.

Approximately 1,500 men and women of all classes and denominations attended the ten-day meeting. It was not uncommon to find
most of them at the very first early morning prayer and praise service,
sharing in prayer or testimony in the Methodist style, clergymen and
laymen declaring the spiritual joys already experienced or eagerly
anticipated before the meetings should end. W. G. Pascoe reported to
the *Advocate of Christian Holiness*, that the Oxford meetings "more nearly
approach to one of your National Camp Meetings than anything we

have hitherto seen in England....″[40] The Rev. Evan H. Hopkins one of the fathers of the Keswick Conference, R. Pearsall Smith, and others recognized the continuity with the American revival as well. Hopkins said, following the August 1874 meetings,

> We have attended many conferences, including a ten-day convention in America, the prototype of that at Oxford, but in most respects this excelled them all. It is the fruit and flower of those which have gone before—of those at Barnet and Mildmay, and Perth and other places at home, *as well as at Manheim, and Vineland and Round Lake in the United States*...[emphasis mine].[41]

The Methodists were there in significant numbers, but they stayed in the background so that there would be no suspicion that they were somehow executing a denominational coup. Smith consistently declared, in his public addresses, that the experience which he advocated was thoroughly Biblical and, therefore, nondenominational; at the same time he rarely failed to speak of the debt which he felt the whole Christian Church and especially he himself, owed to the "Holiness Methodists" for their clear proclamation of the possibilities of "the life of faith and Christian holiness." He was now sharing their "depositum" with the whole European evangelical world.[42]

The significance of such a meeting at the home of the Tractarian movement in the Established Church, as well as the place where the Wesleys and Whitefield had formed their "holy club," was not lost on some. The *Zion's Herald* editorialized that to the Methodists present,

> It must have been a suggestive spectacle to see old Oxford, the birthplace of Methodism, the scene of a great convention, composed of hundreds of Church of England clergymen, as well as representatives of other churches, entirely devoted, through a week or more to prayer, meditation, and consultation respecting "Scriptural holiness," the great theme which Wesley, almost alone, mediated within the University more than a century ago, ...[43]

Inundated with a flow of enthusiastic public and private correspondence and the personal reports of Smith and others who returned to the United States at the end of the year, William McDonald's excitement surfaced in the first editorial of the *Advocate* for the year 1875.

The witnesses to entire sanctification are now enumerated by the thousands....It promises even now to leaven the whole lump of Christianity. It is evident a new and progressive development of spiritual religion is possessing and moving the churches. The Baptists, Presbyterians, Congregationalists, Quakers, Episcopalians, and most other ecclesiastic bodies, are ...directing attention to the higher privilege or obligation of Christians.

He then threw out the same challenge to American Methodism which Smith had presented to British Methodism in an effort to excite Wesley's descendants to renewed holiness emphasis and experience. He warned:

Indeed some of these fellowships are getting to be so pronounced in the experience and so enthusiastic in the promotion of holiness, that we have had a little excusable apprehension that Methodism by her delinquencies and tardiness, not to say cold neglect and uncharitable opposition, might lose her God-given birthright.[44]

THE HOLINESS REVIVAL ON THE CONTINENT

In late spring of 1875, just prior to a second large convention for the promotion of holiness which was to meet at the resort city of Brighton, on England's southeastern coast in May of that year, Robert Pearsall Smith carried his holiness evangelism to France, Germany, and Switzerland.[45] Theodore Monod, who had attended the summer's convention at Oxford, was anxious to see the revival spread among the Free Churches of France. The response to the meetings Smith held there indicated an active interest in the higher life preaching among these French Protestants.[46] But nowhere did Smith receive such an enthusiastic reception as he did on his German and Swiss tour. The doctrine and experience of Christian perfection were already being preached in Germany prior to Smith's coming by a small, but vigorous, German Methodist fellowship. Their cause was fed by the ministry and writings of Dr. William Nast the father of German Methodism in America, and an active member of the National Camp Meeting Association.[47] The year 1875 marked the twenty-fifth anniversary of Methodism in Germany; in the months preceding the evangelist's arrival, the Methodists already had been holding special holiness meetings. One of these met at Ludwigsburg in the southern part of Germany. A reporter said, "not one of the preachers reminded behind" in seeking and claiming the experience. A similar meeting was convened for the preachers in Switzerland. Evangelists went to the Methodist stations in northern Germany, "preaching and singing full salvation."[48] But, as in England, the leadership for the breakthrough into the Established Churches and other Free Churches had to come mainly from sources other than Methodism.

Several of the ministers of the State Church in Germany had participated in the Oxford meeting in August of 1874. They returned home with the "blessing" and preached the experience in spite of significant opposition. The interest stirred by both proponents and opponents resulted in arrangements for an alliance meeting for entire consecration at Bern. On Smith's way to a similar meeting at Basel, one of the main thrusts of the coming revival occurred at Berlin. There, and in German lands in general, there was weariness with the political pace surrounding the war of 1870 and its aftermath. The Established Church offered little personal religion and the old Pietist cells were usually dormant in their interior quietism; the country was ripe for a transcendental appeal such as Smith introduced.

Hermann Krummacher was one of the German representatives who responded to Philip Schaff's trip to Europe to invite prominent European scholars and churchmen to the 1873 Evangelical Alliance meeting in New York. He described German religious life to the delegates. Krummacher observed that the signs of revival which had appeared in Germany in 1864-1870 among all classes of the nation had almost intensified with the outbreak of the Franco-Prussian War and its nationalistic hopes. With the end of that conflict, however, the hopes had not been realized, and the German nation was moving ahead without Christianity.[49]

August Tholuck, professor of theology at the University of Halle, wrote in a paper read to the same assembly, at the same time, in the same vein, that "the unparalleled victory which God granted to the nation in the last war has not regenerated us in faith...On the contrary the new epoch...proves itself to be an ever proceeding dissolution of positive faith and Christian interest...."[50]

Pressed by such concerns prominent German theologians in Berlin, some of whom had attended the Oxford meetings, invited Smith to come to that city.[51] When the "Vereinhaus" built by the Pietists proved to be too small to accommodate the crowds which attended. the meetings moved to the Military Church by permission of the Emperor and Court-preacher Baur. Four to five thousand people crowded into the meetings day after day. The message which had won over so many adherents in England within the upper classes and the Anglican Church, now brought an even more enthusiastic response from leaders of the established church in Germany as well as the pietistic elements within that church. An observer reported that on the last Sunday night of the meetings, the crowd stood "spellbound" as Smith made his religious appeal through Dr. F. W. Beadecker, his interpreter.[52]

Subsequently, the Secretary of State's house was made available to the evangelist for a meeting with one hundred and fifty of Berlin's scholars and statesmen. Dr. Earl von Hegel, son of the famed philosopher and president of the Brandenberg Consistorium, and Dr. Buchsel,[53] bishop of the German church, among them. The Emperor thanked Smith by letter for his ministry in the city. On the Monday following the close of the public services, Smith spoke to another group of one hundred who had gathered at the American embassy at the invitation of the ambassador, Bancroft Davis. Smith also ministered personally to Empress Augusta and her daughter, Luise, and Grand Duchess of Boston.[54]

From Berlin, Smith and Pastor Ernest Gebhardt,[55] who was singing for him in the services, moved on to Basel for a week of camp meeting-style services, arranged for by the Evangelical Alliance. The meeting hall seated two thousand people, but it soon proved to be too crowded; a large church was opened for the remainder of the services. Five thousand attended the day services. Smith spoke six times each day.

At Stuttgart, an eight-day meeting was held with similar results. Here the Lutherans were not ready to accept the musical services of Pastor Gebhardt; they were prejudiced against him because, as Methodist presiding elder in the Wittenberg area, he had administered the sacraments in his church. However, Smith himself, who never sought to deny his debt to the Methodists for his holiness teachings, was enthusiastically received. Services at Heidelberg, Karlsruhe, and Elberfeld followed. In May 1875, he held the closing meeting in Germany at Barmen with Theodor Christlieb, and D. Fabri. More than sixty German pastors followed him to Brighton at the end of the month. Among them was the respected D. G. Warneck, who with fifty other State Church ministers had defended Smith's ministry in Germany; he later remarked that at Brighton he had received "the strongest impulses to his life of faith."[56]

The Holiness Movement and German Pietism

The most lasting effects of Smith's German ministry, however, grew out of the impact of his preaching among the old Pietist areas of southern Germany; students of the German Gemeinschaftsbewegung, such as Abdel Wentz, one-time professor at Gettysburg Lutheran Seminary, maintain that this modern German Pietist Movement represents a combination of the staid strain of old German Pietism and the vigor-

ous, activistic strain of the American and English holiness movements.[57] Conditioned by the waves of evangelism which swept Germany at the beginning and the middle of the nineteenth century,
traditional Pietism had already begun to move away from its old
separatistic, quietistic ways. By Smith's time, it was ready to hear a
message which called for practical, positive, Christian holiness. The
response to the revival and the new continuing Gemeinschaftsbewegung are ample proof that the rationalism of the century
had not destroyed the old Pietism. The impact upon the German
churches was so significant that it is impossible to read the history of
the German evangelical church from that time to this without understanding these origins of the movement.[58]

The German holiness movement took a different turn from that
found in the ongoing American and English movements. Its converts
formed conventicles within the Established or State Church in the old
Pietistic tradition of small group fellowships or churches within the
church. A scholarly comparison of this tradition with that of the American movement at this point, also, might throw new light on the elements
which enter into the dynamics of such movements vis-a-vis the interpretations which rely chiefly on sociological data.

These German groups had three main emphases: fellowship,
which gave them their name "Gemeinschaftsbewegung," evangelization of the masses, and the promotion of the doctrine of entire sanctification. The national movement finally centered around the famous
Gnadau Conference which first met in 1888. Jasper V. Oertzen who had
been strongly influenced by Johann Wichern, the father of German
Inner Missions, was a leader of the movement. He served as head of the
City Mission at Hamburg from 1873-1893, and was president of the
Schleswig-Holstein Society for Inner Missions. Oertzen was presiding
officer at the first three Gnadau Conferences.[59]

Another leader who left his impress on the movement was Theodor
Christlieb, one of Smith's sponsors and professor of practical theology
at Bonn. He began to agitate for evangelists in the church conferences
and set up a school for evangelists at Bonn which emphasized lay
training; lay participation became an important factor in the new
holiness Pietistic movement.60 A third prominent figure, Theodor
Jellinghaus, was the theologian of the movement. His book, *Complete
Salvation in the Present*, outlines the patterns of the movement's theology
of Christian holiness; it was closer to Keswick's general terms than the
more specific language which the American movement used to give
theological definition to its concepts of entire sanctification. Jellinghaus,
too, saw the value of laypersons in evangelization; from 1885 to 1893

he instructed 73 laypersons in his own house during devotional periods with his theological views and sent them out into the church.[61]

In 1890 a national organizational structure was formed under the name of Committee for the Cultivation of Christian Fellowship and Evangelical Piety, and a paper called *Philadelphia* was started with an initial subscription list of five thousand. Intense evangelization steadily increased the ranks; in 1901 the groups were legally registered as the German Philadelphia Society.[62]

By the second decade of the present century, these voluntary associations of Christians meeting in a particular community for spiritual edification, but without regular church connection, expanded their membership even further. Wurtemberg counted 800 societies, ranging in individual membership from 200 to 1,000; Baden had 150 groups, all of old Pietist derivation. In Hessen and Hessen-Nassau, there were 250; in Palatinate 130; in the lower Rhine, 100; Wesphalia had 400, with 25,000t; Schleswig-Holstein, 250; Saxony, 270, which held over 25,000 meetings in a year, published a paper for over 30,000 subscribers and held conferences with attendances of 3,000 people each; Berlin had 50; Pomerania, 40; West Prussia, 60; Prussia, 50; other parts of Germany had a proportion varying in number with the remaining remnants of Pietistic influence in the particular area. In Denmark there were 462 meeting houses.

Wentz also notes that the Christian Endeavor Societies, the Young Men's Christian Associations, and the University Christian Movements in Germany got almost all of their strength from the new Pietist Movement.[63]

The movement in Germany was severely divided in the second decade of the twentieth century when the Pentecostal movement began to promote its particular emphases on the baptism of the Holy Ghost as evidenced by speaking in tongues. Varying positions on the question were taken by powerful leaders in the movement. More than doctrine and experience were at issue; the strong separationist tendencies of the incipient Pentecostal movement gradually led to a breakdown of the prevailing Pietist concept of a church within the church and produced a church organization of distinct Pentecostal bodies much in the same pattern as the holiness and Pentecostal movements in the United States.[64]

This significant influence of the holiness movement upon the German religious life has not generally been well known to the American holiness movement. The involvement of the ongoing holiness work in the Pietistic circles of the State Churches makes it difficult to identify the movement's total activities and influences; the nature of the organization, also, was not conducive to a continued relationship between the German holiness movement and the American. The German-English language barrier also hindered any enduring communication between the direct descendants of R. Pearsall Smith's work in Germany and the American tradition. The only consistent relationship of the American movement with any segment of German holiness teaching was through its development in German Methodism whose contacts with the holiness advocates were kept alive through ecclesiastical channels and church leaders, such as William Nast.

THE BRIGHTON CONVENTION—TRIUMPH AND TRAGEDY

Robert Pearsall Smith returned from his triumphant meetings on the Continent to immediately enter into the long anticipated convention for the promotion of holiness which met at Brighton on May 29, 1875. As that convention began, Dwight L. Moody told his own London audiences that the Brighton meeting was to be "perhaps the most important meeting ever gathered together."[65] He requested special prayer for its success. If Oxford was the Vineland of the European movement, Brighton was its Manheim. In America the Vineland appeal for a special promotion of holiness had gone out mainly to Methodists who had already shown concern for the advancement of the teaching and experience. The initial response proved to be so positive that the second efforts at Manheim attracted a much broader spectrum of the American church to the movement's message.[66] The experience in England was remarkably similar. Those who had found the "blessing" at Oxford had gone everywhere testifying to new spiritual power and hope.

A German Methodist reported to the *Guide*

> The doctrine of sanctification...has found its way to the European continent and is awakening attention especially in the land of Zwingliius and Luther. Christians from Switzerland and Germany many attending the Oxford meetings conducted by E. [sic] Pearsall Smith, experienced the blessing of perfect love, and felt constrained to preach the doctrine and tell the experience in the Fatherland. The movement has thus found advocates in the Lutheran and Reformed Churches; and, what is most remarkable has been most heartily welcomed and endorsed by almost the entire religious press of Germany....[67]

In Basel, Switzerland, a monthly magazine was published under the title of *Des Christen Glaubensweg* [*The Christian's Way of Faith*].

Indication of the positive publicity, which such new journals provided for the incipient holiness revival on the Continent, is provided by a "Correspondent Krehbfel" who reported to the abovementioned journal that

> everywhere large numbers of professed Christians or heathen have been awakened, and a hungering and thirsting after practical holiness is the result. Many of these have had their longing desires satisfied, by being filled with the Spirit in such a real manner as they had never thought possible in the present life.[68]

The editor of *Earnest Christianity* rejoiced in this new spread of the holiness message which was reaching non-Methodist churches in America and Europe. He observed that, "It is no libel on others to say, that for many years, 'the people called Methodists' were peculiar in...that they made the most strenuous efforts to build the churches in holiness." But now, he continued, "Henry Varley is preaching in Canada and the United States." McDonald and Inskip of the National Camp Meeting movement had "been made a great blessing" in a recent Canadian mission; the Canadian Camps at Grimsby and Thousand Islands were "now to be numbered with the Feasts of Tabernacles," and the Presbyterians, who "for many years past have allowed the Methodists to monopolize these special organizations..." were holding a "grand camp."

The summary goes on to note that Moody's and Sankey's work is "too well known to dwell on," but at the same time

> Messers. Pearsall [*sic*], Mahan, Boardman and others are permitted to behold a work in England such as has hardly been witnessed during the present century; conferences are being held solely that ministers and others may understand the doctrine of holiness more clearly. Rev. Thornley Smith and other Wesleyan ministers are taking part in these holy convocations. Many of the evangelical party are very prominent....
>
> The Continent of Europe has caught the flame of spiritual power. A son of the well-known Fred Monod in France has become an itinerant preacher [T. Monod] and his business now is to travel through France and stir up zeal among the Protestant ranks. Conventions have been held in Germany and Switzerland and great good has been done.[69]

Charles W. I. Christine, an English Methodist, summed up the hope which excited the English revival ranks just prior to the Brighton Convention in May of 1875:

> We may confidently and calmly expect a wondrous outpouring of the hallowing Spirit at the Brighton Meetings. A thousand facts around tell us that with respect to our glorious theme "the winter is past, the rain is over and gone. The flowers appear on the earth; the time of the singing of birds is come, and the voice of the turtle is heard in our land!"[70]

The numerous accounts of the time show that many who anticipated Brighton and participated in it, shared Moody's hopes for the gathering. Whatever the contemporary actors on the scene really expected to issue from the meeting, one can only conjecture; unless one reads too much into their predictions, undoubtedly, results shown by the ensuing history did not fully meet their expectations. But it is certain that the religious repercussions were far more reaching than often has been recognized.

About eight thousand people traveled to Brighton, England, that May of 1875, in response to the call of the sponsors. Three wealthy "English gentlemen" had promised a reserve fund of two thousand pounds to provide for the expenses of the meetings, but none of these funds were finally required. The town offered its three main meeting halls, the Town Hall, the Corn Exchange, and the Dome, free of charge to the sponsors of the meeting. The center of organizational activities was the Royal Pavilion Apartments, which were once the sporting place of George V and William IV. When Victoria became queen they had been sold. [71]

The facilities were crowded from the seven o'clock prayer meeting in the morning until the evening meetings in the main halls. The Smiths were the main speakers; to some, Hannah Whitall Smith was an even more forceful presence than her husband. Her daily Bible readings on various spiritual themes, carried over from a type of service common to the National Camps in America, were the chief center of interest. She also conducted special services for the women who were present. An English newspaper correspondent noted that the crowds were so great at these Bible readings that she had to deliver them first in the Corn Exhange and then in the Dome. The more than six thousand people in these auditoriums, she observed, gave her "a congregation. . . larger than Mr. Spurgeon's." A reporter described the scene:

Punctually to the moment, like Mr. Moody, she steps to the front
of the platform, dressed in almost eccentric Quaker simplicity,
and then speaks for fifty minutes by the clock, without hesitating
a moment. Her freshness, her profound spiritual insight, as as
remarkable as her surpising fluency.

Another reporter wrote:

By all she is recognized as the leading spirit of the convention.
Mrs. Smith has little of the feminine in her style of oratory....De-
cision marks every sentence she utters. The pathetic element is
almost wholly absent. As an expositor of the Bible she is trench-
ant, and often powerful.[72]

For ten days the participants in the convention shared in a kind of
massive dialogue in a quest for the experience of Christian holiness
taught by the Smiths. Formal meetings were commonly followed by
smaller gatherings in which inquiry was made and questions answered
on the "higher life" and Christian holiness. Representatives of many
Protestant churches and sects in Europe and Britain, who came together
with the common understanding that doctrinal questions would not be
allowed to take center stage, had only the common desire and pursuit
of practical holiness. Laymen and ministers were involved on common
terms. Frenchmen and Germans whose national interests still smarted
from the wounds of the Franco-Prussian War shared in frequent public
testimony to common spiritual fellowship.

The prominence given to congregational singing represented another common feature with the American holiness camp meeting.
Pastor Gebhardt,[73] who wrote the hymn, "Jesus erretet mich jetz"
("Jesus Saves Me Now") that bore the revival throughout Germany, was
there, and Theodore Monod listened as his hymn of consecration,
written at Broadlands, was sung. It became a favorite musical expression of the theology and experience of the movement.[74]

The record of testimonies given in the course of the meetings
include that of J. Hudson Taylor, founder of the China Inland Mission.
He said that he had realized the reality of Christian life which was being
promoted in the convention "about seven years" before. A Rev. M.
Hesse of Wurtemberg, Germany, told of his struggle involving theology,
which "was, that a certain quantity of sin was necessary, not to orthodoxy, but to keep us humble.... Now he had learned that as Jesus had
pardoned his past sins, so he was willing and able to keep him from sin
in the future."[75] Elizabeth Charles, author of *Chronicles of the Schoenberg*

Cotta Family, a story about Martin Luther, summed up her view, and apparently that of many others, when she predicted "that the doctrine of sanctification by faith and the blessed experience the doctrine brings are about to occupy the attention of Christians as they never have done before...." She felt that "no qualified observer" could doubt that for a moment. "Nor can we doubt," she said, "that a time will come when the Conventions of Oxford and Brighton shall be historical as the first great efforts [in the development of that movement]...."[76]

The Significance of the European Holiness Revival of 1873-1875

It would be easy to relegate such enthusiasm as Mrs. Charles exhibited to the usual optimism of a revival atmosphere. However, when one reads the judgment of the scholarly, but rather prejudiced, Benjamin Warfield, concerning the European holiness revival efforts of Robert Pearsall Smith and his colleagues in the American holiness movement, he/she can put into better perspective the obvious excitement which infused the contemporary accounts. Warfield said that "there is nothing more dramatic in the history of modern Christianity than the record of this 'Higher Life' Movement,"[77] even though he himself, could find nothing in it except the same old Methodist Pelagianism which he so consistently opposed. And that is basically what Smith's message was—the message which he and the others had imbibed out of their own experience in the American holiness movement, now adapted somewhat for their non-Methodist European audiences. It was essentially the same call to Christian experience which Wesley's evangelists had preached to crowds of poor British laborers a hundred years previously in the same places that the Philadelphia Quaker layman was gathering together the "lords and ladies" of the English upper classes, evangelicals and ritualists of the Anglican Church, Lutheran and Reformed theologians from Germany, and representative laymen and pastors from most of the other churches of the day, for his meetings for the "promotion of holiness." It was Phoebe Palmer's and John Inskip's call for definite consecration, definite faith, and definite witness—in short, a call to the practical possibilities of a life of vital Christianity now, not later. It was the proclamation of the new practical pietism which the holiness revival represented.[78]

The participants at Brighton were conscious that they were standing in some kind of enduring Christian tradition. They testified that it was the truth of "our saviour and his apostles, believed in by the godly of all ages."[79] The *Friend's Quarterly Examiner* reported that the promoters of this movement are constant in their protest against being supposed to possess any *new* truth. What is new in their teaching is simply a *vitalizing of the old*—a making personal and definite that which has always been accepted as true, but in too general a sense.

It is making experimental that which we have held doctrinally, that the whole vigour of our spiritual life consists; and this is the key to the rapid spread of this movement for the promotion of Scriptural holiness...[emphasis theirs].

This was the only explanation the *Examiner* could propose for a meeting of eight thousand Christians "at which no doctrinal questions were... discussed, no resolutions passed, and no fresh church organization attempted...."[80] Mrs. Charles said that it was the life, "which we *all* ought to be living, not merely a few of us; which we ought to be living *always*, and not merely now and then....The tenses of the Christian are not mere narrative tenses. They are present and perfect" [emphasis hers]. Quoting Coleridge, she said, "To restore a common-place truth to its first un-common lustre, you need only to *translate it into action*" [emphasis hers].[81]

The implications of this last quote are very critical to the understanding of what was happening. There was something new, but we can only define that novelty by placing it against the contemporary Victorian scene. An awareness of the frame of mind of the Victorians, who heard the "higher life" message, alone can explain why this activistic American presentation, of what was essentially Wesleyan perfectionism, burst upon the scene with such freshness—it *was, in short, a revival of hope* in the midst of an "age of multiplied doubts and shaken beliefs."[82]

In Walter Houghton's definitive panorama of life in the Victorian age, we have a composite picture of the dynamics of ideological and sociological forces which were tearing at the minds and lives of men and women in England during the period of the revival. Houghton shows that the dominant characteristics of the time were "transition" and "doubt"—the transition of a "bourgeois industrial society" and doubt "about the nature of man, society, and the universe."[83] The pressure of unprecedented change and the resultant uncertainty extended to every level of society; it was "a large public living in an age of 'doubts, disputes, distractions, fears....'"[84] Matthew Arnold, in his essay on "Bishop Butler and the Zeitgeist," declared that " amid that breakup of traditional and conventional notions respecting our life, its conduct, its sanctions," men were looking for "some clear light and some sure stay."[85]

Houghton's description of the tensions the Victorians faced in their religious life speaks even more directly to the response given by the American holiness message and method. He says that the common religious mood was marked by the frustrations of "a daily sense of failure" under the hand of a heavy Puritan theology with its somber Deity.[86] There was an almost universal sense that the church was not demonstrating real Christianity. Wrapped up in the title of William Wilberforce's "evangelical Bible," *A Practical View of Prevailing Religious System of Professed Christians in the Higher and Middle Classes, Contrasted with Real Christianity*, was the story of the age's sense of failure to demonstrate "Monday," as well as "Sunday" religion.[87] Ministers, generally were caught up in the pressures of religious conformity and were assailed by doubt and confusion. The answers which they were attempting to provide for their equally disturbed parishioners seemed to be totally inadequate.[88] Even the liberal trend in men like Matthew Arnold may have prepared the way for the revival appeal. He rejoiced that men could now learn "what Christianity really is—simply a life of piety and virtue."[89]

A general feeling of moral failure, existential loneliness, isolation, and nostalgia for a more sure past prevailed. Bertrand Russell described it as "all the loneliness of humanity amid hostile forces...concentrated upon the individual soul."[90] The threats of the new "faith" in science and the rising tide of Biblical criticism threatened the Biblical authority of the evangelical faith. The return to "Rome," whether to the Anglo-Catholics or the Roman Catholics, worried them as well.[91] All of these feelings undoubtedly contributed to the confession of Canon T. D. Harford-Battersby, fellow graduate student of Matthew Arnold, Lord Coleridge, and Archbishop Fredrick Temple, and also later a leader in the Keswick conventions, to his own state of mind in 1873. He wrote,

> At this moment I am feeling much inward struggle and questioning about this "higher Christian life" which is so much talked and written about....What I have been reading of the experience of others, Mr. Pearsall Smith and his excellent wife and their wonderful boy, "Frank," has made me utterly dissatisfied with myself and my state, I feel I am dishonouring God and am wretched myself by living as I do; and that I must either go backwards or forwards, reaching out towards the light and the glory which my

blessed Saviour holds out to me, or falling back more and more into worldliness and sin![92]

Perhaps, for the first time then, one can begin to comprehend what really lay behind the *Examiner*'s conclusion that the only explanation for the Brighton Convention was

> that an earnest desire for increased personal holiness has been awakened in the Christian Church; and to meet this desire there has arisen a fresh setting forth of the truth concerning the Lord Jesus Christ as a present, indwelling Saviour, living in the soul and working there, "to will and to do of His good pleasure."[93]

It also gives us the interpretive context for the remarks of Rev. J. B. Figgis in the *Evangelical Magazine* for September 1875; not agreeing fully with those who disclaimed any newness in the higher life revival, he attempted to articulate the novelty which he sensed, but could not explicitly identify. "There is 'no small stir about this way,' " he said,

> and this implies a certain amount of novelty and (probably) of truth. Some friends of the movement have been a little too ready to disclaim the former....But *they are new to many,* perhaps new to most, new certainly to us; and glorious news—they are "good news," a very "Gospel," only a Gospel not merely for sinners, but for the saved....and life is a continual triumph [emphasis his].[94]

This articulation of new hope and joy comes through to the researcher of the European holiness revival at every turn. To view it only as an adoption by the British, French, German, and other participants of the inherent optimism of the American movement provides only a partial explanation; it must be contrasted with the picture of intense pessimism which characterized the period to fully comprehend the newness which it represented to them. The message answered for many, apparently, the anxiety created by the frustrating striving, which, Houghton says, was common in Victorian religion. Figgis observed that "the old way used to be too much of an effort—a way of self-control. This [new way] is a way of faith..."[95] The promise of a life of vital sanctification also promised an answer to the longing sense of moral failure which also pervaded the English religious scene in 1875. A witness to the new spiritual experiences he had professed, as a result of the revivals, said that under his old theology "the expectation...was failure; success was a surprise. The rule [he said] is reversed now; it [failure] becomes the exception, and the exception [success] the rule."

The result was not a state of "sinlessness," but of "sunshine." The Victorians who heard Smith felt that they had been freed from the heavy hand of a stern God. They professed a new joy in a relationship in which it was "possible to walk with God, and to...'please' Him.[96] In the midst of a troubled society, the vigorous promotion of a faith relationship, which could produce sustained vitality in a Christian's life, spoke forcibly to the Pietistic Puritanism which still infused much of English evangelicalism. It had also spoken directly to the Pietistic remnants in Germany. The result was "Brighton" and "Berlin" and the initiation of institutions and movements which have left a permanent impress upon Protestant life ever since.

It was part of a "new era of American Pietism" which Perry Miller, the able historian of American ideas, has identified with the rise of holiness literature such as Boardman's *Higher Christian Life* just prior to the Civil War. Miller claimed that this "new piety" was "no longer concerned with doctrine," but rather, only with a "practical Christianity," purely of the heart. The extent to which it was received by people of every class and creed, in both European and American Protestantism in the troubled 1870s, serves as a strong reminder that, in spite of Miller's fear that it represented "the ultimate reaches of the Revival's long efforts to elude the trammels of metaphysics," it did speak to the heart.[97] Many a Victorian was driven into himself as the ultimate refuge from the change and doubt which threatened him from every side. A religious experience which promised to bring order, meaning, and hope in that center was attractive to theologian and intellectual as well as pastor and parishioner. The certainty and the immediateness of the holiness message apparently represented a path to new purpose.[98]

The Tragedy: The Fall of Robert Pearsall Smith

After Brighton, Smith and his followers were exuberant; all Europe seemed to be at their feet. However, the continuing reports of the English revival in the *Advocate of Christian Holiness,* brought the announcement in September 1875 that, "our brother R. P. Smith has been obliged because of failing health to return from his work in Europe to his home in Philadelphia...."

The editor commented that,

> we have not been without fear that such a result would follow from what we could not but regard as an over pressure of his physical system just emerging from a serious breakdown....May God very soon restore him to health and service as such laborers are greatly needed.[99]

The editor's hopes for a continued ministry for Robert Pearsall Smith in the holiness work were never realized. Smith and his wife were scheduled to speak at the first Keswick Convention to be held in July of 1875 following the Brighton Convention. When it suddenly was revealed that they would not attend, some explanation was necessary; stories concerning gross immorality and serious doctrinal deviations were spreading and threatening the whole higher life movement. Smith's friends issued a statement indicating that "in personal conversation" his friends had noted suggestions of doctrinal indiscretions which were "most unscriptural and dangerous...." They announced to their shocked followers that, "there had been conduct which although we were convinced that it was free from evil intention was yet such as to render action necessary on our part...." The action agreed upon was to ask Smith to refrain from all further public work. Smith apparently not only acquiesced in this decision but the statement continued that he "recognized with deep sorrow the unscriptural and dangerous character of the teaching of the conduct in question...." The explanation concluded with a reference to the recurrence of Smith's old illness of the brain which "rendered the immediate cessation from work an absolute necessity.[100]

For nearly ninety years the rumors and questions concerning Smith's "fall" persisted without any explanation beyond the above statement from the committee which had dismissed him from his work. The truth of the situation came out in 1965, when John Pollock discovered Smith's full confession of the whole matter in a letter to Cowper-Temple. As Pollock has indicated, "the truth is pathetic rather than shocking...."[101] It appears now that it would have been much better for all concerned had Smith's friends been more forthright in their handling of the affair. At any rate, the pressure of the crisis proved to be too much for Smith, and the risks for the committee were too great; in a state of nervous prostration, he and his wife returned to America.

In all the currents which flowed around the Smiths during this controversy, Dr. Charles Cullis, Boston physician and lay evangelist, remained their staunchest friend. In August of 1876, he persuaded them to take up their public ministry again in a camp meeting; his hope was to restore them of their former usefulness. Mrs. Smith indicates that she and her husband had no personal feelings in the matter, and in agreeing to go, they were showing gratitude for the good intentions of an old friend. Nevertheless, they "hitched" themselves to "Dr. Cullis's team" and 'concluded the Lord would not be very angry with [them] under the circumstances [though it would serve them] right if He should make the meeting a complete failure...."[102] But the meeting was in no sense a failure.

> There was just the same power and blessing as at Oxford or Brighton....There was every sign of the continual presence of the Spirit. Souls were converted, backsliders restored, Christians sanctified...And Robert and I never worked more effectively. He had all his old power in preaching and leading meetings....As for me, thee knows that I am not much given to tell of my own successes, but...I shall have to tell thee that I was decidedly "favored" as the Friends say.[103]

Dr. Cullis's hopes for restoration of Robert Pearsall's image of pulpit effectiveness seemed to be amply fulfilled as the fame of the meeting began to spread. Urgent invitations for Smith and his wife to hold public meetings in various places followed in increasing numbers. The Smith themselves, however, dashed the hopes to the ground forever, "without a longing thought, only too thankful to be released." The future course was set: "Henceforth home and homelife for us," they said. Both of them had "hated the adventure cordially."

> it was all a wearisome *performance* to us. We did it over an impassible gulf. The flood had come since the last time, and changed all things to us.There was no interest, no enthusiasm. The meetings were a bore, the work was like a treadmill. We counted the hours until we could get away and hailed the moment of emancipation with unspeakable joy.[104]

The incident baffled Hannah Smith; she was not sure whether her lack of concern in the matter was due to such an advance in grace that she was utterly indifferent to anything but the will of God, or that she had become "utterly irreligious" and a "lazy fatalist." In spite of the doubts, neither she nor her husband hesitated in their decision to leave the scene of holiness evangelism forever. Later, she said, "I was utterly unmoved; both Robert and I came away more confirmed than ever in our feelings of entire relief from everything of the kind. *We are done!* Somebody else may do it now."[105]

As for the future, she personally testified that her ever broadening views of "the limitless ocean of the love of God that overflows all things" had thrown her "orthodoxy" to the winds. The only certain conclusion which she could draw from the perplexing events was the belief that God "means us to be good human beings in this world, and nothing more."[106] She spent the rest of her life doing just that. Her husband still suffered from his physical and psychological afflictions. Never as resolute a person as his dynamic wife, he endured the rest of his days in disappointment and remorse, but his name still echoes through the mountain tops as well as the valleys of the history of the holiness revival and the holiness movement today.

THE INSTITUTIONALIZATION OF THE ENGLISH REVIVAL

The holiness movement in Europe was shaken by the dissension over Smith, but not finally daunted.[107] Jack Ford lists Wesleyan oriented groups which sprang up as a result of the revival. In addition to his own Church of the Nazarene, he mentions Cliff College (1884), the Southport Convention (1885), the Faith Mission (1886), the Star Hall (1889), the Pentecostal League (1891), the Salvation Army (1878), the Holiness Church (*ca.* 1880), and the Independent Holiness Movement (1907).[108]

But the continuing movement which sprang most directly from the evangelism of the Smiths was the Keswick Convention. The sudden return of the Smiths to America in 1875 precluded their presence at the first convention for the promotion of holiness held at Keswick, England. A decision was made to go ahead with the meeting, nevertheless. Rev. H. W. Webb-Peploe—later Prebendary—was called upon to take Smith's place in the convention. He with men like Rev. Evan H. Hopkins; Robert Wilson, a Quaker; Canon Harford-Battersby, vicar of St. John in Keswick; and Handley Moule, Principal of Ridley Hall and later Bishop of Durham, determined the early course of the Convention. Annual meetings "for the Promotion of Scriptural Holiness" have been held to the present time.[109] Their ongoing history represents the most enduring form of what might properly be called the Calvinistically or non-Methodistically oriented results of the holiness revival. Its structure and purpose, in many ways, faithfully reflects its Oxford-Brighton parentage.

Its purpose was the same. A letter from Canon T. D. Harford-Battersby, the vicar of St. Johns in Keswick, to another of its founders, the Quaker, Robert Wilson, proposed that the promotion of "the full sanctification of believers" was to be the object of the convention.[110]

The lack of predesigned programs or even addresses, yet the general sense of order and continuity which prevailed, the tarrying for the mind of the Spirit, and prominence given to the dialogue of testimony and congregational song, all were common to the patterns which had already developed in the meetings and conventions of the American movement and continue in much of the philosophy of the movement even to this day. As has already been observed in the previous discussion on the American camp meeting, strong personalities who guided the course of the "open ritual" of the gatherings, kept order through a combination of their own personal ability, charisma, semi- or official position and the final appeal to their sense of the "leadings of the Spirit."[111]

The higher life message of Keswick strongly influenced evangelical religious organizations around the world through such men as A. T. Pierson, Hudson Taylor, F. B. Meyer, Andrew Murray, Theodore Monod, and Dr. Eugene Stock. The English evangelical community came under its continuing influence through the ministers and laymen who gathered annually at Keswick under the leadership of men like Webb-Peploe, Harford-Batterersby, and Handley Moule, later Bishop of Durham. Similar higher life conferences standing in an informal relationship to Keswick through their teaching and speaking personnel, were begun in Europe and the United States; through F. B. Meyer and others, the holiness message came back in full circle to American Calvinistic publics, which the Methodist based message often had not been able to penetrate. This influence has remained a vital factor in American Evangelical life ever since, particularly through Dwight L. Moody, as it reinforced his own earlier contacts with the movement. Adoniram J. Gordon and Arthur T. Pierson, both active in the evangelical student movements at the turn of the century introduced the "Spirit-filled life" concepts into those groups. How close to home it had come, has continually been shown in the stream of polemic which has flowed between the closely related Methodist and Calvinist wings of the movement since that time.[112]

SUMMARY

A study of the European expansion of the revival has been considered essential to the development of this thesis basically because it gives us a view of the response to American holiness revivalism in a non-American context. This European view of the movement was far removed from the American frontier, from all other distinctly American sociological factors, and just as importantly, was largely removed from the close involvement with American Methodism. The latter involvement, frequently has tended to make identification of the issues in American perfectionist revivalism difficult. The European revival history provides a unique interpretive control situation.

It may be that an analysis of the factors at work in this non-American situation could be used much more widely than they have been to achieve more accurate evaluations of what was really occurring in the United States and Canada. The close relationship, which seems to be evident, between the effectiveness of the message and methods of the American movement and the prevailing circumstances of English life, would appear to be an extremely important factor in the interpretation of movement wherever it was active. The response generated by its strongly perfectionist, pietistic appeal, apparently was capable of arousing almost instant, broad scale reaction in favor of experiential religion as the only adequate answer to the dual threats of transitoriness and doubt.

What was true of the revivalism in England, was also true of its acceptance and influence in Germany and other European countries. In Germany, in particular, it proved the basic nature of its appeal by reviving the old pietistic cells, while at the same time, attracting to itself men from all levels of society as well as Established churchmen. The disappointments in the religious life of the nation, after the success of the Franco-Prussian War and the dissatisfaction of increasing numbers of individuals with the answers of a sterile rationalism, provide us with a rationale for the amazing scenes in which the learned doctors of the church sang the simple revival chorus, "Jesus Saves Me Now," and testified to receiving the most powerful impulses of their spiritual lives.

Finally, the European story is important because of the numerous movements, which sprang from Smith's evangelism and that of others who continued his work; the basically pietistic impulses, strongly energized by the American movement's optimism and activism, shaped a new concept of the Christian life, not only for many in the Free Churches of England and Europe, but also for many in the evangelical elements of the Established Protestant Churches as well. New institutions, especially dedicated to the revival's holiness doctrines, came into being in England and Europe as they did in America. In the Germany and Switzerland of that day, the revival took up the "Inner Missions" movement and gave it a new dynamic, as an influential force within the State Churches.

NOTES

1. *Supra*, p. 61. The finest analysis of this British-American interaction is Richard Cawardine's *Trans-atlantic Revivalism: Popular Evangelicalism in Britain and America, 1790-1865* (Westport, CT: Greenwood Press, 1978).

2. *Advocate of Christian Holiness*, III (January 1873), 156; Palmer, *Four Years*, p. 105. *Ibid.*, p. 262, notes, "And thus the flame kindled when we were at Hamilton is spreading to Europe."

3. *Ibid.*, p. 105; Orr, *op. cit.*, p. 63.

4. *Supra*, pp. 59ff. The opposition of the Primitive Methodists was especially paradoxical; they themselves had been born in a revival movement sparked by

Lorenzo Dow, an eccentric American Methodist evangelist of the early nine-teenth century. "Crazy Dow," as he was known, ranged far and wide across the United States of his day like a "comet in the religious world." Many thought him more madman than preacher, but the record of his accomplishments as the first Methodist missionary to what was, in 1799, Lower Canada (now the Province of Quebec); his brief camp meeting ministry in England which inspired Hugh Bourne and William Clowes, the founders of Primitive Methodism, and his lesser-known achievements must modify any criticism of his strange maverick lifestyle. See Joseph Riston, *The Romance of Primitive Methodism* (London: Edwind Dalton, 1909), pp. 56-58; Schaff-Herzog, *op. cit.,* 111, 497.

5. Edward Goulburn's *Pursuit of Holiness* (London: Rivingtons, 1870), pp. 212ff., gives a classical statement of the doctrine, paralleling the movement's theology of Christian perfection. William Arthur, a leading advocate of holiness promotion in the Wesleyan Methodist churches in England, published his *Tongue of Fire* in 1856; it was widely read both in England and America in its time and continues to exercise influence within holiness and higher-life ranks today through constant reprints. Richard Poole's *Center and Circle of Evangelical Religion, or Perfect Love* (London: Jarrold and Sons, 1873), sold 10,000 copies in its first year. Stephen Barabas, *So Great Salvation: The History and Message of the Keswick Convention* (Westwood, NJ: Fleming H. Revell, 1952), p. 16, lists the works of Upham and Mahan as also arousing interest in the experience of holiness; but Barabas indicates that Boardman's *Higher Christian Life* was most important. To these must be added all the works of the Palmers, who were well known in England through their Civil War period ministry, and the writings of Robert and Hannah Smith. There was a strong desire-fulfillment circle at work; Charles F. Harford, *The Keswick Convention: Its Message, Its Method, and Its Men* (London: Marshall Brothers, 1907), p. 124, gives Canon Harford-Battersby's statement of the effect upon him of Hannah Whitall Smith's account of her deceased college-age son who had professed to receive a "second blessing" while a student at Princeton, *Frank, the Record of a Happy Life* (Philadelphia: Printed for Private Collection, 1873): "It would be impossible to report the revolution in my religious thought and life effected by that book. No book I have read has had anything like the same effect. *I suspect that today I should find nothing in it of special import; but then it spoke with the voice of God to my inmost condition"* (emphasis mine).

6. *Advocate of Christian Holiness,* III (December 1872), 121.

7. *Ibid.* (January 1873), 156, as quoted from the *King's Highway.*

8. *Ibid.*

9. *Ibid.*

10. *Ibid.,* p. 155; *ibid.,* IV (April 1874), 231.

11. *Ibid.* (March 1873); *ibid.* (June 1873), p. 281.

12. *Ibid.* (May 1873), p. 255.

13. *Ibid.* (June,1873), p. 281.

14. *Ibid.,* IV (April 1874), 232. Also see Paulus Scharpff, *History of Evangelism, Three Hundred Years of Evangelism in Germany, Great Britain, and the United States of America,* Helga Henry (trans.) (Grand Rapids, MI: Wm. B. Eerdmans Publishing Co., 1966), pp. 192-93.

15. Warfield claims, "The whole whirlwind campaign conducted by Mr. Smith was simply a concerted 'drive' of American Perfectionism on the European stronghold"; see Warfield, *Perfectionism*, I, 513. Warfield seems to neglect the fact that Smith originally went to England only for his health and not a "drive"; see Hannah Whitall Smith, *The Unselfishness of God, and How I Discovered It: A Spiritual Autobiography* (New York: Fleming H. Revell Co., 1903), p. 221; also, Logan Pearsall Smith (ed.), *Philadelphia Quaker, the Letters of Hannah Whitall Smith* (New York: Harcourt, Brace and Co., 1950), p. 15. As a young girl, Hannah had written to her cousin, Annie Whitall, "I think I would love to be a minister....Would it not be grand, and then I could travel all over the world and do *so much* good...." Letter of Hannah Whitall to Annie Whitall, Philadelphia, February 17, 1850, as given in *Philadelphia Quaker*, p. 4. Other leading Quakers in the movement were Dr. Dougan Clark, one-time professor of theology at Earlham College, Richmond, Indiana; evangelist David Updegraff, and evangelists Seth and Hulda Rees. Rees was one of the founders of the International Apostolic Holiness Union, which later became the Pilgrim Holiness Church. The best resource on the Smith family is Barbara Strachey [Halpern's] *Remarkable Relations: The Story of the Peasall Smith Family* (London: Victor Gollancz, 1981).

16. H. Smith, *The Unselfishness of God*, p. 172, see *ibid.*, pp. 169ff., for her own account of her religious experience at this period. Also see Melvin E. Dieter, ed., *The Christians Secret of a Holy Life: The Unpublished Personal Writings of Hannah Whitall Smith* (Grand Rapids, MI: Zondervan, 1994).

17. *Ibid.*, p. 189.

18. *Ibid.*, pp. 195ff.

19. *Ibid.*, pp. 241-42. Also see H. Smith, *Frank, the Record of a Happy Life*, p. 37, and "Believing, Resting, Abiding. Experience of a Member of the Society of Friends," *Guide*, LII (July 1867), 21-23. Garrison, *op. cit.*, pp. 119-30.

20. Her son, Logan Pearsall Smith, said in 1950 that the book had been translated into all the European languages and into some of the Oriental; more than one million copies had been sold; the same, *op. cit.*, p. v. However, the jacket of a 1952 paperbound edition by the original publisher, Fleming H. Revell Company, says that the "authorized edition had sold more than 2,000,000 copies"; it was originally published in 1875 and was one of the first Revell books; Hannah Whitall Smith, *The Christian's Secret of a Happy Life* (Westwood, N J: Fleming H. Revell Co., 1952). L. Smith (ed.), *Philadelphia Quaker*, pp. viiff., contains an excellent biographical note. Mrs. Smith used the circumstances under which she wrote the copy which eventually went into the book as a clear example of her belief that true religion was "an ordinary everyday walking in the path of duty" rather than "great ecstasies of inspiration." She had become an ardent member and officer in the Women's Christian Temperance movement (see Frances E. Willard, *Woman and Temperance: or the Woman's Christian Temperance Union* [Chicago: Women's Temperance Publication Association, 1883], pp. 193-207). Her husband's doctor had ordered him to take wine at dinner for his illness. It was a great trial for her to see him drinking, so she offered to write an article for his holiness paper if he would give it up. The article was so well received that he insisted on a series which finally were compiled into the devotional classic.

"These articles were dragged from me, so to speak, at the point of the bayonet, for I never wrote them in any month until the printers were clamouring for their copy." Therefore she said that she could not say she wrote them out of any compelling feeling, but "to oblige my husband." It was her duty, she had done it, and God had used it, she said, to be as helpful to thousands of people as any other book on "experimental religion" had proved to be; Strachey *Religious Fanaticism,* pp. 252-53.

21. H. Smith, *The Unselfishness of God,* p. 243.

22. *Ibid.,* p. 288.

23. *Ibid.,* p. 289.

24. For example, Wallace, *A Modern Pentecost,* p. 12, "R. Pearsall Smith and his excellent and laborious [*sic*] wife, who at Manheim as never before, received a commission from God which absorbed their being and proved an untold blessing to all the churches through their abundant labors." Smith took part in the evangelistic meetings of the National Association under Inskip in 1871 in California; *Guide,* LX (July 1871), 27.

25. See *supra,* n. 13. Smith suffered a head injury when he was thrown from a horse. His son, Logan Smith, speaks differently of the story. See Logan Pearsall Smith, *Unforgotten Years* (Boston: Little, Brown and Co., 1939), p. 61. His great-granddaughter, Barbara Strachey Halpern, told the author that the family believes Smith was a manic-depressive.

26. *Christian Standard,* VIII (No. 42), 333; also see Pollock, *op. cit.,* pp. 18-19; A. T. Pierson, *Forward Movements of the Last Half Century* (New York: Funk and Wagnalls Co., 1905), pp. 24ff. For the general picture of English Protestantism in this period, see Schaff and Prime, *op. cit.,* pp. 9ff.

27. L. Smith, *Unforgotten Years,* pp. 41-42. Mrs. Smith defined her concept of "The Restitution of All things" in the *Unselfishness of God,* pp. 199ff.; "There is to be a final 'restitution of all things' when 'at the name of Jesus every knee shall bow....' The how and when I could not see, but the one essential fact was all I needed—somewhere and somehow God was going to make everything right for all the creatures he had created." *Ibid.,* p. 205. She became convinced of the belief very early in her life; she wavered in it only briefly during her association with the Plymouth Brethren; she looked on it then as a "dreadful heresy, but later on...[she] learned even the blessed fact...that we are all, the heathen included, 'God's offspring.'..." The doctrine came to her on a streetcar on Market Street in Philadelphia; it may have been, in part, a reaction to the rigid Calvinism of her Plymouth Brethren advisors. *Ibid.,* pp. 83-85 195ff., 205-206.

28. Logan Smith (ed.), *Philadelphia Quaker,* p. iii. The same, *Unforgotten Years,* p. 51.

29. H. Smith, *The Unselfishness of God,* pp. 221-22. L. Smith, *The Unforgotten Years,* pp. 43-45.

30. *Ibid.,* p. 225.

31. A correspondent to the *Advocate of Christian Holiness* reported from England that the *King's Highway* was "always Methodist in its approach"; whereas the *Christian's Pathway of Power* "though giving a view of the doctrine which Methodists cannot always endorse, has, without doubt, led many, who

would not have been reached by a Methodist organ, into a closer walk with God."
See *Advocate of Christian Holiness*, V (November 1875), 108. Also Walter B. Sloan,
These Sixty Years: The Story of the Keswick Convention (London: Pickering and
Inglis, 1935), p. 24.

32. *Advocate of Christian Holiness*, IV (September 1873), 65; *ibid.* (July 1873),
15.

33. *Ibid.*, p. 15.

34. Mrs. W. E. Boardman says that 2,000 ministers participated in the
breakfast meetings held by Smith and Boardman in the spring of 1873. The same,
op. cit., pp. 156-59. Pierson, *op. cit.*, pp. 18-19, said the breakfasts were sponsored
by Samuel Morley, Congregationalist and member of Parliament.

35. *Advocate of Christian Holiness*, IV (May 1874), 262. Also see *Christian
Standard and Home Journal*, VIII (December 19, 1874), 45.

36. *Advocate of Christian Holiness*, IV (January 1874), 159, and preceding. See
Pollock, *op cit.*, p. 33; as quoted from the *Record*, a Church of England paper:
"Pearsall Smithism…[is] a new peril imported from America which substitutes
sentimentalism and visionary mysticism for solid piety and Scriptural experi-
mentalism founded on the word of God." Pollock also notes, *ibid.*, that Lord
Shaftesbury and John Charles Ryle opposed the meetings; the latter claimed that
the difference between Moody and Brighton "is the difference between sunshine
and fog." Note that Moody himself hardly agreed with Ryle; see *infra*, p. 174.

37. Charles Harford, *op. cit.*, pp. 25-26. As a boy, Logan Pearsall Smith was
present at the Broadlands Estate during the meetings. He says that Amanda
Smith, the well-known black woman holiness evangelist,took part in the meetings; Smith also notes that Dante Gabriel Rossetti may also have been there; he
painted some of his pictures and wrote some of his poems at Broadlands; Mrs.
Cowper-Temple, "the queen of Evangelicals," as Smith calls her, was the patron
of the Pre-Raphaelite school of artists; she was also the Egeria of Ruskin, who
describes his first seeing her in Rome in 1840 in his Praeterita; L. Smith, *Unforgotten Years*, pp. 55-56, 51, 46.

38. *Webster's Biographical Dictionary* (Springfield, MA: G. & C. Merriam Co.,
Publishers, 1943), p. 1100.

39. *Guide*, XXIII [New Series] (May 1875), 150; *ibid.* (June 1875), 184; *ibid.*
(August 1875), 56.

40. *Advocate of Christian Holiness*, V (November 1874), 113.

41. Evan Hopkins, "Preliminary Stages," Harford, *op. cit.*, p. 30. The ten-day
pattern of the American holiness camp meeting carried over in these meetings.

42. A full account of the proceedings is given in *Account of the Union Meeting
for the Promotion of Scriptural Holiness, Held at Oxford, Aug. 29 to Sept. 7, 1874*
(Chicago: Fleming H. Revell, 1875). For further current accounts of the Oxford
Convention, see: *The Christian Standard and Home Journal*, VIII (November 7,
1874), 353; *ibid.* Novmber 5, 1874), 385. *Advocate of Christian Holiness*, V (December
1874), 134-35; *ibid.* (November 1874), 113. The *Methodist Magazine*, XVII (1874),
992ff.

43. *Guide*, XXIV [New Series] (February 1876), 54. R. P. Smith; reported to a
Philadelphia preacher's meeting in December 1874 that when the suggestion was

made for the Oxford Meeting, one of those present had responded, "Yes, the very center of Ritualism is the place." *Christian Standard and Home Journal*, VIII (December 19, 1874), 405. Ritualism, a part of the Tractarian movement begun about 1833 to move the Anglican Church closer to Catholic creed, was the stage of that movement on the English church scene at the time of the holiness conventions. It sought to move the teachings of the Tractarians into the ritual or externals of the church; see Schaff-Herzog, *op. cit.*, X, 49-55. It too was a perfectionist movement of its own stripe. See Walter E. Houghton, *The Victorian Frame of Mind: 1830-1870* (New Haven, CT: Yale University Press, 1957), pp. 230-31. Thus the holiness movement crossed its path and touched base where some of its own initial impulses had been born in the "Holy Club" of the Wesleys and Whitefield in the preceding century. Another Oxford Movement more closely related to it than Ritualism was the later Buchmanite movement known as the "Moral Rearmament Movement." Scharpff, *op. cit.*, pp. 277-78, says that Buchman's movement was actually inspired by a visit to Keswick in 1908 and a spiritual experience he had there. Also see Sangster, *Methodism Can Be Born Again*, pp. 52-64 for the parallels between Methodist [and holiness] small-group patterns and practices and the Oxford Movement's.

44. *Advocate of Christian Holiness*, V (January 1875),163.

45. See Smith's account in the *Christian Standard and Home Journal*, VIII (December 19, 1874), 405. *Guide*, XXIII (January 1875), 24-25, and *Christian Advocate and Home Journal*, VIII (December 5, 1874), 389, give reports of continuing revival after the Oxford meetings.

46. For an account of the Free Churches in Europe at this time, see Schaff and Prime, *op. cit.*, pp. 76-77, 551. Monod's account of his religious experience, including his involvement in the Revival of 1858 while a law student in America, is given in "Seven Weeks of Trust," quoted from the *Pathway of Power* by the *Advocate of Christian Holiness*, V (December 1874), 139. His father was Dr. Fredrick Monod, a prominent French Free Church leader.

47. Methodist membership in Germany in 1874 was 7,022. See Paul F. Douglass, *The Story of German Methodism, Biography of an Immigrant Soul* (New York: Methodist Book Concern, 1939), p. 127; *ibid.*, chap. viii, gives the history of early Methodist missions in Germany beginning in 1850. This biography of Nast fails to recognize Nast's involvement in the National Camp Meeting Association. It was very significant for the movement, however, because through Nast's great personal influence and his extensive holiness writings, the revival's influences were consistently fed into the life of both German Methodism in America and in Germany as well as to the United Brethren and Evangelical Churches, both of which were German and Methodist-related. See *Advocate of Christian Holiness*, VI (June 1875), 17. A L. Drummond, *German Protestantism Since Luther* (London: The Epworth Press, 1951), contains summaries of the relation of Pietism, German Methodism, and R. P. Smith.

48. *Ibid.*

49. Hermann Krummacher, "Christian Life in Germany," Schaff and Prime, *op. cit.*, pp. 78-84.

50. August Tholuck, "Evangelical Theology in Germany," *ibid.*, pp. 85-89.

51. Smith's revivalism in Germany is summarized in: Fr. Winkler, "Robert Pearsall Smith und der Perfectionismus," *Friedrick D. Kropatscheck, Biblische Zeit-und Streitfragen zur Afklärung der Gebildeten,* Series ix (Berlin-Lichterfelde: Edwin Runge, 1914), pp. 401-22; *Advocate of Christian Holiness,* Vl (June,1875), 17-18. *Earnest Christianity,* I (July 1875), 444. Scharpff, *op. cit.,* pp. 220ff.

52. *Earnest Christianity,* I (July 1875). 444, quoting "a Berlin paper." Baedecker was known as the "German George Miller of Bristol." Scharpff, *op. cit.,* p. 222.

53. *Ibid.* Buchsel is reported to have said on the occasion, "Brethren, we have of late been throwing ourselves with all our force into politics—secular politics, ecclesiastical politics—but we have neglected the politics of the heart. Let us listen to our brother's voice and practice these."

54. *Ibid.* Scharpff, *op. cit.,* p. 216.

55. Gebhardt was one of the pioneer German Methodists, noted for his contributions to the music of the free church movement. See Douglass, *op. cit.,* pp. 120-21; Scharpff, *op. cit.,* pp. 204, 220-21. Scharpff himself was the son of German "holiness" Methodists; *ibid.,* ix. Also see H. Brandenburg, "Heiligungsbewegung," *Die Religion in Geschichte und Gegenwart. Handwörterbuch für Theologie und Religionswissenschaft* (Tübingen: J. C. B. Mohr, 1859), III, pp. 182ff. Hereafter referred to as *RGG.*

56. *Advocate of Christian Holiness,* VI (June 1875), 17-18; Douglass, *op. cit.,* p. 120. Winkler, *op. cit.,* p. 415.

57. Abdel R. Wentz, *Germany's Modern Pietistic Movement* (n.p., n.n., n.d.), is an excellent monograph on the movement which developed out of the holiness revival; see *ibid.,* p. 3: "…In the seventies there came across the Channel a second stream of influence [the first was the mid-century impulse] which united with the remaining legacy of the 17th and 18th century Pietism to bring about the modern Pietistic Movement." Scharpff calls it "The Pietist Fellowship Movement." Scharpff, *op. cit.,* pp. 170, 203, and *RGG,* II, 1366ff., also discuss the movement. Also, L.Tiesmeyer. "Was jederman von der christlichen Gemein-schafts-bewegung in Deutschland wissen muss," *RGG,* II, 1751ff. P. Fleisch, "Heiligungsbewegung," *ibid.* II, 975ff.; *ibid.,* V, 586. The same, *Die Moderne Gemeinschaftsbcwegung in Deutschland: ein Versuch dieselbe nach ihren Ursprung darzustellen und zu würdigen* (Leipzig: H. G. Wallman, 1903).

58. Wentz, *op. cit.,* p. 2. Winkler, *op. cit.,* p. 402.

59. *Ibid.,* p. 4. H Krummacher, "Christian Life in Germany," Schaff and Prime, *op. cit.,* p. 81, defines German "Inner Missions" as a society for combatting social evils—gambling, drinking, prostitution, Sabbath desecration—by direct social action. On Wichern, see Scharpff, *op. cit.,* pp. 207-208, 232-33; *RGG,* 11, 1367.

60. Wentz, *op cit.,* p. 4; Scharpff, *op. cit.,* pp. 224-26. *RGG, loc. cit.*

61. Wentz, *op. cit.,* pp. 4-5. Scharpff, *op. cit.,* p. 219. Otto Stockmayer and Carl Rappard, along with Jellinghaus, became the "theologischen Vertreter" of the movement, *RGG,* III, 182. For an article critical of the movement's claims, see D. Gennrich, *Wiedergeburt und Heiligung mit Berzug suf die gegenwärtigen Strömungun des religiösen Lebens* (Leipzig: A. Deichert, 1908).

62. Wentz, *op. cit.,* p. 6. Scharpff, *op. cit.,* pp. 233-34.

63. Wentz, *op. cit.*, p. 8. *RGG*, II, 1367.

64. See H. Brandenburg, "Heiligungsbewegung," *RGG*, III, 182ff. Paul Fleisch, "Pfingstbewegung," *RGG*, IV, 1153ff. Brandenburg says that "die Einseitigkeit der Heiligungsbewe-gung fürhte im extremen Flügel zur Pfingstwegung." Wentz, *op. cit.*, p. 2.

65. *Record of the Convention for the Promotion of Scriptural Holiness Held at Brighton, May 29 - June 7, 1875* (Brighton: W. J. Smith, n.d.), pp. 47, 319.

66. R. Smith wrote to J. Inskip from the Brighton meeting: "…The meeting was to Oxford, what Manheim was to Vineland…."; *Advocate of Christian Holiness*, VI (August 1875), 37. By this time the National Association had an agent in England publishing holiness tracts. See L. R. Dunn, *Holiness, What Is It?* (London: F. E. Longley, 1875); Longley was the agent.

67. *Guide*, XXII [New Series] (April 1875), 20.

68. *Ibid.*

69. *Earnest Christianity*, I [New Series] (June 1875), 282-83.

70. *Advocate of Christian Holiness*, V (May 1875), 284.

71. *Sunday School Times*, XVII (June 26, 1875), 413:"While Messers [*sic*] Moody and Sankey are gathering thousands in London to religious meetings, another American evangelist, Mr. R. Pearsall Smith has collected nearly as many thousands at Brighton." Other current reports maybe found in the *Guide* and the *Advocate of Christian Holiness* issues following the convention. Most other accounts are found in histories of the Keswick convention such as E. Hopkins, "Preliminary Stages"; Harford, *op. cit.*, pp. 32ff.; Sloan, *op. cit.*, pp. 18ff.; Barabas, *op. cit.*, pp, 23ff. ; Pollock, *op. cit.*

72. *Advocate of Christian Holiness*, V (August 1875), p 36; also quoted by *Sunday School Times*, *loc. cit.*; both are quoting unidentified English papers.

73. Smith claimed that this was the only phrase he knew in German at that time; Gebhardt picked it up as the theme of the gospel song. The *Guide*, XXIII (August 1875), p. 55, gives the English translation of this song which became the theme song of the European holiness movement. There were seven verses. The chorus read:

> "Jesus saves me now.
> Jesus saves me now
> Yes, Jesus saves me all the time—
> Jesus saves me now!"

Smith undoubtedly acquired this emphasis under the tutelage of John Inskip in the American movement. At the Landisville National Camp Meeting, at the close of the first meeting, Inskip said to the audience, "Wait, the Lord is going to save the people. Whisper it all around to one another, *'Jesus saves me now.'* Tell it all over the ground." (Emphasis mine.) Also see Scharpff, *op. cit.*, pp. 220-21. Winkler, *op. cit.*, p. 419, n. 1.

74. *Gospel Hymns Consolidated, Embracing Numbers 1, 2, 3, and ... for Use in Gospel Meetings and Other Religious Services* (Cincinnati, OH: The John Church

Co., 1883), p. 268. Also see *Brighton Convention Report*, p. 23; Pollock, *op. cit.*, p. 21. Harford, *op, cit.*, p. 28.

75. *Advocate of Christian Holiness*, VI (September 1875), 81-62.

76. *The Brighton Record*, p. 429.

77. As quoted by L. Smith, *Unforgotten Years*, pp. 59-60.

78. In a rather negative fashion, one of America's foremost historians has supported our thesis: *infra* p. 183.

79. *The Brighton Record*, p. 416.

80. *Ibid.*

81. *Ibid*, pp. 424-25.

82. Houghton, *op. cit.*, p. 10. This work is critical not only to this thesis, but to any effort to speak to the social currents of the Victorian Age, which Houghton generally defines as 1830-1870. His definition of 1870 as a critical point of transition is especially significant for our discussion of the revival. All of the Victorian trends intensified from that point on; *ibid.*, p. 14.

83. *Ibid.*, pp. 1-22.

84. *Ibid.*, p. xvi.

85. As quoted by *ibid.*, p. 287, from Matthew Arnold, *Last Essays on Church and Religion* (1877), p. 287.

86. Houghton, *op. cit.*, p. 62.

87. *Ibid.*, pp. 228, 405. See especially 228-39. Pierson, *op. cit.*, p. 15, notes that the successive waves of religious excitement created by the Puseyite, Oxford, Cambridge, evangelical, and Plymouth Brethren movements had left the second generation unsatisfied. "Their supposed religious standing and their lives of practical failure were in startling contrast."

88. *Ibid.*, pp. 402-403.

89. *Ibid.*, p. 49, as quoted from the *New Republic*, pp. 51, 227-28.

90. *Ibid.*, p. 87, n. 112, as quoted from Bertrand Russell, "A Free Man's Worship," *Selected Papers of Bertrand Russell* (New York, n.n., n.d.), pp. 11-12.

91. *Ibid.*, pp. 96-102.

92. *Memoir of T. D. Harford-Battersby: By Two of His Sons* (London: Seely and Co., 1890), p. 58.

93. *The Brighton Record*, p. 416.

94. *Ibid.*, p. 422.

95. *Ibid.*, p. 423.

96. *Ibid.*, p. 422.

97. Perry Miller, *The Life of the Mind in America from the Revolution to the Civil War* (New York: Harcourt, Brace and World, Inc., 1965), p. 93.

98. Canon Harford-Battersby's remarks to the members of the Evangelical Union for the Diocese of Carlisle a few weeks after the Oxford Convention in 1874 bear this out: "There was a difference. There was a definiteness of purpose at these meetings, and a directness of aim in the speakers....That purpose was...'the promotion of Scriptural holiness.' The aim of the speakers therefore was to bring about this result by an ordered scheme of teaching out of the Holy Scriptures...."; *Account of the Union Meeting...at Oxford*, pp. i-vii, as quoted from Barabas, *op. cit.*, pp.22-23.

99. *Advocate of Christian Holiness*, VI (September 1875), 70.

100. Warfield, *op. cit.*, I, 505-508.

101. Pollock, *op. cit.*, pp. 34-37. For an account of how the whole matter looked to his son, see L. Smith, *Unforgotten Years*, pp, 60-64.

102. L. Smith, *Philadelphia Quaker*, p. 31. Mrs. Smith observed that the camp "ought not to have been called a 'Convention for the promotion of holiness,' but a 'Convention for the promotion of Pearsall Smith.' " Also see the same, *Unforgotten Years*, pp. 66-69.

103. L. Smith, *Philadelphia Quaker*, p 31.

104. *Ibid*, p. 33.

105. *Ibid*, p. 32.

106. *Ibid, p. 34.* Her son, Logan Smith, says that "the experience confirmed in her the belief which she always fervently preached, namely, that religion should be an affair, not of the feelings, but of the will." L. Smith, *Philadelphia Quaker*, p. xiii.

107. *Ibid.*, p. xvi. Smith died in 1898, "unhappy, bitter, disappointed, his larger designs wrecked, although during the short period of his noticeable work his influence had been immense; nor did it perish with his unfortunate retirement." Hannah continued to take an active interest in the movement, answering the hundreds of letters which came to her annually requesting spiritual advice. She participated at times in the continuing Broadlands Conventions. The Smith's English home became a center for such friends of their children as Roger Fry, Bernard Berenson, R. C. Trevelyan, the Sidney Webbs and Bertrand Russell, whose first wife was Alys Smith, Pearsall and Hannah's daughter. Mrs. Smith died in 1911. Also see Strachey, *op. cit.*, p. 15, and L. Smith, *Unforgotten Years*, p. 72; Barabas, *op. cit.*, p. 27; Pollock, *op. cit.*, p. 36; *Guide*, XXIV (May 1876), 150; *Advocate of Christian Holiness*, VIII (May 1877), 14-15; *ibid.* (September 1877), 214-15. Boardman and Mahan continued their ministry; *Divine Life*, a magazine for the promotion of holiness edited jointly by Mahan and Asbury Lowrey, carried accounts. McDonald and Searles, *op. cit.*, p. 317.

108. Ford, *op. cit.*, pp. 29-30. See also *To the Uttermost: Commemorating the Diamond Jubilee of the Southport Methodist Holiness Convention, 1885-1945* (London: The Epworth Press, 1945). I. R. Govan, *Spirit Revival: Biography of J. G. Govan, Founder of Faith Mission* (London: The Faith Mission, 1938).

109. The latest official history of the movement is Pollock, *op. cit.* Also see R. Duane Thompson, *Keswick: Historical Origin and Doctrine of Holiness* (Marion, IN: n.n., 1963).

110. Harford, *op. cit.*, p. 62.

111. Pierson, *op. cit.*, p. 31; see *supra*, p. 115.

112. Robert Wilder was introduced to the holiness experience by a Salvation Army officer in Carlisle, England, in 1891 at the age of twenty-eight while on his way to Keswick. His contacts there led to the founding of the Student Volunteers in Scotland and Great Britain; Pollock, *op. cit.*, p. 112. A. J. Gordon gave the opening message to the First International Convention of the Student Volunteer Movement; see the same, "The Holy Spirit in Missions," *Report of the First Student*

Volunteer Movement for Foreign Missions Held at Cleveland, Ohio, U.S.A., February 26, 27, 28 and March 1, 1891 (Boston: T. O. Metcalf and Co., n.d.), pp. 7-20.

Chapter 5

A Tradition in Dilemma

The Revival in the Gilded Age

The year 1875, which had proven to be so significant for the expansion of the influence of the American holiness movement to both England and the Continent, also ushered in a dramatic period of change for both the American nation and the American churches. The very success of the revival efforts helped to produce increased tensions between the loosely organized holiness associations and the rapidly solidifying patterns of denominational bureaucracy. It was a critical period for the movement as well as a critical period for American religion in general.[1] Crucial forces were at work in every area and at every level of the nation's life. All of them had a share in shaping the future work of the holiness revival forces, now largely under the leadership of the National Camp Meeting Association.

The swift expansion of the economy, along with industrialization and the concomitant growth in the nation's wealth, merely helped to intensify those "backslidings" of the Methodist and other churches which had become one of the major concerns of the holiness reform movement. William Warren Sweet labels the increase in wealth, particularly from 1880 to the century's end, as "the most significant single influence in organized religion in the United States" during that time.[2] The Methodist Church through its rapidly increasing membership shared fully in the new wealth and the changes that it helped to produce within the churches.[3]

By 1875 the Methodists were swiftly becoming a middle-class church. They began to glory in the mass and beauty of their buildings, in their political influence in local communities as well as in national affairs, and in their status among other established churches in the religious community of the nation.[4] Bishop Matthew Simpson had been a close, wartime adviser of President Lincoln. At the celebration of the Centenary of American Methodism in 1866, the descendants of the church's pioneers in America rejoiced that they were now recognized as equals by the other large churches of the country.[5] In fact, the triumph of Arminianism and a renewing emphasis on Wesley's doctrine of perfection within American revivalism had put them in a place of leadership which they were not hesitant to acknowledge.[6]

A third factor which strongly influenced the patterns of development in the American churches during this era was the rapid growth of the cities.[7] The sources of the migration which fed this urban expansion were two-fold: the one involved masses of people coming from Europe to America; the other less dramatic, but just as important, involved the large numbers of people moving from America's rural areas to its urban centers. The latter movement is especially significant for the story of the development and institutionalization of the holiness movement. As Charles Jones has shown, it was this rural class which formed the backbone of the holiness churches and strongly shaped their institutional patterns.[8]

Only a few leaders in the churches at the time were really aware of the magnitude of the problem and what was happening in the religious communities within the expanding urban centers. Henry Ward Beecher expressed his concerns in 1874 when he noted that, in, "the average churches in New York and Brooklyn—from Murray Hill downward…it will be found that the aristocratic and prosperous elements have possession of them, and if the underclass, the poor and needy, go to them at all, they go sparsely, and not as to a home."[9]

Beecher was one of the few to note the trends so early in their development. And Beecher's New York was not unique. The situation was repeated in city after city in America. The gap between the city churches with their newfound wealth, their rented pews, their robed choirs, their professional musicians, their ritualistic worship, their elaborate architecture, and the revivalistically oriented simple worship patterns and the atmosphere of the country family church was not effectively bridged. Abell says that, "even the Baptist and Methodist faiths, once religions of the poor, now displayed almost frantic solicitude for the spiritual welfare of the rich."[10]

The Methodists, among these rural immigrants, probably felt these differences most keenly, for more than in any other church, during this period, the city churches of that denomination accelerated their turn to liturgical patterns.[11] These tendencies showed up even more starkly than they might have in some other communions because of their direct contrast with former patterns of Methodist induced freedom of expression, personal involvement, and even enthusiasm. Worship in the established city churches seemed to be no part of the religion the new city dweller had previously known; the name on the church and the Discipline were the same, but little else made him feel at home.[12]

A fourth factor at work in the growing alienation between any individual church members and the middle class churches was the type of minister that the newly founded seminaries of the church were supplying in increasing numbers. In these schools, the younger faculty members who knew little of Wesley, began to wrestle with the problems raised by their theological education. Consequently, the "holiness question," which had agitated the church for nearly a hundred years, was often sloughed off as an irrelevant irritant among much more interesting and important issues. This tendency merely served to strengthen the conviction of the advocates of the revival that new and foreign elements were threatening original Wesleyanism within Methodism. This tension fed the revival movements within that church as well as other churches where German theology began to make its influences felt in the schools and consequently in the ministry.[13]

A fifth factor, one which has commonly been overlooked in assessing the changing Methodist reaction to the holiness movement during this period, was the influx of an unusually large number of new men into the total ministerial force of the church. Bishop Matthew Simpson observed in 1875 that more than one-third of the total number of Methodist ministers then serving the church had had less than ten years of experience.[14] The postwar expansion of the church, much of it due to revivalism itself, had demanded an immediate increase in the pastoral supply. Many of those new men were neither indoctrinated in, nor interested in, the issues which entered into the holiness controversy. Furthermore, the dynamic growth situation undoubtedly vaulted many of them into positions of influence in all levels of the church's structure much earlier than would have been so under more normal growth patterns. The infusion of these new leaders was hardly favorable to the puritan-pietist orientation of the reforming movement.

The usual membership growth of the revival churches, particularly of the Methodist Episcopal Church, during the postwar years was a sixth factor that contributed to the developing differences between the denominations and the revival forces. The very fact of the success of the general revival efforts, the holiness revival among them, helped to create a crisis of discipline in the churches. The enrollment of thousands of new converts in the churches' ranks helped to overwhelm the regular patterns of Christian discipline and instruction. Many of the new members were sincerely seeking to become mature Christians; on the other hand, many were probably joining out of varying peer pressures.[15] They had little appreciation for the traditional puritan-pietistic ethic and standards of the Christian life which Methodism had commonly emphasized in its class meetings and *Discipline.*

There was a concurrent, gradual relaxation of the prohibitions against worldly amusements, fine dress, dancing, etc.; revivalists had consistently inveighed against such involvements as totally incompatible with sincere Christian commitment. In the holiness advocate's mind, the "worldly" lives of thousands of church members who were enjoying the social position which their growing wealth brought them bore faint resemblance to the lifestyle of Bunyan's "Pilgrim," Wesley's "Methodist," or the revivalist's "seeker after holiness."[16] The roots of the protest went deep into the experiential tradition. Furthermore, the developing breakdown of the class meeting in Methodism laid that church open, particularly, to the appeal of newly developed small groups who offered the fellowship, discipline, and instruction which were characteristic of that unique Wesleyan institution. The purposes and values of the class meeting in the Methodist structure were manifold. Bishop Simpson regarded these weekly meetings as centers which uniquely incited Methodists to "higher Christian experience," accustomed them to "religious conversation and labor," developed "earnest and active Christian workers," brought young Christians into intimate dialogue with more mature Christians, created "bonds of union" within the church, personally involved every member in Christian life, offered forums for the discussion of special topics, and sought the overall goal of the cultivation of a "more vigorous type of Christian piety."[17]

At the same time—1875—the Bishop had to admit to all the world that regular attendance by the membership of Methodist Episcopal Churches at this type of meeting was no longer as common as it should be. In 1866, unable to salvage its former patterns out of the ravages of the war, the Methodist Episcopal Church South had already done away with the mandatory requirements for class meetings attendance among its members.[18] In the northern church, required attendance continued until early in the twentieth century, but as indicated in Bishop Simpson's remarks, its place in Methodism after the war continually waned.

The relationship between the fortunes of this institution and holiness revivalism's reform concerns for the life of the church were clearly shown in some comments by Nathan Bangs on the class meeting during the Revival of 1858. In an article in the *Christian Advocate*, Bangs responded sharply to the charges of some within the Methodist Church that the stringent requirements of the class meeting were denying the church its full share of the thousands of converts of the revival who were seeking a permanent church home. The pressure to relax the rules under such a pretext, he noted, merely indicated that many of the "converts" who had purportedly refused to join the Methodist Church out of their hesitancy to participate in the spiritual exercises of the class meeting were probably not really converted and should not be taken into the church in any case.[19]

If one adds to this, Franklin Littell's judgment that, "of the various institutions John Wesley introduced to plant and cultivate a living faith, none was so representative of his view of the Christian life as the class meetings, and none was more characteristic of Methodism through the generations."[20] one can understand why those holiness elements in the church that claimed to be calling the church back to true Wesleyanism looked with dismay upon the declining influence of these "schools of holiness" within that body. In a parallel development, the position of the class leader, with his responsibility for the spiritual life on the members under the pastor was lessening, and the power of the trustee, who frequently represented the influences of the new social and economic forces at work in the local churches, was increasing; it did not give supporters of the class meeting any encouragement.[21]

A final factor which played an obvious role in the religious crisis of these decades, or one might more properly say showed the extent and nature of the crisis, was the alienation of significant portions of the population from the established patterns of orthodox Christian religion as demonstrated by the cults which rose around the same time. In 1873, Russellism broke upon the American religious scene; in 1875, Helena P. Blavatsky organized her first Theosophical Society in New York City; and in the same year, Mary Baker Eddy was organizing her first Christian Science churches. One cannot divorce the reality of the fractured religious and social milieu which provided fertile soil for these cultic movements from the pressures that were at work in the total religious context of the developing holiness movement. It was obviously a time of great religious dissatisfaction and unrest, and, obviously as well, a time for new movements.

Wittingly or unwittingly caught up by such tensions, it seemed to the holiness advocates that nothing but a revival of Christian holiness, especially among the ministry, could stem the tide of undisciplined worldliness which was sweeping the church or save it from the onslaught of forces such as German "higher criticism" and British "Darwinian evolutionism," both of which they insisted threatened their basic biblical assumptions. Church fairs, dances, drunkenness, Sabbath-breaking, card-playing, and other practices which were a part of popular Christianity, they claimed, could only be remedied by firm Christian discipline based in a total commitment of all concerned to the final authority of God's will and Word alone.[22]

THE NATIONAL ASSOCIATION IN TENSION WITH METHODISM

Within this cultural complex, the increasing tempo of the revivalism of John Inskip and his associates in the work of the National Camp Meeting Association for the Promotion of Holiness greatly increased the potential for confrontation that had existed within the movement and Methodism from the Palmers' earliest efforts in the special promotion of the experience. The ability of Inskip and his cohorts to raise a strong voice against the tendencies to compromise which they believed they discerned in the church and yet to maintain themselves in the general good graces of many of its most influential leaders is a testimony both to their own leadership and the basic integrity of their claims concerning the state of Methodism itself. In 1872, the *Zion's Herald*, a periodical generally sympathetic to the movement, had recognized that Inskip and McDonald had done an admirable job of "holding the horses." The paper warned that continuing opposition to the movement was unreasonable and that unless its opponents relented, schism would be the inevitable consequence.[23]

Conciliatory counsel such as that, however, did not deter continued opposition to the movement by others who were less enthusiastic for the special efforts to generate holiness reform in the church than the *Herald* was. In the mid-seventies, at the height of the National Association's effectiveness, an attack upon Inskip and the National Committee's publishing interests appeared in the New York *Christian Advocate*, the most prestigious voice in Methodism.[24] The paper charged that a $10,000 holiness tract fund, for which Inskip was currently making an appeal, was really an attempt to secure funds that could be used to rescue the Association from its financial difficulties. The article represents a concise picture of the polity questions which were really predominant in the minds of many of those who eventually forced large segments of the holiness element within Methodism to leave the church and sometimes become its bitter critics. The article noted: "When this new publishing movement started we chronicled it as a scheme fraught with methods if not purposes, directly hostile to the connectional interests of the Church."

It saw in this latest venture the verification of that prophecy, and that no sooner than had been anticipated. The writer charged further that,

> under the profession of Holiness—a doctrine justly precious to our people—a few men whose ministerial influence and position have been acquired under our itinerant system...have first, organized themselves into an association to choose their own time and place of service, and, next, have set themselves to the task of establishing a publishing system institution not recognized in our economy, but claiming the support of our pastors and people.

All of this represented a presence within the Church of "an irresponsible agency, the outcome of which will be another and mischievous secession."[25]

The closing prediction of potential schism over issues raised by the holiness question in these, the two oldest periodicals of the Methodist Episcopal Church, within a few years of each other, struck an ominous note for the future—the one predicted schism because of the way the movement was relating to the church and the other predicted the same because of the way some in the church were relating to the movement. This indicated that the problems which continued to arise within Methodism over the holiness revival were due not alone to doctrinal differences, but also to organizational tensions created by what many Methodists considered to be the irregularity of the National Committee's place within the church structure. The leaders of the National Association realized this. At every opportunity they publicized any activities of ecclesiastical leaders in the National Camps or any favorable comments by voices that were respected in the church on the movement or its concern for holiness.[26] These were commonly at hand.

In 1872, Luke Tyerman, the English Methodist biographer of Wesley, wrote to a friend:

> I shall be *specially* thankful if [the revival] helps to revive the glorious old Methodist doctrine of Christian Perfection, a doctrine of late years disastrously neglected but which is now...obtaining more attention in the country [England] than it has done for more than the last twenty years....All who are acquainted with Methodist history are well aware that Methodism has always prospered most when the doctrine of entire sanctification has been most popular [emphasis his].[27]

In the fall of 1879, Bishop William L. Harris of the Methodist Episcopal Church joined Asbury Lowrey, Asa Mahan, and Daniel Steele—all holiness leaders—in the publication of an "Address" which called for a revival of holiness among the ministers of all denominations. The next spring, a similar appeal to all Christian laypersons appeared over the same signatures.[28] Statements at the Centenary Conference of 1884, just subsequent to Inskip's death at Ocean Grove, New Jersey, in March of that year, would have assured the leader of the movement again that the "inner leadings" which had "warmed" his heart at the thought of the first holiness camp meeting at Vineland, New Jersey, had definitely been in the "Divine will." Bishop Merrill, elected in 1872, along with Harris and other bishops favorable to holiness, declared in the pastoral address at the hundredth anniversary of the organization of the church in America:

> Take from Methodism these doctrines of experience...or even the emphasis given them or overlay them with lifeless forms and ceremonies, or mar them by even human speculations concerning the mode of divine procedure in them, or confuse them by any conceivable departure from their simplicity so that they will only become doctrines in the creed, unverified in the soul as the very essence of salvation...and the glory is departed forever.[29]

The bishop was ringing the changes of all the concerns of the holiness advocates in the church. The threats to the promotion of the doctrine and the "glory" of the church, which he voiced, had been part of the perfectionist revival's warnings to the church since the beginnings of the movement in the thirties.[30]

The bishop, in the same address, continued with the statement that, "the mission of Methodism is to promote holiness," and that "this end and aim enters into all our organic life...[and] in all the borders of Methodism the doctrine is preached and the experience of sanctification is urged."[31] His statement contained contradictory implications for the future of the movement in the church. On the one hand, he clearly declared the progress of the movement in awakening the church to its holiness mission; on the other hand, he may have been indicating that the regular organizations of the church were now adequate to carry on the promotion of that mission. The proponents realized that in spite of the revival influence which everyone in the church recognized, either by approbation or opposition, the battle was still far from over.

This would not have been so if the movement had been moving on some kind of false premise that the church could have readily dismissed, but it was not. Methodists everywhere in the church, from the Board of Bishops on down to the laity of the local churches, some of them not sympathetic to the holiness forces, still had a haunting fear that all was not well. Bishop R. S. Foster's concern expressed also on the occasion of the Methodist centennial, was not atypical. Noting the numerous dangers that faced Methodism in its centenary year, he said that they could all be summed up in the one danger of a "fashionable church." "That there should be signs of it in a hundred years from 'sail loft' [seemed]...almost the miracle of history."[32]

Such expressions only served to confirm the fears of holiness reformers, The movement increasingly presented itself as the one last antidote which could counteract the poison that the bishop sensed within Methodism's veins. The appeal was a strong one, so strong that thousands left the church when it seemed to reject the revival, while other thousands continued the battle within the church, believing that the holiness cause would be lost in all of Protestantism if it were lost in Methodism.[33]

THE RISE OF NEW HOLINESS ASSOCIATIONS

Contentions concerning the adequacy of the promotion of holiness through regular means were hardly allowed by these Methodists across the country who were organizing new associations for holiness evangelism. Inspired by the successes of the National Association, similar associations sprang up everywhere after 1870.[34] The leaders of the national organization were hard put to cope with these new elements in the movement. After the second National Camp at Manheim in 1868, they had brought their organization as tightly under the Methodist organization as the structures allowed. The result was that they had become so Methodist oriented that they had been able to maintain a relatively acceptable position within the church. At the same time, however, their ability to relate to the broader movement as it was developing outside of Methodism, was restricted to a proportionate degree.[35]

Many of the new holiness organizations were very loosely associated bands that cooperated around their common interest in promoting entire sanctification. The band concept may have had its roots in two traditions. In the degree in which they were Methodistic, they were related to the bands that Wesley had organized in his societies in England. Their major root, however, probably lay in the religious bands of the frontier. In sparsely settled communities where there were not enough members of any one denomination to formally organize local churches, the band provided a means by which a heterogeneous group of Christians could gather together for a common religious purpose without relinquishing their regular denominational loyalties; there was little need for either requirements of membership or discipline.[36] In many ways the Church of God concept of church order was merely a step away from this elemental concept of Christian fellowship.[37]

The lack of discipline often evident among these lightly organized indiscriminate groups of holiness zealots provided ample ammunition for those who wanted to drive their fears concerning extremism within the movement to their "logical" ends. The movement recognized the problem. An article in the *Good Way*, one of the prominent voices of the Missouri holiness movement, attacked extremists who, it claimed, had surfaced in some fringe elements there. Some taught that "they should not sleep upon beds, but make their couch on the ground...eat crackers out of the dirt...or go without food." The author claimed to have observed another, who to demonstrate her humility, was "led" to "not eat at the table with the unsanctified, not to visit her neighbors who...[did] not profess sanctification,"[38]

What was read as fanaticism, however, was not always that. After a holiness meeting in a Missouri Methodist church, the opposition took the pulpit and referred to the holiness evangelists as "a troupe of traveling gypsies, tramps, wild fanatics, and vagabonds...guilty of all kinds of crime known to human depravity."[39]

The band was led by J. W. Caughlan, a Methodist Episcopal minister, A. M. Kiergan, a minister of the Methodist Episcopal Church South, and Harry May, a Free Methodist minister. All were active in the Southwestern Holiness Association. The affiliation of two of these men with competitive denominations may have added to the severe observations made by the Methodist pastor who was suspicious of the "gypsy band." This same Methodist minister[40] had objected to his conference passing on the character of the Rev. M. C. Robb, because he had "gone off with that gypsy band...that are working against the church." Defenders of Robb pointed out to the conference that at the Des Plaines Camp of the National Camp Meeting Association, Dr. C. H. Fowler, president of Northwestern University and Dr. Raymond, head of Garrett Biblical Institute, had been first to respond to the holiness evangelists' appeals and they had been followed by hundreds "who had pioneered the west for Methodism."[41] To such differences in evaluation, the same reply may have been given which Dr. John Wesley Redfield used to respond to charges of excesses at the St. Charles, Illinois, camp meeting in 1860: there was "full as much mercy," he thought, "for those who served God a little too hard as for those who did not serve him at all."[42]

Such tolerant judgment, however, could hardly be applied to the early Texas holiness movement. In searching out the beginnings of the holiness groups which preceded the rise of portions of the Church of the Nazarene there in the late years of the nineteenth century, Smith concluded that Hardin Wallace, one of the men most active in organizing holiness associations in the west in the early days of the movement, "accepted the ministry of preachers whom neither God nor man, seemingly, had ordained."[43] Such extreme positions as "salvation from sin is salvation from death," that "demons are God's servants sent into men to discipline them," and that holiness included "marital continence" so plagued the first association formed there that the regular Methodist ministry organized a competing association to save the cause from complete disruption.[44]

When one observes the lack of definitive organizational discipline among loosely related individuals who felt more loyalty to the promotion of an experience of entire sanctification than they did to any particular denomination, the marvel is probably not that there was fanaticism in evidence, but rather, that it was not more extensive. This tendency toward radicalism expedited the development of more effective holiness organizations; the majority of the advocates of the doctrine realized that otherwise the cause would suffer more severely at the hands of its professed friends than it would at the hands of its opponents.

THE EARLY GENERAL HOLINESS CONVENTIONS

The Holiness Conventions of 1877

The rapid growth of the holiness movement in the West, as indicated by the organization of area associations and the vigorous opposition which its frontier components generated, was brought to the public attention of the eastern movement in the June 2, 1877 issue of the *Christian Standard and Home Journal*, in which Inskip printed a report of the Illinois work. It referred the publication of the *Banner*, a paper of the Western Holiness Association in Illinois, edited by John P. Brooks.[45] The *Christian Standard* suggested that closer communications between the various elements of the movement were desirable.

In the same issue, Inskip put out initial feelers, seeking reaction to a proposal of Thomas Doty, editor of the Cleveland, Ohio, *Christian Harvester*, for a general holiness convention to be held at Urbana, Ohio in October 1877.

Inskip endorsed the idea, but felt that it should be enlarged into "something rather more general and comprehensive ... a regular holiness conference embracing the whole country." The purposes and nature of such a meeting as shown in the exchanges of the men involved in the planning, reveal several significant things about this very primitive stage of organizational development; the diversity of the movement was already showing; the men in the west generally favored the name "convention" for the meeting, the eastern leaders generally favored "conference." Inskip felt that "conference" was "more in harmony with our denominational phraseology...and would be better understood...by our people."[46] The fact that Inskip thought first in the terms of the church and "our people," the Methodist people, was indicative of a prevailing attitude among the old eastern National Committee leadership; such priorities were already meeting increasing opposition from the western movements led by men less closely related to the church either by their knowledge of its leaders and history or by favorable experience.

The final decision was to use the word "conference" for the meetings in spite of western usage and the protest of the Rev. John A. Woods, one of the instigators of the holiness camp meeting idea, that to call it a "Holiness Conference" might "stir up the old *mad dog, humbug* cry again, 'you will divide the church, and this thing will lead to a new church organization.'"[47]

Doty's expressed aversion to the growing importance of trustee boards in the Methodist Church surfaced during the course of the planning for the convention. It demonstrates the fear of ecclesiasticism felt by many in the western movement. Doty warned that the more wealthy members of the congregation tended to dominate the membership of these boards. He charged that their secular interests tended to favor liberal goals and dilute the traditional power of the class-leader and other lay spiritual directors of congregational life. "Let us keep this out of the present movement, and out of the whole holiness movement..."[48] Doty urged Inskip.

Doty's correspondence to the editor of the *Christian Standard* also carried another theme which became typical of succeeding national conventions, and indeed, of many segments of the later movement—a plea for an open and unstructured convention. He said, "And while you provide something in the line of progress, please do not go largely into that. Give scope to the Holy Ghost, at the time and place of meeting, and, through messages that he shall then and there call out."[49]

This demand for nonstructured meetings represented a degree of anti-ecclesiasticism and political fear of yielding too much directive leadership to any single segment of the fluid movement; but beyond that, as the quote above indicates, it had a theological base in the very spiritual nature of the doctrine of the movement that taught that in everything the Holy Spirit must give leadership and whatever ritual of preplanned program there was, everyone must be ready to yield to the program of the Spirit. The freedom on the camp meeting reinforced this theology and placed its heavy imprint upon the movement. Its extremes were to show up in the Church of God (Anderson, Indiana) and the Holiness Church of California.[50]

In the services of most of the holiness churches, this extreme did not become the pattern, but there has been a general concern for "the mind of the Spirit" in all services so that at any time human designs might be set aside for what the Lord was telling someone to do, whether it be the minister or a layperson in the pew. To the ritualist, the results would frequently have represented chaos, and in some cases it may have been that, through abuse of this openness; nevertheless, it had the advantage of every open situation in intercommunication between individuals. There apparently was a development of personal fulfillment and community fulfillment in a fellowship in worship that would be the envy of those today who seek to emphasize the concept of the church as the people of God and encourage the individual priesthood of the believer. It grew out of the insistence in holiness preaching for sensitivity to the leadership of the Holy Spirit in the individual's life or the church's life. It was an attempt to create worship on the "Pentecostal" or "Holy Ghost line," phrases commonly used by the members of the movement as they sought to extrapolate holiness experience into a system of faith and order.

The anticipated hopes for the usefulness of such a convention also illustrate conditions which enveloped the movement ten years after Vineland. J. P. Brooks felt that "the prime business of the conference should be...to secure...a unification or, at least, an assimilation of all holiness agencies and plans, with a view to the more harmonious and more successful prosecution of our great holiness work."[51]

This same note ran through the suggestions of Inskip and others. This desire for a united front in the promotion of holiness evangelism became a fervent search for unity and order which lay at the heart of each of the succeeding conventions. It was never fully achieved within that context. Order finally was to come only with sect formation and other institutionalization of the movement.[52]

Inskip suggested further that the proposed conference could be of immense value as an occasion for the holiness workers scattered across the nation to "compare notes" and "communicate" with one another, to learn the condition of the work and "determine upon the best measures to promote it."[53] Certain of the validity of the revival movement in the church of its day, but themselves, unstructured, disorganized, and uncertain about the next or proper moves, the proponents of the revival were already setting patterns, just ten years after Vineland, by which the revival would institutionalize itself for its own perpetuation.

The proposed holiness "conference" finally became two holiness "conferences," the one held at Cincinnati, Ohio, beginning November 26, 1877, and the other held at New York City, beginning December 17, 1877.[54] Apparently, some planning went into the conferences in spite of the fears that they would be overstructured. The records of the proceedings contain prewritten addresses by a number of men who were prominent in the movement at that time. Dr. William Nast of the German Methodist Conferences in America reported on the German and European holiness work: J. E. Searles, one of the early historians of the movement, gave a brief historical sketch of the holiness revival and the origins of the National Camp Meeting Association for the Promotion of Holiness; C. W. Ketchum, the presiding elder of the West Cincinnati District of the Methodist Episcopal Church, read a paper prepared by C. A. Van Anda, then a Methodist pastor at Rochester, New York.[55]

The Significance of the Conventions: The Address of J. P. Brooks

Two of the most significant implications of these first conferences are found in a speech given by J. P. Brooks, entitled, "What are the Chief Hindrances to the Progress of the Work of Sanctification Among Believers."[56] Brooks concluded that the hindrances to the movement were both external and internal. The western editor's comments on exterior obstacles were not designed to encourage unity in the movement. He observed that, in his opinion, the holiness message was too closely tied to Methodism and, therefore, too restricted. This observation cut sharply across the strong Methodist orientation of most of the leaders of the original movement. Brooks claimed that this sectarian emphasis was restricting the acceptance which the truth deserved; other denominations, he claimed, were rejecting it, sight unseen, as merely an effort to expand Methodism's borders through an irregular, but very Methodistic organization. Brooks went on to note that this suspicion was not a particularity of the denominations themselves, but rather a particularity of the sectarian spirit itself, which, he said, tends to be "ever wary and suspicious."[57] This indicated that Brooks' ideas concerning the nature of the church, as an open fellowship in the "Church of God' concept, already were being shaped by his theology of holiness and his dedication to its promotion. Sects, by their very nature as sects, were a hindrance to the spread of the doctrine; nonsectarianism and the Church of God concept of church order were a natural consequence.

Brooks allowed that it was "lawful" for the Methodists to reinforce the authority of the doctrine as it was propagated in the Methodist Church, by referring to it as a Methodist doctrine. But he questioned the "expediency" of the approach even in Methodism:

> it would seem wise...to hold forth and enforce holiness as an altogether Catholic doctrine—Catholic because belonging in the sense of property to no one sect, but to all Catholic, because coming to the people of God more from the general Gospel than from the catechism, more from the Bible than from the *Discipline.*

This catholic approach, he claimed, would provide the truth "a more general welcome and cordial acceptance." It would produce a "general holiness movement."[58]

In this appeal for a broader movement, Brooks had laid down the gauntlet for a contest within the movement to successfully incorporate into the American movement non-Methodist people and the non-Methodist concepts which they often brought with them. This, by its very nature, demanded a greater nonsectarian emphasis on the part of the older National Camp Meeting Association leaders at the very moment when they were coming under increasing criticism for participating in an organization whose very existence was threatened in its Methodist home.

The threat to the movement's future relationship with Methodism was even more strongly intimated in a further observation of Brooks on the situation the movement faced in "wordly-minded" churches:

> So long as there remains in the churches this unrighteousness and darkness, and so long as carnal counsels prevail in and rule over the churches, so long will the doctrine of holiness be held aloof, and so long will its witness be discountenanced and proscribed.[59]

The approaching polarization of positions, both in significant portions of the Methodist Church and in the new revival forces, shows even more starkly in the aggressive position Brooks took toward the work of the evangelist. Holiness reform, he said, required:

> open and unrestricted access to peoples and places. Such access it has not had in the past; it has not in the present. That it may

have, hereafter, will depend much upon the spirit of its champi-
ons,—upon the *wisdom* and the *courage* shown...on the part of
those who have been divinely commissioned for its advocacy"
[emphasis his].

The question of access, he continued, was of "immense moment."
The opposition to the work must not in any degree deter those who
"come under solemn vows to God in the guidance of this great reform."
He maintained that there was given to the evangelists of the movement
a

divine prerogative of *making access*, where it is not. Where entrance into new fields can be gotten without asking it ought to be
taken. When entrance can only be gotten *by the asking* it ought to
be asked. Where entrance *has* not been secured and *cannot* for the
asking then should entrance be procured anyhow, independent
of all considerations and all conditions but the command of God
[emphasis his].[60]

The appeal of this "divine prerogative" became the rationale for
the holiness evangelists in the churches for the next twenty-five years.
Without such aggressiveness the movement would never have moved
beyond Methodism, nor would there have been much promise of a
future in Methodism. This aggressiveness was demonstrated in varying
degrees of intensity, depending upon the temper and perspective of the
individual evangelist. It created tensions between established pastors
and holiness evangelists that sparked much of the controversy of this
period. It appears in this developing history that as long as the holiness
movement largely restricted its evangelism to those people who were
willing to come to their special camps and the communities which
opened up their churches, generally Methodist, to them, the antagonism between the movement and the large mass of Methodist pastors,
to whom the movement was suspect, was kept at a tolerable level; but
when the free-ranging evangelists of the early band organizations
began to insist that the holiness message had a right to be heard by
everyone, and sought access to every community whether invited or
not, a new element of intensity and finality entered the conflict that had
always prevailed. Here were nineteenth century overtones of the ancient struggle in the early church between the prophets, who felt they
were Spirit-commissioned, and the bishops of established churches
who sought to bring order to the Christian community. It was a question
of how much openness a structure was able to tolerate, how many free

agents it could assimilate. The ancient prophet, because of the lack of recourse within the social and religious structure of the Constantinian Age, generally had to yield to the established order.[61] In the America of the latter nineteenth century, the separation of church and state, and voluntary church membership opened up other alternatives to him. Brooks' speech demonstrated that he knew this.

The intensifying presence of holiness proponents in the local congregations made the holiness question an ever-widening issue, one which every pastor had to face, not only for his congregation, but for himself as well. When he had been ordained to the Methodist ministry, he had promised to go on to perfection; now the holiness movement challenged him to perform his vows for his own soul's sake and the sake of the church. Many men were not prepared to accept these alternatives; their opposition combined with the negativeness of those in the church who were believers in the Wesleyan doctrine of Christian perfection, but who were not ready to allow any threat to the church's institutional life from special instruments for its promotion, hastened the ultimate rejection by the church of these elements in the movement who felt that their holiness witness was being repressed and that the institution's whole set of mind was irrevocably against them.

The third major element of Brooks' address to the 1877 Convention was the recognition of hindrances to the work which were generated by weaknesses in the movement itself. He listed six of these; with the possible exception of number four, they continued to show themselves again and again in the future:

(1) Imperfect teaching....Every possessor of holiness is a competent and qualified witness—but not necessarily a competent and qualified teacher...Public teaching...by those who possess no natural or gracious aptness as instructors...whose teachings must hence be crude and imperfect, perhaps essentially incorrect, [makes] the cause to suffer....

(2) Unthorough experiences....[Because of some people who are] regarded by the Church and the world as being representatives of holiness, while their lives are inconsistent and unholy, holiness stands compromised and loses influence....

(3) A form of holiness that is unaggressive and inert....The Church and community where such people live are impressed that holiness is a spiritless, forceless thing that has no inspiration of active well-doing in it....

(4) Unedifying and misleading testimonies....Some say—"I am not tempted"—"I cannot sin"—"I am infallibly saved, I *cannot*

fall." All these testimonies are untrue, misleading and mischievous....

(5) A temptation to Church unaffiliation.

(6) Excessive and extravagant experiences. (Extremes such as those listed above.)[62]

The Weaknesses of the General Conventions

If these first general holiness conventions demonstrated that the movement had a critical self-awareness of the difficulties it had to face both externally and internally, they also proved that the fears of these dangers were not sufficiently grave to force the already diverse elements within its borders to unite under one organizational framework. A committee appointed by the conference chairman, John Inskip, at the request of the Cincinnati Conference, which was "to take into consideration the subject of combining in some way, in harmonious action, the various organizations interested in the holiness movement...." could come to no other conclusion than to report the anticipated activities and plans of the various groups represented in the conference.[63] Failure at this critical point in this first effort at national unity, foretold similar lack of success in such efforts in 1880 at Jacksonville, in 1882 at Round Lake and at Chicago in 1885 and 1901.

This inability to come to joint decisions for future action, not only delayed the search for unity and order, but generally weakened the positive significance of these several general meetings held during these formative transitional years. The conventions listed above undoubtedly played a vital informal role in providing a continuing fellowship and a channel of direct communication between leaders of the movement which no other instrument could provide at that time. They also provided a forum that kept critical issues to the fore. But they were never legislative bodies and their committees, at best, were *ad hoc* groups, whose influence and vitality inevitably died with the convention which created them. In no case was the committee commonly appointed at each of the conventions to call another convention ever officially responsible for such. Each effort was a child of the pressures of the movement, even though the involvement of the same individuals provided considerable historical and organizational continuity.

By conscious design, the meetings were to be in the pattern in which the movement felt most at home; the unstructured atmosphere of the holiness camp prevailed. Prayer, preaching, inspiration were considered more important than human organization. The Holy Spirit would lead in bringing about what was best for the furtherance of God's work at this high level of national organization. The same men who often worked arduously for organization and discipline at other levels, by resigning all activism to the Holy Spirit at this level, were admitting that the diversity in the movement could be reconciled only in this way. Outside of a common dedication to holiness, the movement was seething with too many variant factors in other areas to allow for a more definite organization.[64]

It was genuinely a movement, and its composition was complex. There were Methodists and others, thoroughly committed to the doctrine, yet just as thoroughly committed to complete loyalty to their own sect; these hoped to work from within their organizations to call, what they regarded as increasingly worldly churches, back to Christian purity and power. There were also Methodists and others who were rapidly being driven to the conclusion that the "old bottles" were not pliable enough to tolerate their vital experience; some of these had already begun to lead the exodus from the old sects. Out of the pure necessities of fellowship and order, they created the primitive organizations which broke the trail for the many thousands who eventually followed them out of the established denominations, either out of force of ecclesiastical pressures, or out of individual desire. There was also a third group involved who were members of established holiness sects such as the Wesleyan Methodist Connection and the Free Methodist Church. The latter church was especially active within the movement during these fluid years; it was young and aggressive and dedicated to a very radical standard of holiness and life. The former, although equally committed by its doctrines to the cause of Christian perfection during most of the nineteenth century, was more interested in social reform than in evangelism. Its organization was very loose; the denominational pattern was not conducive to any concerted appeal to the converts of the revival outside of its own gates.

The fourth group, a group only in the sense of a classification of those who shared a common religious condition, were the unchurched who had been converted to the cause. Their only religious attachment was frequently to the holiness evangelist who held the protracted meeting in the schoolhouse, town hall, barn, or tent where they received their religious experience. The tension between the evangelist and the local pastors frequently legislated against his referring them to the local church where he, himself, may have been denied place or support for his holiness meetings.

The evangelist was usually committed to moving on to the next center of revival or back to his secular or religious work through which he supported himself. He could not stay. It was the plight of these refugee converts that made the conscientious evangelist feel that he was continually leaving behind him a trail of religious orphans without adequate means for fellowship and proper nurture; this constituted one of the most influential rationales for the organization of holiness churches.[65] These unchurched converts, in combination with the evangelist, who was usually supported by holiness sympathizers in some organized church body, provided the combination for hundreds of holiness groups which developed by the end of the century; they eventually turned away from the churches to their own fellowships "on the holiness line." This grass roots, localized origin of so much of the movement provided the most common cause for the diversity displayed throughout the movement's subsequent history; it also accounts for the difficulty in ordering its forces in a more consistent pattern.

By 1877, a tradition which had aroused a renewed interest in Christian holiness within all Christian churches by means of a specialized meeting for its promotion, a specialized theology for its attainment, a specialized terminology for its expression, a specialized journal for its propagation, and a specialized organization of evangelists for its leadership, was now ready for the ultimate step in this organized promotion of the doctrine of Christian holiness—the organization of specialized holiness churches. In the world of 1877, only a few men like J. P. Brooks were ready to openly admit that the next step in the promotion of holiness might involve such drastic measures. The straw man, often created by the opponents of the special methods for polemical purposes—separatism—was about to come to life.

SUMMARY

As the holiness revival, at the peak of its worldwide influence in 1875, moved on into the last quarter of the nineteenth century, it was encompassed by social forces that were taking America and the world through a period of change at a giddy pace. The validity of Charles Jones's sociological study of the National Association for the Promotion of Holiness within this cultural context cannot be questioned. However, it would appear that all such studies illuminate only one series of facts in a very complex phenomenon.

This study has also sought to recognize that an understanding of the interplay between the movement and these contextual forces is essential to any proper analysis of its significance to the whole. However, as Stoeffler has suggested, along with the sociological factors operative in the American culture, one must take into account the concept of an enduring experiential tradition in the Christian Church.

The "oppositive" element in Stoeffler's definition of Pietism, which was especially useful in interpreting the European revival, is also helpful in understanding the same period in the American revival. Particularly when applied to American Methodism and the holiness movement, it helps to define the changing religious emphases within Methodism in regard to its own strongly pietistic, revivalistic heritage. Had it not been that significant numbers of people were aware of such trends, the movement obviously would not have emerged as it did; nor, would the conflict within the churches have been as intense and prolonged as it became. Basic religious concerns must be considered in the interpretation of the movement at every period.

The issues were distinctly sharpened by the sociological forces at work in both church and society in general; but there was something much deeper than that at stake—the quality and nature of the Christian life and fellowship, as understood within a long standing Christian tradition, were being challenged. The elemental characteristics of experiential Christianity were scarcely focused more pointedly than they were in those members of the National Committee and the holiness advocates in other American revivalistic churches, who constituted the leading edge of the revival after the Civil War. The picture of the tendencies in American churches and national life almost baited a direct response. Perhaps, at no point in the history of the American churches, and among no other group, is a recognition of this interpretive factor more necessary or valid.

The conditions outlined at the beginning of the chapter constituted a threat at every turn, to the basic Biblical, puritan-pietism of the holiness movement. An individual response to the holiness evangelists' call for a personal, inward conversion experience and a subsequent experience of entire sanctification both claiming their authenticity from the Word of God and personal inner assurance, was the foundation of all Christian relationships and the reality of the church fellowship. In view of this, they felt that all that they believed was being mocked by the tendencies toward increasingly loose standards for church membership. These tendencies had allowed an influx into the churches of large numbers of members who were not required to testify to a personal experience of religion. When the fellowship had been sufficiently permeated with such members, the disciplinary powers of the body were weakened to such an extent that they felt that the church was no longer pure and, therefore, was incapable of maintaining either the individual priesthood or each believer, or a vigorous corporate witness for the world's redemption. Their position within the American churches was strikingly similar to that of the Pietists and Puritans in Germany and England within the Establishment Churches.

Moreover, the anxiety for the level of fellowship and discipline was amplified by the collective effects of the growing urban churches upon these pietistic strivings. In large group worship, the collective responses and the liturgical trends, and, in large congregations, the need for increased organization along businesslike lines, all apparently left many individuals of a pietistic bent highly dissatisfied. It seemed to contradict the individuality, simplicity, and freedom of the experiential tradition. It was not the simplicity of the Gospel.

The challenges which Biblical higher criticism and new theories in the scientific world presented to the authority of the Bible, as pure and simple Word for every man, as well as for the life of the fellowship, seemed to endanger the basis of their spiritual life. At the same time that these were looked upon as destroying the Word by emasculating it, it seemed to them that others such as the Mormons and the Christian Scientists, were destroying it by adding to it their own purportedly equally authoritative word. These threats to the Bible also constituted a threat to both the preaching and the devotion of these pietists, for it was the source of both.

Finally, the holiness movement was concerned, beyond all else, with the practical sanctification of the Christian life, a characteristic of all pietistic movements, but especially set aside by Wesley and the Methodists in their call to entire sanctification as a possibility in this life, a "second blessing." In the view of the holiness people, the doctrine was being set aside by the one church to whom God had trusted the responsibility for its promotion. There was a wide acceptance of the revival of holiness in that church by the 1870's, but not wide enough to overcome the growing tendencies toward institutionalization, which the very success of the revival encouraged. There was increasing despair among loyal Methodists concerning the possibility of the recovery of the disciplinary standards which they believed necessary to the maintenance of the spiritual life of the church. In tension with a rapidly changing church, and often pressed by radical disruption of their sense of community in other relationships as well, many began to look to the institutionalization of the one certainty they had—their commitment to the holiness revival.

NOTES

1. See Arthur M Schlesinger, "A Critical Period in American Religion, 1875-1900," *Massachusetts Historical Society, Proceedings*, LXIV (1932), pp. 523-47; H. S. Smith et al., *American Christianity*, II, 217. A recent and extensive review of the period is Paul A. Carter's *Spiritual Crisis of the Gilded Age.*

2. Sweet, *The Story of Religion in America,* p. 495; also see Sweet, *Methodism in American History,* pp. 332-68.

3. *Ibid.* Also see R. S. Foster, "State of the Church," *Christian Standard and Home Journal,* XIX (June 6, 1885), 2. In 1864, the Methodist Church had 928,320 members and 1,580,559 in 1875; Matthew Simpson, *A Hundred Years of Methodism* (New York: Nelson and Phillips, 1876), pp. 185-86, 347.

4. Abel Stevens, *The Centenary of American Methodism* (New York: Carlton and Porter, 1865), pp. 200, 201-11, 233. Stevens said: "Its people, originally the poorest in the land have become, under its beneficent training, perhaps the wealthiest"; *ibid.,* p. 225.

5. Simpson, *A Hundred Years of Methodism,* p. 208. *Ibid.,* p. 340, notes that according to the 1870 census, Methodism in the United States had one-third of the church buildings (21,337) and one-fifth of the church property values ($69,854,121). Six years later the Methodist Episcopal Church alone had church property valued at $80,893,181; Simpson, *Cyclopedia,* p. 597.

6. *Ibid.,* pp. 333ff.

7. Henry F. May, *Protestant Churches and Industrial America* (New York: Harper and Brothers, 1949), p. 119. *The Rise of the City, 1878-1898,* ed. A. Schlesinger (Vol. X, "History of American Life" Series; New York: Macmillan, 1933). In relation to Methodism, see A. Boisen, *op. cit.,* pp. 130-31.

8. *Supra,* p. 114. Also see similar thesis in W. E. Mann, *op. cit.*

9. As quoted in Herbert M. Morais, *Deism in Eighteenth Century America* (New York: Columbia University Press, 1934), p. 20. Also see George Hedley, *The Christian Heritage in America* (New York: Macmillan, 1946), p. 143. Quoting the *Methodist,* the *American Wesleyan* warned in 1880 that if the church wanted to be a power in the future it had to befriend the "poor and almost friendless young man [who]…is a stranger in a strange city…lonely and homesick"; *American Wesleyan,* XXVIII (April 28, 1880), 5.

10. Aaron Abell, *The Urban Impact on American Protestantism, 1865-1900* (Cambridge, MA: Harvard University Press, 1943), pp 4, 6; also see Sweet, *The American Churches,* p. 56.

11. *Ibid.*

12. Mann, *op. cit.,* p. 55. Abell, *op. cit.,* p. 6. These conditions may have accounted for the lament of the Bishops of the Methodist Episcopal Church in their Pastoral Address to the 1880 General Conference: "The condition of Methodism in our large cities has been a subject of discussion, and its small relative advance has been contrasted with its more rapid growth in rural populations." As quoted by *Guide,* LXXV (June,1880), 178.

13. R. S. Foster, *loc. cit.*

14. Simpson, *A Hundred Years,* p. 205.

15. B. K. Kuiper, *The Church in History* (Grand Rapids, MI: Wm. B. Eerdmans, 1951), pp. 470-71; Foster, *loc cit.* Littell, *From State Church to Pluralism,* pp. 140-42.

16. *Ibid.* Also see Simpson, *A Hundred Years,* p. 204. Two-fifths of the Methodist Church members had been added within the past ten years. The holiness churches themselves later faced similar problems as they developed more city congregations; see Val B. Clear, *op. cit.,* pp.2-3.

17. Simpson, *Cyclopedia*, p. 229. Also see John Atkinson, *The Class Leader* (New York: Nelson and Phillips, 1874); Charles Keys, *The Class Leader's Manual* (New York: Carlton and Phillips, 1856); W. M. Prottsman, *The Class Leader* (St. Louis: Methodist Book Repository, 1856); L.Rosser, *Class Meetings* (Richmond, VA: privately printed, 1855); W. J. Sasnett, "Theory of Methodist Class Meetings," *Methodist Quarterly Review* (So.), V, No. 2 (1851), 265-84.

18. *Ibid.* Also see George G. Smith, *The Life and Times of George Foster Pierce with His Sketch of Lovick Pierce, D.D., His Father* (Sparta, GA: Hancock Publishing, 1888), p. 466, who says that "the regular class meetings had been suspended by the absence of their leaders...."

19. Nathan Bangs, "The Recent Revival," *Christian Advocate and Journal,* XXXIII (July 29, 1858), 117; also see *ibid.* (January 21, 1858), 9.

20. Franklin H. Littell, "Class Meeting," *World Parish,* IX (February 1961), 15. Sangster, *Methodism Can Be Born Again*, p. 60, said that "the decay of the class meeting is a tragedy which the denominational historian will find it hard to exaggerate."

21. Sweet, *History of Methodism*, p. 341. *Ibid.,* pp. 341-45, develops the thesis that the holiness movement arose mainly because of spiritual decline of the Methodist Church. Sangster said that when the fellowship of the class meeting was gone, "the hunger which the class deeply satisfied was still there, a hunger which could not be met in public worship or mass meetings. Finally it burst out in groups." Sangster, *loc. cit.*

22. G. Smith, *op. cit.*, p. 19.

23. *Advocate of Bible Holiness,* XIII (September 1882), p. 260, quoting an unidentified issue of the *Zion's Herald.*

24. As quoted by the *Christian Standard and Home Journal,* VIII (November 27, 1875), 380. It is difficult to reconcile a statement of John Inskip to his friends in ibid. in which he says the finances of the Association "were never in as good condition before" with a rather lengthy account of his biographers, McDonald and Searles, about the financial crisis which threatened to take the whole venture into bankruptcy until Inskip with the financial support of one of his converts, the wealthy Indiana glass manufacturer, Washington DePauw, was made editor of both the *Advocate* and the *Christian Standard and Home Journal.* He weathered the difficulties; before his death in March 1884, the stock of the company had been restored almost to par value; *op. cit.*, pp. 299-302. See a November 24, 1875, letter from Inskip to Curry in the Daniel Curry file of the manuscript section of the Drew University archives. In a handwritten note on Inskip's letter, probably Curry's, is the statement that the attack was carried in the paper of which Curry was then editor without his knowledge. Curry later spoke at Inskip's funeral; he said that the latter's expression of the experience of entire sanctification was "the most rational of any he had ever heard"; McDonald and Searles, *op. cit.*, p. 367.

25. *Christian Standard and Home Journal, loc. cit.*

26. For example, a report in *Divine Life* (January 1880), p. 19, related that Alfred Carman, Bishop of the Methodist Episcopal Church of Canada, was "the first and most pronounced witness and advocate of entire sanctification..." at the St. Clair, Ontario, camp meeting; *ibid.* (May 1880), pp. 207-209, gives an

account of Carman's Christian experience. *Ibid.* (October,1879), pp. 61-67; *ibid.* (March 1880), pp. 161-66.

27. "Letter of L. Tyerman to E. C. Estes from Stanhope House, Clapham Park, April 19, 1872," cited in *Advocate of Christian Holiness,* III (July 1872).

28. *Divine Life* (October 1879), 61-67; *ibid.* (March 1880), 161-66.

29. Stephen M. Merrill, "Pastoral Address," Carroll, *Proceedings of the Methodist Centennial Conference,* p. 319.

30. See *supra,* pp. 49,. 50, 97-8, 105.

31. *Ibid.,* p. 320.

32. Cf. R. S. Foster, *Centenary Thoughts for Pew and Pulpit* (New York: Phillips and Hunt, 1884), p. 166.

33. *Infra,* p. 272.

34. An illustrative but by no means comprehensive list includes Ohio Holiness Association (1870); The Nebraska State Association (1871); The Western Holiness Association (1871) centered in Illinois was instrumental in forming a number of other holiness associations under the leadership of men like L. B. Kent and Hardin Wallace; Southern Ohio Holiness Association (1875); Iowa Holiness Association (1879) long under the leadership of Isaiah Reid; Southwestern Association (1879); New England Association (1879); Indiana State Association (1880), D. J. Warner, who later withdrew from such associations because of his no-sectism, is listed as first vice-president. Southern California and Arizona Holiness Association (1880); Kansas State Association (1884). Since records were often poorly kept, and more than one association may have taken the same state name, this summary, constructed mainly from periodical references, differs in some dates with Jones, *op. cit.,* pp. 147-48.

35. Supra, p. 109.

36. See Simpson, *Cyclopedia,* pp. 85-86; W. E. Boardman began his ministry in such a band; Mrs. Boardman says that it was the custom in that day [Sterling, Illinois, 1840] to form what was called a "band composed of Christians of different denominations who united together to have services on the Sabbath." Boardman, *op. cit.,* p. 39. B. T. Roberts held his groups of followers together in such bands after their expulsion from the Methodist Episcopal Church, hoping that from these temporary organizations they could move back into the church again. Marston, *op. cit.,* p. 227. For the organization and activities of a typical band, see Mrs. S. A. Cooke, *The Handmaiden of the Lord or Wayside Sketches* (Chicago: T. B. Arnold, 1896), *passim.* See *infra,* pp. 238ff.

37. See D. W. M'Laughlin, "Sectizing Holiness," *Good Way,* V (September 5, 1883), p. 2; M'Laughlin, favorable to the organization of independent holiness churches, warned that where such bands are not organized the holiness work commonly went into dissolution or into the hands of the Free Methodists. He called such bands "Embryo Churches." *Infra,* pp. 257ff.

38. *Good Way,* III (October 15, 1881), 2.

39. *Ibid.;* also see *ibid.* (November 5, 1881), p. 1.

40. *Ibid.,* p. 4.

41. *Ibid.*

42. As quoted by Marston, *op. cit.*, p. 334, from J. G. Terrill, *The St. Charles Camp Meeting* (Chicago: T. B. Arnold, 1883), p. 13.

43. T. Smith, *Called Unto Holiness*, p. 31.

44. *Ibid.*; also see C. B. Jernigan, *Pioneer Days of the Holiness Movement in the Southwest* (Kansas City, MO: Pentecostal Nazarene Publishing House, 1919), pp. 150-57; Macum Phelan, *A History of the Expansion of Methodism in Texas, 1867-1902* (Dallas, TX: Mathis, Van Nort and Co., 1937), pp. 118-19. One of the most enlightening volumes on religious fanaticisms including many related to the holiness revival is Strachey, *op. cit.* Mrs. Smith says, *ibid.*, p. 30, that her first introduction to fanaticisms other than that which she got from her Quaker background, which she says "was a good deal, came through the Methodist doctrine of entire sanctification. That doctrine has been one of the greatest blessings of my life, but it has also introduced me into an emotional region where common sense has no chance and where everything goes by feelings, voices and impressions." See especially in reference to Texas revival, *ibid.*, pp. 143-44, the account of "The Women's Commonwealth," a group of "sanctified women" in the Texas revival of 1876 led by Mrs. Martha Mac Whirter, who with other followers were finally forsaken by their husbands and driven from town because of their opposition to the denominations and organized religion. They thereupon formed the "Women's Commonwealth," went into the hotel business and prospered, one of them being elected to the local "board of trade." In 1904 they still existed in Washington state, surviving the death of their founder. Hannah Smith was as objective an observer as someone within the movement could be. She often chided herself for lack of religious feeling and emotion and her common sense approach to her religious life. See *supra*, pp. 161-162.

45. "The Work in Illinois," *Christian Standard and Home Journal*, XI (June 2, 1877), 172.

46. *Ibid.*

47. "Holiness Conference," *ibid.; ibid.* (June 16, 1977), 188; *ibid.* (June 23, 1877), 197-98.

48. *Ibid.* (July 7, 1877), 213.

49. *Ibid.*

50. *Supra* p. 142, n. 44.

51. As quoted from the *Banner of Holiness* in the *Christian Standard and Home Journal*, XI (July 21, 1877), 228.

52. See Timothy L. Smith, "Congregation, State, and Denomination: The Forming of the American Religious Structure" *William and Mary Quarterly*, Third Series, XXV (April 1968), p. 162; Smith speaks of the case with which the people of pioneer New England "fell easy prey to the emotionalism and egotism of the magnetic personalities whose teachings highlighted their sense of social and spiritual estrangement." The same may be said of the socially and religiously displaced converts of the revival.

53. *Christian Standard and Home Journal*, XI (June 2, 1877), p. 172.

54. See *Proceedings of Holiness Conferences held at Cincinnati, November 26th, 1877 and at New York, December 17, 1877* (Philadelphia: National Publishing Association for the Promotion of Holiness [1878]), *passim*.

55. *Ibid.*, p. 31.

56. *Ibid.*, pp. 85-102.

57. *Ibid.*, p. 96. Brooks developed these ideas further in the most systematic statement on ecclesiology which the movement ever produced, *The Divine Church. A Treatise of the Origin, Constitution, Order, and Ordinances of the Church; Being a Vindication of the New Testament Ecclesia, and an Exposure of the Anti-Scriptural Character of the Modern Church of Sect* (Columbia, MO: Herald Publishing House, 1891 [reprinted at Eldorado Springs, MO: Witt Printing, 1960]). See especially *ibid.*, chap. xvi, pp. 267-83.

58. *Ibid.*

59. *Proceedings of Holiness Conferences*, p. 100.

60. *Ibid.*, pp. 86-87.

61. See F. F. Bruce, *The Spreading Flame: The Rise and Progress of Christianity* (Grand Rapids, MI: Wm. B. Eerdmans Publishing, 1954), pp. 81-90.

62. *Proceedings of Holiness Conferences*, pp. 31, 111-12.

63. *Ibid.*, p. 31.

64. For example, differences on ordinances, millennialism, prudentials, church polity, divine healing.

65. The Methodists used the same rationale to justify Wesley's "societies." Simpson, *Cyclopedia*, p. 588, says, "This was done [organizing of societies] not because he designed to constitute any separate church, but because the converts came to him for instruction and longed for the fellowship of kindred spirits."

Chapter 6

In Search of Order

By 1880, the revival, as a movement within all of Protestantism, began to change its character. Thousands of Christians in the Methodist and other churches had responded in varying degrees to the perfectionist message of the holiness evangelists. After 1880, the story became one of gradual organization in the face of their increasingly sharp struggle with those in the churches who reacted to this new evangelism. It is a story even more complex than the general pattern of American religion after 1870, because of the revival's unorganized nature and the involvement of hundreds of ordinary laypersons and pastors who engaged in the most aggressive activities on behalf of their cause. This extensive, grass-roots activity makes the total impact of their work difficult to assess.[1]

The history of these "bands" and "associations," which formed the nucleus of the first holiness churches, is well told in the works of Timothy Smith, Charles Jones, and Vincent Synan.[2] Smith and Jones, particularly, place the movement within the larger struggle for order in American society, to which Robert Wiebe speaks in *The Search for Order*.[3] It is Wiebe's thesis that the late nineteenth century saw the breakdown and reordering of society; the process involved the disruption of the "island communities, the earlier dominant social unit, and the effort to create the newer social patterns structured as a result of the unbroken acceleration of the rural to urban migration. The gathering together of the holiness people into the institutional units which the movement began to spawn after 1880 was part of what Wiebe describes as a crisis precipitated by "a widespread loss of confidence in the powers of the community," which led to attempts "to preserve the society that had given their lives meaning."[4]

Within this context, the holiness churches which developed out of the revival are generally regarded as "transplantations," or, attempts to recreate "village churches" in the midst of the city, "churches identical to warmly remembered ones in town or country...in a found attempt to create at least one bulwark against urban demoralization."[5] The highly puritanical pietism of holiness religion was particularly evident in the rural areas; its reaction to the "worldliness" that it saw as a prevailing feature of the rapid social change occurring in both church and community progressed concurrently with that change. It was accompanied by participation in the common fears of the rapidly growing powers of the industrial and political establishment. Even in these realms, as Wiebe points out, there was a call for "purity and unity." The cry of the populists for "self determination" resulted from those demands.[6]

The general purposes of this paper on revivalism and holiness, however, speak more directly to another observation of Wiebe, that "the more [anxious the search for answers]...the more serious society's predicament, the more grandiose the visions of perfection following that single correction."[7] It is possible, therefore, to see some of the early efforts to orient the holiness revival after 1880 in this light; as a perfectionist revival with perfectionist answers to the problems of both individuals and society, its revivalism and perfectionism strongly molded the nature of both the problems, which the movement encountered in its search for order, and the answers which the movement gave to those problems. Perry Miller has identified the hermeneutical principle that is involved here in his classical study of *The Life of the Mind in America;* speaking to his development of the evangelical basis of that mind, he said that in the nation's "religious mentality," by the end of the Civil War, "the simple fact of the Revival was central. Whether it produced formal unity or created new churches was of less import than the omnipresence of the Revival."[8] The "omnipresence" of the revival in the "religious mentality" of the holiness converts, and, therefore, holiness advocated, is a critical factor in properly understanding what was occurring in this period as well.

THE REVIVAL AND THE CHURCH QUESTION

It has already been pointed out in the summary of the address of J. P. Brooks to the first conference of the general movement in 1877, that the special promotion of holiness was raising trying issues, both external and internal to the movement. At that early point, the difficulties of properly relating the vigorous evangelism of the holiness revivalists to the established structure of the churches, was a problem. Holiness was a reformatory principle; how to most effectively apply its purifying principles to the churches so that they might in turn be restored to the hoped-for primitive holiness and power, was by no means clear to them, and certainly not to the churches. Furthermore, the question of how to reconcile the tendencies to create divisions, both within the churches and within the movement with the principles of perfect love which were to make all the sanctified one, was ever present. This question was seriously raised for some, by the inability of the first conference to come to any kind of unified pattern of organization for the future of the movement.[9] The flurry of "church of God" thinking, even before 1880, indicates how serious it had become.

REVIVALISM'S PARADOX

The Tendency to Divisiveness

The question of access for the holiness evangelists, also raised by Brooks in 1877, pointed up the issue which rapidly became the crucial problem between the organized churches and the revival. Bands of holiness evangelists, often representing several denominations, became increasingly active and aggressive in their evangelism, as the intensity of the holiness question and the growing response and reaction among the churches seemed to move along hand in hand. These bands were loosely organized, and frequently unregulated, except by the most simple peer pressure or a charismatic leader. Their very efforts to refrain from taking on the nature of a second church—their members, in the early period, were all members of some other regulated religious body—prejudiced the groups against any tight internal control. It allowed free spirits, who sometimes were escaping to the group from discipline in some other religious society, or were feeding their own sense of individuality, to readily find a home and an outlet for their ambitions. Moreover, the strong emphasis within the preaching of the movement, upon the development of an obedience to the leadings of the Holy Spirit, above the voice of any person or group of people, often was used to reject the measure of peer discipline which was exercised even in such informal organizations.[10]

This tendency to a lack of discipline created a problem both internally and externally for the movement and this is indicated by the way in which it was addressed at the first gathering of the general movement in 1877;[11] how serious a matter it was for some, was indicated also by the reaction which even the minimal efforts of the next convention at Jacksonville to regulate members created.[12] It was mentioned consistently thereafter in the conventions which followed.[13] Inskip, McDonald, Walter Palmer, George Hughes, and the many others in the leadership of the disciplined Methodist mainstream of the movement in the Palmer tradition, refuted, both by argument and example, the charges that such problems were inevitably inherent in the movement; but, as has been indicated, even they, with the strong support of high ecclesiastical authorities, had been constantly reminded of the tendencies of side effects to schism.

By the 1870s, they too, were increasingly being attacked as irregulars because of their expanding numbers of cohorts in special holiness promotion through holiness associations and, especially, through the numerous holiness papers which supplemented the effectiveness of the *Guide* and the *Advocate of Christian Holiness*.[14]

In the light of these facts, it is not difficult to see why the holiness bands and the holiness evangelists, at the local levels of the church, progressively agitated those pastors and members who were totally unsympathetic to, or uninterested in, their work. It also agitated others who were in general sympathy with the doctrines, but not in sufficient degree to encourage its promotion to the disruption of the churches.[15] The result of these tensions was that the opposition to the revival continued to increase, in spite of the fact that the holiness evangelist was getting a wider and wider hearing in more and more communities, as the laypersons and small-town pastors took the regular promulgation of the doctrine into any place which would invite them—and just as often, into any place which would not.[16] The end result was that by 1880, thirteen years after the postwar phase of the revival had begun, at the Vineland National Camp Meeting, the contest within the Methodist Church over the Holiness question, which Bishop Hamline had eagerly looked forward to, was forcing difficult decisions concerning church loyalties not only upon many Methodists, but upon many non-Methodists as well.

The Sense of Unity

It was against this background of growing strife, resulting from the aggressive efforts of the holiness associations and bands to win the churches to their holiness reform, that their equally perfectionist statements concerning Christian unity sounded so contradictory to some. The basic origin of the Christian unity theme, undoubtedly, developed mainly as a natural consequence of their Biblical orientation.[17] The logical relationship of their sanctification concept to the removal of those selfish prejudices and personal interests, which were commonly regarded as the source of individual differences, introduced the practical problem into every life situation. Perfection in love, as preached by the movement was certainly foreign to such self-centeredness, whether in individuals or in churches. It will be seen that its implications, when driven to their logical ends by some persons within the early movement, raised serious questions within the revival's rank concerning the very nature of the church itself, and the pattern of denominationalism, which had grown out of the voluntaristic organization of the American churches.

The force of the rhetoric which was common to the unity theme within the holiness revival could be illustrated by the record of almost every holiness meeting that is available to the researcher. But it was probably the rhetoric of the National Committee itself and of the other dominant sources of influence in the fluid movement—the holiness periodicals—which provided the most valid examples of the perfectionist ultraism inherent in the holiness message. At the Landisville, Pennsylvania, National Holiness Camp Meeting in 1873, John Inskip, the recognized leader of the general movement until his death in 1884, said to those who had gathered for the first service of the camp:

> We come here not so much to argue as to assert, demonstrate, proclaim, and announce the truth as it is in Christ Jesus....This is not fair, you say. Yes, it is fair. *You get this blessing and we'll take your creed,* whatever it may be, that is we'll find then that there is very little difference between us....This is the lazy way to fight. *Any of us can be tripped up if we go into speculative questions.* Let us keep to the fundamental idea [emphasis mine].[18]

At the same camp, Dr. Edgar M. Levy, long-time Baptist participant in the movement, gave a typical statement of the optimism that was generated on the unity theme by the "Beulah Land" experiences of the fellowshipping holiness community. He said that after all previous efforts to achieve Christian unity had been thwarted because of the "impossibility of creating uniformity in the expression of belief in the constitution of the church, and in the administration of the ordinances," now,

> at last we have discovered the basis for Christian unity. The sanctification of the believers of every name, create unity in the great Christian brotherhood, such as no creed has ever been able to accomplish. Here...we have...an exhibition of Christian unity as thrills one's soul to behold. A unity not in ordinances; a unity not in church government; a unity not in forms of worship; a unity not in mere letter of creed—but in...the baptism of the Holy Spirit. As it is the nature of sin to separate, disintegrate, and repel, *it is*

the nature of holiness to unite and adjust and harmonize [emphasis mine].[19]

The Implications of Revivalism for Church Unity

The paradox which the holiness evangelists and converts of the revival faced in the schism-unity syndrome, which so strongly fastened itself upon the consciousness of the movement, was certainly not foreign to American revivalism as a tradition. The tension between the polarizing and the unifying tendencies in revival efforts was ever present. Revivalism, with its impatient call for immediate decision in the areas of the most deep-seated loyalties, had always caused divisions within religious communities; it became a commonplace in the nation's religious history. Perry Miller says that, in fact, it was virtually bound "to do so." The divisions in New England after the First Great Awakening, the Presbyterian schisms, the secession of the Cumberland Presbytery, and the establishment of the Disciples of Christ—all testify to that, he said.[20]

On the other hand, witnesses are replete in the history of the holiness revival and American revivalism, in general, that the sense of oneness which the members of diverse religious communities enjoyed in the revival atmosphere exceeded that to be found in any other religious situation. The example of the Cane Ridge camp meeting, where Methodists, Baptists, and Presbyterians had worked together as one body of Christians, became an example of the fact for all future time. It was "a mighty symbol of concordance...."[21] Robert Baird had forthrightly adopted this apparent paradox of "unity in diversity" to provide a rationale to his European readers for the "scandal" which the numerous American sects represented to them under the American voluntaristic system.[22] It became part of the American mind.

It especially fixed itself in revivalistic thought, because in the revival meeting it often came closest to reality; there as they worked together in their highest calling, the oneness was felt more poignantly than at most other times in the relationships between the churches. It was in revivals that the dream of unity was moved along most directly. It was there that most men, even as early as the period when the holiness revival began, located the hope of its ultimate realization. The *Christian Spectator* wrote in 1832, that in the fellowship of the revival, "we find a principle of affinity, which, just in proportion as the widespread medium of spiritual emotion becomes purified, will draw all classes of Christians nearer still nearer, until the practical ends even of external unity shall be fulfilled."[23]

The interdenominational realities, and the strong future anticipa-
tions of greater unity, and less and less sectarian feeling, found in the
pre-Civil War holiness movement, have already been noted.[24] It, too,
was part of a general hope for the future of the churches. William Starr,
a somewhat controversial Congregational pastor in Elgin, Illinois,
wrote just before the War:

> The union for which I look and long, is to be brought about by a
> certain change of views among Christians; not by their coming to
> a common doctrinal basis…[but by] inplicit faith in the Lord Jesus
> Christ…proven not by their agreeing to what dogma you attrib-
> ute Christ, but "by their fruits.…" [25]

The unity which holiness advocates professed in their meetings,
and the unity among the heterogeneous groups, which the holiness
evangelistic bands represented, seemed to them to seal the certain
promise that the eschatology of the revival's hoped-for unity was at the
threshold of actuality. This mentality persisted generally in holiness
ranks. The absence of a grass-roots character which Miller noted in most
of the associated religious efforts engaged in among the denominations
before the Civil War, definitely was not true of these postwar bands of
men and women from all revivalistic churches.[26]

Perfectionism and the Promise of Unity

In fact, the application of the holiness ideology to the revival dream
of one church acting redemptively in the work of the evangelization of
society seemed to them to show the way at last to achieving the goal.
This reinforcement of one of the basic rationales of American revivalism
by the dynamics of the unifying, adjusting, and harmonizing powers
which men such as Levy claimed for the Spirit-baptizing experience
they were proclaiming, demonstrates once again the manner in which
the perfectionist tended to modify the basic elements, which were
characteristic of revivalism as it had developed by the period the new
perfectionism arose in the third decade of the nineteenth century. Its
ultraistic tendencies had already led it into deeper life evangelism; into
new and more aggressive methods of revivalism; and, through its call
to complete consecration of the individual, to a life of holiness, into an
intensification of the puritanical moralism, advocated by the preaching
of such revivalists as Finney. These same tendencies now naturally led
some pioneers in the movement into more radical concepts of ecclesiology than the vast majority of holiness people were willing to accept.

THE CONTINUING MOOD OF OPTIMISM

The problem was further intensified by the fact that at the same time that the movement believed that it had found a new principle which would move the churches on rapidly to the unity which the revival tradition had always held out to them, the churches, as ecclesiastical structures, they felt, were increasingly rejecting both their methods and their message.[27] Moreover, in their minds, the churches were ignoring the Spirit of God who was testifying to his intentions for the age, not only by the spread of what they saw as the most extensive holiness revival in church history, but also by "wonderfully" unifying, adjusting, and integrating all of history for the reformation of the world.

In the same year that Josiah Strong made his penetrating analysis of the mission of the American nation and its churches, just prior to the turn of the century, William Jones, one of the movement's evangelists, published a book which illustrates the mood that helped to produce the apocalyptic atmosphere within, which the movement regarded as its mission. In *From Elim to Carmel*, Jones, speaking to questions not commonly touched upon in holiness literature, discussed the churches' responsibility to the "turbil stream of immigration" which was emptying "its ever-increasing flood" upon the nation's shores, as well as to the millions of the illiterate and imbruted ex-slaves," and the "fetid Indians that still linger in squalor and filth upon our Western borders." These grave obligations and the degenerative spiritual inclinations in the life of the churches raised, he said, the all important question as to whether or not the church would "be true to God in the whole broad realm of Christian thought and Christian activity?" He believed it would, and contemplated "the near approach of [that] ultimate victory" with "inexpressible pleasure." He continued,

The tremor of the invisible forces that now pervades all lands and thrills and agitates all peoples, is the product of that spirit that is inherent in the gospel. The impulse to a better life is manifest everywhere; it throbs in the heart of all peoples. Everywhere the struggle of all peoples is toward light....Nation is calling to nation...and the muffled tread of the gathering throng, startles conservatism from its death of sleep. Thrones are crumbling, and crowns are falling like stars in an apocalyptic vision. Empires of spiritual oppression are dissolving into light....

In the projection of railroads into the heart of Africa, he heard the "footsteps of Jehovah...in his omnipotent tramp to his final conquest." Like the engineer who had carefully tunneled into the rocks at Hell's

Gate, set his explosive charges, and then "loosed the electric spark that converted the potential energy into actual energy," so, "God is tunneling the world and packing it with his truth.When the church gets ready, when the world is filled with pure Christian thought, when the ministry shall believe in the Holy Ghost, and accept his fiery baptism...the Father will let slip one spark of the Pentecostal fire...."[28] and the whole earth will become the Kingdom of God. It was with such rhetoric of "crumbling thrones," "falling crowns," "dissolving empires," and the explosive potential of "one spark of Pentecostal fire," ringing in their ears, that the holiness leaders faced the question of the nature of the church. That some should propose new answers to the questions raised is not surprising. The combination was a powerful one; its elements were basic to the mood, and must be kept in mind when one attempts to explain the cast of the perfectionist mind as the period of organization began to set in about 1880.

THE RADICAL HOLINESS REFORMERS

The import of the earliest secessions from the established churches over the holiness question can be illustrated in the answers to the church question given by the men who were most prominent in leading the groups of early schismatics. These commonly became known to the movement and to its opponents in the churches as "the come-outers." A brief review of the contribution of three of these men will illustrate why this period of sect formation deserves more attention than it has commonly received. These leaders were Daniel S. Warner,[29] founder of the Church of God (Anderson, Indiana); John P. Brooks,[30] leader in the independent movement in Missouri, out of which the Church of God (Holiness) rose; and James F. Washburn,[31] leader, with his wife, Josephine, of the Southern California and Arizona Holiness Association, out of which the Holiness Church was ultimately organized. In the past, the historians of the movement have lent significance to these earliest holiness secessionist movements, mainly, because their rural puritan-pietism, and their often undisciplined and enthusiastic, evangelistic bands were a source of embarrassment to the leaders of the mainstream Methodist holiness movement.[32] The latter leaders were already hard put to defend their loyalty to the discipline of the church as well as the relevance of their special concern for holiness promotion in a church gradually shifting away from Wesleyan perfectionism and New Testament standards of life. Criticized by the more conservative element in the movement for their "compromises" in lifestyle and their failure to cast their reform efforts within a more radical framework in relation to church loyalty versus movement loyalty, it was difficult for these mainstream Methodists to appreciate any aspect of "come-ou-tism."[33] The history of the church question, within the institutionaliza-tion of the main forces of the movement, can largely be written around the way in which the National Association leadership controlled the successive geneal holiness conventions and successfully blocked the efforts of the radical reformers to bring their concepts of the kind of reform, which the holiness revival implied, before the larger public in any official way. By the time that the last convention was held in Chicago in 1901, the incipient patterns for the organization of the strong center of the movement were more to the liking of a National Associa-tion leadership, by then, considerably more liberal themselves, in their views of church loyalty and the holiness question, because of the increasing rejection of the movement within the churches.[34]

The significance of this radical movement, however, should no longer be relegated so completely to so negative a context. When one develops the fuller implications of what is only hinted at in Smith's statement that D. S. Warner "carried the nonsectarian traditions of the holiness revival to such extremes that he rejected entirely the idea of an organized denomination,"[35] he finds the interesting fact that their participation in the holiness revival had raised, for such men as Warner, deeper issues than the immediate, practical questions of church mem-bership. In each of the three examples that will be considered, the individual, after being challenged by his respective church on the issue of holiness evangelism, sought to apply the logic of Christian perfec-tionism, with all the ultraistic inclinations of the perfectionist mentality, to the church question.

Daniel S. Warner and the Church of God Movement

The first to propose such radical applications of the revival's promise of unity among all true Christian believers was Daniel Sidney Warner. Warner was born in Wayne County, Ohio, in 1842. He served for a time in the Union Army. After the war, he attended Oberlin College for a brief period and later Vermillion College in Hayesville, Ohio, then under Presbyterian auspices. Converted as a young man, under no particular denominational influence, he left his profession as a school teacher in 1867 to prepare to enter the ministry. He preached his first sermon in a Methodist protracted meeting in a schoolhouse not far from where he lived; but finally he cast his lot with the Church of God (Winebrennerian), a small sect formed out of the German Reformed Churches of Pennsylvania after they had rejected the revivalism of John Winebrenner. They claimed to hold no creed except the Bible, repudi-ated sectarianism, baptized by immersion, and practiced the ordinance of foot washing as well as the Lord's Supper. Undoubtedly, many of Warner's later concepts on the church question in relation to the holiness movement were strongly influenced by his ten years of ministry with that church.[36]

Warner's introduction to the holiness movement and his personal profession of the experience of entire sanctification came like Inskip's, mainly, through the influence of his wife. While visiting some relatives of hers in Upper Sandusky, Ohio, she had claimed the experience in a holiness band meeting. The band was in contact with National Association evangelists. Another important influence upon him was his association with a Baptist minister who was active in the Ohio Holiness Alliance, R. C. R. Dunbar.[37] Warner immediately plunged into holiness evangelism within the Winebrennerian churches. His attempts to promulgate his newly found "light" within his own church produced one of the first examples of the familiar pattern by which many of the holiness proponents, especially those who were active ministers, were separated from the established churches. He had served the Winebrennerians for ten years. Less than three months after he began to preach entire sanctification, he was presented with charges by the church for his holiness advocacy, but after trial was allowed to retain a restricted license to preach; after a brief stay on a new pastorate, he resigned from those duties to become a full-time holiness evangelist, continuing to work within his own denomination. On January 30, 1878, he was charged and tried again for "dividing the church"; the charges were sustained and his license withheld.[38]

The Church of God Concept

How strongly his basic ideas on the relationship of holiness and the nature of the church were cast by the sectarianism which he felt had rejected him and his message is indicated by an entry in his diary in March of the same year, in which he said:

> On the 31st of last January, the Lord showed me that holiness could never prosper upon sectarian soil, encumbered by human creeds, and party names, and he gave me a new commission to *join holiness and all truth together and build up the apostolical* [sic] *church of the living God"* [emphasis mine].[39]

January 31 was one day after he had been ejected from the Winebrennerian ministry. As will be seen below, the truth to which Warner related the truths of holiness, as he understood them in the American holiness revival tradition, especially in the fuller development of his thought, proved to be adaptations of some of the fundamental concepts of the church and its reformation, as developed in the classic tradition of Joachim of Fiore.[40] The result was a remarkable system for the final reformation of the Christian church, built upon Biblical proof texts, the dispensational view of history in the ideological patterns of Joachim, modified at times by the dispensationalism contemporary with his times and the free application of the Old Testament and New Testament prophecies by types and symbols to the church and its history. The whole was integrated by Warner's concept of the holiness revival as an instrument of the church's final reformation, final because of its universal extent and the ability of its purifying message to destroy the last element of sin in the church—sectarianism. In this "Age of the Spirit," the one "invisible" church which was hidden away in the mass of denominational members, much as the true church had been hidden away within the Catholic Church from the time of Constantine to Luther, could be called out one by one, as through entire sanctification, they were cleansed from the "mildew" of sectarianism, to represent the one, visible Church of God.[41]

In September 1868, about a year after Warner was licensed to preach, he purchased a copy of William Henry Starr's *Discourses on the Nature of Faith*. Starr, himself somewhat of an irregular among his fellow Congregational ministers in Illinois, felt that he was being ill-treated by the church establishment which was forcing him into an uncomfortable conformity to its demands. Strong statements in his book protested against the sectarianism which he felt was stifling his freedom to preach as he would. Sometime before 1880, Warner wrote a note on one of the pages of his copy of Starr's book; it followed a strong exhortation by Starr for men to rise up against sectarianism and bring to the world the reality of a "holy and united church." Warner responded to his appeals in the following annotation: "If this holy man, perceiving only the eavil [sic] of division is thus moved to cry out, what must be the guilt of one who sees both the eavil [sic] and remedy and yet will close his mouth and see the world go to ruin."[42]

The call to the reformation movement which Warner began to announce, as the central theme of his holiness evangelism, was already apparently ringing in his own ears.

Warner's earliest extensive treatment of his views of radical holiness reform are found in three consecutive chapters of his first book, *Bible Proofs of the Second Work of Grace...Including a Description of the Great Holiness Crisis of the Present Age, by the Prophets*. In these chapters, Hebrews 12:25-29 is utilized as the key for an interpretation of what he considered to be the Old Testament's prophetic description of the "great work of holiness" of his day. He said that the Holy Spirit had given him that Scriptural key on "the 30th of August, 1879...in a special manner...."[43] In the double shaking spoken of in the Scripture passage, Warner saw a shaking of the world first and then, secondly, of the church. In the restoration that the prophets promised to fallen Israel, which he saw as a type of the church, the latter would enjoy not only the glories of the primitive church, but was to exceed them, "that preceded the dark age of captivity."[44] He said the warnings of Ezekiel to the pastors applied to the pastors of the sectarian churches. "I will seek out my sheep and will deliver them out of all places (sectarian coops) where they have been scattered (into several hundred parties) in the cloudy and dark day....The perfect reign of the Messiah...is to succeed the dark days of party confusion."[45]

The passages surrounding Ezekiel's vision of the valley of dry bones provided a picture of the fallen Catholic church in the type of "Mt. Seir," and the chapters following the vision pictured the Protestant sects which were patterned after the Roman sectarian error. The resurrection of the dry bones was a prophetic picture for him of the ordering of the true church out of this "Babylon of confusion" through the effective working of entire sanctification, preached by the holiness revivalists until the "true Israel" would be unified again as indicated by Ezekiel's parable of the "one stick of Judah," Sectism, because it resisted this unity, was represented as Gog and Magog. They create "war in the camp and a general commotion in the heavens and the earth." In all of this Warner believed that there seemed to be "a reference to the primitive power of the Church and its restoration again after the lapse of the 'years of many generations' of darkness." It would come through "the sin consuming flames of the Sanctifier, the baptism of the Holy Ghost," which corresponded with "the shaking of the Church," Warner appealed to the widespread stir created by the holiness revival as a fulfillment of this great struggle; its universality indicated that this holiness reform was different from those which had preceded it.[46]

He reinforced his antisectarian logic by arguments proposed both outside and inside the movement. William Starr's protest against his treatment at the hands of sects obviously had a strong influence upon him.[47] Within the movement, he drew on the copious supply of statements on holiness as a unifying experience which appeared regularly in the holiness journals. Citing proof for his position from an article by Thomas Doty in the *Christian Harvester* which admitted that there was "*not one word in the Bible favorable* to denominations or sects...that "denominations are directly or indirectly the result of sin remaining in the great body of professors"; and that "thorough and widespread holiness would soon destroy denominations" (emphasis his);[48] he refuted Doty's qualification of these statements in allowing that reform cannot come "until holiness more widely prevails." Warner would have none of such delay. His perfectionism carried strong tones of the holiness advocates involved in the abolitionist movements of the pre-Civil War period: "But for the love of truth I am constrained to differ with the position that sects are a present necessity. They originated from sin in the church; and shall we admit that the fruit of sin is necessary under any circumstances?"[49] The nature of the radical holiness reform proposed by those men must be seen then, in significant measure, as a valid consequence of their perfectionism brought to the support of their essentially pietistic revivalism, fortified by the rural milieu.

Having put forth these arguments, Warner called for each sanctified individual to reject sectarianism in his own heart and leave his denomination "to join the only holy Church of the Bible, not bound together by rigid articles of faith, but perfectly united in love, under the primitive glory of the Sanctifier, continuing steadfastly in the Apostles's doctrine and fellowship, and taking captive the world for Jesus."[50] Warner concluded his arguments with the restatement of his conviction that "the great holiness reform" could not go forward until "every vestige of denominational distinction" had been consecrated and done away with, and God had perfected into "*one* indeed and in truth—all the sanctified" (emphasis his).

> It will then be discovered who for Jesus will be,
> And who are in Babylon the saints then will see;
> The time of division then will *fully be known,*
> Between the pure kingdom and defiled Babylon. (emphasis his.)[51]

About ten years after Warner had published the substance of his new thinking on the church question in relationship with the holiness revival, he began to record a much fuller treatment of his views; they were cast in a much more apocalyptic mood and showed obvious reaction to the Adventist teaching of Uriah Smith, which must have come to his attention between the writing of the first and second books.[52] His efforts to explicate the basis of his reform message now included, not only the apocalypticism of Revelation, but also involved a mild attempt at countering the date-setting of the Adventists, who obviously loomed large in his thinking at the time, along with some projections of his own.[53] But on the whole, the later work is an enlargement of the three chapters of the *Proofs.*

The dominant theme, however, was the strong primitivism which was present in all holiness concepts of the church. The original Pentecost experience and the church which lived close to that period were looked upon as the models of the pure church. In Warner's mind, "the real presence of God in his church is the substance and joyful realization of that which his abode in the tabernacle and temple was but a faint type…" this was "the peculiar heritage of the present dispensation."[54] Both in individual Christians and collectively, "the Holy Spirit now comes and dwells in the true sanctuary of the church of the living God."[55] Warner's perfectionism came to the fore as he continued that the "Spirit" could not dwell among a divided people,

> therefore, the confused and disintegrated factions of sectism cannot be the temple of God….No one of them is a church, nor do all together constitute that holy temple; but the 'spiritual house' of God is made up of the spiritual. In other words the church of the living God includes all saved in Christ.[56]

The "Spirit" was working in his time through the holiness revival to cleanse the church from "all rubbish of creeds, traditions and inventions of sectism which the dark ages of the past have heaped upon her….But all this wood, hay, and stubble, the fire of holiness is consuming, and the temple of God appears in view again in primitive glory."[57]

He then described the "Heroic Age" of the church which lay back "over the 1,260 years of utter night that extend far beyond, even into the third century." He saw it as "one," "visible," "holy," "universal" church with an order formed by the God, "who really organizes the church himself."[58]

But the church as a whole fell, in the Constantinian Age, from its pristine state; as a result, in the third century, "the living church retired gradually within the lonely sanctuary of a few solitary hearts." And there it continued as a "Church in the Wilderness" during the creedal church's "Great Apostasy," for the 1,260 years until the sixteenth century Reformation. That reign of Catholicism was the dark night of the church and the visible church became the "great whore."[59]

The restitution of the church began with the Reformers, but only progressed spasmodically, because whenever a truly spiritual reformation was begun such as that of the reformers themselves, or of Wesley, or of another, a creedal sect was formed and the true church that was gathering was again divided. The Protestant sects became images of the Catholic Church before them, as they perpetuated its doctrines and services—e.g., the rite of sprinkling, infant baptism, confirmation, etc.

The organization of the sects was the disorganization of the church of God. In the fall of Babylon, depicted by John the Revelator, he saw the fall of the Protestant churches. The loss of holiness caused the downfall of the church.[60]

Now, in the new holiness revival, he declared, God was again restoring to the church her original holiness. During all the dark ages of the fallen church, it had been a "mystery," hidden in the "book written within and on the backside, sealed with seven seals," which "no man in heaven or earth could open." But the "Lion of the Tribe of Judah" took the book and opened it; it was the plan of "salvation and redemption," it was the cleansing of the sanctuary by "holiness and truth...[which] burn the false religions of the world and restore the true worship of God as in the days of yore—as it existed in apostolic times."[61] Another note, written by Warner sometime before 1880, in the pages of his copy of Starr's *Discourses,* indicated that the progressive revelation of the "mystery" was already in his thinking. In response to one of Starr's strongly antisectarian comments, Warner wrote, "It is evident from the above remarks that the author was fully awake to the eavils [sic] of divisions but had not discovered the remedy for the eavil [sic] —which is to use the universal name, 'Church of God'."[62] The mystery was at last revealed.

It is impossible to review these two works of Warner's together with the contents of a rather complete journal that he kept during this period, without being impressed with the fact that in the expression of his concepts of the Biblical truth as he saw it, there were propositions obviously imprinted with classical Anabaptist views of the church and church reform. If one compares them with the views of the church held by the sixteenth century reformers as outlined by Franklin Littell in his *Origins of Sectarian Protestantism*—an ironic title to introduce into the interpretation of a group which preached the end of all sectarianism— he can see apparent crossovers from the older tradition to the one under consideration. However, one must always keep foremost, a principle, also stated by Littell, "that Christianity is a historical religion with a sacred book in which all reforms seek their inspiration and confirmation. Since the norm provided by the book was itself diverse, it was, in turn, selectively applied in the light of the real problems of the age."[63]

That caution applies to the review of Warner's relation to the classical tradition. He, too, claimed that he had received these truths by inspiration of the Spirit and the Word and was applying them "in light of the real problems" of his age. Nevertheless, one can still say that Warner's system was expressed in many conceptual patterns which show the strong influence of classical Anabaptism. Through him they were introduced into the holiness movement at this early period of its institutional development. As indicated in the outline of his teaching already given above, his development of the church as the dwelling place of the Spirit, the baptism of believers only, the centrality of the Word of God in the midst of the congregation as the "universal law," the strong sense of mission as a reformer, the strongly apocalyptical tone, and even the retention of the rite of foot washing as an ordinance of the church—all may be closely identified with the Anabaptist tradition.[64]

These were all strongly Biblical; their application in reform movements throughout all church history proves that. In Warner's case, however, there is good reason to conclude that the identification of thought between him and the radical sixteenth century tradition is a result of more than their common Biblical source and the fact that both were in conflict with the prevailing church structures in their day.

The Winebrennerian Church of God must have encouraged some of Warner's earliest thinking, not only in the area of his expansion of their "church of God" concept under the aegis of his consequent holiness perfectionism, but also in the fact that the Winebrennerian Church drew heavily upon "free church" principles in its separation from the German Reformed Church. In its polity and practice there were elements of Anabaptist ideology such as foot washing, the believer's church, the concept of the fall of the church from its "Heroic Age," and consequently its own strong primitivism. It was especially exposed to such ideology by its geography, for it had shaped its own structures of independency, surrounded by the large concentrations of Mennonite and other "peace church" groups of east central Pennsylvania, northern Ohio, and Indiana.[65]

Warner's own contacts with earlier Anabaptist concepts of the nature of the church and its reformation, probably came from more direct association than his former church relationships. Warner had ample opportunity to know their teachings, as they were practiced and preserved by their descendants in America. His diary mentions meetings with the Dunkards and other "peace groups," and that he preached for them. But most important of all, at one point in his religious quest, after he was ejected from the Winebrennerian ministry, he had associated for a short time with the Northern Indiana Eldership of the Church of God. This group had dissociated themselves from the Winebrennerians because of the refusal of the latter to deny membership to those who belonged to secret orders.[66]

As a member of the Northern Indiana Eldership, Warner took part in union talks with a Mennonite association known as the United

Mennonite Church. His diary records that he and they had met in Hawpatch, Indiana, September 24-26, 1879, and their hearts were "wonderfully knit together in love."[67] On December 5, 1879, as he was "pushing" his book, *Bible Proofs*, to completion, he left to attend the joint meeting of the committees on union, which were to draw up an agreement for merger of the two groups. But at the joint convention, resolutions for union were agreed upon. They provided for union as soon as it could be consummated, a common recognition of the Word of God as the true basis of Christian union, and the provision for bringing all points of difference to "the truth as it is in Christ Jesus" in the belief that it could be "ascertained" and that all were "morally bound to learn and abide its decision."[68]

The fact that Warner's group and the United Mennonites never did consummate the merger is not of consequence to our purpose here. But it is consequential that, in addition to the impact of others upon his thinking, during the period in which he was writing his first defense of the "Church of God" idea, he had spent several days of serious discussion with a Mennonite group about the nature of the church and church union. The import for the history of the holiness movement is that the "come-outer" movement, at least as associated with men like Warner, had some contacts with strong traditions of the church behind it. As Littell said, they were "selectively applied," for the time,[69] but their goal of the restoration of the true church in its primitive holiness was one. It was another demonstration of the manner in which the perfectionist movement tended to be modified by, and to modify, a tradition with which it interacted.

Fully dedicated to his new reform ideas, Warner attempted to persuade the Indiana Holiness Association, which he had served as a vice-president, to modify its membership statement on church membership to allow men like himself to continue to participate in the activities of the association. Warner was already in contest with men like Thomas Doty, and especially with the Free Methodists who, under B. T. Roberts, were avidly trying to rally their own reform movement to a single denominational loyalty. Warner's suggestions were rejected.[70]

Warner had proposed that the association's rules which provided that it should "consist of members of various Christian organizations and seek to work in harmony with all these societies," should be changed to read: "It shall consist of and seek to cooperate with, all true Christians everywhere." It is probable that both sides had essentially polarized their positions before the meeting.[71]

He and his friends who accompanied him to the meeting in Terre Haute, he said, "were positively denied membership on the ground of not adhering to any sect." Consequently, they declared, "we wish to announce to all that we wish to cooperate with all Christians, as such in saving souls—but forever withdraw from all organisms that uphold and endorse sects and denominations in the body of Christ."[72] This point marked the final organizational separation of Warner and his followers from the mainstream National Association movement. It was not until recent years that the Church of God provided a rationale for organization of its work which allowed for identification again with the present components of the Christian Holiness Association. The latter is the direct successor of the National Association from which Warner and his friends "forever" withdrew in 1881.[73]

The attractiveness of Warner's approach to holiness evangelism, for many people, is demonstrated by the fact that the Church of God (Anderson, Indiana) which grew around his revivalism became the third largest of the holiness groups.[74] The appeal lay largely in the simple alternatives that his democratic structures provided for people who were increasingly fearful of, what they regarded as, a complex ecclesiasticism. That ecclesiasticism, they believed, was threatening the religious simplicity which, in the Church of God order, they attributed to the primitive church and pure religion. They sought to maintain that simplicity in the midst of the rapid social change of the last two decades of the nineteenth century. Warner's promise of a group, gathered together under the guidance and instruction of the sanctifying Spirit, free of denominational and sectarian trammels, as he pictured them, combined with a reformatory, eschatological thrust, carried a certain populist magnetism. It continued to demonstrate its democratic effectiveness as the church of God concept was even more widely used among the Pentecostal sects in the next century, especially in the black pentecostal movements.[75] To many it offered the simplest form of organization by which an informal revival group could conceive of themselves and the church. This may have been its most obvious Anabaptist characteristic. These features obviously provided one answer to the call for a broader movement by those who were not Methodists and those to whom Methodism was secondary to the revival. The Church of God came to represent a more equal balance of Methodists and non-Methodists in its early constituency than the other holiness bodies of similar size.[76]

John P. Brooks and the Church of God Concept

John P. Brooks was an Illinois Methodist minister. He was closely associated with the activities of the Western Holiness Association, formed in 1871, following a holiness movement revival in the state. Brooks' voice, in the early stages of the movement's search for order, was widely heard through the *Banner of Holiness,* the official voice of the Western Association, published at Bloomington, Illinois. In 1882 he was tried by the Illinois Conference on charges relating to alleged slanderous articles in the *Banner.* He was acquitted.[77] Soon thereafter, be became deeply involved in the movements toward independency among the associations of the rural, more conservative holiness converts of the area. Many of the groups had been particularly aggressive in their holiness evangelism. In no other area of the movement was the revival more wracked with extremisms of every kind. The agitation ultimately centered in the Southwestern Holiness Association, active in Missouri and Kansas.[78]

Because of the accusations of its enemies and the fears of its friends, that the undisciplined nature of some of the evangelistic bands was damaging the reputation of the whole movement; a holiness convention was called by the western leaders at Jacksonville, Illinois, in December, 1880.[79] Its purpose was to try to answer the charges of their detractors, that the movement "had no administrative authority over those who compose its own body of workers."[80] The National Association's leadership, possibly reinforced by the Free Methodists who were present, controlled the proceedings to the extent that the convention urged that all holiness evangelists should be members of "some Evangelical Church...."[81] The strength that the independent movement had already gained at this early date is demonstrated, however, in the fact that the above statement was qualified by the exception of those individuals who had been "expelled for the teaching of holiness."82 The tensions within the convention are best illustrated by the tenor of the addresses presented by men who represented each of the two main factions, the conservative and the radical. John W. Caughlan, at that time editor of the *Good Way,* the paper of the Southwestern Association, reviewed the history of the holiness work in the Association's area, beginning in 1872. He concluded with the observation that the work had had permanent results

> only in those places where a regular Holiness Band is organized. In those places where out of regard to ecclesiastical influences, such organizations have been omitted, the holiness work has come to naught. *Those who work for Christ have to consecrate the Church, and go forward."* Loyalty to Christ is the first duty [emphasis his].[83]

Thomas K. Doty, a Wesleyan Methodist, associated with a loose connection of churches, rather than a more highly organized denomination, made equally strong stabs at "denominationalism." Although urging the representatives at the convention to work in their church, if they were in a church, he quickly set the priorities of loyalty for the holiness evangelists, by saying, "Bring everything in your church work to bear on the work of holiness. While you do this, you must be saved from the church. You must use your church meetings to promote this work." According to the transcribed record of the address, a voice broke into his remarks with the question. "But what if they will not allow you?" Doty replied:

> If they turn you out of the synagogue, I have no objection. I don't believe in this denominational idea as God's idea. He permits it and so must we....The time will come when these denominations will all crumble; and the sooner the better, if we can build on a better basis.[84]

In contrast with the more radical calls of men like Caughlan and Doty, M. L. Haney, one of the more irenic holiness evangelists, cautioned against any tendency to follow "the *come-outers*, who insist on the silly dogma of no-churchism, and favor the disorganization of all Christian forces." He also warned against those who "have desired and advocated the organization of a distinctively *Holiness church*." He said that the holiness movement had always been "designed of God to spread scriptural holiness in existing churches, and thus fit them to subjugate the world to Christ."[85]

The New Testament Church

The confusion over the church question demonstrated, in the record of proceedings of the Jacksonville Convention, illustrates the milieu within which the church of God or New Testament church idea, as it was at first known, began to develop within the ranks of the Southwestern Holiness Association. C. E. Cowan, in his history of the Church of God (Holiness), indicates that the concept was generated more or less out of the pragmatic answers which the independents, separated from their former churches and not yet certain of how to reorganize, gave to the situation in which they found themselves.[86] That answer began to be hammered out in the pages of the *Good Way* soon after the conclusion of the Western Union Holiness Convention; it finally led to the formation of the early independent Holiness Churches after 1882.[87]

It was not until 1887, when John P. Brooks became the editor of the *Good Way*, the paper then representing the independent movement, that he began to develop his treatise on the church of God ideas which had been generated within the movement.[88] *The Divine Church*, which he published in 1891, in many ways, stands in stark contrast with Warner's presentations, in either his initial development in the *Bible Proofs*, or the more extensive development in *The Cleansing of the Sanctuary*. Warner's work is that of reformer, proclaiming the message from God in strong Biblical terms. Brooks' effort is what he claims for it in its subtitle—a treatise, a systematic rationale for a system of congregational organization which had already developed.[89] The atmosphere of Brooks' work is one of theological defense; the work of the scholar, the preface indicated that he realized that his ideas would not be well received, but he offered them with the hope that in the process of time, reasonable men would accept them and act upon them.[90] The atmosphere of Warner's work, as we have already indicated, is apocalyptic, proclamatory, and urgent—the reform was already begun and every sanctified member of the sectarian bodies was called to a revivalistic response.[91] The expositions of the editor of the *Good Way* were an attempt to inject some kind of order into disorder which had arisen out of the extreme independency of the western radical movement. Warner's ideas had become the basis for the eastern movement from the beginning. The work of Brooks was an attempt to explain a group of people who had already worked out a church of God congregational system for themselves out of a disarray of extremism and individuality; the thinking of Warner offered a comprehensive idea to which the individual committed himself before he came into the fellowship.[92] The difference between the nature of the two men's works in their attempts to answer the question of church order in the holiness revival, with the concepts of the church of God idea, probably is best shown in their continuing impact upon the holiness revival and its institutionalization. The Church of God (Anderson) became a worldwide movement and one of the larger bodies within the revival's ranks; the Independent Churches, to whom Brooks was speaking, had already set a pattern of local congregationalism and individuality. Together with the conservatism and even extremism in which the western movement was born, it has greatly restricted the growth and apparent appeal to the movement in general.

Warner's Influence Upon the Independent Holiness Churches

The basic concepts of the ideal church of God as proposed by both men are remarkably similar. The parallels are particularly striking in the outlines by each of them in the pattern of the New Testament Church in its Old Testament types,[93] of the essential characteristics of the pristine New Testament Church,[94] of the nature of the fall of the church from its original purity,[95] the evaluation of the intervening period of sectarian rule,[96] the subsequent failure of the Protestant reforming movements to retain the purity of their reform because of sectarian organization,[97] and the necessity and dynamic of the holiness movement as the hoped for agent for the final destruction of sectarianism and the establishment of the fully visible church of God.[98] The question naturally arises as to what influence Warner, who was publicly proclaiming his views in some systematic rationale for some time before Brooks, may have had on the early development of the idea among the Independent Churches.

Warner's concepts not only helped to set the pattern for the New Testament Church idea, but may have even been the reason for its adoption in the early 1880s. It appears, from the discussion which follows, that one can properly conclude that the fact of direct contacts between Warner and Brooks, during the early period of Warner's reform efforts, and the concurrent beginnings of the agitation of the church of God question in Brooks' area, can be established. If they had not met previously in the common dedication to the work of holiness associations related to the National Association, they did meet and spent four days together as representatives to the 1880 Western Union Holiness Convention. Both men were prominent in the activities of that convention. Brooks served on the committee which drew up the official report for the convention; Warner was appointed to the committee responsible for the planning of any succeeding conventions. Warner was brought prominently to the attention of the convention as one of its main speakers. He may have been introduced as representing the Church of God; his registration was in that name. It is difficult to believe that his thinking on the church question, already published in his *Bible Proofs*, but not referred to in his public address to the convention, was not discussed. The church question was the foremost one on everyone's mind.[99]

There is evidence, both circumstantial and actual, that his views injected themselves into the accelerated discussions of the church question among the western independents, in the years immediately following the 1880 meeting. The proceedings of the Jacksonville convention, as published with the roll of registrants, showed Warner and two others registered as members of the Church of God.[100] Ordinarily, this might not have been noteworthy to those who read the proceedings, except that the church name probably was not as familiar to them as were the names of the other churches represented; moreover, in combination with the publication of Warner's address and his appointment to help to arrange for future conventions, attention was called to him as one of the recognized leaders among others who had been at the forefront for a much longer time.[101] These are all strong indicators that both he and his views on the question which was pressing itself most urgently upon every one in the movement at the time were brought to the attention of this area of the movement.

Such reasoning must modify, to some extent, Cowan's claim, noted above, that the western independents came to their views on the "New Testament Church" based on the "two outstanding ideas...—Holiness and the church." They had come to these beliefs, they reasoned, out of their search of the Scriptures and the practical exigencies of their lack of organization.[102] A significant number of the most prominent leaders in the Southwestern Association and the Independent movement were at the Jacksonville Convention in 1880. Although some of them left the Association at a later date, because of disagreement with its "come-outer" tendencies, they all were deeply involved in the discussions on the church of God question. These included Rev. John H. Allen, Methodist Episcopal; Justice Morris, Methodist Protestant; Rev. J. W. Caughlan, Methodist Episcopal; Rev. Isaiah Reid, Presbyterian; Rev. W. B. M. Colt, Free Methodist; and Rev. A. M. Kiergan, Methodist Episcopal Church South.[103] Kiergan's presence at Jacksonville with Warner is especially significant to the establishing of possible connections between Warner's and Brooks's concepts of the church of God. It was Kiergan who was the central figure in encouraging independency and defending the church of God or New Testament church idea in the movement. It was he who reminisced thirty-seven years later that the Southwestern Association's ideas had developed "without any conscious understanding of the New Testament polity of the church."[104]

The initiation of Warner's own holiness publishing career as associate editor for the holiness page of the *Herald of Gospel Freedom*, the official paper of the Northern Indiana Eldership of the Church of God, and his editorship of the newly established *Gospel Trumpet*, soon thereafter, spread his early views widely throughout the movement.[105] His widespread views were further publicized by the general reaction to his withdrawal from the organizations of the movement in 1881. Discussions of his "come-outism" and of his rationale for denying "no-churchism" filled the movement's journals.[106]

Definite evidence that the line of reasoning, outlined above, is not entirely circumstantial, is provided by an article by F. H. Sumpter, entitled "One Church," which appeared in the *Good Way* for June 3,

1883.[107] The publication date was only one day after Sumpter, with eight others, had been ordained to the ministry of the Southwestern Association at Centralia, Missouri, by a presbytery headed by Isaiah Reid.[108] On the same day that the article appeared, Reid, a Presbyterian pastor in Nevada, Iowa, until he was expelled by the Iowa Synod for his holiness evangelism, preached the sermon for the dedication of the church building which had been erected by the Centralia organization.[109] It was the first of a number of such churches that quickly followed.[110] It is striking that in his article, Sumpter makes reference to Warner's church of God thinking in support of his contention. Consequently, he declared that the time had "fully come for that part of the church of God that has the light on Bible holiness and is determined to walk in it to unite into independent organizations."[111] In combination with the circumstances outlined above, this represents strong evidence that Warner's ideas were under consideration within the inner circle of men who made the first steps toward the Independent Churches in that area.

In conclusion, it appears that Warner must be considered not only as the originator of the church of God concept, as modified by the preaching of the holiness revival, and around which the Anderson, Indiana group gathered, but he must also be regarded as a direct contributor to the rise of the church of God concept around which the independency movement in the Southwestern Holiness Association rallied just a few years later. The latter development came through the familiarity of the prominent leaders in that movement with Warner and his ideas at the time of their earliest efforts to establish some kind of New Testament order in their disorganized ranks. These conclusions do not negate the reality of the Biblical and pragmatic context in which these early leaders later placed the struggle which resulted in their adoption of the New Testament Church of God church order;[112] but they do indicate again, that no movement, especially no Christian movement, can divorce itself from history. The continuity of tradition is always there even within those churches who make the strongest appeals to the essentially Biblical sources of their life and order. In the light of the above contentions, the question arises as to why Brooks nowhere in his extensive treatise refers to Warner by name, in spite of their agreement upon the implications which they saw in the holiness movement for the church question. The answer probably lies, in part, in the fact that, contrary to the intervention of Warner's ideology at a critical point in the organization of the New Testament Church movement, he himself was not personally involved with that movement. But more probably, the reason that no credit was given to his views among the Missouri and Kansas Church of God groups, after the early period, is due to the strong mutual antagonism that developed between the two movements as their evangelistic efforts crossed paths. Warner's reports on his evangelism in Mississippi in 1889 contain numerous, strong recriminations against the "Straight Holness" people of Scott, Kansas, and their paper, the *Good Way,* then under Brooks' editorship.[113] Warner regarded their work as the chief hindrance to his own work there. This sharp contest between the two groups was taking place at the same time at which Brooks was writing *The Divine Church;* it was highly unlikely that he would refer directly to Warner under those circumstances. It also explains why there has been little contact between the two groups at any time since then.

James F. Washburn: Churches "on the Holiness Line"

The question of the nature of the New Testament Church, as it was raised among the first groups of converts of the holiness revival in California, surfaced in the Southern California and Arizona Holiness Association. The Association had been organized at Artesia, California on July 1, 1880 out of the revivalism of Rev. Hardin Wallace, an aged minister of the Methodist Episcopal Church, and veteran holiness evangelist. Rev. Harry Ashcraft, a young evangelist of the Free Methodist Church, and James Jayns, a Methodist Gospel singer, assisted Wallace.[114] All were from Illinois. Mr. and Mrs James F. Washburn, living at that time in the Azusa Valley of California, became the prominent leaders in the holiness evangelism of the Association in the Los Angeles area.

Under their leadership, the organization of the revival's adherents within new holiness structures followed the common pattern. The converts of the revival, first of all, gathered together into bands which gradually assumed the nature of a simple church fellowship, with standards for membership and standards of discipline for their workers. The purchase, or renting of places for their meetings, the increasingly organized activity, brought the groups intensified opposition from pastors who were not sympathetic with the movement.[115] The opposition tended to expand the activities of the bands and associations, and thus one feeding on the other, the most ardent advocates of radical action eventually turned their semiformal, interdenominational associations into full-fledged churches; they provided basic statements of faith and rules for order. These included a provision for the ordination of a ministry and the administration of the sacraments.[116] The conservation of the fruits of their revival efforts is the most common reason given for the moves to final organization. "A few of us...heard the bleating of the starving, dying sheep.... And before high heaven we promised the Lord in the oaken groves of Santa Barbara that we would feed the sheep."[117]

The *Pentecost*, the official journal of the Southern California and Arizona Holiness Association, provided a contemporary account of the evolution of one of the first Holiness churches. Of the organization of the Downey, California "Holiness" church, he said,

> Some members of the Baptist denomination having professed that God had sanctified them wholly were tried by their churches and excluded from the membership because they would not recant....Some Methodists had withdrawn from the M. E. Church South and others felt that they could no longer support preachers who were opposing the holiness movement and preaching against sanctification....Some of them were visited by the pastor and urged to withdraw from the Holiness Band or leave the Methodist Church. Some of them told them to drop their names from the roll. Their names were dropped as in the case above, sometimes without the consent of the one whose name was dropped.
>
> The Downey Band was at first composed altogether of those who held membership in some Christian denomination or sect, but in this respect has undergone a gradual change until now only one or two members have their name on any other church book....
>
> In the year 1884 the Downey Band appointed a committee of five to draw up a constitution and bylaws to be submitted to the Band for its adoption. In August 1884 the committee made their report and submitted...a constitution and bylaws very much like that of the Holiness Church at San Bernardino....The word "Band" was retained in the name to avoid expense...the words "or church" were added. The name is "Downey Holiness Band or Church." It is "free and independent" subject to no ecclesiastical control.[118]

The Downey California Church was not the first to be organized out of the Southern California Holiness Association. The chapels at Azusa, Pomona, Downey, San Bernardino, and Santa Barbara erected by the Holiness Bands for regular services on "the Pentecost line" in 1882 and 1883 were actually churches.[119] At first they held their meetings Sunday afternoon and Tuesday evening, but finally as unchurched converts joined the denominationally attached band members, they began to meet during the same hours as the established denominations.

"It was soon made evident the Lord should have the best hours in the day for holiness."[120]

The "Holiness" Church of California

The unique contribution that the California group made to the work of the radical reformers represented another application of the perfectionist impulses of the revival at work in the undisciplined formative years. It did not involve the breadth of concept which had swept Warner into what he proclaimed as the final reformation of the church, nor were its principles ever developed in a lengthy treatise such as Brooks had provided for the New Testament Church groups which grew out of the Southwestern Association. Washburn had not attended college as both Brooks and Warner had. His approach to the church question was more pragmatic than either of theirs had been. The statement above, tracing the history of the organization of the Downey church, illustrates that pragmatism.

However, Washburn's ideas, like those of the other two men under consideration, did not develop in isolation. In fact, there was very little isolation within the diverse movement; the constant flow of periodical literature and its peripatetic evangelists who circulated continuously among the local groups and in the general camp meetings, provided a complex, yet efficient network of communication. Washburn was in direct contact with the areas in which the Independent Churches were developing in the mid-west. As we have noted, Wallace and Ashcraft were from Illinois; they continued their contacts with the California movement. Moreover, there were family ties that took prominent members of the California movement back to the same area.[121] His views on the church question were carried by the papers of the Independent Church movement. The fact that such links existed between California and Illinois and the fact of the links that have already been shown between that area and Warner and his reform movement, seem to indicate that this early period of church organization, between 1800 and 1885, should be studied in the light of these relationships—possibly they constituted components parts of a single movement in spite of their geographical separation.[122]

The best outlines of the reasoning by which the first "come-outers" justified their decisions for leaving the churches and creating new holiness band-churches of their own are provided by another Washburn who was active in the California Association—B. A. Washburn. His most extensive treatment of the church question was given in his book, *Holiness Links,* published in 1887. Washburn defended their separation from the denominational churches because "the sanctified" were no longer tolerated in their congregations. Since, in most cases, the sheer disparity of numbers between them and the "sinners" made it impossible for the "saints" to purify the local churches, he recommended, therefore, that thet latter should organize themselves into independent churches in which they could set in order a congregation more amenable to their holiness interests.[123]

In the same book, Washburn answered questions concerning that new order. It was very primitive at first and extremely congregational. Elders were elected by the congregation for no more than a year and frequently, for briefer periods; the only ordination that was required was "the baptism of fire." If one received that experience, he was "ordained enough" "The men, women and children" were free to take part in the services "as led by the Spirit." No one was given a special commission to preach at any particular service. The use of musical instruments was relegated to the Old Testament dispensation and had no place in the congregation of "the saints." Washburn said that it was "high noon-tide" then, and in the dispensation of the Holy Ghost, "every sanctified soul" was "a harp of a thousand strings" and the "baptism of fire" had set "them all going." He saw such small holiness band-churches, as places where "the poorest of the poor" could have the Gospel preached to them. The plainness of their service, of the churches and their life-style, they believed, helped to guarantee that.[124]

The basic, practical conclusions on the implications of the holiness revival for the future of church order had been outlined in two letters which were sent by B. A. Washburn and James Swing, of the California Association, to the General Holiness Assembly which met in Chicago, at the Park Avenue Methodist Church from May 20 to May 26, 1885.[125]

Other than in their unique concept of the basis for membership required by the California independents discussed below, they represented a concise statement of the rationale by which all of the radical reformers explained their separatist actions. Both documents were denied any formal hearing at the convention. They were labeled by the National Association forces, who continued to exercise discipline over the movement as a whole through the general conventions, as "a perfect charge of dynamite come-outism."126

When one compares the reasoning of these men with the conclusions of the convention as interpreted by the National Association's journal, he can see why the charge was made against them by the main group of loyal Methodists who represented the heart of the movement. The Christian Standard and Home Journal said that the convention had denied that the holiness people had any right "to sever connection with the Church even if the Spirit of holiness did not prevail in the congregation."[127] On the other hand, James Swing and B. A. Washburn contended that many of the converts had no church home. "They [could not] endorse the the modes and customs of the religious denominations around them." Many of them had been "turned out" of their congregations because they had joined the holiness associations; their zeal became a "living rebuke" to the churches. These, they continued, had been joined by large numbers of others whom the revival had won who never joined any denomination; "This is the people's movement and is as broad as the universe." Furthermore, the holiness people have the right to "set things in order" without consulting or receiving the approval of any other denomination.

Their independent churches, they said, were essential not only to sustain the spiritual life of holiness people who often found little food or fellowship in the larger churches, but also to check the growing ecclesiasticism which all of these groups feared. "Many small independent churches," he said, "prevent pride of denominational glory and give poor people a chance." Finally, he appealed again to the obvious "success" of their efforts as a sign of divine blessing upon them. In light of the prevailing circumstances, he asked the Assembly to "declare to the world that the permanent salvation of souls is vastly more important than methods regular or irregular. Speak out," he said, "voice freedom over the earth by declaring in favor of 'Independent Holiness Churches with pentecost sanctification as a basis for membership."[128]

Entire Sanctification: A New Basis for Church Membership

This concluding appeal of B. A. Washburn to the Chicago Holiness Assembly identifies the unique results of another application of the perfectionist impulses of the revival to the church question. The "Holiness" churches in California were to be fellowships of the "entirely sanctified." In most other aspects of their organization, they demonstrated many of the prominent characteristics of the congregations which had formed around the church of God concept in the other two areas under review. Most prominent among these was their attempt to restore the purity of the church within local congregations gathered by the Spirit around the Word of God, as previously outlined. They were responsible only to the direction of the Spirit in the congregation. The emphasis in the California groups upon such leadership was probably the most extreme of any of these three reform groups. Complete disorder was checked by the recognition that personal impulses had to somehow come under the teaching of the Scripture as generally accepted by the congregation.[129]

The strong emphasis of all the holiness people upon the centrality of Spirit guidance in the worship of the congregation, and, in the radical groups under consideration, in church polity as well, created classic situations for the operation of what Franklin Littell saw as one of the pivotal points of Free Church concern. In his discussion of the origin of the Anabaptist believers churches, he noted that "among the Anabaptists the Bible was opened in the congregation and the Spirit gave guidance to interpret the meaning of the Word." He said that this resulted in their claim to the right to change their minds about truth. "The same attitude was taken to church law and structures: the Spirit, and not the letter ruled. But the Spirit was the one who gave order, not atomism and anarchy."[130]

This professed openness to the Spirit in the midst of the congregation, in the holiness context described above, provides one with useful insight into the dynamics of the radical holiness reform movements. Such a context helps to account for the "pentecost sanctification" basis for church membership proposed by James Washburn "in the early eighties."[131] As was true of the discovery of the basic thought of the other two movements, Washburn's reflections on the nature of the church carried him back across the centuries, past the history of the sectarian origins of the churches which were now rejecting holiness as he believed, to what he saw as the pure life of the New Testament Church. But, Washburn envisioned that church, not only as a group of true Christians, but as a group of entirely sanctified Christians. He had brought the "second blessing" revivalism message into the ordering of the restored church of the Holy Ghost dispensation in which he and all holiness people believed they were living. The church was to be once more a visible gathered company of the "saints"—and "saints," for Washburn, meant those who were entirely sanctified Christians. The result was an effort to regain the purity of the congregation by demanding the highest standard of Christian profession ever proposed for church membership.[132]

Like Warner and Kiergan, Washburn attributed this new insight to the direct inspiration of the Spirit's unveiling of Biblical truth. In what he believed to be "a vision, revelation direct from Jesus Christ," he claimed that John the Revelator's picture of the spiritual deficiencies of the "Seven Churches of Asia" flashed as a "panorama" before his eyes. It was further revealed to him, that each deficiency in those churches which, for him, were representative of the denominations of his time, had developed because of a lack of holiness in their membership. They too had consisted of mixtures of sinful people who had rejected holiness and God had demanded repentance and sanctification as remedy for their sin. He finally concluded that God was revealing to him the pattern for the restoration of apostolic purity and order, for "the Spirit, at the same moment seemed to speak in audible words, saying: 'What God required at the beginning, will he require at the end'."[133]

It became obvious to him that "through this clear revelation"...it had been made quite clear that the establishing of the New Testament or Christ's Church was founded on Holiness or Sanctification." This light of Divine Revelation," he said, "spread rapidly, as a forest fire."[134]

On this "holiness line," the Holiness Church of California was ultimately organized out of Washburn's Southern California and Arizona Holiness Association bands. In 1946, having failed to experience any significant growth under this radical organizational basis, it merged with the Pilgrim Holiness Church. In that merger, its churches abandoned Washburn's concept and took up the Pilgrim's requirement of conversion and a willingness to pursue holiness as the standard church fellowship. The latter represented the common pattern for membership in the holiness churches.[135]

THE MAINSTREAM'S REJECTION OF THE "COME-OUTERS"

Regardless of the fact that the three early holiness separatists movements which have been reviewed above represented a classic example in American church history of efforts to apply the doctrine of the Holy Spirit to the questions of church order in the Free Church tradition, the results constituted too much of an irregularity for the Methodist mainstream holiness movement. B. A. Washburn's independency was undoubtedly a much greater issue to the 1885 General Holiness Assembly than his "pentecost sanctification" requirement for local church membership. Methodism could tolerate almost anything easier than it could tolerate independent, irregular methods which conflicted, in any significant degree, with its own tightly knit structures. The whole movement learned the reality of that fact by the end of the century, according to Charles Ferguson's recent history of Methodism.[136]

The independent movements of the 1880s constituted an unbearable embarrassment to the leaders of the moderate holiness center who were pursuing their own holiness reform almost exclusively in terms of their Methodist loyalist context. The torment of these men, whose optimistic hope for the perfection of the churches was irrevocably related to the success of the Methodist churches as holiness churches, became increasingly evident as the pressures, which had created the radical reform groups, intensified in the next two decades. In 1890, the *Guide's* editor, George Hughes, remembering the happier days of the

Palmer movement in Methodism, chided the independents for their "voluntary" withdrawal from "the several churches" or "the sects," as they called them. He deplored "the spirit of 'COME-OUTISM' " which had seized these "friends of holiness." He wrote plaintively, "In doing this they have wounded the cause of holiness in the house of its friends, and they have done serious harm in making the allotment harder on those who determine to remain in the Church of their choice. That is not acting on the golden rule, we think."[137]

Looking back from a twentieth-century vantage point, it appears that the reformers were merely ahead of their time. They were acting out of the exigencies of the moment in an attempt to discover an answer to their relationship with the universal church. With the possible exception of Warner, they recognized that they were reacting as pragmatists— although Biblical pragmatists.[138] They felt that they had been rejected by churches, which, for them, no longer represented believers churches and especially not holiness churches. They brought into play all the conscious or unconscious influences from historical Christian traditions which had been infused into their thinking and experience.

The goal they were seeking was to try to establish new believers' fellowships, in which the doctrines and lifestyle that they adhered to could be nourished, and above all, propagated. Their efforts to express the universality of the church in their "church of God" and their "church of the saints" concepts, the attempt to express the equality of the worth and contribution of each member, their strong emphasis on the separateness and holiness of the fellowship, and their impelling sense of mission were not new. They were well known as the Free Church tradition.[139] What made their efforts somewhat unique was the holiness hermeneutic by which they interpreted that tradition in their contemporary application of it. Their perfectionist tendencies and the special concern for the primacy of freedom in the Holy Spirit strongly reinforced the basic elements of the tradition. Their efforts marked the final interaction between revivalism and perfectionism within the framework of the movement. In this instance, it was not the message or the method of its propagation, but the manner of its perpetuation within the church structures which was in view. They were proving Sperry's contention that "it is in the bodies which inherit the Reformation passion for a church purged from worldliness and purified after the primitive pattern that we find in America those schisms and subschisms of the more evangelical types of Protestantism." Sperry continued, "Here is the truth of most of our excessive denominations."[140]

Although the answers at which they arrived were rejected by the main body of holiness people at the time, and eventually modified by the groups themselves, these early separatists, with their radical demands for a place within the structure of the American denomination, were merely the pioneers of a pattern that was repeatedly followed by others within the movement over the next fifteen years.[141] Among the later group were many who had to defend themselves against the same charges of "come-outism" which had been directed against the earlier group.[142] By the time of the denunciation of the movement's raison d'etre—its special promotion of the doctrine of Christian holiness—in the episcopal address to the Methodist Episcopal Church South in 1894, the die had been cast for many who had once stoutly resisted the early separatist tendencies.[143] They had probably learned from the bitter experience of the first independent movement. The leaders of the later movements were often men of broader experience, both within their denomination and the holiness revival. They set the course of their own independency within patterns more acceptable to the Methodistic orientation of the movement. These new organizations provided church homes for the majority of those adherents of the revival who did not choose to stay within the established churches.[144] "A strange silence shrouded the subject of holiness" in the churches which they left, for it seems that with their separation, not only the controversy over the doctrine, but the zeal in its proclamation waned. The lure, which the call to perfection still carried, was demonstrated in the success of the evangelism of the new holiness churches. That evangelism, together with that of the pentecostal sects which also sprang from the revival's milieu, eventually attracted a constituency which approximated that of worldwide Methodism itself.[145]

SUMMARY

Pressed by the rapidly changing patterns of life in their postwar communities and churches, many of the converts of the holiness revival turned to the incipient institutions of the movement to find identity and community. These holiness bands or associations shared in the sense of unity, which had become common among members of American evangelical churches who met and worked together in joint evangelism. Out of those experiences, revivalists had boldly spoken of a coming day when the revival would eventuate in one united church. In the restoration, they said, a true, spiritual brotherhood would subsume the differences among what to them were the obviously deficient denominations. The visible unity of the church would be restored.

The rhetoric of the holiness partisans concerning the unity which the general acceptance of the holiness experience would bring among the churches was stronger than the rhetoric on Christian unity in any other segment of the American revival. Faced with opposition in their own churches, which they felt were progressively falling away from the puritan pietism lifestyle, which the Holiness advocates commonly recognized as an integral part of genuine Christian witness, they adopted new strategies. They applied the combined teleology of the logic of their message of perfectionism and their doctrines of present purification by the Holy Spirit to the questions of their church relations and the nature of the church itself.

That logical union, reinforced by the vitality of the idealistic dreams represented by the expansive mood of America's belief in her manifest destiny, resulted in a challenge to the holiness movement and the American "sects" to fulfill the revival's promise of a pure, unified, visible church. A small group of radical pioneers began to call for a radical reformation of the churches. In the real perfection in love which they believed the Holy Spirit had made possible for every Christian now, they saw the potential for the restoration of the perfection of the primitive church of Pentecost, in which the "saints" and the "sanctified" would gather together once again in undivided Christian witness. The divine patterns of that church, they felt, had been obscured by the accumulation of human creeds and ecclesiasticism. Out of their own commitment to perfectionism, they proclaimed that God had revealed the mystery of the restoration of his true church; it was to be a church of God, pure and one, comprised of people who were freed from selfish partisanship by entire sanctification by faith. For them, the holiness revival was the testimony to this new "age of the Spirit."

It was a bold new dream, made even bolder by the growing negative reaction of the churches to the perfectionist's optimistic claims. There was little hope, therefore, that the denominations would accept the ultimate conclusions of the radical application of that perfectionism to their own structure. Moreover, at this point, most segments of the holiness movement, itself, were equally unprepared to accept the radical reformer's conclusions. They were genuinely dedicated to Methodism's own commitment to order and organization. Beginning with Methodism, though admittedly increasingly reluctant Methodism, they continued to hope to usher in the long anticipated reformation of the many churches into one great holiness crusade.

NOTES

1. This can best be seen by following the activities of the various associations in their periodicals referred to throughout this book. More readily available sources that illustrate the type of personnel who made up such bands and their band activities are Josephine F. Washburn, *History and Reminiscences of Holiness*

Church Work in Southern California and Arizona (South Pasadena, CA: Record Press [1912]); or Sarah A. Cooke, *op. cit.*, The work of the numerous individual evangelists who were continually carrying on informal evangelism wherever "the Spirit led them" can be reviewed in the work of the black Methodist evangelist Amanda Smith, *An Autobiography* (Chicago: Meyer and Brothers, Publishers, 1893); or Jennie Smith, *From Baca to Beulah* (Philadelphia: Garrigues Brothers, 1880).

2. T. Smith, *Called Unto Holiness*, pp. 27-242; C. Jones, *Perfectionist Persuasion*, pp. 194-234; Vinson Synan, *The Holiness-Pentecostal Movement in the United States* (Grand Rapids, MI: Wm. B. Eerdmans Publishing, 1971), pp. 44-76.

3. Robert Wiebe, *The Search for Order: American Society, 1877-1920*, Vol. V of "Making of America," American Century Series (New York: Hill and Wang, 1967).

4. *Ibid.*, pp. xiii, 12, 27, 44; also see Mann, *op. cit.*, pp. 154-55, Paul Kramer and Fredrick L. Holborn (eds), *The City in American Life: A Historical Anthology* (New York: G. P. Putnam's Sons, 1970), pp. 263-64.

5. *Ibid.*, 247. T. Smith, *Called Unto Holiness*, p. 29, Val Clear, *op. cit.*, p. 3.

6. Wiebe, *op. cit.*, p. 44, C. Jones, *op. cit.*, pp. 146-47; T. Smith, *Called Unto Holiness*, p. 28; Hudson, *op. cit.*, p. 307, notes that during this period, the Greenback and the Farmer's Alliance movements of the 1870s and 1880s were soon followed by the Populists of the 1890s. His statement that the eastern papers described the agrarian protesters as "dangerous characters" may throw some light on the reaction of the National's leaders to the rural reformers of the holiness movement. Hudson claims that "the evangelical religion of the rural and village churches of the Midwest and South...was implicated in the farm revolt and contributed to its continuing impetus." The "relationship" between the two, he says, "has received little study."

7. Wiebe, *op. cit.*, p. 62.

8. Perry Miller, *op. cit.*, p. 23.

9. The committee appointed at the 1877 Holiness Conference in Cincinnati to achieve "harmonious action" among the participants in their holiness promotion could only produce a report of the future plans of each of them; *Proceedings of Holiness Conferences*, pp. 31, 111-12.

10. A. M. Kiergan, *Historical Sketches of the Revival of True Holiness and Local Church Polity from 1865-1916* (n.p.: Published by the Board of Publication of the Church Advocate and Good Way [1972]), p. 40. "A Survey of the Field," *A Survey of the Field and Strictures Thereon*, by J. P. Bro,oks reviewed by T. J. Bryant (n.p.: n.n. [1882]), pp. 4-9. The "Survey of the Field," had appeared as an editorial in the *Central Christian Advocate*, one of the many Methodist "Advocates"; it was a sharp attack upon the holiness movement in the Illinois area for what the editor claimed were the large numbers of people involved in it whose lives "were not up to the common standards of Christian morals" and who were "lacking in the spirit of Christ...." Those individuals, he said, were "captious, arrogant, ready in finding fault, wanting in Christian courtesy, [and] overanxious, apparently, to assert and show their disregard for proper authority"; *ibid.*, p. 3. J. P. Brooks, editor of the *Banner*, charged that the attack was an attack on the doctrines of

entire sanctification which the movement was propagating, that there were irregularities among some he could not deny, but he claimed that they were due to the fact that people in the holiness associations were human and subject to the problems which had faced all Christian revivals of religion. He claimed, however, that the western holiness movement was subject to fewer such faults than some others; *ibid.*, pp. 9-14. That Bryant was probably the less prejudiced of the two may be indicated by the fact that he was generally a friend of the movement. Only a year before he wrote his review, he had said that "Nobler and purer men than Hardin Wallace, M. L. Haney and L. B. Kent are not to be found in or out of Illinois," and that in spite of fanaticism in "the work at Williamsville" the holiness people on the whole were just as true to their professions of religion as were those who made no claim to such an experience; *Good Way*, III (November 12, 1881), 4. The *Good Way*, III (October 15, 1881), 7, carried an advertisement of five sermons by Bryant in support of the movement and its central doctrine. Also see *supra*, p. 214.

11. *Proceedings of Holiness Conferences*, pp. 100-102.

12. "The Holiness Movement an Error," *Good Way*, IV (November 1884), 2. "Address of General Western Union Holiness Convention, to the Friends of Holiness..." *Proceedings of the Western Union Holiness Convention Held at Jacksonville, Illinois, December 15th-19th, 1880* (Bloomington, IL: Western Holiness Association, 1881), p. 81.

13. "The Holiness Convention: Round Lake, N.Y.," *Advocate of Bible Holiness*, XIII (August 1882), p. 227.

The report of the convention was signed by "J. S. Inskip, President" and "J. N. Short, Secretary"; Short later was a dominant figure in the unions which created the Church of the Nazarene. For the 1885 Chicago Assembly's "Declaration of Principles," see *Guide*, LXXVI (July 1885), 26-28.

14. See "That Illinois Conference Report," *Advocate of Christian Holiness*, X (December 1879), 283-84. The paper noted that when every Methodist minister became a preacher of perfect love as the conference recommended there would be "no further need of 'Associations,' 'Evangelists' or 'periodicals,' for the special promotion of holiness..."

15. For example, T. J. Bryant mentioned above and particularly the friends of the movement among the church's hierarchy.

16. One of the main divisions of the Western Convention "Address" was titled "Aggression"; *Proceedings of the Western Union Holiness Convention*, p. 82; their "aim," they said, was *"pushing the whole truth of God* upon the attention of the whole population around them." (Emphasis theirs.)

Some of the best examples of both the extreme aggressiveness and the extreme reaction are found in Kiergan, *op. cit.*, pp. 11-34 et passim.

17. The strong statement on Christian unity in the prayer of Christ in John 17, which carried great import for the whole Christian Church, carried a special import for them because it immediately followed a statement on sanctification which was widely used in the teaching of the movement.

18. Wallace, *op. cit.*, p. 15.

19. *Ibid.*, p. 144.

20. Miller, *op. cit.*, pp. 22-23.

21. *Ibid.*, p. 43.

22. *Ibid.*, pp. 46-47.

23. *Ibid.*, p. 46.

24. *Supra*, pp. 37-40.

25. William H. Starr, *Discourses on the Nature of Faith and Kindred Subjects* (Chicago: D. B. Cook and Co., 1857), p. 35. Starr was particularly put out with the denominational establishment because of what he considered to be their shabby treatment of him at his ordination. "It is thought there is more liberty at the West than at the East," he wrote, "With the people perhaps it is so. Yet with the ministry, I should think it the reverse....But the handle of our pap-spoon is at the East, and so we have to turn our faces that way to get the bowl to our mouths. This makes us wonderfully orthodox." This book was apparently one of the most influential books in the development of the views of Daniel S. Warner's "church of God" concepts; *infra*, p. 248. It may also be significant that it was written in Illinois and probably well known there where the independency movement of the Southwestern Holiness Association, a movement ideologically related to Warner's, began.

26. For example, Daniel Sidney Warner, *Bible Proofs of the Second Work of Grace or Entire Sanctification as a Distinct Experience, Subsequent to Justification, Established by the United Testimony of Several Hundred Texts, Including a Description of the Great Holiness Crisis of the Present Age, by the Prophets* (Goshen, IN: E. U. Mennonite Publishing Society, 1880), p. 397, said, "I have...heard the charge that these holiness bands are a 'conglomeration of all sects,' etc. Well here is a striking evidence of the Divinity [*sic*] of the whole movement. What but the power of God could join into such loving bands of union...elements from the various disintegrated and selfish parties of Israel...." Only "the all resolvent and utilizing virtues of holiness" could accomplish it, he concluded. The largely rural Southwestern Holiness Association said the same thing: "We do not...aim to labor only on denominational lines, but to secure in the different tribes of our common Israel 'the unity of the Spirit in the bonds of peace' and bring about the desire of the redeemer's heart 'that they may be one.'" Clarence E. Cowan, *A History of the Church of God (Holiness)* (Overland Park, KS: Herald and Banner Press, 1949), p. 18, as quoted from the *Good Way* (October 16, 1880). Also see Kiergan, *op. cit.*, p. 10.

27. See *supra*, pp. 134-36.

28. William Jones, *From Elim to Carmel* (Boston: Christian Witness, 1885), pp. 78-81. Also see Clebsch, *op. cit.*, p. 202; Hudson, *Religion in America*, pp. 320ff. The holiness people were reading the *Zeitgeist* and placing their movement within it. James Buckley, editor of the *New York Christian Advocate*, said in 1898, *ibid.*, LXXIII, No. 2, 65, that "the number of believers who look for the speedy fulfillment of all that is meant in the dispensation of the Holy Ghost is rapidly increasing." In June of the same year, William B. Godbey, one of the movement's most prominent evangelists, declared that the holiness movement was "the last call of the Gospel age." Its acceptance would "give the Church power and glory such as she had never known." *Guide*, CII (June 1898), 179.

29. A discussion of the work of Warner and the two other men listed here follows below. Warner's work is most fully outlined in A. L. Byers, *Birth of a Reformation Or the Life and Labors of Daniel S. Warner* (Anderson, IN: Gospel Trumpet, 1921); it is especially useful for the long passages from Warner's diary. Other accounts of Warner's life and work are found in Charles Ewing Brown, *When the Trumpet Sounded: A History of the Church of God Reformation Movement* (Anderson, IN: The Warner Press, 1951) and John W. V. Smith, *Heralds of a Brighter Day: Biographical Sketches of Early Leaders in the Church of God Reformation Movement* (Anderson, IN: Gospel Trumpet, 1955).

30. Brooks is best known for his treatise on the church and church order, *The Divine Church*, previously cited in chapter 5. Until he joined the Independent Church movement, he was a member of the Central Illinois Conference of the Methodist Episcopal Church.

31. Washburn's work is best told in Josephine M. Washburn, *op. cit.*, and the *Pentecost Magazine*, where most of the material in the book was originally printed; also see mostly from the same source, L. A. Clark (ed.), *Truths of Interest: Bible Doctrine and Experience as Advocated by "The Holiness Church"* (El Monte, CA: The Standard Bearer Publishing House, 1939).

32. T. Smith, *Called Unto Holiness*, pp. 28-33, 160.

33. S. B. Shaw, long active in the movement in the Michigan Holiness Association and editor of the *Michigan Holiness Record*, was one of their most vocal critics. Shaw reported on a National Association camp in Lansing, Michigan. He admitted that "the preaching was good as far as it went." But he thought "the teaching and the explanations regarding consecration were not sufficiently definite." He also decried the National's use of gate fees and renting of tenting space for "unreasonable rates"; *Michigan Holiness Record*, II (June 1884), 21, The National's workers present at the camp were William McDonald, George D. Watson, John A. Wood, E. I. D. Pepper, and Dougan Clark. "All of them seem honest," he noted, "and some of them [were] dear, good men of God who are in sympathy with our radical holiness work"; *ibid.* Also see T. Smith, *Called Unto Holiness*, p. 33. The Free Methodists generally worked actively in the expanding movement, but they too had criticism for the National's Methodist leadership at times; see "An Unkind Insinuation," *Advocate of Bible Holiness*, XIII (September 1882), 263, Also see *Christian Standard and Home Journal*, XIX (February 21, 1885), 5.

34. For example, George Hughes' editorial, "An Awful Drift," *Guide*, CII (March 1898), 82-83; the same, *Holiness Yearbook: 1893*, as cited by Peters, *op. cit.*, p. 147.

35. T. Smith, *Called Unto Holiness*, p. 28.

36. A. L. Byers, *op. cit.*, pp. 30-42; Brown, *op. cit.*, pp. 42-54; J. W. V. Smith, *op. cit.*, pp. 20-25. John Winebrenner, "History of the Church of God," *History of All Religious Denominations in the United States: Containing Authentic Accounts of the Rise and Progress, Faith and Practice, Localities and Statistics of the Different Persuasions...*(Harrisburg, PA: Published by John Winebrenner, V. D. M., 1848); the same, *Doctrinal and Practice Sermons* (Lebanon, PA: Published by Authority of the General Eldership of the Church of God, 1868).

37. Byers, *op. cit.*, pp. 103-109; Brown, *op. cit.*, pp. 62-68; J. W. V. Smith, *op. cit.*, pp. 17-20.

38. Byers, *op. cit.*, pp. 132-33, 154-56; Brown, *op. cit.*, pp. 68-72.

39. As quoted from Warner's journal for March 7, 1878 in Brown, *op. cit.*, pp. 71-72.

40. In their efforts to develop a rationale for their movements and their place within the Christian Church, Warner and the other radicals under discussion exhibited a classic illustration of a persistent Christian tradition which may be traced back to Joachim of Fiore (*ca.* 1145-1202). Joachim, out of his study of the Scriptures and in his earnestness for reform of the church as he knew it, divided the history of the church into seven periods, dominant among which were the Constantinian fall and restitution of the church under a new Constantine in the end time. His further division of history into the dispensations (status) of the Father, Son, and Spirit with the "age of the Spirit" as the greatest and last is especially represented in its long passage through men and movements in subsequent church history. It recurs in the concept of the "Holy Ghost and last Dispensation" which, as we have seen, was so important to the holiness movement and particularly to the perfectionism of the radical reformers. They saw their age as corresponding with the end time, which Joachim, in his scheme, had seen as the time "when the Spirit and Life" would be in the church in "the time of the eternal Gospel." It was the time as well of the battle against evil in the person of the "last and worst anti-Christ, in Gog." Victory over Gog, in turn would usher in "the final judgment and the great Sabbath of consummation...." S. M. Deutsch, "Joachim of Fiore and the 'Everlasting Gospel,' " SchaffHerzog, *op. cit.*, pp. 184-85. Franklin Littell has shown how these ideas constantly surfaced in the Anabaptist groups of the Reformation period. Joachim's "thought has influenced the underground of Christian dissent ever since..." Littell says. Its influence or recurrence in basic but adapted forms is indicated in the discussion which follows. See Littell, *The Anabaptist View of the Church*, pp. 51-53. Also see Brown, *op. cit.*, pp. 24-35.

41. Warner, *Bible Proofs*, pp. 415-19.

42. Starr, *op. cit.*, p. 231.

43. Warner, *Bible Proofs*, p. 367.

44. *Ibid.*, pp. 367-73.

45. *Ibid.*, p. 376.

46. *Ibid.*, pp. 375-85; "The 'seven months' that are required to bury Gog and cleanse the Church, it is probable, is prophetic time—'a day for a year'—making 210 years; but whether the Wesleyan reformation, or the present more general movement be the point to reckon from, I am unable to say." *Ibid.*, p. 386. Although Warner at times speculated cautiously with dates as he did here, he rarely pressed his conclusions.

47. According to his inscription in his copy of Starr's *Discourses* in the Warner Collection of Anderson School of Theology Library, Anderson, Indiana, Warner purchased the book in 1868 at the start of his ministry. It is the only source he identifies outside of the holiness periodicals cited below. See *ibid.*, pp. 420, 422-25, 430-31.

48. Warner, *Bible Proofs*, p. 419.

49. *Ibid.*, p. 420, as quoted from Starr.

50. *Ibid.*, p. 429. Immediately preceding this passage, Warner specifically claims that he is not "advocating the no-church theory that we hear of in the west...."

51. *Ibid.*, p 436.

52. D. S. Warner and H. M. Riggle, *The Cleansing of the Sanctuary: Or The Church of God in Type and Antitype, and in Prophecy and Revelation* (Moundsville, WV: The Gospel Trumpet Publishing, 1903). Warner was especially concerned because Adventist theology applied the "cleansing of the sanctuary" concept, which he had applied to the holiness reform of the day, to "a cleansing in heaven...to begin in 1844." *Ibid.*, p. 38 *et passim.*

53. *Ibid.*, p. 389.

54. *Ibid.*, pp. 225-26.

55. *Ibid.*, pp. 227-28.

56. *Ibid.*, p. 229.

57. *Ibid.*, pp. 229-30.

58. *Ibid.*, pp. 230-35, 283, 291-315. The "Heroic Age" is a term used by Littell for the early church prior to the Constantinian fall. *The Anabaptist View*, p. 57 *et passim.*

59. *Ibid.*, pp. 237, 298-335, 349.

60. *Ibid.*, pp. 375-79. He saw the second "beast" of Rev. 13 as the type of the Reformation sects; the first "beast" represented, for him, the Catholic Church. His most recent fulfillment of the type was applied to the sectarian spirit of the Free Methodists under B. T. Roberts. He said that they began to shout, "We're free, we're free!" But when they organized, they became "as dead spiritually as their mother."

61. *Ibid.*, pp. 435-36, 448ff.; see Littell, *The Anabaptist View*, p. 52. Here was the "eschatologicl accent" which Littell saw in the Anabaptist movement. Like them, Warner and the other radical reformers, and indeed the movement as a whole, looked on "themselves as the secret meaning and bearers of the New Age...." *Ibid.*, pp. 76-77. Just prior to these passages Warner had described the final battle of Gog and Magog as a struggle between the sects and the true church of God, which the holiness revival was calling together out of all denominations; *ibid.*, pp. 411ff.

62. Handwritten note on p. 221 of Warner's copy of Starr's *Discourses.*

63. Littell, *The Anabaptist View*, p. 77.

64. Charles Ewing Brown, Church of God (Anderson, Indiana) historian, emphasized the links with this tradition and others such as Pietism; see the same, *When the Trumpet Sounded*, pp. 30-35; the same, *When Souls Awaken: An Interpretation of Radical Christianity* (Anderson, IN: Gospel Trumpet, 1954), pp. 34-37.

65. Winebrenner, *Doctrinal and Practical Sermons*, pp. 37, 88, 119-20, 177-83, 211, 266-67, 283, 285-90, 333-70; the same, *The Religious Denominations*, pp. 173-82.

66. Byers, *op. cit.*, pp. 124, 190-91; 177-79. Brown, *When the Trumpet Sounded*, pp. 72-73.

67. Byers, *op. cit.*, p. 191.

68. *Ibid.*, pp. 193-94.

69. The Evangelical Mennonite Publishing House at Goshen, Indiana, published Warner's *Bible Proofs*.

70. Byers, *op. cit.*, p. 261; the date was April 22, 1881. In the same year the first Church of God congregation was established at Beaver Dam, Indiana; *ibid.*, p. 269.

71. *Ibid.*

72. *Ibid.*

73. *Supra*, p. 107. The Church of God (Anderson, Indiana) has not officially joined the Christian Holiness Association, but does have members of its official family who participate in its activities and serve on some of its committees.

74. The largest holiness denominations are: The Church of God (Anderson, IN), 224,846 U.S. and Canada, 532,624 total worldwide (1994); The Church of the Nazarene, 609,540 U.S. and Canada, 1,138,504 worldwide (1994); The Free Methodist Church, 83,584 U.S. and Canada, 358,253 worldwide (1993); The Salvation Army 446,403 U.S. and Canada; The Wesleyan Church, 122,116 U.S. and Canda, 223,662 worldwide (1994).

75. Among the churches of the Churches of God which followed was the Church of God (Cleveland, TN). According to Brown, A. J. Tomlinson, founder of the southern church, may have been involved in the Church of God movement of Warner in his earliest ministry; he also purportedly took the Church of God name from the Warner group's use of it. Brown, *When the Trumpet Sounded*, pp. 362-63, xii. It adopted the name Church of God in 1907.

76. Val Clear, "The Church of God: A Study in Social Adaptation" (Unpublished Ph. D. dissertation, University of Chicago, 1963), p. 117, as cited by Ralph Eugene Price, "The American Holiness Movement, 1830-1910" (Unpublished B. D. thesis, Anderson School of Theology, Anderson, Indiana, 1957), pp. 2-3. Clear, in a detailed study of the early *Gospel Trumpet*, examined the published letters to the editor and found that of 99 persons mentioning the group from which they came, 44 came from non-Methodist groups and 45 came from Methodist denominations.

77. *Advocate of Bible Holiness*, XIII (May 1882), 157. Also see ibid. (February 1882), p. 62; apparently Brooks had considered resigning his editorship of the Banner to become editor of the Free Methodist. McDonald, editor of the *Advocate*, wrote: "We are fully persuaded that the interests of Holiness in the West will be conserved by this decision," The *Good Way*, III (November 8, 1882), p. 4, reported that he joined the Free Methodists, but there is no further record of this.

78. Kiergan, *op. cit.*, pp. 31, 51-57. These involved some of the first evidences of the "tongues" phenomenon in the holiness movement's context; *ibid.*, p. 31. Charges of "free lovism" and other moral irregularities were rampant. Kiergan denies that these were tolerated in the Independent Church movement, and that the fact that they did exist more widely in the undisciplined holiness associations was one of the reasons he and others pressed for the organization of local holiness congregations; *ibid.*, pp. 40-42. Also see Byers, *op. cit.*, pp. 365-67. Bryant, *op. cit.*, pp. 4-6.

79. The conveners of the convention were careful to explain that they were not planning to "give law to the work." However, one of the main topics placed on the agenda was the consideration of "Teachers—the proper kinds; preservation of the work from the damaging influence of those who have proven themselves unfit..." *Proceedings of the Western Union Holiness Convention*, pp. 2-3; also see *Good Way*, VI (November 1, 1884), 2. *The Bible Standard*, a Wesleyan Methodist holiness periodical,

reported that the delegates to the convention were determined that the "work of holiness shall go forward. in spite of the interdiction of preachers, Churches or Conferences"; *Ibid.*, XIII (January 1881), p. 30. Also see Peters, *op. cit.*, p. 136.

80. Bryant, *op. cit.*, p. 5.

81. *Proceedings of the Western Union Holiness Convention*, p. 81.

82. *Ibid.*

83. J. W. Caughlan, "Some Account of the Holiness Work in Missouri and West," *ibid.*, p. 21. Kiergan in his reminiscences written many years later makes much of this statement as a critical point in the independency movement; see Kiergan, *op. cit.*, pp. 28-29. It is of more than passing interest to the development of the independency movement that Kiergan in this same passage attributed the origin of the key phrase, "consecrating the church," to a "Sister M. E. Scott," a Baptist holiness evangelist who was active with the Southwestern Association at that time. She had caused "a furor," he said, "among the ultra interholiness folks [interdenominational holiness groups] in Illinois some years before by saying she had 'consecrated her church.' " She was active in the Missouri work as early as 1880; *ibid.*

84. Thomas K. Doty, "Right and Wise Methods of Promoting Holiness," *Proceedings of the Western Union Holiness Convention*, p. 23. Nowhere does the confusion of the movement at this early stage of its effort to find its place for the future within the prevailing pattern of the revival churches show itself more than in Doty's speech. He concluded: "Sometimes you hardly know what to do..." *Ibid.*, p. 26.

85. M. L. Haney, "Current Errors among Teachers of Holiness," *ibid.*, pp. 44, 43-49.

86. Cowan, *op. cit.*, pp. 20-21; Kiergan, *op. cit.*, p. 38.

87. See, for example, *Good Way*, III (October 15, 1881); *ibid.* (November 12, 1881); *ibid.*, IV (March 4, 1882); *ibid.* (April 1, 1882); *ibid.*(September 23, 1882); *ibid.* October 21, 1882); *ibid.* (November 18, 1882); *ibid.*, V (June 2, 1883). Also see *infra*, pp. 263ff.

88. Cowan, *op. cit.*, pp. 43, 48.

89. Brooks, *op. cit.*

90. *Ibid.*, "Preface."

91. Warner, *Bible Proofs*, pp. 431-32, made his appeals personal; the "enormous sin [of sectarianism] must be answered for by individual adherents to...sects....The divisions of the church are caused by...deposits of the enemy, which exist in the hearts and practices of individual members, involving their responsibility and requiring their personal purgation....These facts make *your duty* plain" (emphasis his).

92. It appears that the individual who was most influential in the pragmatic development of the movement which Brooks undertook to explicate in his treatise was A. M. Kiergan. The first churches were organized around six principles which Kiergan had outlined in a series of unpublished articles early in 1882. They show the simple pattern of organization common to these early movements:

(1) This congregation shall be called "The church at___."

(2) "The Church at ____ " takes the Word of God as its confession of faith and rule of conduct and agrees to live and teach by that alone.

(3) The bond of union between "The Church at ____ " and any and all other congregations of "the church" shall be simply the unity of the Spirit and God shed abroad in the heart.

(4) Let offenders be dealt with or disposed of by admonition, or if incorrigible, simply by withdrawal from the fellowship, according to directions laid down in the New Testament.

(5) "The Church at ____" shall exercise its coherent right to "ordain elders" by the laying on of hands of the presbytery.

(6) The temporal affairs of the church shall be administered by "deacons" chosen by the congregation.

The similarity of this pattern with basic Baptist or other congregational organization of the local church may have been due to direct influences from Baptist, Congregational, and Disciples groups who were prominently associated with Kiergan and the Southwestern Association. A. B. Earle, New England Baptist holiness evangelist, had held holiness revivals among the Baptists in Missouri which brought about the eventual separation of small groups of "holiness Baptists" from their churches. These people did not find a congenial home in the Methodist churches.

Their association with Kiergan and the other independents apparently was very close. Many joined the independent movement. Their concepts of church organization must have contributed directly to Kiergan's thinking on congregational organization. Moreover, one of the six men who marked the beginning of the main "come-outer" movement with their agreement in March, 1881 to leave their churches was a Dr. J. W. Blosser of Macon, Missouri, a Congregationalist minister. See Kiergan, *op. cit.*, pp. 3-5, 29, 32, 39.

93. Brooks, *op. cit.*, pp. 1-17. Warner and Riggle, *op. cit.*, p. 98 *et passim*.

94. Brooks, *op. cit.*, pp. 63-92. Warner and Riggle, *op, cit.*, pp. 230ff.

95. Brooks, *op. cit.*, pp. 32-36. Warner and Riggle, *op. cit.*, pp. 317-23.

96. Brooks, *op. cit.*, pp. 36-39. Warner and Riggle, *op. cit.*, pp. 323-33.

97. Brooks, *op. cit.*, pp. 39-42, 242-66. Warner and Riggle, *op. cit.*, pp. 37 5-90.

98. Brooks, *op. cit.*, pp. 267-83. Warner and Riggle, *op. cit.*, pp. 435-43.

99. Kiergan, *op. cit.*, pp. 28-29; *Proceedings of Western Union Holiness Convention*, pp, 18-26, 44, 81-83.

100. *Ibid.*, p. 12.

101. *Ibid.*, pp. 13, 16.

102. Kiergan, *op. cit.*, pp. 44; Cowan, *op. cit.*, p. 26.

103. *Proceedings_of the Western Union Holiness Convention*, pp. 7-1.

104. Cowan, *op. cit.*, pp. 20-21; Kiergan, *op. cit.*, pp. 34-42.

105. Byers, *op. cit.*, pp. 178-81, 237-41, 259-60.

106. *Ibid.*, pp. 263-66. Warner's separation from the Northern Indiana Eldership of the Church of God in October of 1881 caused a widespread stir in the holiness press; *ibid.*, pp. 266, 272. Warner recognized that he was receiving considerable attention at this period; at the beginning of 1882, he wrote: "Nearly all the professed holiness periodicals have been hauling barrels of water and pouring on the altar of God's truth...." See articles from the *Gospel Trumpet* in reply to some of these as quoted in papers; *ibid.*, pp. 275-89.

107. F. H. Sumpter, "One Church," *Good Way*, V (June 2, 1883), Sumpter was one of the six original "come-outers" who took part in the March, 1881, meeting at Macon, Missouri. Kiergan, *op. cit.*, p. 39.

108. *Good Way,* V (June 9, 1883); Kiergan, *op. cit.,* pp. 44-49, gives a complete account of the events. He is in error on the date, however; he gave it as May 1883, instead of June; *ibid.* Cowan, *op. cit.,* pp. 26-27.

109. Kiergan, *loc. cit.* Cowan, *loc. cit. Good Way,* III (November 12, 1881), p. 4.

110. Kiergan, *loc. cit.*

111. Sumpter, *loc. cit.* An article by J. H. Allen, another of the prominent leaders in the early holiness work in Missouri, appeared in the same periodical later in the year entitled "Sectism Doomed." It requested the editor to publish a letter by D. W. McLaughlin which offered the holiness people an alternative to either the undesirable "come-outism" or Free Methodism, which he looked upon as an attempt to "patch up or resuscitate dying Methodism...." *Good Way,* V (September 23, 1882), p. 2. The significance for the present argument is that McLaughlin was writing for Warner's *Gospel Trumpet* in defense of Warner's ideas at the same time; see Byers, *op. cit.,* pp. 286-88.

112. Kiergan, *op, cit.,* pp 1-51, and Brooks, *op. cit.,* pp. 266-75.

113. See accounts from Warner's journal for his claims that the "Fort Scott creed" people, as he called them actually stirred up mobs against him Byers, *op. cit.,* pp. 370-71, 366; also see *ibid.,* pp. 368-69 for his charges against their moral conduct and ethics. It should be remembered that the Missouri independency movement created absolute autonomy for the local congregation and the discipline which was exercised depended completely on its local administration; that varied greatly among these churches. See Kiergan, *op. cit.,* p. 41. Byers, *op. cit.,* p. 285, also cites an article from the *Gospel Trumpet (ca.* 1381) in which Warner said that under pressure from M. L. Haney and L. B. Kent, Brooks had failed to put "radical truth" in the *Banner.* Warner called the former "temporizers" and said Brooks had yielded and backslid "from Holy Ghost power." This hardly encouraged warm relationships between the men or the movements.

114. Washburn, *op. cit.,* p. 7; Clark, *op. cit.,* p. 1.

115. *Ibid.,* p. 2; Washburn, *op. cit.,* pp. 10, 19, 24.

116. Clark, *op. cit.,* p. 2.

117. B. A. Washburn, *Holiness Links* (Los Angeles: Pentecost Office, 1887), pp. 155-56.

118. George E. Butler, "Holiness in Downey," *Pentecost,* I (February 28, 1886), 8; Clark, *op. cit.,* pp. 3-5.

119. The first formal organization was that at San Bernardino in 1884 by James Swing, a leader in the early years of the Association; Clark, *op. cit.,* p. 2; also see B. A. Washburn, *Holiness Links,* pp. 189-200, for rules and policy adopted by these congregations.

120. *Ibid.,* p. 155. Clark, *op. cit.,* p. 4.

121. Dennis Rogers, *Holiness Pioneering* (Hemet, CA, 1944), p. 13.

122. This may be true in spite of their differences and antagonisms. Their common goal for a method of applying the holiness revival's message to local church organization and their simultaneous and not unrelated rise make such common study profitable.

123. B. A. Washburn, *op. cit.,* p. 155.

124. *Ibid.,* pp. 165-81.

125. *Ibid.,* p. 184.

126. B. A Washburn, *op. cit.*, pp. 184ff., gives the contents of James W. Swing's letter to the 1885 convention. Washburn's letter is published in the *Good Way*, VII (May 23, 1885), 1. Cowan, *op. cit.*, pp. 24-25, gives it from that source. Both, however, were widely broadcast across the movement by their publication in the *Good Way* and the *Banner of Holiness*; B. A. Washburn, *op. cit.*, p. 184.

Brooks, editor of the *Banner*, was the one who tried to force the letters to the floor of the convention. According to Kiergan in spite of Brooks' statement that he would be heard "if he had to get on a goods box in front of the door," and the support of L. B. Kent against the ruling of the chair against the hearing of the California documents, the "communication was pigeon-holed in the chairman's pocket"; Kiergan, *op. cit.*, p. 63. Kiergan also points up the opposing points of view in quotes from two men; E. Davis, "a Methodist preacher from Massachusetts, rock-ribbed sectarian, said: 'What do we want better than we had? What we want is not machinery so it will run better.' Bro. Doty replied to the above remarks, that 'We are not here to bind hands or hearts, but to give our brethren something that will do them good and help them in their work.' " Kiergan, *op. cit.*, p. 62. Kiergan's account, though written late in life, is the best account we have of the inner workings of the convention; *ibid.*, pp. 64-65. Kiergan had been elected as Secretary of the Chicago Assembly, but did not serve because of his duties as a reporter for the *Good Way; ibid.*, p. 62. The conclusion of the independents was that they had attended "a National prayer meeting." *Loc. cit.* The official report of the proceedings is given in *Proceedings of the Gen. Hol. Assembly, Held in the Park Ave. M. E. Ch., Chicago, May 20-26, 1885* (Grand Rapids, MI: S. B. Shaw, 1885), The *Guide*, through its editor George Hughes, reported that in the Assembly "there was a disposition on the part of a few to discuss 'come-outism'; this was decidedly checked and on the whole there was a great unity of spirit and action." *Ibid.*, LXXVI (July 1885), 26.

127. *Christian Standard and Home Journal*, XIX (June 6, 1885); 8.

128. B. A. Washburn, *op. cit.*, pp. 174-210.

129. *Supra*, p. 142, n. 44; also see Washburn, *op. cit.*, p. 139; Swing and James Washburn never talked about who was to preach. They waited for the Spirit. L. B. Kent, as late as 1900, reported on a meeting of the Holiness Church which he attended: "Aiming to have the meetings Pentecostal, formal order and ordering were unknown, and free-speaking, prophesying and testimony, were quite in excess of preaching and not a few of the Lord's handmaidens spoke and prophesied to edification, exhortation, and comfort." *Ibid.*, p. 278. Kent was still president of the Illinois Holiness Association at that time. This freedom of, or from, liturgy was typical of the movement, although not commonly in this extreme. It arose both out of the movement's teaching on the Holy Spirit's leadership of the individual and the freedom of the camp meeting atmosphere which was so dominant in shaping all the holiness churches, even the bodies which had first left Methodism—the Free Methodists and the Wesleyan Methodists. E.g., see David B. Updegraff's remarks on the programming at Mountain Lake Park Camp Meeting, Maryland: "The meetings are remarkably free of prearrangement and programme." Dougan Clark and Joseph Smith, *op. cit.*, p. 175. Churches like the Holiness Churches gradually brought more order to their services; see Josephine Washburn, *op. cit.*, p. 359. The most complete single collection of source material on the "Pentecostal order" as used by this church is in Clark, *op. cit.*, pp. 44-48.

130. Littell, "Concerns of the Believer's Church," *The Chicago Theological Seminary Register,* LVIII (December 1967), p. 14.

131. Josephine Washburn, *op. cit.,* pp. 58-59; *Pentecost,* I (February 5, 1886), 2; Clark, *op. cit.,* pp. 39-40.

132. *Ibid.* For the Holiness Churches' explanation of the church relationship of those who were not entirely sanctified, see J. W. Swing, "The Relation of Justified People to Christ's Holy Church"; in summary he likens it to the citizen who was undergoing naturalization, he did not have full rights until he was finally declared a citizen; this happened for the Christian when he was finally sanctified; *Pentecost,* XXI (September 28, 1905), 1, quoting from a pamphlet of Swing's originally printed in 1889.

133. Josephine Washburn, *op. cit.,* p. 58; Clark, *op. cit.,* p. 53-68.

134. *Ibid.,* p. 59.

135. *Ibid.,* pp. 112, 132-34, 146, 276, 241; *Manual of the Pilgrim Holiness Church, Revised by the International Conference of 1966, Edited by the Committee* (Indianapolis, IN: The Pilgrim Publishing House [1966]), p. 14.

136. *Organizing to Beat the Devil* (Garden City, NY: Doubleday and Co., Inc., 1971), p. 277; Ferguson said, "Holiness was one thing, but disturbance was another"; pp. 282-83; T. Smith, *Revivalism and Social Reform,* p. 132; the same, *Called Unto Holiness,* pp. 52-53.

137. "No Schism in the Body," *Guide,* LXXXV (April 1890), 122.

138. The exception of Warner is made because his reform concepts seemed to involve a much broader scope of thinking than the other two men under discussion. This was possibly why he was the only one to specifically call his movement a reform movement. The others frankly admitted their pragmatism; *supra,* pp. 261ff., 266ff.

139. Littell, *Register,* pp. 15-18.

140. Sperry, *op. cit.,* p. 76. Peters, *op. cit.,* p. 190, says, "It is sometimes assumed that the movement was primarily an expression of an economically and culturally submerged group finding in the high promises of religion compensation for their poverty in other areas. It may be possible to illustrate this thesis by examples from later periods. But the post-Civil War revival of holiness cannot be so explained. Economic and social factors undoubtedly played a part. But the more basic motivation for those who were active in the holiness movement within the Methodist Church must be sought for in the realm of theology and psychological predisposition." The period at which this paper concludes probably marks the beginning of the "later period" Peters referred to.

141. Synan said, "Never before in the history of the nation had so many churches been founded in so short a time"; *op. cit.,* p. 53. Also see T. Smith, *Called Unto Holiness,* p. 36; "A dozen denominations...set sail in the narrows between 'anarchy' and ecclesiasticism."

142. For example, Phineas Bresee, founder of the Church of the Nazarene, asked in *The Nazarene,* IV (June 28, 1900), 3, why there was a Salvation Army, why a Keswick Movement "filling already so largely the minds of people interested in a better spiritual life in Europe and America? Simply, because of the failure of Methodism to continue to preach the pure Pauline doctrines of entire sanctification by a second definite work of grace....Why the Church of the Nazarene? Simply because Methodism will not brook holiness revivals and be an agency for the distinctive work of sanctification. It is no child's play to go out under the blue sky,

without means and agencies and try to create them." He said that anyone would prefer to work with existing agencies than to have to go out "single handed, mistrusted, misunderstood, and misrepresented. Nothing but dire necessity would compel any man to do. [*sic*]" In *ibid.* (July 26, 1900), p. 1, he noted that the logic against establishing new churches has always been the same: "All are unnecessary, unwise, uncalled for; if only the promoter [would] have had the superior wisdom which 'we' possess, they would have found a better way."

This he said was applied to Luther, the Independents in Great Britain, the Free Churches of Scotland, the Friends and the Methodists; also see *ibid.* (August 2, 1900), p. 1, "Whether a man leaves his fellowship or not is entirely up to his own situation"; *ibid.* (November 8, 1900, p. 1, "All the churches were new once, and we are unable to see what difference it makes whether a church is one year old or a thousand."

143. The bishops in their address observed; "But there has sprung up among us a party with holiness as a watchword; they have holiness associations, holiness meetings, holiness preachers, holiness evangelists, and holiness property.…We do not question the sincerity and zeal of these brethren; we desire the church to profit by their earnest preaching and godly example; but we deplore their teaching and methods in so far as they claim a monopoly of the experience, practice, and advocacy of holiness, and separate themselves from the body of ministers and disciples"; as quoted by Synan, *op. cit.*, pp. 50-51. Also see Peters, *op. cit.*, p. 148; T. Smith, *Called Unto Holiness*, p. 41; Jones, *op. cit.*, p. 456.

144. Of the new holiness churches that eventually were organized out of the revival, The Church of the Nazarene, under Bresee rapidly gathered together the largest number of holiness adherents. See *infra* p. 285, n. 74; the second largest was the Pilgrim Holiness Church which grew by a series of mergers out of the Apostolic Holiness Union and Prayer League started by Martin Wells Knapp and Seth Cook Rees in Cincinnati, Ohio, in 1897. In 1968, at its merger with the Wesleyan Methodist Church, in their joint formation of The Wesleyan Church, it reported a membership in the United States and overseas of 56,607; *Minutes of the Twenty-Sixth International Conference of The Pilgrim Holiness Church: June 25, 1968, Anderson, Indiana* (Marion, IN: The Wesleyan Publishing House, 1968), p. 31.

145. Ferguson, *op. cit.*, pp. 283-85, Synan, *op. cit.*, pp. 213-15.

Chapter 7

"The Rest of the Story"

The Holiness Churches
at the Turn of the Century

Most holiness leaders and lay adherents had vigorously rejected the "come outer" movements of the earlier period. To understand why they themselves later came to the decision to move major elements of the movement into newly formed denominations and agencies, one has to look at the comprehensive network of people and movements which constituted the holiness movement of the time. By the 1880s, an extensive, polycaepholous network of holiness adherents was active across the United States and Canada, and indeed around the world wherever Protestant missions had established Christian outposts.

Timothy Smith, in a revised edition of his now classic work, *Revivalism and Social Reform in Nineteenth Century America* recognized that, in that work, he had tended to look at the holiness revival too narrowly as an almost exclusively, Methodist phenomenon.[1] In addition to rallying the faithful within Methodism, the holiness revivalists also had significant success in bringing large numbers of unchurched people into the movement in the closing decades of the century. These new converts joined the movement with no direct loyalties or attachments to Methodism or other organized religious entities. It was the movement's claim to biblical authority and its proposed social and spiritual response to the declining piety and loss of spiritual power its followers perceived in the existing churches and society that attracted them. The holiness camp meetings, revival meetings, Bible conferences, books, and periodicals constituted the spiritual room and board of these otherwise unattached adherents.

The coordination of these disparate units was not achieved through up-line or down-line authority or planning. Rather it was an informal, but dynamic, network of peripatetic, often charismatic, holiness evangelists who became the recognized leaders of the numerous associations. Like their Methodist progenitors, riding the preaching circuits of a century before, they made their annual rounds of evangelization and institutional formation. They travelled by rail instead of on horseback and the points on their circuits were camp meetings instead of established preaching points. But their aim was the same calling men and women to faith in Christ and sanctification in the Spirit. Through their presence and preaching at revivals and, most important of all, the campmeetings which gathered the faithful together every summer to refuel the spiritual energies, they rallied the faithful and set the ethos and mores for the developing movement.

In addition to the charismatic peripatetic leaders who fostered the growth of the holiness associations, an equally vigorous, rapidly proliferating, publishing network shaped and supported this foment of doctrinal and institutional development. The Palmer-sponsored *Guide to Holiness and Pentecostal Life,* as it became known later in the century, continued to serve as the main periodical for the broader interdenominational movement.[2] The National Association's *Christian Witness and Advocate of Bible Holiness* focused more directly on the Methodist movement. Its publishing house in Philadelphia poured out books and tracts, flooding the hundreds of holiness associations inside and outside of Methodism with materials supporting the movement and keeping the zeal of its followers kindled at white heat. The printing presses of the Wesleyan Methodist and Free Methodist Churches, churches who were already full participants in the revival by this time, served the revival as well. As the revival flourished and spread to every area of the rapidly developing nation, scores of other publishing centers and their publications sprang up to support and promote the revival.[3] Publications of the larger and older Wesleyan denominations also abetted the cause. Under the editorship of William Nast, *Der Christliche Apologete,* the organ of the Central German Conference of the Methodist Episcopal Church, fed the revival among German Methodists. Nast was a member of the National Camp Meeting Association. The *Living Epistle* appeared in the Evangelical Association and the *Highway of Holiness* in the United Brethren Church. The Keswick Convention in England, its related mission agencies, along with its American relatives in the movement among constituents of such leaders as Dwight L. Moody, A. J. Gordon, A. T. Pierson and others in the non-Methodist higher-life movement, promoted the Spirit-filled life with their publications as well.[4]

THE KESWICK/HIGHER-LIFE MOVEMENT

In addition to the failure to take into account the importance of evangelistic successes of the revival among the unchurched, there has also been a failure to pay enough attention to the significance of the non-Wesleyan holiness/higher-life groups' influence upon the mainstream Wesleyan holiness revival. The most significant Wesleyan penetration into the Reformed evangelical traditions was the spread of holiness/higher-life teaching promoted by the English Keswick Convention. It became the most popular and pervasive of the non-Wesleyan expressions of the holiness revival. The Keswick understanding of the experience of holiness and life in the Spirit represented a re-shaping of the American Methodist holiness revival's experience of entire sanctification by English, largely Reformed, evangelicals. Low-church Anglicans such as Evan Hopkins, Webb-Peploe, and Handley Moule continued the Keswick Convention after the American leadership faltered because of questions about Smith's doctrinal and moral integrity.[5]

The consequent reformulation of the holiness message of the victorious Christian life under the Keswick banner allowed holiness teaching to penetrate the non-Methodist churches of America more broadly than had been possible under the original revival movement with its heavy Methodist perfectionist flavor. The experience of daily victory sin was the promise of both theologies. The Calvinistic Keswickians, however, would claim only that, in the fully consecrated believer's life, the power of the old nature of sin was countered by the presence of the indwelling Spirit, not cleansed away as commonly maintained by their Wesleyan compatriots. The Methodist holiness movement clung to its Wesleyan theology and terminology for the experience, but tolerated considerable terminological freedom in heralding the experience until continuing theological definition brought the Wesleyan and Keswick camps into open conflict at the turn of the century.[6] Keswick spirituality, strongly tinged with Wesleyan understanding and experience, still haunts the self-understanding of many of contemporary evangelicalism's institutions and movements.[7]

The widespread pietistic bent in conservative Protestantism undoubtedly allowed this cross-fertilization of theologies of the holy life across such radically opposed evangelical theological traditions. Perry Miller recognized the shift in American religion which allowed a shared piety to become a channel for a shared theology in his influential work *The Life of the Mind in America*.[8] On the one hand this brought new theological forces into play in non-Methodist churches as the Arminianism and Wesleyanism of the revival penetrated more Reformed and even Catholic traditions. On the other hand the theological currents which were at work in the churches of the Reformed tradition were also making their way back through the same network of relationships to influence the ethos and theology of the largely Methodist-shaped movement. This cross-bridging has altered the theological perspectives of both. It has introduced perspectives, which have sometimes proven difficult to reconcile with the traditions upon which they impinged on either side.[9]

THE RISE OF A PENTECOSTAL PRIMITIVISM

Along with the shared habits of piety that kept the Wesleyan and Reformed wings of the holiness revival on parallel course in spite of theological stresses, a growing Pentecostal primitivism began to move through all of Protestant Anglo-Saxon revivalism as the end of the century approached. Spirit Baptism and Pentecostal motifs and language increasingly interlaced the Wesleyan/Higher-Life interdenominational network. American Methodism's widespread familiarity with John Fletcher's use of Pentecostal imagery and Spirit-baptism terminology to explain the dynamics and essence of Wesley's holiness perfectionist theology played a significant part in its origin and spread.[10] British Methodist William Arthur's popular *Tongue of Fire*,[11] riding the tide of the Layman's Revival of 1857-58 encouraged this renewed emphasis on the contemporary work of the Holy Spirit in the church and the world. It fanned the expectations for a new "Age of the Spirit" which would restore the power of primitive Christian spirituality to the church, reenergize its evangelism, and hasten the establishment of the Kingdom of God on earth. Along with other similar works,[12] it provided a persuasive working paradigm for the revival's self-understanding and its explication of it place in the church and history.

The anticipation of some impending, vague but revolutionary, "new age" which was to follow the wrenching experience of the Civil War was stirring the nation even before Appomattox. The readers of Bruce Catton's *A Stillness at Appomattox* sense it as they join the men in the trenches that circled Richmond and Petersburg in the Spring of 1865.[11] The nation had been redeemed in a baptism of blood and somehow it seemed that the terrible cost could only be justified by becoming both a redeemed nation and a redeemer nation among the nations of the world.[12] The postwar holiness movement found both the mood and the rhetoric of the society's expectation of a new age for the nation a nurturing cultural milieu for its own growing anticipation of an approaching "new age of the Spirit."

The revivalists' expectations of what they believed would be the dawning of this new Pentecostal age encouraged a growing proclamation of God's readiness to demonstrate the Spirit's presence and power in the world. The promise of a renewal of miraculous signs and wonders as great or even greater than those in apostolic times mingled with the movement's primary concern for the promotion of the experience of entire sanctification within the churches. Evangelists and pastors increasingly raised the theme that the powers released at Pentecost were promised anew to a church which would put itself under the full command of the Holy Spirit. The church of Pentecost became the model for many in the holiness movement. It was a Christian primitivism, not seeking to return to the doctrinal formulas or ecclesiastical structures of the early church, but, rather, to experience again the power and purity which they believed the first Christians had experienced because of Pentecost.[15]

This renewed emphasis on the direct and dynamic divine intervention in human history, rooted in a Pentecostal theology, encouraged the holiness movement to espouse and participate in two significant theological thrusts within American evangelicalism in the last quarter of the century: the faith healing movement and the replacement of the gradualism of traditional evangelical postmillennial view of history with the crisis-centered, apocalyptic patterns of dispensational premillenialism. Growing attention to the Pentecostal theme created increasing tensions within the movement between those who believed that the proclamation of the new message was intimately involved with the continued successful promotion of its central theme of Christian holiness and those who felt that it would lead to undue attention to involvement in "side issues"[16] which would distract the movement from its historical evangelistic focus.

THE HEALING MOVEMENT

Prominent among these "side issues" was a growing emphasis on the renewed presence and power of the Holy Spirit in the world. It opened up the way for holiness adherents to play a major role in the growth of the divine healing movement in American revivalism. Its Wesleyan Pentecost-centered, theology had in it elements of scriptural and experiential understanding which proved to be more encouraging to the development of healing doctrines than those offered by other strands of American religion. John Wesley himself had believed in the efficacy of faith and prayer in the healing of the body and the expectation of the powerful intervention of the Spirit in human lives and events, but only in rare and extraordinary circumstances. The Pentecostal imagery increasingly fostered among his American Methodist/holiness successors, however, opened the way for the more regular expectation of such intervention. Moreover, the widening understanding of the Spirit-filled life revived the expectation of the reactivation of the gifts of the Spirit in the lives of Christians for ministry in the church and the world.[17]

In most instances, divine healing teaching found friendlier acceptance within those holiness associations that were most interdenominational in makeup. The National Holiness evangelists all under regular appointment by the Methodist Episcopal Church commonly refused to promote faith healing teaching in camp meetings which they sponsored; however, they still espoused many of the tenets of the healing movement and, therefore, encouraged their spread throughout the movement. None other than John Inskip witnessed to a miraculous divine healing under the ministry of Dr. Charles Cullis. Renowned railroad evangelist Jennie Smith's widely read biographies witnessing to her miraculous divine healing after decades of invalidism also fired interest in the teaching throughout the movement.[18]

Cullis, an Episcopalian, homeopathic physician, was the father of the healing movement in the holiness movement and in its close relative, the Pentecostal movement. The latter eventually gave it much more prominence than the former did. Cullis, founder of a faith home for consumptives in Boston, was one of the first in the United States to recognize the spiritual element in healing. W. E. Boardman, author of *The Higher Christian Life*; A. J. Gordon, prominent Baptist deeper life pastor; and most significantly of all, A. B. Simpson, founder of the Christian and Missionary Alliance movement, were strongly influenced by Cullis' work. All these leaders were active in the holiness revival and proclaimed their faith healing message throughout the revival network.[19] They, in turn, were influenced by the work of Pastor Blumhart and Dorothea Trudel in Switzerland, who also had joined a pietistic holiness theology to a fuller understanding of faith and spiritual healing in their convalescent homes.[20]

As the faith healing teachings proliferated throughout late nineteenth-century evangelicalism, differences concerning the true biblical doctrine of faith healing continued to trouble the movement. The early teaching of the holiness healing movement, influenced by such leaders as Cullis and Boardman, held that in the same manner that Christ's work of the cross had provided present forgiveness and sanctification for all who claimed them by faith, so believers in atonement through Christ could also claim present and complete deliverance from disease and sickness by faith alone.

After some years of experience and biblical reflection, R. Kelso Carter, a member of the Christian and Missionary Alliance, who earlier had accepted the above view, came to gradually reject the ultraism it represented without rejecting belief in the possibility or even the expectation of divine healing itself. Carter developed his initial views in his *The Atonement for Sin and Sickness; or, A Full Salvation for Soul and Body.*[21] His revision of these views is outlined in his *"Faith Healing" Reviewed after Twenty Years.*[22] In the latter, he affirmed the mystery of the overriding providential will of God and insisted that faith does not command healing but receives it if it is the providential will of God for that individual at that moment; therefore, the prayer for healing unlike the prayer for salvation must always end with the petition, "If it be Thy will." The nature of the prayer of faith for physical and mental healing, therefore, divided holiness, and later, Pentecostal teachers. The differences continue to the present. The understanding of divine healing finally espoused by most of the holiness churches was to be rooted in the later understanding of healing as represented by Carter. The more radical position, which may more properly be called "faith healing" developed into the healing theology common to the Pentecostal movement of the twentieth century, although some in the holiness tradition continued to stand with the Pentecostals in including healing in the atonement along with redemption from sin.[23]

THE MOVEMENT AND PREMILLENNIALISM

The second development within American revivalism that strongly influenced the holiness movement was the rise of dispensational premillennialism which originated largely within the Darby wing of the Plymouth Brethren in England. This understanding of history and of the nature of the church made its way to America through the ministry of John Nelson Darby himself, abetted by its advocacy within the Moody movement which was at the same time strongly infused with higher life holiness teaching, largely Keswick in origin. Moody's voice was influential within the holiness revival because he himself had testified to having experienced a "second blessing" after two Free Methodist women had spoken to him about his need of the filling of the Spirit.[24] By the close association of Wesleyan and deeper-life Calvinistic holiness adherents in holiness associations and conventions and especially by the literature which freely made its way back and forth through both movements, premillennialism began to overcome the postmillennial view of the church's mission in history which had dominated Methodism and the holiness revival from its beginning.

The more traditional National Holiness Association leaders had the same concerns about the rise of premillennial teaching that they had about the rise of the healing movement. They regarded any undue emphasis upon it as another "side issue." In their mind, its promotion, as with any aggressive espousal of the healing movement, threatened to weaken the main thrust of holiness evangelism. Postmillennialists in their ranks, such as Daniel Steele, stoutly resisted the signs of the new teachings in holiness circles. He insisted that the biblical and doctrinal bases of the premillennialism were foreign to the optimism inherent in the Wesleyan understanding of the gospel and the work of the church in the world. But in spite of such worthy defenders postmillennialism gradually began to give way to premillennialism in much of the movement. Dispensational premillennialism promised to bring a solution to the problems of history and world in a dramatic moment of divine intervention. It meshed easily with the movement's message of the central importance of the direct intervention of the Holy Spirit in cleansing the hearts of Christians and establishing them in perfect love in the crisis of entire sanctification.[25]

The influence of A. B. Simpson, founder of the Christian Missionary Alliance, is very obvious here. His "Four-fold Gospel" of salvation, sanctification, healing, and the second coming eventually became the doctrinal standard for many of the organized groups which later consolidated into holiness churches, the Pilgrim Holiness Church among them. Both of its founders, Seth Cook Rees and Martin Wells Knapp were members of the Alliance before it took on a more traditional denominational organization in 1897.[26] James McClurkan's Pentecostal Mission and Bible Institute in Nashville, Tennessee, was another holiness movement center closely related to Simpson's work. The mission later merged with the Church of the Nazarene to form the center of much of that group's expansion in the southeastern United States. Nevertheless, the Church of the Nazarene, the largest of the American holiness bodies, kept away from explicit premillennial terminology in its doctrinal statements and continued to hold diverse opinions on the question.[27]

Another influential center for the promotion of premillennialism in the movement was the Kentucky holiness circle dominated by H. C. Morrison, the Methodist Episcopal Church South evangelist of Asbury College and Seminary fame. His associate, L. L. Pickett of Louisville, Kentucky, was the most ardent proponent of the position.[28] The Wesleyan Methodists also became predominantly premillennial, but because of their more formal Methodist tap-roots there were always a significant number of postmillennial adherents within the denomination. Premillennialism eventually became the dominant eschatological position of most holiness adherents, but other views never lost out completely. The Church of God (Anderson) took up an alternative commonly referred to as amillennialism.[29]

THE SECOND WAVE OF CHURCH FORMATION

The growing stresses generated by the movement's successes tested the tolerance of the existing denominational structures. Tensions were particularly evident within Methodism, north and south. Methodism remained the dominant force within the movement for much of the latter part of the century. Its Methodist home had provided the movement a rich milieu for the development of structures and resources by which it could survive the separation that was to come at the end of the century. The support came from a holiness party within the Methodism that claimed to be fostering renewal of the one biblical truth that had distinguished Methodism among other Christian movements. These Methodists continued to look upon the revival as Methodism's best hope for preserving its historic piety and vital spirit. Continuing Methodist connections, resources, and historical awareness constantly fed the revival even after their separation nurtured the early holiness churches.

Tensions between such loyal Methodist leaders who sought to keep the revival within Methodism and the leaders of the broader separatist movement which took in clergy and laity of every non-Methodist stripe, or of no denominational stripe at all, surfaced in various ways. At the general conventions of holiness leaders, the broader more populist wing of the revival was constantly pressing the National Holiness Association leadership to set the revival free from the heavy hand of domination by the already existing churches and let it do its work as the Spirit directed. The National Committee leadership found it difficult to stem the tide. The failure of the National Holiness Association leadership to rally the institutional power of Methodism to the support of the holiness crusade at the peak of the revival's influence upon the church in the 1870s, their inability to thwart the first wave of holiness church formation, and the growing importance of the "side issues"[30] are indicators of the weakened position of their leadership as the movement entered the last two decades of the nineteenth century. As a result, new organizations, largely based in the hundreds of local and state holiness associations which sprang up wherever the revival spread, moved much of the movement out of the existing denominations and into more independent and inclusive arenas of influence and control.[31]

At the same time that the movement's Methodist leadership, represented most prominently by the National Holiness Association, was fighting to remain loyal to Methodism, an emerging new leadership in Methodism was tiring of the long struggle over the "holiness question." The movement and the church were like two ships passing in the night. Institutional Methodism, as we have already noted, was moving along a trajectory of acculturation and popular approval which, by the end of the century, would make the church almost as "American" as apple pie. For those who had opposed the revival and many of the newer clergy and laity who had little interest in the issues, the holiness proponents represented a revivalistic and pietistic past which many wanted to forget and leave behind. The final issue between many in Methodism and the holiness movement became not some "side-issue," or the doctrine of holiness itself, but rather the theological authority of Wesley himself in the future Methodism. Critics of the revival often had charged that the preaching of the Christian perfection which became characteristic of the revival was un-Wesleyan because the context of American revivalism tended to create significant variations from Methodism's standard teachings of the doctrine. That judgment, how-ever, never won the day. When the conflict over the place of the holiness movement in Methodism came to a head towards the end of the century it was not, tragically, that Methodism was freeing itself from a deviant Wesleyanism to preserve an authentic Wesleyanism, as some had con-tended. Rather, in spite of its purported novelties or even fanaticisms, the holiness movement was so closely identified with traditional Methodism and Wesleyan doctrine and life that Methodist opponents of the revival were forced to distance themselves from Wesley and the standard authors of prevailing Methodist theology to resolve the strug-gle with the holiness elements within the church.[32]

Supported by a radical transition in the scholarship in its theologi-cal institutions in the last decade of the century, the church turned to the new and greener pastures in more modern teachers and theolo-gies.[33] The legacy of entire sanctification, with whatever modifications may have been made to it during the course of the American deeper life revival, was now being surrendered, in large part, to the holiness movement; it had become difficult for the tradition to survive within its original Methodist Episcopal Church and Methodist Episcopal Church South home.

As a result, at the turn of the century, more new denominations became active on the American religious scene than at any other period prior to that time. In this process, often a wrenching one, some holiness adherents, undoubtedly, were lost to both the existing churches and the movement as a result of the trauma and stress that marked these divisions. Most of them, however, remained within the movement as it went on to create its own institutional life for the preservation and further promotion of the tradition.[34]

The so-called "come outer" holiness churches of the first wave of institutionalization—the Church of God(Anderson); the Church of God (Independent Holiness) and the Holiness Church of California—were already a generation old by the turn of the century. The Warner movement had proved to be the most vigorous of the three and by that time was already on its way to being one of the more significant of the numerous holiness groups which grew out of the revival. Both its radical "Church of God" ecclesiology which allowed it to function as a denomination and yet to deny that it was just another Christian sect, and its aggressive evangelism tended to keep its adherents in the recently constructed fold as newer holiness organizations began to develop.[35] The Independent Holiness movement in the Midwest and the Holiness Church of California were more deeply affected by the end-of-the-century reorganization than the Anderson movement was. The first, torn by the antiordinance controversy,[36] and the second, hindered by its unique requirement of a personal testimony to the experience of entire sanctification as the basis for full church membership, failed to reap much advantage from the transition of thousands of holiness adherents from their former denominational or associational homes into one kind or another of avowedly holiness denominations and agencies. Another early grouping of holiness churches, the Heavenly Recruit Association, an urban holiness movement also had began its work on the streets of Philadelphia and adjoining cities in 1882. Much of its work, too, was absorbed over the years into other organizing holiness groups as the movement coalesced.[37]

Another major institutionalized actor already on the holiness revival scene before the "second wave" of holiness movement organization was the Salvation Army. William Booth's religious and social activists were making their American revival beachheads at Philadelphia, Boston, New York, and Chicago at almost exactly the same moment that the first "come outers" were forming the first holiness churches. The historic relationship between William and Catherine Booth and the early holiness movement revivalists in England combined with the Booths own roots in the Wesleyan evangelical tradition established Wesley's doctrine of Christian holiness as a central emphasis in the Army's teaching and practice. It became the dynamic of its evangelism and social movements.

The Army's particular brand of enthusiasm, its strict military-like organizational structures, and its rejection of the accepted teaching of much of the movement on the sacraments, however, were unattractive to many of the holiness adherents looking for new church homes.[38] To the American public in general and even to the unattached members of holiness associations at century's, end its model of organization and evangelism was not main-line enough to be an attractive model for further organization. Nevertheless, the Army in America quickly took its place among the early holiness organizations.[39]

It would seem that of all the holiness organizations existing at the time of the "second wave" of the movement's reorganization, the long-established small Methodist holiness denominations such as the Wesleyan Methodist Connection and the Free Methodist Church should have found themselves more strategically positioned to reap significant institutional benefits from this period of fluidity and transition than any other groups. They officially had acknowledged themselves to be "holiness" churches from the time of their separation from the Methodist Episcopal Church in 1843 and 1860 respectively. They became full partners in the holiness crusade of the post-Civil War period. It is true that both of them experienced significant membership growth during this critical period of the movement's denominationalization. However, students of the movement have to ask, "Why didn't more of the revival forces than did find a home in these established holiness denominations which largely represented the vision and ethos of the revival? Why did so many holiness believers feel it was desirable to create new denominations and agencies to preserve and advance the cause?"

An adequate answer to these questions cannot be developed fully here. At times undoubtedly, the personal ambition and a reluctance to relinquish power by individual charismatic leaders contributed to the fact that the movement produced so many new holiness denominations. In defense of the integrity of most of the early leaders, however, one must say that the larger part of the movement, in spite of its extreme diversities and inclinations toward independency, ultimately came together under only a select few of the many new organized holiness banners to which the movement rallied for the future.

When one looks beyond these personal dynamics to other factors in play at the time that reorganization was in process, however, one can make several observations about why it moved in the patterns it did. In the case of Wesleyan Methodism, that church's appeal to the body of unattached or transferring holiness men and women at century's end was watered down by its continuing organizational lassitude. The American Wesleyan Methodists had organized in 1843, mainly out of the Methodist Episcopal Church, around Wesleyan and republican principles. The call for the immediate abolition of slavery buttressed by perfectionist ideals fired its vision and energies. After the success of the

Union cause in 1865 largely fulfilled its organizing vision, the church floundered for a generation or more as it sought to find a new balance between its continuing reform commitments, such as the anti-Masonic temperance and women's rights crusades, and its dedication to evangelism and the holiness crusade.

At the same time, a denomination which had originally organized as a loose "connection" of churches was gradually grasping for more centralized administration and leadership. Furthermore, the group's shift in emphasis from a major on social reform and a minor in revivalism to a major on revivalism and a minor on social reform was still in process while holiness revival's reorganization was at its critical stage. In the 1890s, when the opportunity arose to invite into its fellowship the thousands of holiness followers who now wanted to be part of an aggressively evangelistic holiness church with strong leadership, the Wesleyan Methodists found themselves without either strong denominational structures or leadership in place. The Wesleyan Methodist image still lacked clear definition. It was not organizationally attractive to many holiness believers.[40]

The Free Methodist Church also was firmly rooted in the holiness tradition from the time of its founding in 1860. Like the Wesleyan Methodists before them, they withdrew from the Methodist Episcopal Church over issues of freedom as they perceived them. The immediate issue was their contention for free rather than rented pews; it grew out of their concern for making the gospel and the fellowship of the church available to the poor on an equal basis with those who-could rent personal worship space. Freedom for the slaves was also an issue in contest with an episcopal Methodism which they believed lacked the courage to speak boldly on the greatest moral question that faced the nation. The new church also placed itself squarely within the holiness ranks by espousing the holiness revival. B. T. Roberts, the church's founder, was not hesitant to charge the Methodist Episcopal Church with forsaking the old Wesleyan doctrines, especially Wesley's teachings on Christian perfection and compassion for the poor for theologies and lifestyles more agreeable to its rising status as the largest and most influential American Protestant denomination. Like the Wesleyan Methodists, it saw Free Masonry as a quasi-Christian fellowship masking its competition with true Biblical Christianity behind its secret oaths and rituals. Under the leadership of Roberts and a denominational vision of creating a new Methodist church entirely consecrated to primitive Christianity's demands for holy living and concern for the poor, the Free Methodists quickly became major participants in the holiness revival. Their strong commitment to holiness evangelism, reform, education, and primitive Methodism was set in a strong administrative context. It was a Methodism modified mainly by democratic concerns for the role of laypersons in the church which seemed to position them ideally to invite the dislocated elements of the holiness movement to find a new institutional home among them.

Several factors legislated against the realization of these logical expectations. One of the most telling of these was that Roberts and his people had been so successful in retaining an image of historical Methodism that many of the holiness people of the time were hesitant to flee from what they believed to be the oppressive power structures of a highly organized Methodist Episcopal Church, north or south, into the arms of another avowedly Methodist body, even though its holiness credentials were impeccable. It is true that, for some Methodist holiness loyalists, the opportunity to continue as Methodists in a church very much like the one they were leaving made Free Methodism attractive to them. But, most others set adrift at the time, wanted to get as far away from organized Methodism as they could. They were gun-shy because of the powerful organizational fire-power that they believed official Methodism had used against them as it had tried to contain the heady wine of the revival within its rather inflexible organizational wineskins. Persons of this mind were not about to live again under bishops, even though the bishops be Free Methodists general superintendents (later bishops) with greatly restricted powers.

Free Methodism's distinct emphasis on denomination building also cut both ways. It produced a marked loyalty among its membership which served it well throughout this turbulent period. To those outside, however, it created an image of exclusiveness that did not sit well with the inclusiveness that marked many of the loosely affiliated, interdenominational holiness associations looking for a new church home. Robert's concerns that Free Methodist members might give too much time to independent holiness promotion at the expense of denomination building were well known throughout the movement.[41] Furthermore, the church's disciplines of lifestyle and worship were severe even beyond the restrictive and often legalistic limits common to the movement as a whole. A dress style commonly adopted by its ministers not unlike the simple uniform style of the Mennonites and its disciplinary prohibitions against the use of musical instruments in its worship services created formidable obstacles for many holiness adherents who otherwise would have felt at home with the theological commitments of the group.[42]

There were other churches that had been organized before the general reorganization of the movement at century's end that had also joined the ranks of holiness loyalists. Significant elements in the Society of Friends and among churches in the Anabaptist tradition underwent their own transformations into active holiness movement participants. Thomas Hamm's study outlining the overwhelming impact of evangelical revivalism upon the Quakers in America in the last half of the nineteenth century tells that story well. By the period under discussion, the holiness revival, set within its context of evangelical revivalism, brought such a revolution to contemporary Quaker teaching and practice that the traditionalists charged the young holiness evangelists with "Methodizing" Quakerism. A new order—camp meetings, revival meetings, prayer meetings, youth meetings, altar calls, paid-preachers, and above all, the introduction of the visible ordinances of baptism and the Lord's Supper—rapidly replaced or significantly modified the old order in most of the Friends' annual meetings. Quakerism in America was never to be the same again. The Evangelical Friends, as many of these Quaker holiness eventually became known, quickly took their place within the holiness movement at its reorganization. Their numbers grew steadily through aggressive evangelism, but their tradition, in spite of its turn toward Methodism, was still too parochial to be attractive to the mass of holiness believers who were searching for a new church order. In fact, like other smaller American churches who espoused the Wesleyan/Holiness revival and were deeply affected and even revolutionized by it, the "Holiness Friends" were more prone to loose significant numbers of their evangelists to the newer holiness churches such as the Pilgrims and the Nazarenes. Quaker evangelists and missionaries were especially prominent in the early history of the former group.[43]

The other extant non-Methodist tradition which the revival affected most directly was the Mennonite. From the time of the Mannheim (1868) and Landisville (1872) National Holiness campmeetings within the Amish/Mennonite/Dunkard homelands in Pennsylvania and later across the Niagara Falls region of Canada, the affinities between holiness piety and concerns for unaffected lifestyle reinforced by effective revivalism excited many in these Anabaptist, peace church, traditions. The introduction of the Wesleyan doctrine of entire sanctification into these well-established communities proved to be as traumatic and revolutionary as it had among the mainline denominations before them. By the period under review, The Brethren in Christ and the Missionary Church had become so deeply committed to the holiness camp meeting movement that they became Wesleyanized in ways reminiscent of the holiness Quakers.[44] However, these groups contributed little to the solution of the "church question" for the movement at century's end.

Most of the holiness adherents looking for a new church home were too much a part of the mainline religious culture to find the culture of these more radical expressions of Christianity attractive to them. Nevertheless, the continual interaction between both Quaker and Anabaptist cultures and the predominantly Methodist culture of the larger part of the movement had reinforced the pietistic and antiestablishment emphases already native to the holiness movement.

THE NEW HOLINESS CHURCHES

For these reasons the mass of holiness believers looking for new church homes continued to reject already existing ecclesiastical structures, even those above which had proved themselves as holiness churches. A majority of the members of the interdenominational holiness associations moved inexorably toward new denominational structures. What was to grow to be the most sizeable of these new denominations had its origins in developments within Methodism and the holiness movement in the mid-1890s on the west coast under leadership of Phineas Bresee. Bresee, a Methodist minister for thirty-eight years, pastor of the largest Methodist church in Los Angeles, and member of the board of trustees of the University of Southern California, requested an appointment by his bishop to work among the poor of the city with the Peniel Missions, a holiness movement agency. When the bishop, who made no effort to conceal his distaste for the holiness element in the Methodist Episcopal Church, refused to make the appointment Bresee moved out of Methodism and into the new work. In 1895, he organized his Church of the Nazarene, then a local congregation in Los Angeles. Thirteen years later, in conjunction with like-minded groups in New England, the middle-Atlantic states, the South, and the Midwest, he and his supporters created a national denomination The Pentecostal Church of the Nazarene.[45]

The Nazarenes, as they are commonly known, gathered together a strong cadre of experienced leadership who had given up on established Methodism or on whom established Methodism had given up, marginalized, and forced out of their places within the denominations. Some of the most seasoned leaders within the National Holiness Association with its widely scattered, loosely organized interdenominational, parachurch, holiness associations eventually opted for "organized holiness" under the Nazarene banner. They were joined by other able men and women from various non-Methodist traditions who, because of their holiness commitments, had suffered the same disruptions in their prior denominational relationships. Because of Bresee's previous National Holiness Association and Methodist associations and this diversity of prior experience, the early leadership of the movement put together a denomination whose membership requirements expressed a more moderate view of holiness lifestyle expectations than that considered essential to the holiness ethos and mores in some of the more radical wings of the revival. Strict rules and expectations for full-membership were by no means lacking, but the *Manual* of the Pentecostal Church was less demanding on the "side issues" which had been a bone of contention between the movement's more moderate and more radical leaders. The statements of faith were expressed broadly enough to allow holiness advocates with varying views on such questions as millennialism and divine healing to gather together in its fold. This combination of leadership and moderation enabled the Church of the Nazarene to gather together a larger number of holiness adherents than any other of the holiness denominations in Canada and the United States.[46]

The institution of the American camp meeting as it was gradually adopted and adapted by the holiness movement as an instrument of holiness worship and promotion ultimately became an instrument of holiness movement communication and organization. The Church of the Nazarene and similar holiness churches are first generation descendants of the American camp meeting. They literally took the camp meeting's intensity of evangelistic preaching, its community of experience, the freedom of worship, and the focus on holiness promotion indoors into the mission halls, tabernacles and modest chapels that housed most of the early holiness congregations. The ambience and ethos of the Methodist/Holiness camp meeting of the last quarter of the nineteenth century thoroughly fashioned the ambience and ethos of these holiness churches as well. The founding and formative leadership of the Church of the Nazarene reflected the holiness camp meeting movement in its combination of Methodist and non-Methodist revivalistic traditions.

What eventually became known, in 1922, as the Pilgrim Holiness Church represented the second largest coalition of revival forces to come out of holiness revivals and camp meetings of the latter part of the century. At the same time that Bresee's Nazarene Church was organizing in California, another Methodist, Martin Wells Knapp, pastoring in Michigan, a strong center for the holiness movement in the Methodist Episcopal Church, was eager to do something for the revival. When, for health reasons, he failed to secure an appointment as a missionary under Bishop William Taylor, a Methodist missionary bishop and himself a member of the National Holiness Association, Knapp began to publish a holiness periodical, *God's Revivalist*, moved to Cincinnati and organized a Bible College, camp meetings, city missions, and other social and evangelistic agencies "on the holiness and faith lines."[47]

God's Bible School soon became a center for a somewhat different coalition of holiness adherents. It was there, in 1897, that Knapp together with Seth Cook Rees, a widely known Indiana Quaker holiness pastor and evangelist, and C. W. Ruth, an evangelist of the Holiness Christian Church organized the Apostolic Holiness Union and Prayer Band. Although, in their formative years, the leadership and life of the Union on the one hand, and of God's Bible School and the *Revivalist* on the other were so closely interrelated in practice that the public looked on them as one organization. They were always two. After Knapp's untimely death in 1901 the interests of the two groups tended to become more distinct.[48]

The intimate, almost hundred-year relationship, between the Church of the Nazarene and the Pilgrim Holiness Church, provides an illustration of the unusual unity in diversity which marks the holiness movement, even in its institutional phase. Differences in numbers of constituents and the background and experiences of the early leadership introduced significant variants in their approach to the so-called "side issues." Rees and Knapp at one time or another had both been associated with early elements of A. B. Simpson's Christian and Missionary Alliances. Through these associations, they became much more aware of the holiness movement as it had reshaped the revivalistic theology of Presbyterian Simpson and the noted holiness/deeper-life pastor and evangelist Adoniram J. Gordon.[49] The divine-healing and premillennial themes in the holiness teachings of Simpson's "Four-fold Gospel" reverberated much more prominently in the preaching of Knapp and Rees than that of Bresee. For the former, they became "articles of faith" rather than "side issues, or "adiophora." The Pilgrims, in essence, became the Wesleyan/Holiness expression of Simpsons "Four-fold Gospel." This more inclusive theology combined with a more exclusive expression of acceptable parameters of "sanctified" lifestyle formed the theological and philosophical distinctive which have marked the relationships of the Nazarene and Pilgrim movements from the beginning. The distinctions were not so definitive as to prohibit the continuing cooperation of the churches in the common promotion of the revival under the broader aegis of the holiness movement; but, abetted by the social dynamics of smaller versus larger group and their competing appeals to a common holiness constituency, they have been significant enough to keep the two on their separate organizational paths for almost a hundred years in spite of repeated initiatives for their federation or even merger, especially in recent years.

These newly formed churches organized out of the fruits of the revival, together with the Wesleyan Methodists and the Free Methodists, gave to most of the new holiness churches a Wesleyan and Methodist flavor. Most of the groups that eventually organized out of the holiness revival retained a Methodist affinity in their articles of faith, structures, spirituality, and sense of mission which reached far beyond their fervent advocacy of Methodism's central doctrine of entire sanctification.[50] They never completely cut themselves off from Methodism. They maintained close relationships with such holiness organizations as Henry Clay Morrison's Holiness Unions which stayed within the Methodist Episcopal Church South.

Morrison was a dominant figure in the life of Asbury College and was the founder and first president of Asbury Theological Seminary. The holiness adherents and the significant cadre of Methodist holiness evangelists which rallied around Morrison's popular *Pentecostal Herald* moved freely in and out of both mainline Methodism and the holiness groups that broke away or were forced out of mainstream at the turn of the century. Holiness evangelists continued to minister in Methodist Episcopal Churches north and south and National Association evangelists ministered in holiness churches and camp meetings. Both groups cooperated in joint camp meeting ventures and supported independent holiness colleges such as Asbury and Taylor and interdenominational missionary agencies like OMS International and the World Gospel Missionary Society.

By the end of WW1, the reorganization of the movement was essentially complete. Distinct in their particular mix of Wesleyanism and American revivalism, but never completely divorced from historic Methodism, the new holiness churches took their place in American and worldwide religious life.[51]

NOTES

1. (Baltimore: The Johns Hopkins University Press, 1980), p. 259.

2. Since the publication of the first edition of *The Holiness Movement*, two excellent interpretations of the life and work of Phoebe Palmer have appeared: Harold Raser, *Phoebe Palmer: Her Life and Thought* (Lewiston, NY: Mellen Press, 1987) and Charles Edward White, *The Beauty of Holiness: Phoebe Palmer as Theologian, Revivalist, Feminist, and Humanitarian* (Grand Rapids, MI: Francis Asbury Press, 1986).

3. Jones' extensive but incomplete list names more than 100 publications. *Guide*, 74-80.

4. Martin Marty notes the movement "is one of the better noticed, recorded, and preserved among modern Christian phenomena." See Donald W. Dayton, *Theological Roots of Pentecostalism* (Grand Rapids, MI: Zondervan Publishing House, 1987), p. 930.

5. See above, pp. 154-157.

6. The theological differences produced open conflict as the holiness movement increasingly began to use the "eradication" of the carnal nature as the central paradigm for its teaching on the Wesleyan doctrine of cleansing from all sin. This strengthened the persistent evangelical Calvinist perception that the movement was promoting a sinless perfectionism. In the closing years of the century, F. B. Meyer, with the subsequent support of Dwight L. Moody, charged the holiness advocates at this point. When hiliness leaders such as A. M. Hills challenged these contentions of the higher-life leaders, a wedge was driven between two holiness movements that for a generation had reinforced each other in their common mission to deepen the spiritual life of the churches. The fullest review of these developments is in David Bundy's "The Wesleyan/Holiness and Keswick Traditions: 1875-1912," (Unpublished paper, 1989). For a summary of holiness theology see Melvin E. Dieter, "The Development of Holiness Theology in Nineteenth Century America," in *Theological Themes in the American Protestant World: Modern American Protestantism and its World*, Martin Marty, ed. (Westport, CT: Meckler, 1991).

7. For example, Campus Life, Moody Bible Institute, Gordon-Conwell Seminary, Columbia Biblical Seminary (S.C.), and significant elements within the Southern Baptist Convention. Note the many holiness and Keswick hymns on sanctification, Pentecost, and the Holy Spirit incorporated in the latest Souther Baptist hymnal, even the gospel song most native to the movement—"The Comforter Has Come." See George M. Marsden, *Fundamentalism and American Culture: The Shaping of Twentieth Century Evangelicalism, 1870-1920* (Oxford: Oxford University Press, 1980), 72-85. Marsden gives recognition to the holiness component in the broad revivalist tradition but still fails to recognize that it was as central a formative driving force as it really was.

8. Miller notes in his *Life of the Mind in America from the Revolution to the Civil War* (New York: Harcourt, Brace, and World, 1965), p. 93, that certain key publications which appeared immediately before the Civil War, such as William E. Boardman's *Higher Christian Life*, marked "the ultimate reaches of the Revival's long effort to elude the trammels of metaphysics and serve as a starting point for a new era in American pietism which, no longer concerned with doctrine, would seek a 'practical Christianity,' purity of heart."

9. The controversy raised in Wesleyan holiness ranks by the introduction of largely Reformed-centered premillennialism represents a classic example of this. On the other hand, the ready acceptance of womens' ministry in interdenominational holiness associations was difficult for many in the Reformed tradition. The tensions inherent in the contemporary relationships between some Wesleyan and Calvinistic evangelicals, whether neo or fundamentalist, in spite of their common biblical commitments, can be attributed in large part to a failure on both parts to understand the history of this cross-fertilization.

10. See *The Works of the Reverand John Fletcher* (reprint, Salem, OH: Schmul Publishers, 1974), especially his *Sixth Check to Antinomianism* and his *Portrait of St. Paul*, pp. 166-73.

11. (New York: Harper and Brothers, 1856).

12. Such as S. H. Platt, *The Gift of Power: or The Special Influences of the Holy Spirit, the Need of the Church. Introduction by Rev. Nathan Bangs* (New York: Carlton and Porter, 1856); and George S. Phillips, *The American Republic and Human Liberty Foreshadowed in Scripture* (Cincinnati: Poe and Hitchcock, for the Author, 1864).

13. (New York: Simon and Schuster, 1953), p. 361.

14. See William A. Clebsch, *From Sacred to Profane America: The Role of Religion in American History* (New York: Harper and Row, 1969), pp. 188-91 and "Chosen Race...Chosen People," Chapter 7, in Ernest Lee Tuveson, *Redeemer Nation: The Idea of America's Millennial Role* (Chicago: University of Chicago Press, 1968), pp. 137-86 among many others.

15. See Melvin E. Dieter, "Primitivism in the American Holiness Tradition," *Wesleyan Theological Journal* 30 (Spring 1995):1:78-91. For a classic reference, see Seth C. Rees, *The Ideal Pentecostal Church* (Cincinnati, OH: The Revivalist Office, 1897).

16. A perjorative term used by those in the holiness ranks who felt that the attention given to healing and premillennial teaching by certain elements of the holiness movement would only serve to divert the movement from its focus on the holiness theme.

17. See Donald Dayton, *Theological Roots of Pentecostalism* (Grand Rapids, MI: Francis Asbury Press, 1987), pp. 115-41, for a more extensive summary of the development and significance of the healing movement within the context of the holiness and later the Pentecostal revival.

18. W. Mcdonald and John E. Searles, *The Life of John S. Inskip, President of the National Association for the Promotion of Holiness* (Chicago: The Christian Witness Co., 1885), pp. 279-80. Jennie Smith, *From Baca to Beulah* (Cincinnati, OH: Press of Jennings and Pye, 1880), pp. 185-203.

19. The healing views of these leaders circulated throughout the movement through such books as Charles Cullis, *Faith Cures. or, Answers to Prayer in the Healing of the Sick* (Boston: Willard Tract Repository, 1879); W. H. Daniels, *Dr. Cullis and His Work* (Boston: Willard Tract Repository, 1885); W. E. Boardman, "The Lord that Healeth Thee" (London: Morgan and Scott, 1881); A. J. Gordon, *The Ministry of Healing: Miracles of Cure in All Ages* (Boston: H. Gannett, 1882); and A. B. Simpson, The Gospel of Healing, rev. ed. (New York: Christian Alliance Publishing, 1915).

20. See *Dorothea Trudel; or, the Prayer of Faith*, with an introduction by Charles Cullis, 3rd ed. (Boston: Willard Tract Repository, 1872).

21. (Boston: Willard Tract Repository, 1884).

22. (Boston: Christian Witness Co., 1897).

23. The author remembers his father, Dr. Harold D. Dieter, early Pilgrim Holiness educator, and Dr. R. G. Glexon, noted Pilgrim Holiness evangelist and denominational official, debating this issue. Dieter defended the position that the atonement did not include the healing of the body in the same sense that it

did redemption from sin. He maintained, with most in the holiness tradition, that there was healing for the body by divine intervention by the prayer of faith, but only in the providential permissive will of God and not in any sense of universal appropriation by right bought by Christ. "If it be thy will" must always be appended to the prayer of faith for physical healing or any other material and physical need, but not to the prayer for forgivenss and salvation from sin.

24. Sarah A. Cooke, *The Handmaiden of the Lord, or Wayside Sketches* (Chicago: T. B. Arnold Publisher, 1896), pp. 42, 42; J. C. Pollock, *Moody: A Biographical Portait of the Pacesetter in Modern Mass Evangelism* (New York: Macmillan, 1963), pp. 84-91.

25. See his *Jesus Exultant, or Christ, No Pessimist* (Boston: The Christian Witness Co., 1899); for a summary analysis, see Dayton, *Roots of Pentecostalism*, pp. 164-67.

26. See Melvin E. Dieter, "The Post-Civil War Holiness Revival: the Rise of the Campmeeting Churches," in Wayne E. Caldwell, ed., *Reformers and Revivalists: The History of the Wesleyan Church*, Weslayan History Series, Vol. 3 (Indianapolis, IN: Wesley Press, 1992), p. 150. Portions of the above adapted for this essay are used with permission of Wesley Press.

27. Charles Edwin Jones, *A Guide to the Study of the Holiness Movement* (Metuchen, NJ: Scarecrow Press, 1974), pp. 244-47; Timothy L. Smith, *Called unto Holiness, the Story of the Nazarenes: the Formative Years* (Kansas City, MO: Nazarene Publishing House, 1962), 181-84; John T. Benson, Jr., *A History 1898-1915 of the Pentecostal Mission, Inc., Nashville, Tennessee* (Nashville, TN: Trevecca Press, 1977), p. 45.

28. One of Pickett's most widely read books was *The Blessed Hope of His Glorious Appearing* (Louisville, KY: Pickett Publishing Co., 1901); Morrison wrote the introduction.

29. In spite of the fact that the sentiments of many if not a majority of holiness adherents would still be more sympathetic to premillennialism than any other eschatological view, official stances are changing. The premillennial article in the doctrinal statment of the Pilgrim Holliness was not carried over into the doctrinal statement of the merged church adopted at their union with the Wesleyan Methodist Church to form The Wesleyan Church in 1968. Since that time, the author has been involved in theological discussions about the retention of the modifier "imminent" found in official statements on the return of Christ in both The Wesleyan Church and Asbury Theological Seminary. There is concern in both instances that the use of the phrase may still be too closely related to dispensational premillennialism and too prejudicial to postmillennialists and others in the movement who do not hold to the generally prevailing premillennial view.

30. To oppose one so-called side issue did not necessarily mean one was opposed to the other as well. Daniel Steele strongly attacked Darbyite premillennialism, but he actively espoused Cullis's work. The premillennial stance strongly offended his Wesleyan optimism, and the healing movement strongly affirmed it.

31. Smith, *Called unto Holiness*, pp. 38-47 outlines the dynamics of the struggle between the associations and its Methodist critics as it related to the formation of the Church of the Nazarene.

32. Ibid., pp. 42-44.

33. See Robert C. Chiles, *Theological Transition in American Methodism: 1790-1936* (New York: Abingdon Press, 1965), pp. 62-72.

34. Vinson Synan, *The Holiness Pentecostal Movement in the United States* (Grand Rapids, MI: William B. Eerdman Publishing Company, 1971), p. 53 and Smith, *Called unto Holiness*, p. 36.

35. For an excellent history of the Church of God, see John W. V. Smith, *The Quest for Holiness and Unity: a Centennial History of the Church of God* (Anderson, Indiana) (Anderson, IN: Warner Press, 1980).

36. See Charles Edwin Jones, "Anti-Ordinance: A Proto-Pentecostal Phenomenon?", *Wesleyan Theological Journal* 25 (Fall 1990), 2:7-23.

37. See Jones, *Guide*, p. 224 and Smith, *Called unto Holiness*, p. 77. The denomination now is known as the Evangelical Christian Church.

38. For the most recent history of the Army in the United States, see Edward H. McKinley, *Marching to Glory: The History of the Salvation Army in the United States* (New York: Harper and Row, 1980).

39. Over the years, the Salvation Army has become the largest of the worldwide holiness organizations. In the United States and Canada, particularly, it remains one of the most active participants in ecumenical holiness promotion.

40. See Robert E. Black, "Becoming a Church: Wesleyan Methodism, 1895-1935," Caldwell, *Reformers and Revivalists*, pp. 191-94.

41. For example, see a Free Methodist criticism of the National Holiness Association, January 12, 1871.

42. The latest general history of Free Methodism is Leslie Ray Marston, *From Age to Age a Living Witness: a Historical Interpretation of Free Methodism's First Century* (Winona Lake, IN: Light and Life Press, 1960). Marston's history of the church is structured around the thesis that Free Methodism has always been true and ongoing Methodism, the emphasis that turned many disillusioned Methodist mainliners away from the church as the holiness movement was reorganizing.

43. *The Transformation of American Quakerism: Orthodox Friends, 1865-1918* (Indianapolis: University of Indiana Press, 1986). Hamm's excellent work rests on the premise that early nineteenth-century Quakerism was traditional Quakerism. Actually it was a troubled tradition, because the Quakerism of the time may not have been as close to traditional Quakerism as were some of the evangelicals who were promoting revival within the Friend Yearly Meetings. Methodist perfectionism may have been much closer to the heart of the historical Friend's movement than that existing at the time. See Arthur O. Roberts, "The Concept of Perfection in the History of the Quaker Movement," (Unpublished B.D. thesis, Nazarene Theological Seminary, 1951). Much of the Friends' holiness movement is now gathered into the Evangelical Friends Church.

44. See William C. Kostlevy, *Holiness Manuscripts: A Guide to Sources Documenting the Wesleyan Holiness Movement in the United States and Canada* (Metuchen, NJ: Scarecrow Press, 1994).

45. T. Smith, Called unto Holiness, 205-223.

46. E. A. Girvin, *Phineas F. Bresee: A Prince in Israel* (Kansas City, MO: Nazarene Publishing House, 1916), pp. 84-116. For the history of the formative years of the Church of the Nazarene, see Smith, *Called unto Holiness;* subsequent denominational history is outlined in W. T. Purkheiser, *Called unto Holiness, Volume 2: The Second Twenty-Five Years, 1933-58* (Kansas City, MO: Nazarene Publishing House, 1983).

47. See Aaron Merritt Hills, *A Hero of Faith and Prayer: or, Life of Rev. Martin Wells Knapp* (Cincinnati, OH: Mrs. M. W. Knapp, 1902).

48. On the development of the Pilgrim Holiness Church, see Paul Westphal Thomas and Paul William Thomas, *The Days of Our Pilgrimage: The History of the Pilgrim Holiness Church;* Wesleyan History Series, Melvin E. Dieter and Lee M. Haines, Jr., eds. (Marion, IN: The Wesley Press, 1976). God's Bible School continues its educational work to the present, mainly serving the churches of the Interchurch Holiness Convention—a group of more conservative holiness bodies organized out of the older holiness churches in still a "third wave" of reorganization following World War II. See H. E. Schmul, et al., compilers, *Profile of the Interchurch Holiness Convention: A Retrospect of 40 Years of IHC Ministry* (Salem, OH: Interchurch Holiness Convention, 1992).

49. Dieter, "The Post-Civil War Holiness Revival: the Rise of the Campmeeting Churches," in *Reformers and Revivalists,* p. 150.

50. Thomas C. Oden, *Doctrinal Standards in the Wesleyan Tradition* (Grand Rapids, MI: Zondervan, 1988), 127-172.

51. In their revisionist study, *The Churching of America, 1776-1990: Winners and Losers in Our Religious Economy* (New Brunswick, NJ: Rutgers University Press, 1992), Roger Finke and Rodney Stark contend that Methodism was the "ultimate loser" in its rejection of the holiness movement. They believe that the decline in Methodism, which followed the loss of the holiness movement to mainline Methodism, and the rapid growth of the Baptists during the same period are the result, in large part, of Methodism's inattention to the central concerns of the holiness revival.

Bibliography

PRIMARY SOURCES

Unpublished Material

Inskip, John S. "Letter" to Daniel Currey, November 24, 1875. Currey Folder, Drew University Archives Manuscript Collection.

Merritt, Timothy. "Autobiographical Note." Merritt Folder. Drew University Archives Manuscript Collection.

Palmer, Walter and Phoebe. Nineteen "Letters" to Walter and Phoebe Palmer. Palmer Folder. Drew University Archives Manuscript Collection.

_____. "Letters." Catalog Nos. 460, 461. New York Methodist Historical Society Collection.

_____. "Letters." Inventory No. 439, Methodist Episcopal Church Records Collection. New York Public Library Manuscript Collection.

Taylor, William. "Letter" to Dr. and Mrs. Palmer, January 25, 1867. Taylor Folder Drew University Archives Manuscript Collection.

Wesleyan Methodist Church Original "Record of the Wesleyan Convention," held at Utica, N.Y., 1843. Archives of The Wesleyan Church, Marion, Indiana.

Periodicals

Advocate of Christian Holiness. 1870-1882.

African News. 1889.

American Wesleyan. 1860-1880.

Beauty of Holiness. 1857, 1860.

Biblical Repository and Review. 1848.

Bibliotheca Sacra and Biblical Repository. 1860, 1865, 1866.

Chester Times (Pa.). 1883.

Christian Standard and Home Journal. 1874-1877.

Congregational Quarterly. 1876.

Divine Life and International Expositor of Scriptural Holiness. 1879, 1886.

Earnest Christianity. 1873, 1875.

Fraser's Magazine. 1875.

God's Revivalist and Bible Advocate. 1901.

Good Way. 1881-1886.

Guide to Christian Perfection (Guide to Holiness). 1839-1901.

Harper's Weekly. 1873.
Ladies Repository. 1860-1870.
Living Epistle. 1866, 1871, 1886, 1888.
Methodist Quarterly Review. 1841-1878.
Methodist Quarterly Review (So.). 1851.
Michigan Holiness Record. 1883-1885.
Nazarene Messenger. 1910.
New York Christian Advocate and Journal. 1855-1885.
Pentecost Magazine. 1886-1900.
Pentecostal Herald. 1899.
Philadelphia Public Ledger. 1867-1868.
Sunday School Times. 1875.
Zion's Herald and Wesleyan Journal. 1837-1860.

Books and Articles

Abbott, Jacob. "The Higher Christian Life," *Bibliotheca Sacra and Biblical Repository,* XVII (July 1860), 508-535.

Account of the Union Meeting for the Promotion of Scriptural Holiness, Held at Oxford, Aug. 29 to Sept. 7, 1874, Chicago: F. H. Revell, 1875.

Agnew, Milton S. *Manual of Salvationism.* N.p.: The Salvation Army, 1968.

Aitken, W. Hay. The Highway of Holiness: Helps to the Spiritual Life. London: J. F. Shaw, n.d.

Akers, Lewis, R. *God's Specific for Sin.* N.p.: n.n., n.d.

Alexander, James Waddell. *Forty Years' Familiar Letters of James W. Alexander. Constituting with Notes, a Memoir of His Life.* 2 vols. Edited by John Hall. New York: Scribner, 1860.

_____. *The New York Pulpit in the Revival of 1858: A Memorial Volume of Sermons.* New York: Sheldon, Blakeman and Co., 1858.

_____. *The Revival and Its Lessons.* New York: Anson D. F. Randolf, 1859.

Allis, Matilda. *Holiness Briefs.* Fort Scott, KS: Monitor Publishing House, 1889.

Alsop, Christine Majolier. *Memorials of Christine Majolier Alsop.* Compiled by Martha Braithwaite. Philadelphia: H. Longstreth, 1882.

American Almanac: 1885. Edited by R. Ainsworth Spofford. New York: The American News Co., 1885.

The American Christian Record: Containing the History, Confession of Faith and Statistics of Each Religious Denomination in the United States and Europe. New York: W. R. C. Clark and Meeker, 1860.

Arnold, J. M. *Selections from the Autobiography of Rev. M. Arnold, D.D. and from His Editorial Writings on the Doctrine of Sanctification.* Compiled and arranged by M. A. Boughton. Ann Arbor, MI: Endex Publishing House, 1885.

Arthur, William. *The Tongue of Fire: Or the True Power of Christianity.* New York: Harper and Brothers, 1880.

Atkinson, John. *The Class Leader.* New York: Nelson and Phillips, 1874.

Atwood, Anthony. *The Abiding Comforter: A Necessity to Joyful Piety and Eminent Usefulness.* Philadelphia: Adam Wallace, 1874.

_____. *Causes of the Marvelous Success of Methodism in This Country within the Past Century.* Philadelphia: National Publishing Association for the Promotion of Holiness, 1884.

Ayars, J. E. *The Holiness Revival of the Past Century: Commerative of the National Camp Meeting Association, Its Work and the Philadelphia Friday Meeting with Chronological Notes from the Writer's Journal—Supplementary.* Philadelphia: J. E. A., 1913.

Baker, Sheridan. *Living Waters: Being Bible Expositions and Addresses Given at Different Camp Meetings and to Ministers and Christian Workers on Various Other Occasions. Introduced with the Author's Experiences in Spreading Holiness.* 3d. ed., corrected and enlarged. New York: Phillips and Hunt, 1888.

_____. *A Peculiar People: Being Expositions, Addresses and Posthumous Papers by Sheridan Baker.* Edited by G. F. Oliver. Introd. by Bishop Isaac W. Joyce. Boston: McDonald, Gill and Co., 1890.

Bangs, Nathan. *The Necessity, Nature and Fruits of Entire Sanctification.* New York: Phillips and Hunt, 1851.

_____. *Prospects and Responsibilities of the Methodist Episcopal Church.* New York: Lane and Scott, 1850.

Barchwitz-Krauser, Oscar van. *Six Years with William Taylor in South America.* Boston: McDonald, Gill, Office of the Christian Witness, 1885.

Belman, J. C. *The Great Revival at Roberts Park M. E. Church and Other Churches.* Indianapolis: Journal Co., 1881.

Bennett, William W. *A Narrative of the Great Revival Which Prevailed in the Southern Armies.* Philadelphia: Claxton, Remsen and Haffelfinger, 1877.

Binney, Amos. *The Theological Compend.* Cincinnati: OH: Swormstead, 1858.

Boardman, Henry A. *The Higher Life of Sanctification as Tried by the Word of God.* Philadelphia: Presbyterian Board of Publication, 1877.

Boardman, William Edwin. *Faith Work under Dr. Cullis in Boston.* Boston: Willard Tract Repository, 1874.

_____. *The Higher Christian Life.* Boston: Henry Hoyt, 1858.

_____. *The Lord that Healeth Thee.* London: Morgan and Scott, 1881.

_____. *In the Power of the Spirit.* Boston: Willard Tract Repository, 1875.

Boardman, Mrs. William Edwin. *Life and Labors of the Rev. W. E. Boardman.* New York: D. Appleton and Co., 1887.

Boland, J. M. *The Problem of Methodism: Being a Review of the Residue Theory of Regeneration and the Second Change Theory of Sanctification and the Philosophy of Christian Perfection.* Nashville, TN: Publishing House of the M. E. Church South, for the Author, 1888.

Booth, Catherine. *Aggressive Christianity.* Boston: McDonald, Gill and Co., 1883.

_____. *Godliness: Being Reports of a Series of Addresses.* Boston: McDonald, Gill and Co., 1893.

_____. *Popular Christianity.* Boston: McDonald, Gill and Co., 1888.

Bowman, H. J. (comp.). *Voices on Holiness from the Evangelical Association.* Cleveland: Published for the Author at the Publishing House of the Evangelical Association, 1882.

Boynton, J. *Sanctification Practical: A Book for the Times.* New York: Foster and Palmer, 1867.

Bristol, Sherlock. *Paracletos: Or the Baptism of the Holy Spirit*. New York: F. H. Revell, 1892.

Brooks, John P. *The Divine Church: A Treatise on the Origin, Constitution, Order and Ordinances of the Church; Being a Vindication of the New Testament Ecclesia, and an Exposure of the Anti-Scriptural Character of the Modern Church of Sect*. Columbia, MO: Herald Publishing House, Printers and Binders, 1891.

Brooks, John R. *Scriptural Sanctification. An Attempted Solution of Holiness Problem*. Nashville, TN: Publishing House of the M. E. Church South, 1899.

Brown, H. D. *Personal Memories of the Ministry of Dr. Phineas F. Bresee*. Seattle, WA: H. D. Brown, 1930.

Brown, James Baldwin. *The Higher Life: Its Reality, Experience and Destiny*. London: Henry S. King and Co., 1875.

Byers, A. L. *Birth of a Reformation: Or the Life and Labors of Daniel S. Warner*. Anderson, IN: Gospel Trumpet Co., 1921.

Caldwell, Merritt. *The Philosophy of Christian Perfection*. Philadelphia: Sorin and Ball, 1848.

Carradine, Beverly. *Beulah Land*. Boston: The Christian Witness Co., 1904.

_____. *Sanctification*. Cincinnati, OH: God's Revivalist Office, 1890.

Carter, Russell Kelso. *The Atonement for Sin and Sickness Or a Full Salvation for Soul and Body*. Boston: Willard Tract Repository, 1884.

_____. *"Faith Healing" Reviewed after Twenty Years*. Boston: The Christian Witness Co., 1897.

Caughey, James. *Arrows from My Quiver: Pointed with the Steel of Truth and Sent Winged by Faith and Love*. New York: W. C. Palmer, Jr. Publisher, 1867.

_____. *Conflicts with Skepticism*. Boston: George C. Rand and Avery, 1860.

_____. *Earnest Christianity Illustrated: Or Selections from the Journal of the Rev. James Caughey*. Boston: J. P. Magee, 1854.

_____. *Methodism in Earnest: Being the History of a Great Revival in Great Britain*. Selected and arranged from "Caughey's Letters" by Rev. R. W. Allen and edited by Dan Wise. Boston: C. H. Pierce, 1850.

Cheever, Henry T. "Life and Writings of Madame Guyon," *Biblical Repository and Review*, IV (October 1848), 608-644.

Clark, Dougan. *From Elim to Carmel*. Boston: The Christian Witness Co., 1895.

_____. *The Holy Ghost Dispensation*. Chicago: Association of Friends, 1892.

_____. *The Offices of the Holy Spirit*. Philadelphia: The National Association for the Promotion of Holiness, 1879.

Clark, Dougan, and Smith, Joseph. *H. David Updegraff and His Work*. Cincinnati, OH: Published for Joseph H. Smith by Martin Wells Knapp, Revivalist Office, 1895.

Clark, L. A. (ed.). *Truths of Interest: Origin and Distinctive Teachings of the "Holiness Church."* El Monte, CA: Standard Bearer Publishing House, 1939.

Conant, William C. *Narratives of Remarkable Conversions and Revival Incidents*. New York: Derby and Jackson, 1858.

Constitution and Bylaws of the Churches of Christ in Christian Union. 1968 Edition. Circleville, OH: The Advocate Publishing House, 1968.

Cooke, Sarah A. *The Handmaiden of the Lord: Or Wayside Sketches*. Introd by. L. B. Kent. Chicago: T. B. Arnold, 1896.

Cookman, Alfred. *The Higher Christian Life*. Boston: Christian Witness Co., 1900.

Cowen, Clarence Eugene. *A History of the Church of God (Holiness).* Overland Park, KS: Herald and Banner Press, 1949.

Crane, J. T. *Popular Amusements.* Cincinnati, OH: Hitchcock and Walden, 1869.

_____. *Holiness the Birthright of All God's Children.* New York: Nelson and Phillips, 1875.

Cullis Charles. *History of the Consumptives Home, No. 11 Willard Street and Other Institutions Connected with a Work of Faith. Being the Five Annual Reports.* Boston: A. Williams and Co., 1869.

_____. *Faith Cures, or, Answers to Prayer in the Healing of the Sick.* Boston: Willard Tract Repository, 1879.

Curnick, Edward T. *A Catechism of Christian Perfection.* Chicago: The Christian Witness Co., 1885.

Danforth, Samuel A. *Spreading Scriptural Holiness.* Chicago: Christian Witness Co., 1913.

Daniels, Morris S. *The Story of Ocean Grove: Related in the Year of Its Golden Jubilee, 1869-1919.* New York: Methodist Book Concern, 1919.

Daniels, W. H. *Dr. Cullis and His Work.* Boston: Willard Tract Repository, 1885.

Davies, Edward. *The Believer's Hand-Book on Holiness for Christians of Every Name.* Reading, MA: Published by the Author, 1877.

_____. *The Bishop of Africa: Or Life of William Taylor, D.D., with an Account of the Congo Country and Mission.* Published for the Benefit of the Building and Transit Fund of William Taylor's Mission. Reading, MA: Holiness Book Concern, 1885.

_____. *Frances Ridley Havergal.* Reading, MA: Holiness Book Concern, 1885.

_____. *The Gift of the Holy Ghost: The Believer's Privilege.* Reading, MA: Rev. E. Davis, 1877.

_____. *He Leadeth Me.* New York: Nelson and Phillips, 1873.

_____. *History of Silver Lake Camp Meeting.* Reading, MA: Holiness Book Concern, 1899.

_____. *Illustrated History of Douglas Camp Meeting.* Boston: McDonald, Gill and Co., 1890.

Degen, H. V. *The Promise of the Father.* Boston: Henry V. Degen, 1859.

Dodsworth, Jeremiah. *The Better Land: Or the Christian Emigrant's Guide to Heaven.* Columbia, S C: L. L. Pickett, 1857.

Dorothea Trudel, or, The Prayer of Faith, with an introduction by Charles Cullis, 3rd ed. Boston: Willard Tract Repository, 1872.

Doty, Thomas K. *Lessons in Holiness.* Cleveland, OH: Published by the Author, 1881.

_____. *The Two- Fold Gift of the Holy Spirit.* Chicago: T. B. Arnold, 1891.

Dunn, Lewis Romaine. *The Gospel in the Book of Numbers.* New York: Hunt and Eaton, 1889.

_____. *Holiness—What Is It?* London: F. E. Longley, 1875.

_____. *A Manual of Holiness and a Review of Dr. James B. Mudge.* Cincinnati, OH: Cranston and Curtis, 1895.

_____. *Relations of the Holy Spirit to the Work of Entire Holiness.* New York: W. C. Palmer, 1883.

_____. *Sermons on the Higher Life.* Cincinnati, OH: Walden and Stowe, 1882.

Earle, A. B. *Bringing in the Sheaves.* Boston: James H. Earle, 1870.

_____. *The Rest of Faith*. Boston: James H. Earle, 1876.

Fairchild, James H. "The Doctrine of Sanctification at Oberlin," *Congregational Quarterly*, LXX (April 1876), 237-259.

Fenelon, Francois de Salignac de La Mothe. *Christian Perfection*. New York: Harper and Brothers, 1947.

Fenélon, Guyon and Lacombe. *Spiritual Progress*. New York: Dodd, Mead and Co., n.d.

Ferguson, Mamie Payne. *T. P. Ferguson, the Love Slave of Jesus Christ and His People and the Founder of Peniel Missions*. Los Angeles: n.p., n.d.

Figgis, J. B. *Christ and Full Salvation*. Cincinnati, OH: Cranston and Curtis, 1893.

Finney, Charles Grandison. *Memoirs of Rev. Charles G. Finney Written by Himself*. New York: Fleming H. Revell Co., 1908. (Originally published in 1876.)

_____. *Power from on High*. London: The Victory Press, 1957.

_____. *Revivals of Religion*. New York: Fleming H. Revell Co., n.d.

_____. *Sermons on Gospel Themes*. New York: Fleming H. Revell Co., 1876.

_____. *Sermons on Important Subjects*. New York: John S. Taylor, 1836.

_____. *Views on Sanctification*. Oberlin, OH: James Steele, 1840.

Fisch, George. *Nine Months in the United States during the Crisis*. London: J. Nisbet, 1863.

Fish, Henry Clay. *Primitive Piety Revived: Or the Aggressive Power of the Christian Church. A Premium Essay*. Boston: Congregational Board of Publication, 1855.

Fiske, Daniel T. "New England Theology," *Bibliotheca Sacra and Biblical Repository*, XXII (July 1865).

Foster, Randolph S. *Nature and Blessedness of Christian Purity*. Introd. by Bishop Janes. New York: Lane and Scott, 1851.

Franklin, S. *A Critical View of Wesleyan Perfection*. Cincinnati, OH: Methodist Book Concern, 1875.

Fraternal Camp Meeting Sermons Preached by Ministers of the Various Branches of Methodism at the Round Lake Camp Meeting, New York, July 1874, with an Account of the Fraternal Meeting. Phonographically reported by S. M. Stiles and J. G. Patterson. New York: Nelson and Phillips, 1875.

The Free Methodist Yearbook: 1968. Winona Lake, IN: The Free Methodist Publishing House, 1968.

Garrison, S. Olin. *Forty Witnesses, Covering the Whole Range of Christian Experience*. Freeport, PA: The Fountain Press, 1955. (Reprint of the 1888 edition).

Gibson, William. *The Year of Grace: A History of the Revival in Ireland, A. D. 1859*. Boston: Gould and Lincoln, 1860.

Godbey, William B. *Autobiography of Rev. William B. Godbey*. Cincinnati, OH: God's Revivalist Office, 1909.

_____. *Happy Nonagenarian*. Zarapheth, NJ: Pillar of Fire, 1919.

_____. *Holiness Clergy Bureau*. Greensboro, NC: Apostolic Messenger Office, n.d.

_____. *Holiness or Hell*. Louisville, KY: Pentecostal Publishing Co., 1899.

_____. *Psychology and Pneumatology*. Cincinnati, OH: God's Revivalist Office, n.d.

_____. *Woman Preacher*. Atlanta, GA: Office of the Way of Faith, 1891.

Gordon, Adoniram J. *Ecce Venit: Behold He Cometh*. New York: Fleming H. Revell, 1889.

_____. *How Christ Came to the Church: The Pastor's Dream, A Spiritual Autobiography*. Philadelphia: American Baptist Publishing Society, 1895.

_____. *The Holy Spirit in Missions*. Harrisburg, PA: The Christian Alliance Publishing Co., n.d.

_____. *The Ministry of Healing: Miracle Cures in all Ages*. Boston: H. Garrett, 1882.

_____. *Yet Speaking: A Collection of Addresses by A. J. Gordon*. New York: Fleming H. Revell Co., 1897.

Gorham, B. W. *God's Method with Man*. Boston: Published by the Author, 1885.

Goulburn, Edward M. *The Pursuit of Holiness*, 2nd ed, London: Rivington, 1870.

Govan I. R. *Spirit of Revival: Biography of J. G. Govan, Founder of the Faith Mission*. London: The Faith Mission, 1938.

Guyon, Jeanne Marie (Bouvier de La Mothe). *Sweet Smelling Myrrh: The Autobiography of Madame Guyon*. Edited by Abbie C. Morrow, Cincinnati, OH: God's Revivalist Office, n.d.

Haney, Milton Lorenzo, *The Inheritance Restored: Or Plain Truths on Bible Holiness*. Chicago: Christian Witness Co., 1904.

_____. *Pentecostal Possibilities. Or Story of My Life*. Chicago: Christian Witness Co., 1906.

Canon Harford-Battersby and the Keswick Convention. Edited by two of his sons, London: Seely and Co., n.d.

Harford, Charles F. (ed.) *The Keswick Convention: Its Message, Its Method and Its Men*. London: Marshall Bros., 1907.

Hart, Edward P. *Reminiscences of Early Free Methodism*. Chicago: Free Methodist Publishing House, 1903.

Haven, Gilbert. *Sermons, Speeches and Letters on Slavery and Its War*. Boston: Lee and Shepherd, 1869.

Haygood, Atticus G. (ed.). *Bishop Pierce's Sermons and Addresses: With a Few Special Discourses by Dr. Pierce*. Nashville, TN: Southern Methodist Publishing House, 1886.

Haynes, B. F. *Fact, Faith and Fire*. Nashville, TN: B. F. Haynes Publishing Co., 1900.

Hazen, E. A. *Salvation to the Uttermost*. Lansing, MI: Darius D. Thorpe, 1892.

The Heavenly Recruit Association: Its History, Articles of Faith, and Proceedings of Conference Held at Reading Pa., January 25, 26, 27, and 28, 1892.

Hermiz, Thomas. *What We Teach: A Summary of the Doctrines of the Churches of Christ in Christian Union*. Circleville, OH: The Advocate Publishing House, 1965.

Hills, Aaron Merritt. *Scriptural Holiness and Keswick Teaching Compared*. Manchester: Star Hall Publishing Co., 1900.

Hoke, Jacob. *Holiness: Or the Higher Christian Life*. Dayton, OH: United Brethren Printing Establishment, 1870.

Holiness Miscellany: Essays of Adam Clarke, Richard Watson; Experiences of Bishop Foster, George Peck, Alfred Cookman J. A. Wood, Edgar Levy, and Daniel Steele. Philadelphia: National Publication Association for the Promotion of Holiness, 1882.

Horner, R. C. *Notes on Boland: Or Mr. Wesley and the Second Work of Grace*. Boston: McDonald, Gill and Co., 1893.

Hughes, George. *The Beloved Physician, Walter C. Palmer, M.D,: His Sunlit Journey to the Celestial City.* Introd. by F. G Hibbard. New York: Palmer and Hughes, 1884.

_____. *Days of Power in the Forest Temple: A Review of the Wonderful Work of God at Fourteen National Campmeetings from 1867 to 1872.* With an Introduction by Bishop Haven. Boston: John Bent and Co., 1873.

_____. *The Double Cure: Or Echoes from the National Campmeetings.* Boston: The Christian Witness Co., 1894.

_____. *Fragrant Memories of the Tuesday Meeting and the Guide to Holiness and Their Fifty Years' Work for Jesus.* New York: Palmer and Hughes, 1886.

_____. *Ministerial Life Pictures.* With an introduction by Alfred Cookman. Philadelphia: Methodist Home Journal Press Establishment, 1869.

Hughes, John Wesley. *Autobiography.* Louisville, KY: Pentecostal Publishing Co., 1923.

Hunt, John. *Entire Sanctification: Its Nature, the Way of Its Attainment, Motives for Its Pursuit.* London: John Mason, 1860.

Huntington, DeWitt Clinton. *What Is It to Be Holy?: Or the Theory of Entire Sanctification.* Rochester: Benton and Andrews, 1869.

Inskip, John S. *Methodism Explained and Defended.* Cincinnati, OH: H. J. and J. Applegate, 1851.

_____. (comp.). *Songs of Triumph Adapted to Prayer Meetings, Camp Meetings and All Other Seasons of Religious Worship.* Philadelphia: National Publishing Association for the Promotion of Holiness, 1882.

Janes, Edmund S. *Sermons on the Death of Nathan Bangs.* New York: Carlton and Porter, 1862.

Jernigan, Charles Brougher. *Pioneer Days of the Holiness Movement in the Southwest.* Kansas City, MO: Pentecostal Nazarene Publishing House, 1919.

Jones, J. William. *Christ in the Camp: Or Religion in Lee's Army.* Richmond, VA: 1877.

Jones, William. *Elim to Carmel.* Boston: Christian Witness Co., 1885.

Journal of the General Conference of the Methodist Episcopal Church. New York: Carlton and Porter, 1864.

Journals of the General Conference of the Methodist Episcopal Church: 1848-1856. New York: Carlton and Porter, 1856.

Keen, Mary J. *Memorial Papers: Or the Record of a Spirit-filled Life.* Cincinnati, OH: M. W. Knapp, 1899.

Keen, S. A. *Salvation Papers.* Cincinnati, OH: Revivalist Office, 1896.

Keys, Charles C. *The Class Leader's Manual.* New York: Carlton and Phillips, 1856.

Kiergan, A. M. *Historical Sketches of the Revival of True Holiness and Local Church Polity from 1865-1916.* N.p.: Published by the Board of Publication of the Church Advocate and Good Way, [1972].

Kimbrough, Mary D. His Way with Me: Life Story and Poems Overland Park, Kan.: The Herald and Banner Press, 1967.

Kring, James A. *Trumpet Blasts to the Unsaved.* College Mound, MO: Herald Printing, 1907.

Landis, Charles K. *The Founder's Own Story of the Founding of Vineland, N.J.* Published by the Vineland Historical and Antiquarian Society. Vineland, NJ: The Vineland Printing House. 1903.

_____. "The Settlement of Vineland in N.J.," *Fraser's Magazine*, XI [New Series] (January 1875), 129ff.

Lee, Luther. *Wesleyan Manual: A Defense of the Organization of the Wesleyan Methodist Connection*. Syracuse, NY: Samuel Lee Publisher, 1862.

Lowrey, Asbury. *Possibilities of Grace*. Chicago: Christian Witness Co., 1884.

McDonald, William. *John Wesley and His Doctrine*. Boston: McDonald, Gill and Co., 1893.

_____. *Life Sketches of Rev. Alfred Cookman*. Cincinnati, OH: The Freedman's Aid and Southern Education Society, 1900.

_____. *Marquis de Renty: Or Holiness Exemplified by a Roman Catholic...to Which Is Appended...Some Account of Madame Guyon and F. W. Faber*. Philadelphia: National Publishing Association for the Promotion of Holiness, 1881.

_____. and Hartsough, L. *Beulah Songs: A Choice Collection of Popular Hymns and Music, New and Old Especially Adapted Camp Meetings, Prayer and Conference Meetings, Family Worship, and All Other Assemblies Where Jesus Is Praised*. Philadelphia: National Publishing Association for the Promotion of Holiness, 1881.

_____. and Searles, John E. *The Life of Rev. John S. Inskip, President of the National Association for the Promotion of Holiness*. Chicago: The Christian Witness Co., 1885.

McLaughlin, G. A. *Old Wine in New Bottles*. Chicago: Christian Witness Co., 1897.

McLean, A. and Eaton, J. W. (eds.). *Penuel: Or Face to Face With God*. New York: W. C. Palmer, Jr., 1869.

Mahan, Asa. *Autobiography*. London: T. Woolmer, 1882.

_____. *The Baptism of the Holy Ghost*. New York: W. C. Palmer, Jr., 1870.

_____. *Out of Darkness into Light: Or the Hidden Life Made Manifest*. Louisville, KY: Pickett Publishing Co., n.d. (Originally published in 1876.)

_____. *Scripture Doctrine of Christian Perfection*. Boston: D. S. King, 1839.

Manual of the Pilgrim Holiness Church: Revised by the International Conference of 1966. Edited by the Committee. Indianapolis, IN: The Pilgrim Publishing House, [1966].

Marvin, E. M. *The Doctrinal Integrity of Methodism*. St. Louis, MO: Advocate Publishing Co., 1878.

Mead, Amos P. *Manna in the Wilderness: Or the Grove and Its Altar, Offerings, and Thrilling Incidents, Containing a History of the Origin and Rise of Camp Meetings and a Defense of This Remarkable Means of Grace; Also an Account of the Wyoming Camp Meeting, Together With Sketches of Sermons and Preachers, With an introduction by J. B. Wakely of New York*. Philadelphia: Perkinpine and Higgins, 1860.

Merrill, Stephen M. *The Aspects of Christian Experience*. New York: Walden and Stowe, 1882.

_____. *Sanctification: Right Views and Other Views*. Cincinnati, OH: Jennings and Pye, 1901.

Merritt, Timothy. *The Christian's Manual*. New York: Published by N. Bangs and J. Emory for the Methodist Episcopal Church, 1827.

Meyer, Fredrick Brotherton. *The Soul's Pure Intention*. Samuel Bagster and Sons, 1907.

Miley, John. *Treatise on Class Meetings*. Cincinnati, OH: Poe and Hitchcock, 1866.

Miller, H. E. *Reply to F. B. Meyer.* Boston: Christian Witness Co., 1898.

Minutes of Several Conversations Between The Rev. Thomas Coke, L.L.D., The Rev. Francis Asbury and Others ... in the Year 1784. Composing a Form of Discipline for the Ministers ... of the Methodist Episcopal Church in America. Philadelphia: Chas. Cist, 1785.

Minutes of the Twenty-Sixth International Conference of the Pilgrim Holiness Church: June 25, 1968, Anderson, Indiana. Marion, IN: The Wesleyan Publishing House, 1968.

Moberly, George. *The Administration of the Holy Spirit in the Body of Christ.* London: J. Parker and Co., 1868.

Moody, Dwight Lyman. *Power from on High.* London: Morgan and Scott, n.d.
_____. *Secret Power.* Chicago: Fleming H. Revell Co., 1881.

Morell, James Fletcher. *A Perfect Christian and How He Became So.* New York: Phillips and Hunt, 1881.

Morrison, Henry Clay. *Life Sketches and Sermons.* Louisville, Ky.: Pentecostal Publishing Co., 1903.
_____. *Open Letters to the Bishops, Ministers and Members of the Methodist Episcopal Church South.* Louisville KY: Pentecostal Publishing Co., n.d.
_____. *Some Chapters of My Life Story.* Louisville, KY: Pentecostal Publishing Co., 1941.

Moule, Handley Carr Glyn. *The Cross and the Spirit.* London: Pickering and Inglis, Ltd., n.d.
_____. *Veni Creator.* London: Hodder and Stoughton, 1892.

Mudge, James. *Growth in Holiness Toward Perfection: Or Progressive Sanctification.* New York: Hunt and Eaton, 1895.
_____. *The Perfect Life in Exposition and Doctrine: A Restatement.* With an introduction by Rev. Wm. F. Warren. New York: Eaton and Mains, 1911.

Murray, Andrew. *Holy in Christ.* New York: Fleming H. Revell Co., 1887.
_____. *The Two Covenants and the Second Blessing.* New York: Fleming H. Revell, 1898-99.

National Association for the Promotion of Holiness. (Booklet for 1907-1908.) Chicago: The Christian Witness Co., [1908].

Nelson, Thomas H. *Life and Labors of Rev. Vivian A. Dake, Organizer and Leader of the Pentecost Bands: Embracing and Account of His Travels in America, Europe and Africa with Selections from His Sketches, Poems and Songs.* Chicago: T. B. Arnold, 1894.

Osborn, Lucy Reed Drake. *Heavenly Pearls Set in a Life: A Record of Experiences and Labors in America, India and Australia.* New York: Fleming H. Revell Co., 1893.
_____. *Pioneer Days of Ocean Grove.* New York: Printed for the Author by Methodist Book concern, n.d.

Palmer, Phoebe. *Faith and Its Effects: Or Fragments from My Portfolio.* New York: Published for the Author at 200 Mulberry St., 1854.
_____. *Four Years in the Old World: Comprising the Travels, Incidents and Evangelistic Labors of Dr. and Mrs. Palmer in England, Ireland, Scotland, and Wales.* New York: Foster and Palmer, Jr., 1867.
_____. *Incidental Illustrations of the Economy of Salvation, Its Doctrines and Duties.* Boston: Henry V. Degen, 1860.

_____. (ed.). *Pioneer Experiences: Or the Gift of Power Received by Faith and Confirmed by the Testimony of Eighty Living Ministers of Various Denominations.* Introduction by Rev. Bishop Janes. New York: W. C. Palmer, Jr. Office for Works on the Higher Christian Life, [1868].

_____. *A Present for My Friend on Entire Devotion to God.* New York: Published for the Author, 1853.

_____. *The Promise of the Father: Or a Neglected Specialty of the Last Days.* New York: Foster and Palmer, 1866.

_____. *Some Account of the Recent Revival in the North of England and Glasgow.* Manchester: W. Bremner [1859].

_____. *Sweet Mary.* London: Simpkin Marshall and Co., 1862.

_____. *The Way of Holiness.* New York: Palmer and Hughes, 1867.

Palmer, Walter Clark. *Life and Letters of Leonidas L. Hamline, D.D.* New York: Carlton and Porter, 1866.

Parker, Theodore. *Autobiography, Poems, Prayers.* Edited with notes by Rufus Leighton; vol xiii; his Works Centenary ed.: Boston: American Unitarian Association, 1910.

Pearse, Mark Guy. *Thoughts on Holiness.* Chicago: The Christian Witness Co., 1884.

_____. *The Christian's Secret of Holiness.* Boston: Ira Bradley and Co., 1886.

Peck, George. *The Scripture Doctrine of Christian Perfection Stated and Defended.* New York: Lane and P. P. Sanford, 1842.

Peck, George B. *Steps and Studies: An Inquiry Concerning the Gift of the Holy Spirit.* Boston: H. Gannett, 1884.

Peck, Jesse T. *The Central Idea of Christianity.* Boston: H. V. Degen. 1856.

Pepper, E. I. D. (ed.). *Memorial of Rev. John S. Inskip.* Philadelphia: National Publishing Association for the Promotion of Holiness [1884].

Perfect Love Or the Speeches of Rev. E. L. Janes, Rev. Hiram Mattison, D.D., Rev. D. Currey, D.D., Rev. J. M. Buckley, and Rev. S. D. Brown, in the New York Preachers Meeting in March and April 1867 upon the Subject of Sanctification: also Bishop Janes' Sermons of Sin and Salvation. New York: N. Tibbals and Co., 1868.

Phonographic Report of the Debates and Addresses together with the Essays and Resolutions of the New England Methodist Centenary Convention Held in Boston, June 5-7, 1866. Boston: B. B. Russell Co., 1866.

Pickett, Leander Lycurgus. *Entire Sanctification from 1799-1901.* Louisville Ky.: Pickett Publishing Co., 1901.

_____. *The Blessed Hope of His Glorious Appearing.* Louisville, KY:Pickett Publishing, 1901.

_____. *Faith Tonic I and II Combined.* Louisville, KY: Pentecostal Publishing Co., n.d.

_____. *A Plea for the Present Holiness Movement.* Louisville, KY: Pickett Publishing Co., 1896.

Platt, Smith N. *Christ and Adornments.* Cincinnati, OH: American Reform Tract and Book Society, 1858.

_____. *Christian Holiness: Its Philosophy, Theory and Experience.* Brooklyn, NY: The Hope Publishing Co., 1882.

_____. *Christian Separation from the World:...With Especial Reference to Popular Amusements*. With an introductory letter by Theodore L. Cuyler. Winsted [CT]: Printed at the Winsted Herald Office, 1868.

_____. *The Gift of Power: Or the Special Influences of the Holy Spirit: The Need of the Church*. New York: Carlton and Porter, 1856.

Pomeroy, B. *Visons from Modern Mounts: Namely, Vineland, Manheim, Round Lake, Hamilton, Oakington, Canton, with Other Selections*. Albany, NY: Van Benthuysen Printing House, 1871.

Poole, Richard. *The Center and Circle of Evangelical Religion: Or Perfect Love*. London: Jarrold and Sons, 1873.

The Present State of the Methodist Church: A Symposium. Edited by George R. Crooks. Syracuse, NY: Northern Christian Advocate Office, 1891.

Prime, S. Iraneus. *The Power of Prayer, Illustrated in the Wonderful Displays of Divine Grace at the Fulton Street and Other Meetings*. New York: Sheldon Blakeman and Co., 1859.

Proceedings of Holiness Conferences Held at Cincinnati, November 26th, 1877, and at New York, December 17th. 1877. Philadelphia: National Publishing Association for the Promotion of Holiness [1878].

Proceedings of the Western Union Holiness Convention Held at Jacksonville, Ill., December 15th-19th, 1880. Bloomington, IL: Published by Western Holiness Association, 1881.

Prottsman, William. *The Class Leader*. St. Louis, MO: Methodist Book Repository, 1856.

Quaker Sesqui-centennial: 1818-1962. Damascus, OH: The Friends Church Ohio Yearly Meeting, 1962.

Record of the Convention for the Promotion of Scriptural Holiness Held at Brighton, May 29 to June 7, 1875. Brighton: W. J. Smith, n.d.

Rees, Byron J. *Halleluyahs from Portsmouth Camp Meeting Number Three: A Report of the Camp Meeting Held at Portsmouth, Rhode Island, July 29 to August 8, 1898*. Springfield, MA: Christian Unity Publishing Co., 1898.

_____. *Hulda, the Pentecostal Prophetess*. Philadelphia: Christian Standard Co., Ltd., 1898.

Rees, Seth Cook. *The Ideal Pentecostal Church*. Cincinnati, OH: God's Revivalist Office, 1897.

Report of the First Student Volunteer Movement for Foreign Missions Held at Cieveland, Ohio, U.S.A., February 26, 27, 28, and March 1, 1891. Boston: T. O. Metcalf and Co. [1891].

Ridgaway, Henry B. *The Life of Rev. Alfred Cookman: With Some Account of His Father, the Rev. George Crimston Cookman*. Introduction by the Rev. R. S. Foster. New York: Harper and Brothers, 1873.

Roberts, Benjamin Titus. *Holiness Teachings*. North Chili, NY: "Earnest Christian" Publishing House, 1893.

_____. *Pungent Truths: Being Extracts from the Writings of the Rev. Benjamin Titus Roberts while Editor of the Free Methodist from 1886-1890*. Compiled and edited by Wm. B. Rose. Chicago: The Free Methodist Publishing House, 1915.

_____. *Why Another Sect: Containing a Review of the Articles by Bishop Simpson and Others on the Free Methodist Church*. Rochester, NY: "The Earnest Christian" Publishing House, 1879.

Roche, John A. *The Life of Mrs. Sarah A. Lankford Palmer Who for Sixty Years Was the Able Teacher of Entire Holiness.* Introduction by John P. Newman, Bishop of the Methodist Episcopal Church. New York: George Hughes and Co., 1898.

Rogers, Dennis. *Holiness Pioneering in the Southland.* Hemet, CA: n.n., 1944.

Rosser, Leonidas. *Class Meetings.* Richmond, VA: Privately printed, 1855.

_____. *A Reply to the Problem of Methodism.* Nashville TN: Printed for the Author, 1899.

Sage, Charles H. *Autobiography of Charles H. Sage.* Edited by Wm. B. Olmstead. Chicago: Free Methodist Publishing House, 1903.

Schaff, Philip and Prime, S. Iranaeus (eds.). *History, Essays, Orations. and Other Documents of the Sixth General Conference of the Evangelical Alliance Held in New York October 2-12, 1873.* New York: Harper and Brothers Publishers, 1874.

Searles, J. E. *A Sermon Preached by the Request of the National Camp Meeting at Pitman Grove, N.J., August 5 1887 on the History of the Present Holiness Revival.* Boston: McDonald, Gill and Co., 1887.

See, Isaac, M. *The Rest of Faith.* New York: W. C. Palmer, 1871.

Shaw, S. B. (ed.). *Echoes of the General Holiness Assembly Held in Chicago, May 3-13, 1901.* Chicago: S. B. Shaw, [1901].

_____. (ed.). *Proceedings of the General Holiness Assembly, Held in the Park Avenue M. E. Church in Chicago, May 20-26, 1885.* Grand Rapids, MI: S. B. Shaw, [1885].

_____. *Old Time Religion: Including an Account of the Greatest Revivals Since Pentecostal Days, and Telling How to Bring About an Old Time Revival.* Chicago: S. B. Shaw Publisher, 1904.

Simpson, A. B. *Christ Our Sanctifier.* Harrisburg, PA: Christian Publications, Inc., 1947.

_____. *The Four-fold Gospel.* New York: Christian Alliance Publishing Co., 1890.

_____. *The Gospel of Healing,* rev. ed. New York: Christian Alliance Publishing, 1915.

_____. *Wholly Sanctified.* New York: Christian Alliance Publishing Co., 1893.

Smith, Amanda. *An Autobiography: The Story of the Lord's Dealings with Mrs. Amanda Smith, the Colored Evangelist; Containing the Account of Her Life Work of Faith, and Her Travels in America, England, Ireland, Scotland, India, and Africa as an Independent Missionary.* Chicago: Meyer and Bros., Publishers, 1893.

Smith, George G. *The Life and Times of George Foster Pierce with His Sketch of Lovick Pierce, D.D., His Father.* Sparta, GA: Hancock Publishing Co., 1888.

Smith, Hannah Whitall. *The Christian's Secret of a Happy Life.* Westwood, NJ: Fleming H. Revell Co., 1952. (Originally published in 1870.)

_____. *Difficulties of Life.* New York: H. M. Caldwell, 1897.

_____. *Frank: The Record of a Happy Life.* Philadelphia: Printed for Private Collection, 1873.

_____. *The Open Secret.* New York: Fleming H. Revell Co., 1885.

_____. *Philadelphia Quaker: The Letters of Hannah Whitall Smith.* Edited by Logan Pearsall Smith. New York: Harcourt and Brace and Co., 1950.

_____. *Religious Fanaticism: Extracts from the Papers of Hannah Whitall Smith. Edited with an Introduction by Ray Strachey [Rachel Costelloe] Consisting of an Account of the Author of these Papers and of the Times in which She lived; together with a Description of the Various Religious Sects and Communities of America during, the Early and Middle Years of the Nineteenth Century.* London: Faber and Gwyer, Ltd., 1928.

_____. *The Unselfishness of God, and How I Discovered It: A Spiritual Autobiography.* New York: Fleming H. Revell Co., 1903.

Smith, Jennie. *From Baca to Beulah.* Philadelphia: Guarigues Brothers, 1880.

Smith, Logan Pearsall. *Unforgotten Years.* Boston: Little, Brown and Co., 1939.

Smith, Robert Pearsall. *Holiness Through Faith: Light on the Way of Holiness.* Boston: Willard Street Tract Repository, 1870.

_____. *Walking in the Light: Words of Counsel to Those Who Have Entered into "The Rest of Faith."* Boston: Willard Tract Repository, 1872.

Spener, P. J. *Das geistliche Priesterthum.* English Translation in H. E. Jacobs, *A Summary of Christian Faith.* Philadelphia: General Council Board of Publications, 1905, pp. 58-595.

Star Hall Convention. *Addresses on Holiness Delivered at the Star Hall Convention. Manchester, November 9-16, 1890.* Ed. Isabella S. Leonard. London: S. W. Partridge and Co., 1890.

Starr, William H. *Discourses on the Nature of Faith and Kindred Subjects.* Chicago: D. B. Cook and Co., 1857.

Steele, Daniel. *Antinomianism Revived: Or The Theology of the So-called Plymouth Brethren Examined and Refuted.* Toronto: Wm. Briggs, 1887.

_____. *A Defense of Christian Perfection: Or a Criticism of Dr. Mudge's Growth in Holiness towards Perfection.* New York: Hunt and Eaton, 1896.

_____. *Jesus Exultant, or, Christ No Pessimist.* Boston: Christian Witness, 1899.

_____. *Love Enthroned.* Boston: Christian Witness Co., 1875.

_____. *Milestone Papers.* New York: Phillips and Hunt, 1878.

Stevens, Abel. *Life and Times of Nathan Bangs.* New York: Carlton and Porter, 1863.

"A Survey of the Field and Strictures Thereon" by J. P. Brooks. Reviewed by T. J. Bryant N.p.: n.n., n.d.

Taylor, B. S. *Full Salvation.* Des Moines, IA: Northwestern Holiness Publishing Co., 1886.

Taylor, William. *Four Years Campaign in India.* New York: Phillips and Hunt, 1880.

_____. *Seven Years' Street Preaching in San Francisco, California.* New York: Phillips and Hunt, [1856].

_____. *The Story of My Life: An Account of What I Have Thought, Said, and Done in My Ministry of More than Fifty-three Years in Christian Lands and among the Heathen.* New York: Eaton and Mains, 1898.

Ten Years by the Sea: Annual Report of the Ocean Grove Camp Meeting Association. Philadelphia: Published by order of the Association, 1890.

Thoburn, J. M. *The Church of Pentecost.* Cincinnati, OH: Jennings and Pye, 1901.

Torrey, R. A. *The Baptism with the Holy Spirit.* New York: Fleming H. Revell Co., 1895.

_____. *How to Obtain the Fullness of Power in Christian Life and Service.* New York: Fleming H. Revell, 1897.

Tucker, F. de L. Booth. *The Life of Catherine Booth, the Mother of the Salvation Army.* 2 Vols. New York: Fleming H. Revell Co., 1892.

Tyng, Stephen H. *Christ Is All.* New York: Robt. Carter and Bros., 1849.

U. S. Bureau of the Census. *Historical Statistics of the United States, Colonial Times to 1957.* Prepared by the Bureau of the Census with the cooperation of the

Social Science Research Council. Washington, DC: Government Printing Office, 1960. (Statistical Abstract Supplement.)

Van Cott, Maggie N. *The Harvest and the Reaper. Reminiscences of Revival Work.* New York: N. Tibbals and Sons., Publishers, 1876.

Vincent, H. *History of the Camp-meeting and Grounds at Wesley Grove Martha's Vineyard, for the Years Ending with the Meeting of 1869, with Glances at the Earlier Years.* Boston: Lee and Shepard, 1870.

Wallace, Adam (ed.). *A Modern Pentecost: Embracing a Record of the Sixteenth National Campmeeting for the Promotion of Holiness Held at Landisville, Pa., July 23 to August 1st, 1873.* Philadelphia: Methodist Home Journal Publishing House, 1873.

Warner, Daniel Sidney. *Bible Proofs of the Second Work of Grace: Or Entire Sanctification as a Distinct Experience Subsequent to Justification, Established by the United Testimony of Several Hundred Texts—Including a Description of the Great Holiness Crisis of the Present Age, by the Prophets.* Goshen, IN: E. U. Mennonite Publishing Society, 1880.

———. *The Church of God: Or What Is the Church and What Is Not?* Moundsville, WVA : Gospel Trumpet Co. [1902].

———. and Riggle, H. M. *The Cleansing of the Sanctuary: Or the Church of God in Type, and in Prophecy and Revelation.* Moundsviile, WVA: The Gospel Trumpet Publishing Co., 1903.

Washburn, B. A. *Holiness Links.* Los Angeles: Pentecost Office, 1887.

Washburn, Josephine F. *History and Reminiscences of Holiness Church Work in Southern California and Arizona.* South Pasadena, CA: Record Press [1912].

Wesley, John. *Explanatory Notes Upon the New Testament.* London: Epworth Press, 1950.

———. *Plain Account of Christian Perfection.* Boston: The Christian Witness Co., n.d.

———. *The Scripture Way of Salvation.* Waukesha, WI: Metropolitan Church Association, n.d.

———. *Works.* Ed. Thomas Jackson. 14 vols. Grand Rapids, MI: Zondervan Publishing House, 1958. (Photo offset reprint of the authorized ed; London: Wesleyan Conference Office, 1872.)

Wheatley, Richard. *The Life and Letters of Mrs. Phoebe Palmer.* New York: W. C. Palmer, Jr., 1876.

Whedon, Daniel A. *Entire Sanctification: John Wesley's View.* New York: Hunt and Eaton, n.d.

Willard, Frances E. *Woman and Temperance: Or the Work and Workers of the Woman's Christian Temperance Union.* Chicago: Woman's Temperance Publication Association, 1883.

Winebrenner, John. *Doctrinal and Practical Sermons.* Lebanon, PA: Published by the Authority of the General eldership of the Church of God., 1868.

———. *History of All Religious Denominations: Containing Authentic Accounts of the Rise and Progress, Faith and Practice, Localities, and Statistics of the Different Persuasions....* Harrisburg, PA: Published by John Winebrenner, V. D. M., 1848.

Wonders of Grace: Or Instances of the Mighty Cleansing Power of Jesus' Blood. Compiled by Rev. A. Sims, Editor of *The Radical Christian* (Kelvin, Ontario). Toronto: Wm. Lightfoot, n.d.

Wood, John A. *Autobiography.* Chicago: Christian Witness Co., 1904.
_____. *Christian Perfection as Taught by John Wesley.* Boston: McDonald, Gill and
    Co., 1885.
_____. *Perfect Love.* Chicago: Christian Witness Co., 1880.
Yearbook of American Churches with Information on Religious Bodies in Canada.
    Edited by Costant Jacquet, Jr. 40th issue. Nashville, TN: Abingdon Press,
    1972.
Yearbook of the Evangelical Association. Compiled by W. Horn. Cleveland, OH:
    Publishing House of the Evangelical Association, 1907.

SECONDARY SOURCES

Unpublished Materials

Behney, J. B. "Conservatism and Liberalism in the Late 19th Century in American
    Protestantism." Unpublished Doctoral dissertation, Yale University, 1941.
Clear, Valorous Bernard. "The Church of God: A Study in Social Adaptation."
    Unpublished Ph.D. thesis, University of Chicago, 1954.
Emmons, Irvin. "A History of Revivalism in America Since the Civil War."
    Unpublished Th.M. thesis. Princeton Theological Seminary, 1944.
Forrest, Aubrey Leland. "A Study of the Development of the Basic Doctrine and
    Institutional Patterns in the Church of God (Anderson, Ind.)." Unpublished
    Ph.D. Dissertation, University of Southern California, 1948.
Gaddis, Merrill Elmer. "Christian Perfectionism in America." Unpublished
    Ph.D. dissertation, University of Chicago, 1929.
Hughes, Howard Raymond. "The History of Delanco Camp Meeting Associa-
    tion." Unpublished Th.M. thesis, Eastern Baptist Seminary, 1961.
Jones, Charles E. "Perfectionist Persuasion: A Social Profile of the National
    Holiness Movement within American Methodism, 1867-1936." Unpublished
    Ph.D. thesis, University of Wisconsin, 1968.
Knapp, John Franklin. "The Doctrine of Holiness in the Light of Early Theologi-
    cal and Philosophical Conceptions." Unpublished M.A. thesis, University of
    Cincinnati, 1924.
O'Brien, Michael F. "A Nineteenth Century Hoosier Business Man: Washington
    Charles DePauw." Unpublished B.A. thesis, DePauw University, 1966.
Rader, Paul A. "A Study of the Doctrine of Sanctification in the Life and Thought
    of Charles G. Finney." Unpublished B.D. thesis, Asbury Theological Semi-
    nary, 1959.
Roberts, Arthur Owen. "The Concepts of Perfection in the History of the Quaker
    Movement." Unpublished B.D. thesis, Nazarene Theological Seminary, 1951.
Schwab, Ralph K. "The History of the Doctrine of Christian Perfection in the
    Evangelical Association." Unpublished Ph.D. dissertation, University of Chi-
    cago, 1922.
Smith Willard Garfield. "The History of the Church-Controlled Colleges in the
    Wesleyan Methodist Church." Unpublished Ph.D. thesis, School of Educa-
    tion of New York University, 1951.

Sproul, Jerry. "The Methodist Class Meeting: A Study in Its Development, Dynamics, Distinctions, Demise, and Denouement." Unpublished Master's thesis, Asbury Theological Seminary, 1957.

Thompson, Claude H. "The Witness of American Methodism to the Historical Doctrine of Christian Perfection." Unpublished Ph.D. thesis, Drew University, 1949.

Walton, Herbert. "The Pillars of Methodism: A Historical Study of the Class System of the Methodist Church in America." Unpublished Th.M. thesis, Princeton Theological Seminary, 1958.

Wesche, Percival A. "The Revival of Camp Meetings by the Holiness Groups." Unpublished M.A. thesis, University of Chicago, 1945.

Published Books and Articles

Abell, Aaron I. *The Urban Impact on American Protestantism: 1865-1900.* Cambridge, MA: Harvard University Press, 1943.

Acornley, J. H. *A History of the Primitive Methodist Church in the United States of America.* Fall River, MA: Rev. N. W. Marrhuga, 1909.

Albright, Raymond W. *A History of the Evangelical Church.* Harrisburg, PA: The Evangelical Press, 1942.

Anderson, William K. *Protestantism: A Symposium.* Nashville, TN: Commission on Courses of Study, the Methodist Church, 1944.

Arnett, W. M. "Current Theological Emphases in the American Holiness Tradition." *Mennonite Quarterly Review,* XXXV (April 1961), 120-129.

Arnold, W. E. *A History of Methodism in Kentucky.* Louisville, KY: Herald Press, 1936.

Asbury Theological Seminary Fortieth Anniversary Committee. *The Doctrinal Distinctives of Asbury Theological Seminary.* Edited by Harold B. Kuhn. Wilmore, KY: n.n., 1963

Atkins, Glenn C. *Religion in Our Times.* New York: Round Table Press, 1932.

Atkinson, J. Baines. *The Beauty of Holiness.* New York: Philosophical Library, 1963.

Bach, Marcus. *Report to Protestants.* New York: Bobbs Merrill Co., 1948.

Bainton, Roland. *Christian Unity and Religion in New England.* Boston: Beacon Press, 1964.

Baird, Robert. *Religion in the United States of America.* New York: Arno Press and the New York Times, 1969. (Originally printed in 1844.)

Baker, Eric. *The Faith of A Methodist.* New York: Abingdon Press, 1958.

Barabas, Steven. *So Great Salvation: The History and Message of the Keswick Convention.* Westwood, NJ: Fleming H. Revell, 1952.

Barnes, G. H. *The Anti-Slavery Impulse: 1830-1844.* New York: Appleton-Century-Crofts, Inc., 1933.

Bebb, E. Douglas. *A Man with a Concern.* London: Epworth Press, 1950.

Beet, Joseph Agar. *Holiness as Understood by the Writers of the Bible.* New York: Phillips and Hunt, 1889.

_____. *Holiness Symbolical and Real.* London: Robert Culley, 1910.

Begbie, Harold. *Life of William Booth, the Founder of the Salvation Army.* 2 vols. London: Macmillan and Co., 1920.

Bemensderfer, James O. *Pietism and Its Influence upon the Evangelical United Brethren Church.* Annville, Pa. n.n., 1966.

Benson, John T., Jr. *A History, 1898-1915, of the Pentecostal Mission, Inc., Nashville Tennessee.* Nashville, TN: Trevecca Press, 1977.

Bishop, Edward. *Blood and Fire: The Story of General William Booth and the Salvation Army.* London: Longmans, 1964.

Black, Robert E. "Becoming a Church: Weslayan Methodism, 1895-1935." Wayne Caldwell, ed. *Reformers and Revivalists.* Indianapolis, IN: Wesley Press, 1992.

Boisen, Anton T. *Religion in Crisis and Custom: A Sociological and Psychological Study.* New York: Harper Brothers, 1955.

Bossard, James H. *The Churches of Allentown: A Study in Statistics.* Allentown, PA: Jacks the Printer, 1918.

Bouyer, Louis. *The Spirit and Forms of Protestantism.* Westminster, MD: The Newman Press, 1961.

Bowen, Elias. *History of the Origin of the Free Methodist Church.* Rochester, NY: B. T. Roberts, 1871.

Boyd, Robert. *The Wonderful Career of Moody and Sankey in Great Britain and America.* New York: Henry S. Goodspeed and Co., 1875.

Brandenberg, H, "Heiligungsbewegung," *Die Religion in Geschichte und Gegenwart: Handwörterbuch für Theologie und Religionswissenschaft.* Tubingen: J. C. B. Mohr, 1959. Ill.

Brash, John. *Our Lovefeast and Testimonies to the Christian's Full Salvation.* London: Woolmer, 1887.

Brauer, Jerald C. *Protestantism in America.* Philadelphia: The Westminster Press, 1953.

Brickley, Donald Paul. *Man of the Morning: The Life and Work of Phineas F. Bresee.* Kansas City, MO: Nazarene Publishing House, 1960.

Bronkema, Ralph. *The Essence of Puritanism.* Goes, Holland: Oosterban and Lecointre, n.d.

Brown, Charles Ewing. *When the Trumpet Sounded: A History of the Church of God Reformation Movement.* Anderson, IN: Warner Press, 1951.

Bruce, F. F. *The Spreading Flame: The Rise and Progress of Christianity.* Grand Rapids, MI: Wm. B. Eerdmans Co., 1954.

Bucke, Emory, et al. *The History of American Methodism.* 3 vols. New York: Abingdon Press, 1964.

Buckley, James M. *A History of Methodism in the United States.* 2 vols. New York: Harper Brothers, 1898.

Bundy, David, "Bishop William Taylor and Methodist Mission: A Study in Nineteenth Century Social History." *Methodist History* 27, 28 (July, October, 1989): 197-210, 3-21.

Burr, Nelson R. *A Critical Bibliography of Religion in America.* In collaboration with the editors, James Ward Smith and S. Leland Jamison. Vol. IV; "Religion in American Life." No. 5 of Princeton Studies in American Civilization. Princeton, NJ: Princeton University Press, 1961.

Bury, John B. *The Idea of Progress: An Inquiry into Its Origin and Growth.* Introduction by Charles A. Beard. London: Macmillan, 1928. (Reprinted in 1955: New York: Dover Publications, Inc.)

Calliet, Emile. *Pascal: The Emergence of Genius.* New York: Harper and Brothers, 1961.

Campbell, Joseph E. *The Pentecostal Holiness Church, 1898-1948: Its Background and History.* Franklin Springs, GA: Publishing House of the Pentecostal Holiness Church, 1951.

Cannon, William R. *The Theology of John Wesley, with Special Reference to the Doctrine of Justification.* New York: Abingdon Press, 1946.

Carroll, H. K. (ed.). *Proceedings, Sermons, Essays, and Addresses of the Centennial Methodist Conference Held in Mt. Vernon Place Methodist Episcopal Church, Baltimore, Md., December 9-17, 1884.* New York: Cranston and Stowe, 1885.

_____. *The Religious Forces of the United States, Enumerated, Classified and Described on the Basis of the Government Census in 1890.* New York: The Christian Literature Co. (1893).

Carter, Paul A. *The Spiritual Crisis of the Gilded Age.* DeKalb, IL: Northern Illinois University Press, 1971.

Carwardine, Richard. *Transatlantic Revivalism: Popular Evangelicalism in Britain and America, 1790-1865.* Westport, CT: Greenwood Press, 1978.

Cell, George Croft. *The Rediscovery of John Wesley.* New York: Abingdon-Cokesbury Press, 1946.

Chiles, Robert E. "Methodist Apostasy: From Free Grace to Free Will." *Religion in Life*, XXVII (Summer 1958), 438-449.

_____. *Theological Transition in American Methodism: 1790-1935.* Abingdon Press, 1965.

Church, Leslie F. *The Early Methodist People.* London: Epworth Press, 1949.

Clark, Elmer T. *The Small Sects in America.* Rev. ed. New York: Abingdon Press, 1949.

Clark, Robert D. *The Life of Matthew Simpson.* New York: Macmillan, 1956.

Clear, Valorous Bernard. "The Urbanization of a Holiness Body." *City Church*, IX (July-August, 1958), pp. 2ff.

Clebsch, William A. *From Sacred to Profane America: The Role of Religion in American History.* New York: Harper and Row, 1969.

Climenhaga, A. W. *History of the Brethren in Christ Church.* Napanee, IN: E. U. Publishing House, 1942.

Cobbins, Otho. *History of the Church of Christ (Holiness) U.S.A.: 1895-1964.* New York: Vantage Press, 1965.

Cole, Charles C., Jr. *The Social Ideas of the Northern Evangelists: 1826-1860.* New York: Columbia University Press, 1954.

Collier, Richard. *The General Next to God: The Story of William Booth and the Salvation Army.* New York. Dutton, 1965.

Copeland, Kenneth W. "The Magnificent Purpose." *Asbury Seminarian*, XXVI (January 1972), 31-33.

Corbin, J. Wesley. "Christian Perfection and the Evangelical Association through 1875." *Methodist History*, VII (January 1969), 28-44.

Cox, Leo George. *John Wesley's Concept of Perfection.* Kansas City, MO: Beacon Hill Press, 1964.

Cross, Whitney R. *The Burned-Over District: The Social and Intellectual History of Enthusiastic Religion in Western New York, 1800-1850.* Ithaca, NY: Cornell University Press, 1950.

Cumming, J. Elder. "An Exposition of Recent Teaching on Holiness." *Expository Times.* V (1893-94), 164-168.

Daniel, Harrison W. "A Brief Account of the Methodist Episcopal Church South in the Confederacy." *Methodist History,* Vl (January, 1968).

Day, Richard Ellsworth. *Man of Like Passions: A Dramatic Biography of Charles Grandison Finney.* Grand Rapids, MI: Zondervan Publishing House, n.d.

Dayton, Donald W. *The American Holiness Movement: A Bibliographic Introduction.* Wilmore, KY: Asbury Theological Seminary, 1971.

_____. *Theological Roots of Pentecostalism.* Grand Rapids, MI: Zondervan Publishing House, 1987.

DeVoist, S. G. *History of the East Michigan Conference of the Free Methodist Church.* Owosso, MI: Time Printing Co., 1925.

Dieter, Melvin E. "The Development of Nineteenth Century Holiness Theology." *Theological Themes in the American Protestant World. Modern American Protestantism and Its World.* Vol. 4. Martin Marty, ed. Westport, CT: Meckler, 1991.

_____. "Primitivism in the American Holiness Tradition." *Wesleyan Theological Journal* 30 (Spring 1995) 1:78-91.

_____. "The Post-Civil War Holiness Revival: The Rise of the Campmeeting Churches." in Wayne W. Caldwell, ed. *Reformers and Revivalists: The History of the Wesleyan Church.* Wesleyan Church History Series. Vol. 3. Indianapolis, IN: Wesley Press, 1992.

Douglas, W. M. *Andrew Murray and His Message: One of God's Choice Saints.* Fort Washington, PA: Christian Crusade, 1957.

Douglass, Paul F. *The Story of German Methodism: Biography of an Immigrant Soul.* With an introduction by Bishop John L. Nuelson. New York: Methodist Book Concern, 1939.

Drummond, L. R. *German Protestantism Since Luther.* London: The Epworth Press, 1951.

Farish, Hunter D. *The Circuit Rider Dismounts: A Social History of Southern Methodism, 1865-1900.* Richmond, VA: Dietz Press, 1938.

Ferguson, Charles W. *Organizing to Beat the Devil.* Garden City, NY: Doubleday and Co., Inc., 1972.

Fleisch, Paul. *Die Moderne Gemeinschaftsbewegung in Deutschland. Ein Versuch dieselbe nach ihren Ursprüngen darzustellen und zu würdigen.* Leipzig: H. G. Wallman, 1903.

_____. "Pfingstbewegung." *Die Religion in Geschichte und Gegenwart: Handwörterbuch für Theologie und Religionswissenschaft.* Tübingen: J. C. B. Mohr, 1959. IV, 1153ff.

Fleming, Walter L. "The Religious and Hospitable Rite of Feet Washing." *The Sewanee Review,* XVI No. 1, 1-13.

Flew, Newton R. *The Idea of Perfection in Christian Theology: Historical Study of the Christian Ideal for the Present Life.* London: Oxford University Press, 1934.

Ford, Jack. *In the Steps of John Wesley: The Church of the Nazarene in Britain.* Kansas City, MO: Nazarene Publishing House, 1968.

Foss, Martin. *The Idea of Perfection in the Western World.* Princeton, NJ: Princeton University Press, 1946.

Foster, F. H. *A Genetic History of New England Theology.* Chicago: University of Chicago Press, 1907.

Foster, John O. "The First Des Plaines Camp Meeting, Des Plaines, Ill.: August, 1860." *Journal of the Illinois State Historical Society,* XXIV (January 1932).

Freemantle, Anne (ed.). *The Protestant Mystics.* London: Weidenfeld and Nicolson, 1964.

Garrison, W. E. *The March of Faith: The Story of Religion in America Since 1865.* New York: Harper and Brothers, 1933.

Gasper, Louis. *The Fundamentalist Movement.* The Hague: Mouton and Co., 1963.

Gaustad, Edwin S. *The Great Awakening in New England.* New York: Harper and Brothers, 1957.

_____. *Historical Atlas of Religion in America.* New York: Harper and Row, 1962.

_____. *A Religious History of America.* New York: Harper and Row, 1966.

Girvin, E. A. *Phineas F. Bresee, A Prince in Israel: A Biography.* Kansas City, MO: Pentecostal Nazarene Publishing House, 1916.

Goen, C. C. "The Methodist Age in American Church History." *Religion in Life,* XXXIV (1965), 562-572.

_____. *Revival and Separatism in New England. 1740-1800.* New Haven, CT: Yale University Press, 1962.

Gospel Hymns Consolidated: Embracing Numbers 1, 2, 3 and 4 ... for Use in Gospel Meetings and other Religious Services. Cincinnati: OH: The John Church Co., 1883.

Green, John Brazier. *John Wesley and William Law.* London: The Epworth Press, 1945.

Hall, Clarence W. *Samuel Logan Brengle, Portrait of a Prophet.* New York: Salvationist Publishing Co., n.d.

Hamm, Thomas. *The Transformation of American Quakerism: Orthodox Friends, 1865-1918.* Indianapolis, IN: University of Indiana Press, 1986.

Handlin, Oscar. *The Uprooted: The Epic Story of Great Migrations that Made the American People.* New York: Grosset and Dunlap, 1951.

Handy, R. T. "The Protestant Quest for a Christian America: 1830-1930." *Church History,* XXI (1953-54), 11-13.

_____. *American Christianity: An Historical Representation with Representative Documents.* Edited by R. T Handy, L. H. Loetscher and H. Shelton Smith. 2 vols. New York: Chas. Scribner's Sons, 1960-1963.

_____. *A Christian America: Protestant Hope and Historical Realities.* New York: Oxford University Press, 1971.

Harkness, Georgia E. *The Fellowship of the Holy Spirit.* Nashville, TN: Abingdon Press, 1966.

_____. *The Methodist Church in Social Thought and Action.* New York: Abingdon Press, 1964.

Haroutunian, Joseph. *Piety vs. Moralism: The Passing of New England Theology.* New York: Henry Holt and Co., 1932.

Hay, Fanny A., Cargo, Ruth E., Freeman, Harlan. *A History of Adrian College: The Story of a Noble Devotion.* Adrian, MI: Adrian College Press, 1945.

Hedley, George. *The Christian Heritage in America.* New York: Macmillan, 1946.

Henry, George W. *History of the Jumpers: Or Shouting Genuine and Spurious; a History of the Outward Demonstrations of the Spirit.* Waukesha, WI: Metropolitan Church Association, 1909.

Hertzberg, A., Marty, Martin E., Moody, Jos. W. *The Outbursts that Await Us.* New York: Macmillan, 1963.

Hilson, James B. *History of the South Carolina Conference of the Wesleyan Methodist Church of America: 55 Years of Wesleyan Methodism In South Carolina.* Winona Lake, IN: Light and Life Press, 1950.

Hobbhouse, Stephen. *Wm. Law and 18th Century Quakerism.* London: George Allen and Unwin, Ltd., 1927.

Hogue, Wilson T. *History of the Free Methodist Church of North America.* 2 vols. Chicago: The Free Methodist Publishing House, 1915.

Holdrich, Joseph. *The Life of Wilbur Fisk, D.D., First President of Wesleyan University.* New York: Harper and Brothers, 1842.

Holt, John B. "Holiness Religion: Cultural Shock and Reorganization." *American Social Review,* V (1940), 740-747.

Hopkins, Charles H. *History of the Y.M.C.A. in North America.* New York: Association Press, 1951.

Houghton, Walter Edwards. *The Victorian Frame of Mind: 1830-1870.* New Haven, CT: Yale University Press, 1957.

Howard, Ivan. "Wesley vs. Phoebe Palmer: An Extended Controversy." *Wesleyan Theological Journal,* VI (Spring 1971), 31-40.

Hudson, Winthrop. *American Protestantism.* Chicago: University of Chicago Press, 1961.

———. *Religion in America.* New York: Chas. Scribner and Sons, 1965.

Huffman, Jasper Abraham (ed.). *History of the Mennonite Brethren in Christ Church.* New Carlisle, OH: Bethel Publishing Co., 1920.

Inge, W. R. *Mysticism in Religion.* Chicago: University of Chicago Press, 1948.

Inventory of the Church Archives in the City of New York. "The Methodist Church." New York: The Historical Records Survey, 1940.

Jackson, Samuel, et al. (eds). *The New Schaff-Herzog Encyclopedia of Religious Knowledge.* 12 vols. New York: Funk and Wagnalls, 1909.

James, William. *The Varieties of Religious Experience: A Study in Human Nature; Being the Gifford Lectures on Natural Religion Delivered in Edinburgh in 1901-1902.* New York: Modern Library, 1902.

Jervey, Edward D. "LaRoy Sunderland, Zion's Watchman." *Methodist History,* VI (April 1968), 16-32.

———. "Motives and Methods of the Methodist Episcopal Church in the Period of Reconstruction." *Methodist History,* IV (July 1966), 17-25.

Johnson, Charles A. *The Frontier Camp Meeting: Religious Harvest Time.* Dallas, TX: Southern Methodist University Press, 1955.

Johnson, James E. "Charles G. Finney and a Theology of Revivalism." *Church History,* XXXVIII (September 1969).

Jones, Charles Edward. "Anti-Ordinance: A Proto-Pentecostal Phenomenon?" *Wesleyan Theological Journal,* 25 (Fall 1990) 2:7-23.

———. *A Guide to the Study of the Holiness Movement.* Metuchen, NJ: Scarecrow Press, 1975.

———. *Perfectionist Persuasion: The Holiness Movement and American Methodism, 1867-1936.* Metuchen, NJ: Scarecrow Press, 1974.

Katzenbach, Friedrich W. *Die Erweckungsbewegung: Studien zur Geschichte ihrer Entstehung und ersten Zubereitung in Deutschland.* Neuendettlesau: Freimundverlag, 1957.

Kellog, D. O. *Illustrated Vineland.* Vineland, NJ: L. L. Buckminster, Printer, 1897.

Knox, Ronald A. *Enthusiasm: A Chapter in the History of Religion with Reference to the XVII and XVIII Centuries.* New York: Oxford University Press, 1961.

Kostlevy, William. *Holiness Manuscripts: A Guide to Sources Documenting the Wesleyan Holiness Movement in the United States and Canada.* Metuchen, NJ: Scarecrow Press, 1994.

Kramer, Paul and Holborn, Fredrick L. *The City in American Life: A Historical Anthology.* New York: G. P. Putnam's Sons, 1970.

Latourette, K. S. *The Great Century in America, Australia and Africa.* Vol V. "A History of the Expansion of Christianity." New York: Harper and Brothers, 1944.

Lee, Umphrey. *The Historic Backgrounds of Early Methodist Enthusiasm.* New York: Columbia University Press, 1931.

Lindstrom, Harald. *Wesley and Sanctification: A Study in the Doctrine of Salvation.* Translated by H. S. Harvey. London: Epworth Press, 1946.

Littell, Franklin H. *The Anabaptist View of the Church: A Study in the Origins of Sectarian Protestantism.* Second ed., revised and enlarged: Boston: Star King Press, 1958.

_____. "The Concerns of the Believer's Church." *The Chicago Theological Seminary Register,* LVIII (December 1967), 12-21.

_____. *From State Church to Pluralism: A Protestant Interpretation of Religion in American History.* New York: Macmillan, 1971.

_____. "The Methodist Class Meeting as an Instrument of Discipline, I: The Early Phase." *World Parish,* IX (February 1961), 14-24.

_____. "Some Free Church Remarks on the Concept of the Body of Christ." K. E. Skydsgaard, et al. *The Church as the Body of Christ.* Vol I. "The Cardinal O'Hara Series." Robert S, Pelton (ed.). *Studies and Research in Christian Theology at Notre Dame University.* Notre Dame, IN: University of Notre Dame Press, 1963.

McCutchan, Robert G. *Our Hymnody: A Manual of the Methodist Hymnal.* 2nd ed. New York: Abingdon Press, 1937.

Madden, Edward H., and James E. Hamilton. *Freedom and Grace: The Life of Asa Mahan.* Metuchen, NJ: Scarecrow Press, 1982.

MacGregor, G. H. C. "An Exposition of Recent Teachings on Holiness." *Expository Times,* V (1893-94), 28-31.

McKelvey, Blake. *The Urbanization of America: 1860-1915.* New Brunswick, NJ: Rutgers University Press, 1963.

McKinley, Edward H. *Marching to Glory: The History of the Salvation Army in the United States.* New York: Harper and Row, 1980.

McLeister, Ira Ford. *History of the Wesleyan Methodist Church of America.* 3rd ed. revised by R. S. Nicholson. Marion, IN: Wesley Press, 1959. Revised and reprinted as *Conscience and Commitment.* Wesleyan History Series. Lee M. Haines, Jr., and Melvin E. Dieter, eds. Marion, IN: Wesley Press, 1977.

McLoughlin, William, Jr. *Modern Revivalism: Charles Grandison Finney to Billy Graham.* New York: Ronald Press Co., 1959.

McNeill, John T. *Modern Christian Movements.* Philadelphia: Westminster Press, 1954.

Mann, W. E. *Sect, Cult, and Church in Alberta.* Toronto: University of Toronto Press, 1955.

Marsden, George M. *Fundamentalism and American Culture: The Shaping of Twentieth Century Evangelicalism, 1870-1925.* Oxford:Oxford University Press, 1980.

Marston, L. R. *From Age to Age a Living Witness: An Historical Interpretation of Free Methodism's First Century.* Winona Lake, IN: Light and Life Press, 1960.

Martin, Joel. *The Wesleyan Manual: Or History of Wesleyan Methodism.* Syracuse, NY: Wesleyan Methodist Publishing House, 1889.

Marty, Martin E. *Righteous Empire: The Protestant Experience in America.* New York: Dial Press, 1970.

May, Henry Farnham. *Protestant Churches in Industrial America.* New York. Harper and Brothers, 1949.

Mayer, F. E. *The Religious Bodies of America.* St. Louis, MO: Concordia, 1956.

Mead, Sidney Earl. *Nathaniel William Taylor, 1798-1858: A Connecticut Liberal.* Chicago: The University of Chicago Press, 1942.

_____. *The Lively Experiment: The Shaping of Christianity in America.* New York: Harper and Row Publishers, 1963.

Mead, Frank S. *Handbook of Denominations in the United States.* New York: Abingdon Press, 1965.

Miller, Perry. *The Life of the Mind in America from the Revolution to the Civil War.* New York: Harcourt, Brace and World, Inc., 1965.

Morais, Herbert M. *Deism in Eighteenth Century America.* New York: Columbia University Press, 1934.

Morento, J. L. *Sociometry Reader.* Glencoe, IL: Free Press, 1960.

Morrow, Ralph E. *Northern Methodism and Reconstruction.* East Lansing, MI: Michigan State University Press, 1941.

Mudge, James. *History of the New England Conferences of the Methodist Episcopal Church.* Boston: Published by the Conference, 1910.

Muncy, W. C., Jr. *Evangelism in the United States.* Kansas City, MO: Central Seminary Press, 1945.

Nagler, A. W. *Pietism and Methodism.* Nashville, TN: Publishing House of the Episcopal Church South, 1918.

The Nature of the Holy Life: Four Papers from the Anabaptist and Wesleyan Tradition Seminar, December 10, 1960. Mennonite Quarterly Review, XXXV (April 1961).

Neill, Stephen Charles and Weber, Hans-Ruedi (eds.). *The Layman in Christian History: A Project of the Department on the Laity of the World Council of Churches.* Philadelphia: The Westminster Press, 1963.

Neve, J. L. *Churches and Sects of Christendom.* Blair, NE: Lutheran Publishing House, 1952.

Newby, J. Edwin. *Teachings of Evangelical Friends as Gleaned from George Fox's Journal and Friends' Disciplines.* N.p. Messages given to Central Yearly Meeting, 1952.

Nicholson, Roy Stephen. *Wesleyan Methodism in the South: Being the Story of Eighty-Six Years of Reform and Religious Activities in the South as Conducted by*

American Wesleyans. Syracuse, NY: Wesleyan Methodist Publishing Association, 1933.

Niebuhr, Helmut Richard. *The Kingdom of God in America.* Chicago: Willet, Clark and Co., 1937.

_____. *The Social Sources of the Denominations.* New York: Henry Holt and Co., 1929. (Reprinted, New York: Meridian Books, Inc., 1957.)

Noble, W. E. P. *A Century of Gospel Work: A History of the Growth of Evangelical Religion in the U.S. (1776-1876).* Philadelphia: H. C. Watts and Co., 1876.

Nordhoff, Charles. *Communistic Societies of the United States.* New York: Hillary House Publishers, Ltd., 1961.

Nye, Russell E. *This Almost Chosen People: Essays in the History of American Ideas.* N.p.: Michigan State University Press, 1966.

Olmstead, Clifton E. *History of Religion in the United States.* Englewood Cliffs, NJ: Prentice-Hall, 1960.

Orr, James E. *The Second Evangelical Awakening.* London: Marshall, Morgan and Scott, 1955.

_____. *The Second Evangelical Awakening in America.* London: Marshall, Morgan and Scott, 1952.

_____. *The Second Evangelical Awakening in Britain.* London: Marshall, Morgan and Scott, 1949.

Osborn, Ronald E. *The Spirit of American Christianity.* New York: Harper and Brothers Publishers, 1958.

Peters, John L. *Christian Perfection and American Methodism.* New York: Abingdon Press, 1956.

Phelan, Macum. *A History of Early Methodism in Texas: 1817-1866.* Nashville, TN: Cokesbury Press, 1924.

_____. *A History of the Expansion of Methodism in Texas, 1867-1902: Being a Continuation of the History of Early Methodism in Texas.* Dallas, TX: Mathis, Van Nort and Co., 1937.

Pierson, Arthur T. *Forward Movements of the Last Half Century.* New York: Funk and Wagnalls Co., 1905.

Pollock, John Charles. *The Keswick Story: The Authorized History of the Keswick Convention.* London: Hodder and Stoughton, 1964.

_____. *Moody: A Biographical Portrait of the Pacesetter in Modern Mass Evangelism.* New York: Macmillan, 1963.

Pollock, Norman. *The Populist Response to Industial America: Midwest Populist Thought.* Cambridge, MA: Harvard University Press, 1962.

Porter, James. *Revivals of Religion Showing Their Theory, Means, Obstruction, Importance, and Perversions.* New York: Nelson and Phillips, 1878.

Potts, J. H. *Pastor and People: Methodism in the Field.* New York: Phillips and Hunt, 1879.

Preece, Harold and Kraft, Celia. *Dew on Jordan.* New York: E. P. Dutton and Co., 1946.

Prescott, William Ray. *The Fathers Still Speak: A History of Michigan Methodism.* Lansing, MI: Michigan Printing Service, 1941.

Purkheiser, W. T. *Called unto Holiness, Volume 2: The Second Twenty-Five Years, 1933-1958.* Kansas City, MO:Nazarene Publishing House, 1983.

Raser, Harold. *Phoebe Palmer: Her Life and Thought*. Lewiston, NY: Mellon Press, 1987.

Rhodes, Arnold B. (ed.). *The Church Faces the Isms*. New York: Abingdon Press, 1958.

Richardson, E. C. et al. (comp. and ed.). *An Alphabetical Subject Index and Index Encyclopedia to Periodical Articles on Religion, 1890-1899*. New York: Chas. Scribner and Sons, 1907.

Rightmire, Robert David. *Sacraments and the Salvation Army: Pneumatological Foundations*. Studies in Evangelicalism; No. 10. Metuchen, NJ: Scarecrow Press, 1990.

Riston, Joseph. *The Romance of Primitive Methodism*. London: The Primitive Methodist Publishing House, 1909.

Roberts, Philip I. *F. B. Meyer: Preacher, Teacher, Man of God*. By Chester A. Mann, pseud. New York: Fleming H. Revell, 1929.

Rose, Delbert A. *A Theology of Christian Experience: Interpreting the Historic Wesleyan Message*. Minneapolis, MN: Bethany Fellowship, Inc., 1965.

Rosenbaum, Max and Berger, Milton. (eds.). *Group Psychotherapy and Group Function*. New York: Basic Books 1963.

Salisbury, W. Seward. *Religion in American Culture: A Sociological Interpretation*. Homewood, IL: The Dorsey Press, 1964.

Salter, Darius. *Spirit and Intellect: Thomas Upham's Holiness Theology*. Metuchen, NJ:Scarecrow Press, 1986.

Sangster, William E. "The Church's One Privation." *Religion in Life*, XVIII (Winter 1949), 493-502.

_____. *Methodism Can Be Born Again*. New York: The Methodist Book Concern, 1938.

_____. *The Path to Perfection: An Examination and Restatement of John Wesley's Doctrine of Christian Perfection*. London: Epworth Press, 1943.

_____. *The Pure in Heart: A Study in Christian Sanctity*. New York: Abingdon Press, 1954.

_____. "Wesley and Sanctification." *London Quarterly and Holborn Review*, CLXXI (July 1946), 214-221.

Sasnett, W. J. "Theory of Methodist Class Meetings." *Methodist Quarterly Review (So.)*, V (1851), 265-284.

Scharpff, Paulus. *The History of Evangelism: Three Hundred Years of Evangelism in Germany, Great Britain and the United States of America*. Translated by Helga Bender Henry. Grand Rapids, MI: Wm. B. Eerdmans Publishing Co., 1966.

Schilling, S. Paul. *Methodism and Society in Theological Perspective*. Vol. III of "Methodism in Society." New York: Abingdon Press, 1960.

Schlesinger, Arthur M. "A Critical Period in American Religion: 1875-1900." *Massachusetts Historical Society Proceedings*, LXIV (1932), 523-547.

_____. (ed.). *The Rise of the City: 1878-1898*. New York: Macmillan, 1933.

Schmul, Harold E. et al., comp. *Profile of the Interchurch Holiness Convention: A Retrospect of 40 Years of IHC Ministry*. Salem, OH:Interchurch Holiness Convention, 1992.

Schwab, Ralph K. *The History of the Doctrine of Christian Perfection in the Evangelical Association*. Menasha, WI: George Banta Publishing Co., 1922.

Scott, Leland H. *Methodist Theology in America in the Nineteenth Century.* Published by the Microcard Foundation for the American Theological Library Association, 1954.

Simpson. Matthew (ed.). *A Cyclopedia of Methodism.* Philadelphia: Everts and Stewart, 1878.

_____. *A Hundred Years of Methodism.* New York: Nelson and Phillips, 1876.

Sloan, Walter B. *These Sixty Years: The Story of the Keswick Convention.* London: Pickering and Inglis [1935].

Smith, James Ward and Jamison A. Leland (eds.). *Religious Perspectives in American Culture.* Vol. II of "Religion in American Life." No 5 of Princeton Studies in American Civilization. Princeton, NJ: Princeton University Press, 1961.

_____. *The Shaping of American Religion.* Vol. I of "Religion in American Life." No. 5 of Princeton Studies in American Civilization. Princeton, NJ: Princeton University Press, 1961.

Smith, John W. V. *Heralds of a Brighter Day: Biographical Sketches of Early Leaders in the Church of God Reformation Movement.* Anderson, IN: Gospel Trumpet Co., 1955.

_____. *The Quest for Holiness and Unity: A Centennial History of the Church of God.* Anderson, IN:Warner Press, 1980.

Smith, Joseph H. *Things Behind and Things Before in the Holiness Movement.* Chicago: Evangelistic Institute Press, 1916.

Smith, Timothy L. *Called unto Holiness: The Story of the Nazarenes, The Formative Years.* Kansas City, MO: Nazarene Publishing Co., 1962.

_____. "Congregation, State, and Denomination: The Forming of the American Religious Structure." *William and Mary Quarterly,* XXV (April 1968), 156-176.

_____. "Historic Waves of Religious Interest in America," *Annals of the American Academy of Political and Social Science,* No. 332 (1960), pp. 9-19.

_____. *Revivalism and Social Reform in Mid-Nineteenth Century America.* Baltimore, MD:Johns Hopkins University Press, 1980. Originally published New York: Abingdom Press, 1957.

Sperry, Willard L. *Religion in America.* Cambridge: University Press. 1946.

Stark, Rodney and Clock, Charles Y. *Patterns of Religious Commitment,* Vol. I; *American Piety: The Nature of Religious Commitment.* Berkeley and Los Angeles, CA: University of California Press, 1969.

Starkey, Lycurgus, Jr. *The Work of the Holy Spirit.* New York: Abingdon Press, 1962.

Stevens, Abel. *History of the Methodist Episcopal Church in the United States of America.* 4 vols. New York: Carlton and Lanahan, 1864.

Stoeffler, F. Ernest. *The Rise of Evangelical Pietism.* Leiden: E. J. Brill, 1971.

Storms, Everck. *History of the United Missionary Church.* Elkhart, IN: Bethel Publishing Co., 1958.

Strachey, Barbara. *Remarkable Relations: The Story of the Pearsall Smith Family.* London: Victor Gollancz Ltd, 1981.

Strong, Josiah. *The New Era: Or the Coming Kingdom.* New York: Baker and Taylor, 1893.

Sweet, William Warren. *The American Churches: An Interpretation.* New York: Cokesbury Press, 1947.

_____. *Methodism in American History.* Revision of 1953 ed. New York: Abingdon Press, 1961.

_____. *Our American Churches: Studies in Christian Faith*. Edited by Henry H. Meyer. New York: The Methodist Book Concern, 1924.

_____. *Revivalism in America: Its Origin, Growth and Decline*. New York: Charles Scribner's Sons, 1944.

_____. *The Story of Religion in America*. New York: Harper and Brothers, 1950.

Synan, Vincent. *The Holiness-Pentecostal Movement in the United States*. Grand Rapids, MI: Wm. B. Eerdmans Publishing Co., 1971.

Tappert, T. G. "Orthodoxism, Pietism, and Rationalism: 1580-1830." *Christian Social Responsibility*. Edited by Harold C. Letts. Philadelphia: Muhlenberg Press, 1957.

Taylor, Mendell B. *Exploring Evangelism*. Kansas City, MO: Beacon Hill, 1964.

Taylor, W. S. "Perfectionism in Psychology and in Theology." *Canadian Journal of Theology*, IV (July 1959), 170-179.

Tenny, Mary Alice. *Blueprint for a Christian World: An Analysis of the Wesleyan Way*. Winona Lake, IN: Light and Life Press, 1953.

Terrill, Joseph Goodwin. *The Life of Rev. John Wesley Redfield, M.D.* Chicago: Free Methodist Publishing House, 1899.

_____. *The St. Charles Campmeeting*. Chicago: T. B. Arnold, 1883.

Thomas, Paul Nesphal, and Paul William Thomas. *The Days of Our Pilgrimage: The History of the Pilgrim Holiness Church*. Wesleyan History Series. Melvin E. Dieter and Lee M. Haines, eds. Marion, IN: Wesley Press, 1976.

Thompson, A. E. *A. B. Simpson: His Life and Work*. Revised ed. Harrisburg, PA: Christian Publications, 1960.

Thompson, R. Duane. *Keswick: Historical Origin and Doctrine of Holiness*. Marion, IN: n.n., 1963.

Thompson, Robert Ellis. *A History of the Presbyterian Churches in the United States*. New York: Chas. Scribner's Sons, 1895.

Troeltsch, Ernest. *The Social Teachings of the Christian Churches*. Translated by Olive Wyon, with introductory notes by Chas. Gore. New York: Macmillan, 1931. (Reprinted; New York: Harper, 1960. With an introduction by H. Richard Niebuhr.)

Turner, George Allen. *The More Excellent Way: The Scriptural Basis of the Wesleyan Message*. Winona Lake, IN: Light and Life Press, 1951.

Tyler, Alice Felt. *Freedoms Ferment: Phases of American Social History from the Colonial Period to the Outbreak of the Civil War*. Minneapolis, MN: University of Minneapolis Press, 1944. (New York: Harper Torchbooks, 1962.)

Van Duesen, Henry P. "Third Force in Christendom." *Life* (June 9, 1958), pp. 113-124.

Vineland N. J. Centennial. Vineland, NJ: Vineland Centennial, Inc. n.d.

The Vineland Historical Magazine. Edited by Elena J. Darling. Vineland, NJ: Vineland Historical and Antiquarian Society, 1961.

Wall, Ernest. "I Commend unto You Phoebe." *Religion in Life*, XXVI (Summer 1957), 396-408.

Warfield, Benjamin B. *Perfectionism*. 2 vols. New York: Oxford University Press, 1931-1932.

Warren, Austin. *New England Saints*. Ann Arbor, MI; University of Michigan Press, 1956.

Watson, Bernard D. *A Hundred Years' War: The Salvation Army, 1865-1965.* London: Hodder and Stoughton, 1964.

Watson, Richard. *The Life of Rev. John Wesley, A.M., Sometime Fellow of Lincoln College, Oxford, and Founder of the Methodist Societies.* New York: Lane and Tippett, 1847.

Weber, Max. *The Sociology of Religion.* Translated by E. Fischoff. London: Methuen, 1965.

Webster's Biographical Dictionary. Springfield, MA: G. and C. Merriam Co. Publishers, 1943.

Wentz, Abdel R. *Germany's Modern Pietistic Movement.* N.p. n.n., n.d.

Wesley, John. *Christian Perfection as Believed and Taught by John Wesley.* Edited and with introduction by Thomas S. Kepler. Cleveland, OH: World Publishing Co., 1954.

_____. *The Message of the Wesleys: A Reader of Instruction and Devotion.* Compiled and with an introduction by Phillip S. Watson. New York: Macmillan, 1964.

Wheatley, Richard. *The Life and Letters of Mrs. Phoebe Palmer.* New York: W. C. Palmer, Jr., 1876.

White, Charles Edward. *The Beauty of Holiness: Phoebe Palmer as Theologian Revivalist, Feminist, and Humanitarian.* Grand Rapids, MI: Francis Asbury Press, 1986.

Wiebe, Robert. *The Search for Order: American Society, 1877-1920.* Vol. V of "Making of America: American Century Series." New York: Hill and Wang, 1967.

Wilcox, Leslie D. *Be Ye Holy: A Study of the Teaching of Scripture Relative to Entire Sanctification with a Sketch of the History and Literature of the Holiness Movement.* Cincinnati, OH: Revivalist Press, 1965.

Wilson, George. "An Exposition of Recent Teaching on Holiness." *Expository Times,* No. 5 (1893-94), pp. 108-111.

Wilson, George. *Methodist Theology vs. Methodist Theologians.* Cincinnati, OH: Jennings and Pye, 1904.

Winkler, Fr. "Robert Pearsall Smith und der Perfektionismus." Friedrich D. Kopatschek, *Biblische Zeit und Streitfragen zur Aufklärung der Gebildeten.* Series ix. Berlin-Lichterfelde: Edwin Runge, 1915.

Wittke, Carl F. *William Nast, Patriarch of German Methodism.* Detroit, MI: Wayne State University Press, 1959.

Wolf, Richard C. "The Middle Period, 1800-1870: The Matrix of Modern American Christianity." *Religion in Life,* XXII (1952-53), 72-84.

Worcester, Paul W. *The Master Key: The Story of the Hephzibah Faith Missionary Association.* Kansas City, MO: Nazarene Publishing House, 1966.

Yates, Arthur S. *The Doctrine of Assurance.* London: The Epworth Press, 1952.

Yocum, Dale M. (ed.). *The New Testament Church.* Church of God (Holiness) Unification Commission. Overland Park, KS: Witt Printing Co., n.d.

Index

About the Author

MELVIN E. DIETER (A.B., Muhlenberg College; Th.B., United Wesleyan College; M.A., Lehigh University; S.T.M., Ph.D., Temple University) is Professor (emeritus) of Church History and Historical Theology at Asbury Theological Seminary, Wilmore, Kentucky, where he had served on the faculty and as Provost and Vice-President. His extensive research and publication on revivalism and the place and significance of the Wesleyan/Holiness teaching and tradition in American culture quickly made his work a basic resource for further study of these movements. At his retirement from the seminary, he was director of the Wesleyan/Holiness Study Project funded by a grant from the Pew Charitable Trusts. The three-year research project was the first such in-depth study of the tradition. He continues as chairman of the advisory committee to the seminary's new Center for Wesleyan/Holiness Studies established with additional support from the Pew Charitable Trusts. In his retirement he continues his life-long commitments to scholarship and service by writing, serving on accreditation teams, and in various consultative assignments for churches and colleges in the holiness tradition.